PRAISE FOR THE FIRST EDITION OF *HOW LINUX WORKS*

"A great resource. In roughly 350 pages, the book covers all the basics."
—eWEEK

"I would definitely recommend this book to those who are interested in Linux, but have not had the experience to know the inner workings of the OS."
—O'REILLYNET

"One of the best basic books on learning Linux, written with the power user in mind. Five stars."
—OPENSOURCE-BOOK-REVIEWS.COM

"Succeeds admirably because of the way in which it's organized and the level of technical detail it offers."
—KICKSTART NEWS

"This is a very different introduction to Linux. It's unflashy, concentrates on the command line, and digs around in the internals rather than on GUI front-ends that take the place of more familiar MS Windows tools."
—TECHBOOKREPORT.COM

"This book does a good job of explaining the nuts and bolts of how Linux operates."
—HOSTING RESOLVE

HOW LINUX WORKS

2ND EDITION

What Every Superuser Should Know

by Brian Ward

no starch press

San Francisco

HOW LINUX WORKS, 2ND EDITION. Copyright © 2015 by Brian Ward.

Printed in USA
First printing

18 17 16 15 14   1 2 3 4 5 6 7 8 9

ISBN-10: 1-59327-567-6
ISBN-13: 978-1-59327-567-9

Publisher: William Pollock
Production Editor: Laurel Chun
Cover and Interior Design: Octopod Studios
Cover Illustration: Tina Salameh
Developmental Editor: William Pollock
Technical Reviewer: Jordi Gutiérrez Hermoso
Copyeditor: Gillian McGarvey
Compositor: Susan Glinert Stevens
Proofreader: Paula L. Fleming

For information on distribution, translations, or bulk sales, please contact No Starch Press, Inc. directly:

No Starch Press, Inc.
245 8th Street, San Francisco, CA 94103
phone: 415.863.9900; info@nostarch.com
www.nostarch.com

The Library of Congress has cataloged the first edition as follows:

Ward, Brian.
  How Linux works : what every superuser should know / Brian Ward.
      p. cm.
  Includes index.
  ISBN 1-59327-035-6
  1. Linux. 2. Operating systems (Computers). I. Title.
    QA76.76.O63 W3654 2004
    005.4'32--dc22
        2004002692

BRIEF CONTENTS

CONTENTS IN DETAIL

4
DISKS AND FILESYSTEMS   65

5
HOW THE LINUX KERNEL BOOTS 93

6
HOW USER SPACE STARTS 111

7
SYSTEM CONFIGURATION: LOGGING, SYSTEM TIME, BATCH JOBS, AND USERS 149

8
A CLOSER LOOK AT PROCESSES AND RESOURCE UTILIZATION 171

12
MOVING FILES ACROSS THE NETWORK   271

15
DEVELOPMENT TOOLS
309

16
INTRODUCTION TO COMPILING SOFTWARE
FROM C SOURCE CODE
329

17
BUILDING ON THE BASICS   345

BIBLIOGRAPHY   351

INDEX   355

PREFACE

I wrote this book because I believe you should be able to learn what your computer does. You should be able to make your software do what you want it to do (within the reasonable limits of its capabilities, of course). The key to attaining this power lies in understanding the fundamentals of what the software does and how it works, and that's what this book is all about. You should never have to fight with a computer.

Linux is a great platform for learning because it doesn't try to hide anything from you. In particular, most system configuration can be found in plaintext files that are easy enough to read. The only tricky part is figuring out which parts are responsible for what and how it all fits together.

Who Should Read This Book?

Your interest in learning how Linux works may have come from any number of sources. In the professional realm, operations and DevOps folks need to know nearly everything that you'll find in this book. Linux software architects and developers should also know this material in order to make the best use of the operating system. Researchers and students, often left to run their own Linux systems, will also find that this book provides useful explanations for *why* things are set up the way they are.

Then there are the tinkerers—people who just love to play around with their computers for fun, profit, or both. Want to know why certain things work while others don't? Want to know what happens if you move something around? You're probably a tinkerer.

Prerequisites

Although Linux is beloved by programmers, you do not need to be a programmer to read this book; you need only basic computer-user knowledge. That is, you should be able to bumble around a GUI (especially the installer and settings interface for a Linux distribution) and know what files and directories (folders) are. You should also be prepared to check additional documentation on your system and on the Web. As mentioned earlier, the most important thing you need is to be ready and willing to play around with your computer.

How to Read This Book

Building the requisite knowledge is a challenge in tackling any technical subject. When explaining how software systems work, things can get *really* complicated. Too much detail bogs down the reader and makes the important stuff difficult to grasp (the human brain just can't process so many new concepts at once), but too little detail leaves the reader in the dark and unprepared for later material.

I've designed most chapters to tackle the most important material first: the basic information that you'll need in order to progress. In places, I've simplified things in order to keep focus. As a chapter progresses, you'll see much more detail, especially in the last few sections. Do you need to know those bits right away? In most cases, no, as I often note. If your eyes start to glaze over when faced with a lot of extra details about stuff that you only just learned, don't hesitate to skip ahead to the next chapter or just take a break. The nitty-gritty will still be there waiting for you.

A Hands-On Approach

However you choose to proceed through this book, you should have a Linux machine in front of you, preferably one that you're confident abusing with experiments. You might prefer to play around with a virtual installation—I used VirtualBox to test much of the material in this book. You should have superuser (root) access, but you should use a regular user account most of the time. You'll mostly work at the command line, in a terminal window or a remote session. If you haven't worked much in this environment, no problem; Chapter 2 will bring you up to speed.

Commands in this book will typically look like this:

```
$ ls /
[some output]
```

Enter the text in bold; the non-bolded text that follows is what the machine spits back. The $ is the prompt for your regular user account. If you see a # as a prompt, you should be superuser. (More on that in Chapter 2.)

How This Book Is Organized

I've grouped the book's chapters into three basic parts. The first is introductory, giving you a bird's-eye view of the system and then offering hands-on experience with some tools you'll need for as long as you run Linux. Next, you'll explore each part of the system in more detail, from device management to network configuration, following the general order in which the system starts. Finally, you'll get a tour of some pieces of a running system, learn some essential skills, and get some insight into the tools that programmers use.

With the exception of Chapter 2, most of the early chapters heavily involve the Linux kernel, but you'll work your way into user space as the book progresses. (If you don't know what I'm talking about here, don't worry; I'll explain in Chapter 1.)

The material here is meant to be as distribution-agnostic as possible. Having said this, it can be tedious to cover all variations in systems software, so I've tried to cover the two major distribution families: Debian (including Ubuntu) and RHEL/Fedora/CentOS. It's also focused on desktop and server installations. There is a significant amount of carryover into embedded systems, such as Android and OpenWRT, but it's up to you to discover the differences on those platforms.

What's New in the Second Edition?

The first edition of this book dealt primarily with the user-centric side of a Linux system. It focused on understanding how the parts worked and how to get them humming. At that time, many parts of Linux were difficult to install and configure properly.

This is happily no longer the case thanks to the hard work of the people who write software and create Linux distributions. With this in mind, I have omitted some older and perhaps less relevant material (such as a detailed explanation of printing) in favor of an expanded discussion of the Linux kernel's role in every Linux distribution. You probably interact with the kernel more than you realize, and I've taken special care to note where.

Of course, so much of the original subject matter in this book has changed over the years, and I've taken pains to sort through the material in the first edition in search of updates. Of particular interest is how Linux boots and how it manages devices. I've also taken care to rearrange material to match the interests and needs of current readers.

One thing that hasn't changed is the size of this book. I want to give you the stuff that you need to get on the fast track, and that includes explaining certain details along the way that can be hard to grasp, but I don't want you to have to become a weightlifter in order to pick up this book. When you're on top of the important subjects here, you should have no trouble seeking out and understanding more details.

I've also omitted some of the historical information that was in the first edition, primarily to keep you focused. If you're interested in Linux and how it relates to the history of Unix, pick up Peter H. Salus's *The Daemon, the Gnu, and the Penguin* (Reed Media Services, 2008)—it does a great job of explaining how the software we use has evolved over time.

A Note on Terminology

There's a fair amount of debate over the names of certain elements of operating systems. Even "Linux" itself is game for this—should it be "Linux," or should it be "GNU/Linux" to reflect that the operating system also contains pieces from the GNU Project? Throughout this book, I've tried to use the most common, least awkward names possible.

ACKNOWLEDGMENTS

Thanks go to everyone who helped with the first edition: James Duncan, Douglas N. Arnold, Bill Fenner, Ken Hornstein, Scott Dickson, Dan Ehrlich, Felix Lee, Scott Schwartz, Gregory P. Smith, Dan Sully, Karol Jurado, and Gina Steele. For the second edition, I'd especially like to thank Jordi Gutiérrez Hermoso for his excellent technical review work; his suggestions and corrections have been invaluable. Thanks also to Dominique Poulain and Donald Karon for providing some excellent early-access feedback, and to Hsinju Hsieh for putting up with me during the process of revising this book.

Finally, I'd like to thank my developmental editor, Bill Pollock, and my production editor, Laurel Chun. Serena Yang, Alison Law, and everyone else at No Starch Press have done their usual outstanding job at getting this new edition on track.

1

THE BIG PICTURE

At first glance, a modern operating system such as Linux is very complicated, with a dizzying number of pieces simultaneously running and communicating. For example, a web server can talk to a database server, which could in turn use a shared library that many other programs use. But how does it all work?

The most effective way to understand how an operating system works is through *abstraction*—a fancy way of saying that you can ignore most of the details. For example, when you ride in a car, you normally don't need to think about details such as the mounting bolts that hold the motor inside the car or the people who build and maintain the road upon which the car drives. If you're a passenger in a car, all you really need to know is what the car does (transports you somewhere else) and a few basics about how to use it (how to operate the door and seat belt).

But if you're driving a car, you need to know more. You need to learn how to operate the controls (such as the steering wheel and accelerator pedal) and what to do when something goes wrong.

For example, let's say that the car ride is rough. Now you can break up the abstraction of "a car that rolls on a road" into three parts: a car, a road, and the way that you're driving. This helps isolate the problem: If the road is bumpy, you don't blame the car or the way that you're driving it. Instead, you may want to find out why the road has deteriorated or, if the road is new, why the construction workers did a lousy job.

Software developers use abstraction as a tool when building an operating system and its applications. There are many terms for an abstracted subdivision in computer software, including *subsystem*, *module*, and *package*—but we'll use the term *component* in this chapter because it's simple. When building a software component, developers typically don't think much about the internal structure of other components, but they do care about what other components they can use and how to use them.

This chapter provides a high-level overview of the components that make up a Linux system. Although each one has a tremendous number of technical details in its internal makeup, we're going to ignore these details and concentrate on what the components do in relation to the whole system.

1.1   Levels and Layers of Abstraction in a Linux System

Using abstraction to split computing systems into components makes things easier to understand, but it doesn't work without organization. We arrange components into layers or levels. A *layer* or *level* is a classification (or grouping) of a component according to where that component sits between the user and the hardware. Web browsers, games, and such sit at the top layer; at the bottom layer we have the memory in the computer hardware—the 0s and 1s. The operating system occupies most of the layers in between.

A Linux system has three main levels. Figure 1-1 shows these levels and some of the components inside each level. The *hardware* is at the base. Hardware includes the memory as well as one or more central processing units (CPUs) to perform computation and to read from and write to memory. Devices such as disks and network interfaces are also part of the hardware.

The next level up is the *kernel*, which is the core of the operating system. The kernel is software residing in memory that tells the CPU what to do. The kernel manages the hardware and acts primarily as an interface between the hardware and any running program.

Processes—the running programs that the kernel manages—collectively make up the system's upper level, called *user space*. (A more specific term for process is *user process*, regardless of whether a user directly interacts with the process. For example, all web servers run as user processes.)

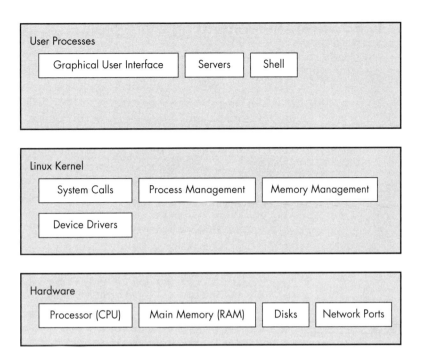

Figure 1-1: General Linux system organization

There is a critical difference between the ways that the kernel and user processes run: The kernel runs in *kernel mode*, and the user processes run in *user mode*. Code running in kernel mode has unrestricted access to the processor and main memory. This is a powerful but dangerous privilege that allows a kernel process to easily crash the entire system. The area that only the kernel can access is called *kernel space*.

User mode, in comparison, restricts access to a (usually quite small) subset of memory and safe CPU operations. *User space* refers to the parts of main memory that the user processes can access. If a process makes a mistake and crashes, the consequences are limited and can be cleaned up by the kernel. This means that if your web browser crashes, it probably won't take down the scientific computation that you've been running in the background for days.

In theory, a user process gone haywire can't cause serious damage to the rest of the system. In reality, it depends on what you consider "serious damage," as well as the particular privileges of the process, because some processes are allowed to do more than others. For example, can a user process completely wreck the data on a disk? With the correct permissions, yes—and you may consider this to be fairly dangerous. There are safeguards to prevent this, however, and most processes simply aren't allowed to wreak havoc in this manner.

1.2   Hardware: Understanding Main Memory

Of all of the hardware on a computer system, *main memory* is perhaps the most important. In its most raw form, main memory is just a big storage area for a bunch of 0s and 1s. Each 0 or 1 is called a *bit*. This is where the running kernel and processes reside—they're just big collections of bits. All input and output from peripheral devices flows through main memory, also as a bunch of bits. A CPU is just an operator on memory; it reads its instructions and data from the memory and writes data back out to the memory.

You'll often hear the term *state* in reference to memory, processes, the kernel, and other parts of a computer system. Strictly speaking, a state is a particular arrangement of bits. For example, if you have four bits in your memory, 0110, 0001, and 1011 represent three different states.

When you consider that a single process can easily consist of millions of bits in memory, it's often easier to use abstract terms when talking about states. Instead of describing a state using bits, you describe what something has done or is doing at the moment. For example, you might say "the process is waiting for input" or "the process is performing Stage 2 of its startup."

NOTE   *Because it's common to refer to the state in abstract terms rather than to the actual bits, the term* image *refers to a particular physical arrangement of bits.*

1.3   The Kernel

Why are we talking about main memory and states? Nearly everything that the kernel does revolves around main memory. One of the kernel's tasks is to split memory into many subdivisions, and it must maintain certain state information about those subdivisions at all times. Each process gets its own share of memory, and the kernel must ensure that each process keeps to its share.

The kernel is in charge of managing tasks in four general system areas:

Processes   The kernel is responsible for determining which processes are allowed to use the CPU.

Memory   The kernel needs to keep track of all memory—what is currently allocated to a particular process, what might be shared between processes, and what is free.

Device drivers   The kernel acts as an interface between hardware (such as a disk) and processes. It's usually the kernel's job to operate the hardware.

System calls and support   Processes normally use system calls to communicate with the kernel.

We'll now briefly explore each of these areas.

NOTE *If you're interested in the detailed workings of a kernel, two good textbooks are* Operating System Concepts, *9th edition, by Abraham Silberschatz, Peter B. Galvin, and Greg Gagne (Wiley, 2012) and* Modern Operating Systems, *4th edition, by Andrew S. Tanenbaum and Herbert Bos (Prentice Hall, 2014).*

1.3.1   Process Management

Process management describes the starting, pausing, resuming, and terminating of processes. The concepts behind starting and terminating processes are fairly straightforward, but describing how a process uses the CPU in its normal course of operation is a bit more complex.

On any modern operating system, many processes run "simultaneously." For example, you might have a web browser and a spreadsheet open on a desktop computer at the same time. However, things are not as they appear: The processes behind these applications typically do not run at *exactly* the same time.

Consider a system with a one-core CPU. Many processes may be *able* to use the CPU, but only one process may actually use the CPU at any given time. In practice, each process uses the CPU for a small fraction of a second, then pauses; then another process uses the CPU for another small fraction of a second; then another process takes a turn, and so on. The act of one process giving up control of the CPU to another process is called a *context switch*.

Each piece of time—called a *time slice*—gives a process enough time for significant computation (and indeed, a process often finishes its current task during a single slice). However, because the slices are so small, humans can't perceive them, and the system appears to be running multiple processes at the same time (a capability known as *multitasking*).

The kernel is responsible for context switching. To understand how this works, let's think about a situation in which a process is running in user mode but its time slice is up. Here's what happens:

1. The CPU (the actual hardware) interrupts the current process based on an internal timer, switches into kernel mode, and hands control back to the kernel.

2. The kernel records the current state of the CPU and memory, which will be essential to resuming the process that was just interrupted.

3. The kernel performs any tasks that might have come up during the preceding time slice (such as collecting data from input and output, or I/O, operations).

4. The kernel is now ready to let another process run. The kernel analyzes the list of processes that are ready to run and chooses one.

5. The kernel prepares the memory for this new process, and then prepares the CPU.

6. The kernel tells the CPU how long the time slice for the new process will last.

7. The kernel switches the CPU into user mode and hands control of the CPU to the process.

The context switch answers the important question of _when_ the kernel runs. The answer is that it runs _between_ process time slices during a context switch.

In the case of a multi-CPU system, things become slightly more complicated because the kernel doesn't need to relinquish control of its current CPU in order to allow a process to run on a different CPU. However, to maximize the usage of all available CPUs, the kernel typically does so anyway (and may use certain tricks to grab a little more CPU time for itself).

1.3.2 Memory Management

Because the kernel must manage memory during a context switch, it has a complex job of memory management. The kernel's job is complicated because the following conditions must hold:

- The kernel must have its own private area in memory that user processes can't access.
- Each user process needs its own section of memory.
- One user process may not access the private memory of another process.
- User processes can share memory.
- Some memory in user processes can be read-only.
- The system can use more memory than is physically present by using disk space as auxiliary.

Fortunately for the kernel, there is help. Modern CPUs include a _memory management unit (MMU)_ that enables a memory access scheme called _virtual memory_. When using virtual memory, a process does not directly access the memory by its physical location in the hardware. Instead, the kernel sets up each process to act as if it had an entire machine to itself. When the process accesses some of its memory, the MMU intercepts the access and uses a memory address map to translate the memory location from the process into an actual physical memory location on the machine. The kernel must still initialize and continuously maintain and alter this memory address map. For example, during a context switch, the kernel has to change the map from the outgoing process to the incoming process.

NOTE   _The implementation of a memory address map is called a_ page table.

You'll learn more about how to view memory performance in Chapter 8.

1.3.3 Device Drivers and Management

The kernel's role with devices is pretty simple. A device is typically accessible only in kernel mode because improper access (such as a user process asking to turn off the power) could crash the machine. Another problem is that different devices rarely have the same programming interface, even if the devices do the same thing, such as two different network cards. Therefore, device drivers have traditionally been part of the kernel, and they strive to present a uniform interface to user processes in order to simplify the software developer's job.

1.3.4 System Calls and Support

There are several other kinds of kernel features available to user processes. For example, *system calls* (or *syscalls*) perform specific tasks that a user process alone cannot do well or at all. For example, the acts of opening, reading, and writing files all involve system calls.

Two system calls, fork() and exec(), are important to understanding how processes start up:

fork() When a process calls fork(), the kernel creates a nearly identical copy of the process.

exec() When a process calls exec(*program*), the kernel starts *program*, replacing the current process.

Other than init (see Chapter 6), *all* user processes on a Linux system start as a result of fork(), and most of the time, you also run exec() to start a new program instead of running a copy of an existing process. A very simple example is any program that you run at the command line, such as the ls command to show the contents of a directory. When you enter ls into a terminal window, the shell that's running inside the terminal window calls fork() to create a copy of the shell, and then the new copy of the shell calls exec(ls) to run ls. Figure 1-2 shows the flow of processes and system calls for starting a program like ls.

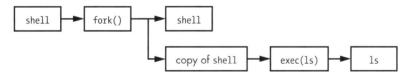

Figure 1-2: Starting a new process

NOTE *System calls are normally denoted with parentheses. In the example shown in Figure 1-2, the process asking the kernel to create another process must perform a fork() system call. This notation derives from the way the call would be written in the C programming language. You don't need to know C to understand this book; just remember that a system call is an interaction between a process and the kernel. In addition, this book simplifies certain groups of system calls. For example, exec() refers to an entire family of system calls that all perform a similar task but differ in programming.*

The kernel also supports user processes with features other than traditional system calls, the most common of which are *pseudodevices*. Pseudodevices look like devices to user processes, but they're implemented purely in software. As such, they don't technically need to be in the kernel, but they are usually there for practical reasons. For example, the kernel random number generator device (*/dev/random*) would be difficult to implement securely with a user process.

NOTE   *Technically, a user process that accesses a pseudodevice still has to use a system call to open the device, so processes can't entirely avoid system calls.*

1.4   User Space

As mentioned earlier, the main memory that the kernel allocates for user processes is called *user space*. Because a process is simply a state (or image) in memory, user space also refers to the memory for the entire collection of running processes. (You may also hear the more informal term *userland* used for user space.)

Most of the real action on a Linux system happens in user space. Although all processes are essentially equal from the kernel's point of view, they perform different tasks for users. There is a rudimentary service level (or layer) structure to the kinds of system components that user processes represent. Figure 1-3 shows how an example set of components fit together and interact on a Linux system. Basic services are at the bottom level (closest to the kernel), utility services are in the middle, and applications that users touch are at the top. Figure 1-3 is a greatly simplified diagram because only six components are shown, but you can see that the components at the top are closest to the user (the user interface and web browser); the components in the middle level has a mail server that the web browser uses; and there are several smaller components at the bottom.

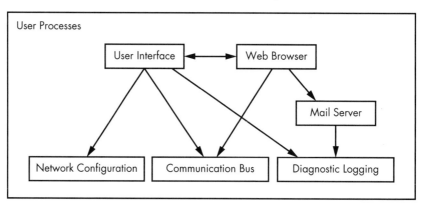

Figure 1-3: Process types and interactions

The bottom level tends to consist of small components that perform single, uncomplicated tasks. The middle level has larger components such as mail, print, and database services. Finally, components at the top level perform complicated tasks that the user often controls directly. Components also use other components. Generally, if one component wants to use another, the second component is either at the same service level or below.

However, Figure 1-3 is only an approximation of the arrangement of user space. In reality, there are no rules in user space. For example, most applications and services write diagnostic messages known as *logs*. Most programs use the standard syslog service to write log messages, but some prefer to do all of the logging themselves.

In addition, it's difficult to categorize some user-space components. Server components such as web and database servers can be considered very high-level applications because their tasks are often complicated, so you might place these at the top level in Figure 1-3. However, user applications may depend on these servers to perform tasks that they'd rather not do themselves, so you could also make a case for placing them at the middle level.

1.5   Users

The Linux kernel supports the traditional concept of a Unix user. A *user* is an entity that can run processes and own files. A user is associated with a *username*. For example, a system could have a user named *billyjoe*. However, the kernel does not manage the usernames; instead, it identifies users by simple numeric identifiers called *userids*. (You'll learn more about how the usernames correspond to userids in Chapter 7.)

Users exist primarily to support permissions and boundaries. Every user-space process has a user *owner*, and processes are said to run *as* the owner. A user may terminate or modify the behavior of its own processes (within certain limits), but it cannot interfere with other users' processes. In addition, users may own files and choose whether they share them with other users.

A Linux system normally has a number of users in addition to the ones that correspond to the real human beings who use the system. You'll read about these in more detail in Chapter 3, but the most important user to know about is *root*. The root user is an exception to the preceding rules because root may terminate and alter another user's processes and read any file on the local system. For this reason, root is known as the *superuser*. A person who can operate as root is said to have *root access* and is an administrator on a traditional Unix system.

NOTE *Operating as root can be dangerous. It can be difficult to identify and correct mistakes because the system will let you do anything, even if what you're doing is harmful to the system. For this reason, system designers constantly try to make root access as unnecessary as possible, for example, by not requiring root access to switch between wireless networks on a notebook. In addition, as powerful as the root user is, it still runs in the operating system's user mode, not kernel mode.*

Groups are sets of users. The primary purpose of groups is to allow a user to share file access to other users in a group.

1.6   Looking Forward

So far, you've seen what makes up a *running* Linux system. User processes make up the environment that you directly interact with; the kernel manages processes and hardware. Both the kernel and processes reside in memory.

This is great background information, but you can't learn the details of a Linux system by reading about it alone; you need to get your hands dirty. The next chapter starts your journey by teaching you some user-space basics. Along the way, you'll learn about a major part of the Linux system that this chapter doesn't discuss—long-term storage (disks, files, etc.). After all, you need to store your programs and data somewhere.

2

BASIC COMMANDS AND DIRECTORY HIERARCHY

This chapter is a guide to the Unix commands and utilities that will be referenced throughout this book. This is preliminary material, and you may already know a substantial amount of it. Even if you think you're up to speed, take a few seconds to flip through the chapter just to make sure, especially when it comes to the directory hierarchy material in Section 2.19.

Why Unix commands? Isn't this a book about how Linux works? It is, of course, but Linux is a Unix flavor at heart. You'll see the word *Unix* in this chapter more than *Linux* because you can take what you learn straight over to Solaris, BSD, and other Unix-flavored systems. I've attempted to avoid covering too many Linux-specific user interface extensions, not only to give you a better background for using the other operating systems, but also because these extensions tend to be unstable. You'll be able to adapt to new Linux releases much more quickly if you know the core commands.

> **NOTE** *For more details about Unix for beginners than you'll find here, consider reading* The Linux Command Line *(No Starch Press, 2012),* UNIX for the Impatient *(Addison-Wesley Professional, 1995), and* Learning the UNIX Operating System, *5th edition (O'Reilly, 2001).*

2.1   The Bourne Shell: /bin/sh

The shell is one of the most important parts of a Unix system. A *shell* is a program that runs commands, like the ones that users enter. The shell also serves as a small programming environment. Unix programmers often break common tasks into little components and use the shell to manage tasks and piece things together.

Many important parts of the system are actually *shell scripts*—text files that contain a sequence of shell commands. If you've worked with MS-DOS previously, you can think of shell scripts as very powerful *.BAT* files. Because they're important, Chapter 11 is devoted entirely to shell scripts.

249

As you progress through this book and gain practice, you'll add to your knowledge of manipulating commands using the shell. One of the best things about the shell is that if you make a mistake, you can easily see what you typed to find out what went wrong, and then try again.

There are many different Unix shells, but all derive several of their features from the Bourne shell (*/bin/sh*), a standard shell developed at Bell Labs for early versions of Unix. Every Unix system needs the Bourne shell in order to function correctly, as you will see throughout this book.

Linux uses an enhanced version of the Bourne shell called bash or the "Bourne-again" shell. The bash shell is the default shell on most Linux distributions, and */bin/sh* is normally a link to bash on a Linux system. You should use the bash shell when running the examples in this book.

> **NOTE** *You may not have* bash *as your default shell if you're using this chapter as a guide for a Unix account at an organization where you're not the system administrator. You can change your shell with* chsh *or ask your system administrator for help.*

✶

2.2   Using the Shell

When you install Linux, you should create at least one regular user in addition to the root user; this will be your personal account. For this chapter, you should log in as the regular user.

2.2.1   The Shell Window

After logging in, open a shell window (often referred to as a *terminal*). The easiest way to do so from a GUI like Gnome or Ubuntu's Unity is to open a terminal application, which starts a shell inside a new window. Once you've opened a shell, it should display a prompt at the top that usually ends with a dollar sign (\$). On Ubuntu, that prompt should look like *name@host:path*\$, and on Fedora, it's [*name@host path*]\$. If you're familiar with Windows, the shell window will look something like a DOS command prompt; the Terminal application in OS X is essentially the same as a Linux shell window.

This book contains many commands that you will type at a shell prompt. They all begin with a single \$ to denote the shell prompt. For example, type this command (just the part in bold, not the \$) and press ENTER:

$ **echo Hello there.**

NOTE   *Many shell commands in this book start with #. You should run these as the super-user (root). These commands usually require extra caution.*

Now enter this command:

$ **cat /etc/passwd**

This command displays the contents of the */etc/passwd* system informa-tion file and then returns your shell prompt. Don't worry about what this file does right now; you'll learn all about it later, in Chapter 7.

2.2.2   cat

The cat command is one of the easiest Unix commands to understand; it simply outputs the contents of one or more files. The general syntax of the cat command is as follows:

$ **cat** *file1 file2 ...*

When you run this command, cat prints the contents of *file1*, *file2*, and any other files that you specify (denoted by ...), and then exits. The command is called cat because it performs concatenation when it prints the contents of more than one file.

2.2.3   Standard Input and Standard Output

We'll use cat to briefly explore Unix input and output (I/O). Unix pro-cesses use I/O *streams* to read and write data. Processes read data from input streams and write data to output streams. Streams are very flexible. For example, the source of an input stream can be a file, a device, a termi-nal, or even the output stream from another process.

To see an input stream at work, enter cat (with no filenames) and press ENTER. This time, you won't get your shell prompt back because cat is still running. Now type anything and press ENTER at the end of each line. The cat command repeats any line that you type. Once you're sufficiently bored, press CTRL-D on an empty line to terminate cat and return to the shell prompt.

The reason cat adopted an interactive behavior has to do with streams. Because you did not specify an input filename, cat read from the *standard input* stream provided by the Linux kernel rather than a stream connected to a file. In this case, the standard input was connected to the terminal in which you ran cat.

Pressing CTRL-D on an empty line stops the current standard input entry from the terminal (and often terminates a program). Don't confuse this with CTRL-C, which terminates a program regardless of its input or output.

Standard output is similar. The kernel gives each process a standard output stream where it can write its output. The cat command always writes its output to the standard output. When you ran cat in the terminal, the standard output was connected to that terminal, so that's where you saw the output.

Standard input and output are often abbreviated as *stdin* and *stdout*. Many commands operate as cat does; if you don't specify an input file, the command reads from stdin. Output is a little different. Some commands (like cat) send output only to stdout, but others have the option to send output directly to files.

There is a third standard I/O stream called standard error. You'll see it in Section 2.14.1.

One of the best features of standard streams is that you can easily manipulate them to read and write to places other than the terminal, as you'll learn in Section 2.14. In particular, you'll learn how to connect streams to files and other processes.

2.3   Basic Commands

Now let's look at some more Unix commands. Most of the following programs take multiple arguments, and some have so many options and formats that an unabridged listing would be pointless. This is a simplified list of the basic commands; you don't need all of the details just yet.

2.3.1   ls

The ls command lists the contents of a directory. The default is the current directory. Use ls -l for a detailed (long) listing and ls -F to display file type information. (For more on the file types and permissions displayed in the left column below, see Section 2.17.) Here is a sample long listing; it includes the owner of the file (column 3), the group (column 4), the file size (column 5), and the modification date/time (between column 5 and the filename):

```
$ ls -l
total 3616
-rw-r--r--    1 juser    users        3804 Apr 30  2011 abusive.c
-rw-r--r--    1 juser    users        4165 May 26  2010 battery.zip
```

```
-rw-r--r--   1 juser    users    131219 Oct 26  2012 beav_1.40-13.tar.gz
-rw-r--r--   1 juser    users      6255 May 30  2010 country.c
drwxr-xr-x   2 juser    users      4096 Jul 17 20:00 cs335
-rwxr-xr-x   1 juser    users      7108 Feb  2  2011 dhry
-rw-r--r--   1 juser    users     11309 Oct 20  2010 dhry.c
-rw-r--r--   1 juser    users        56 Oct  6  2012 doit
drwxr-xr-x   6 juser    users      4096 Feb 20 13:51 dw
drwxr-xr-x   3 juser    users      4096 May  2  2011 hough-stuff
```

You'll learn more about the d in column 1 of this output in Section 2.17.

2.3.2   cp

In its simplest form, cp copies files. For example, to copy *file1* to *file2*, enter this:

```
$ cp file1 file2
```

To copy a number of files to a directory (folder) named *dir*, try this instead:

```
$ cp file1 ... fileN dir
```

2.3.3   mv

The mv (move) command is like cp. In its simplest form, it renames a file. For example, to rename *file1* to *file2*, enter this:

```
$ mv file1 file2
```

You can also use mv to move a number of files to a different directory:

```
$ mv file1 ... fileN dir
```

2.3.4   touch

The touch command creates a file. If the file already exists, touch does not change it, but it does update the file's modification time stamp printed with the ls -l command. For example, to create an empty file, enter this:

```
$ touch file
```

Then run ls -l on that file. You should see output like the following, where the date and time ❶ indicate when you ran touch:

```
$ ls -l file
-rw-r--r-- 1 juser users 0 May 21 18:32❶ file
```

2.3.5 rm

To delete (remove) a file, use rm. After you remove a file, it's gone from your system and generally cannot be undeleted.

```
$ rm file
```

2.3.6 echo

The echo command prints its arguments to the standard output:

```
$ echo Hello again.
Hello again.
```

The echo command is very useful for finding expansions of shell globs ("wildcards" such as *) and variables (such as $HOME), which you will encounter later in this chapter.

2.4 Navigating Directories

Unix has a directory hierarchy that starts at /, sometimes called the *root directory*. The directory separator is the slash (/), *not* the backslash (\). There are several standard subdirectories in the root directory, such as */usr*, as you'll learn in Section 2.19.

When you refer to a file or directory, you specify a *path* or *pathname*. When a path starts with / (such as */usr/lib*), it's a *full* or *absolute* path.

A path component identified by two dots (..) specifies the parent of a directory. For example, if you're working in */usr/lib*, the path .. would refer to */usr*. Similarly, *../bin* would refer to */usr/bin*.

One dot (.) refers to the current directory; for example, if you're in */usr/lib*, the path . is still */usr/lib*, and *./X11* is */usr/lib/X11*. You won't have to use . very often because most commands default to the current directory if a path doesn't start with / (you could just use *X11* instead of *./X11* in the preceding example).

A path not beginning with / is called a *relative path*. Most of the time, you'll work with relative pathnames, because you'll already be in the directory you need to be in or somewhere close by.

Now that you have a sense of the basic directory mechanics, here are some essential directory commands.

2.4.1 cd

The *current working directory* is the directory that a process (such as the shell) is currently in. The cd command changes the shell's current working directory:

```
$ cd dir
```

If you omit *dir*, the shell returns to your *home directory*, the directory you started in when you first logged in.

2.4.2   mkdir

The mkdir command creates a new directory *dir*:

```
$ mkdir dir
```

2.4.3   rmdir

The rmdir command removes the directory *dir*:

```
$ rmdir dir
```

If *dir* isn't empty, this command fails. However, if you're impatient, you probably don't want to laboriously delete all the files and subdirectories inside *dir* first. You can use rm -rf *dir* to delete a directory and its contents, but be careful! This is one of the few commands that can do serious damage, especially if you run it as the superuser. The -r option specifies *recursive delete* to repeatedly delete everything inside *dir*, and -f forces the delete operation. Don't use the -rf flags with globs such as a star (*). And above all, always double-check your command before you run it.

2.4.4   Shell Globbing (Wildcards)

The shell can match simple patterns to file and directory names, a process known as *globbing*. This is similar to the concept of wildcards in other systems. The simplest of these is the glob character *, which tells the shell to match any number of arbitrary characters. For example, the following command prints a list of files in the current directory:

```
$ echo *
```

The shell matches arguments containing globs to filenames, substitutes the filenames for those arguments, and then runs the revised command line. The substitution is called *expansion* because the shell substitutes all matching filenames. Here are some ways to use * to expand filenames:

- at* expands to all filenames that start with at.
- *at expands to all filenames that end with at.
- *at* expands to all filenames that contain at.

If no files match a glob, the shell performs no expansion, and the command runs with literal characters such as *. For example, try a command such as echo *dfkdsafh.

NOTE *If you're used to MS-DOS, you might instinctively type *.* to match all files. Break this habit now. In Linux and other versions of Unix, you must use * to match all files. In the Unix shell, *.* matches only files and directories that contain the dot (.) character in their names. Unix filenames do not need extensions and often do not carry them.*

matcher

?

Another shell glob character, the question mark (?), instructs the shell to match exactly one arbitrary character. For example, b?at matches boat and brat.

If you don't want the shell to expand a glob in a command, enclose the glob in single quotes (''). For example, the command echo '*' prints a star. You will find this handy for a few of the commands described in the next section, such as grep and find. (You'll learn more much about quoting in Section 11.2.)

NOTE *It is important to remember that the shell performs expansions before running commands, and only then. Therefore, if a * makes it to a command without expanding, the shell will do nothing more with it; it's up to the command to decide what it wants to do.*

There is more to a modern shell's pattern-matching capabilities, but * and ? are what you need to know now.

2.5   Intermediate Commands

The following sections describe the most essential intermediate Unix commands.

2.5.1   grep

The grep command prints the lines from a file or input stream that match an expression. For example, to print the lines in the */etc/passwd* file that contain the text root, enter this:

```
$ grep root /etc/passwd
```

The grep command is extraordinarily handy when operating on multiple files at once because it prints the filename in addition to the matching line. For example, if you want to check every file in */etc* that contains the word root, you could use this command:

```
$ grep root /etc/*
```

Two of the most important grep options are -i (for case-insensitive matches) and -v (which inverts the search, that is, prints all lines that *don't* match). There is also a more powerful variant called egrep (which is just a synonym for grep -E).

grep understands patterns known as *regular expressions* that are grounded in computer science theory and are very common in Unix utilities. Regular expressions are more powerful than wildcard-style patterns, and they have a different syntax. There are two important things to remember about regular expressions:

- .* matches any number of characters (like the * in wildcards).
- . matches one arbitrary character.

NOTE *The grep(1) manual page contains a detailed description of regular expressions, but it can be a little difficult to read. To learn more, you can read* Mastering Regular Expressions, *3rd edition (O'Reilly, 2006), or see the regular expressions chapter of* Programming Perl, *4th edition (O'Reilly, 2012). If you like math and are interested in where regular expressions come from, look up* Introduction to Automata Theory, Languages, and Computation, *3rd edition (Prentice Hall, 2006).*

2.5.2 less

The less command comes in handy when a file is really big or when a command's output is long and scrolls off the top of the screen.

To page through a big file like */usr/share/dict/words*, use the command less /usr/share/dict/words. When running less, you'll see the contents of the file one screenful at a time. Press the spacebar to go forward in the file and the b key to skip back one screenful. To quit, type q.

NOTE *The less command is an enhanced version of an older program named more. Most Linux desktops and servers have less, but it's not standard on many embedded systems and other Unix systems. So if you ever run into a situation when you can't use less, try more.*

You can also search for text inside less. For example, to search forward for a word, type /word, and to search backward, use ?word. When you find a match, press n to continue searching.

As you'll learn in Section 2.14, you can send the standard output of nearly any program directly to another program's standard input. This is exceptionally useful when you have a command with a lot of output to sift through and you'd like to use something like less to view the output. Here's an example of sending the output of a grep command to less:

```
$ grep ie /usr/share/dict/words | less
```

Try this command out for yourself. You'll probably use less like this a lot.

2.5.3 pwd

The pwd (print working directory) program simply outputs the name of the current working directory. You may be wondering why you need this when most Linux distributions set up accounts with the current working directory in the prompt. There are two reasons.

First, not all prompts include the current working directory, and you may even want to get rid of it in your own prompt because it takes up a lot of space. If you do so, you need pwd.

Second, the symbolic links that you'll learn about in Section 2.17.2 can sometimes obscure the true full path of the current working directory. You'll use pwd -P to eliminate this confusion.

2.5.4   diff

To see the differences between two text files, use diff:

```
$ diff file1 file2
```

Several options can control the format of the output, and the default output format is often the most comprehensible for human beings. However, most programmers prefer the output from diff -u when they need to send the output to someone else because automated tools can make better use of it.

2.5.5   file

If you see a file and are unsure of its format, try using the file command to see if the system can guess:

```
$ file file
```

You may be surprised by how much this innocent-looking command can do.

2.5.6   find and locate

It's frustrating when you know that a certain file is in a directory tree somewhere but you just don't know where. Run find to find *file* in *dir*:

```
$ find dir -name file -print
```

Like most programs in this section, find is capable of some fancy stuff. However, don't try options such as -exec before you know the form shown here by heart and why you need the -name and -print options. The find command accepts special pattern-matching characters such as *, but you must enclose them in single quotes ('*') to protect the special characters from the shell's own globbing feature. (Recall from Section 2.4.4 that the shell expands globs *before* running commands.)

Most systems also have a locate command for finding files. Rather than searching for a file in real time, locate searches an index that the system builds periodically. Searching with locate is much faster than find, but if the file you're looking for is newer than the index, locate won't find it.

2.5.7   head and tail

To quickly view a portion of a file or stream of data, use the head and tail commands. For example, head /etc/passwd shows the first 10 lines of the password file, and tail /etc/passwd shows the last 10 lines.

To change the number of lines to display, use the -n option, where n is the number of lines you want to see (for example, head -5 /etc/passwd). To print lines starting at line n, use tail +n.

2.5.8   sort

The sort command quickly puts the lines of a text file in alphanumeric order. If the file's lines start with numbers and you want to sort in numerical order, use the -n option. The -r option reverses the order of the sort.

2.6   Changing Your Password and Shell

Use the passwd command to change your password. You'll be asked for your old password and then prompted for your new password twice. Choose a password that does not include real words in any language and don't try to combine words.

One of the easiest ways to create a good password is to pick a sentence, produce an acronym from it, and then modify the acronym with a number or some punctuation. Then all you need to do is remember the sentence.

You can change your shell with the chsh command (to an alternative such as ksh or tcsh), but keep in mind that this book assumes that you're running bash.

2.7   Dot Files

Change to your home directory, take a look around with ls, and then run ls -a. Do you see the difference in the output? When you run ls without the -a, you won't see the configuration files called *dot files*. These are files and directories whose names begin with a dot (.). Common dot files are *.bashrc* and *.login*, and there are dot directories, too, such as *.ssh*.

There is nothing special about dot files or directories. Some programs don't show them by default so that you won't see a complete mess when listing the contents of your home directory. For example, ls doesn't list dot files unless you use the -a option. In addition, shell globs don't match dot files unless you explicitly use a pattern such as .*.

NOTE   *You can run into problems with globs because .* matches . and .. (the current and parent directories). You may wish to use a pattern such as .[^.]* or .??* to get all dot files* except *the current and parent directories.*

2.8   Environment and Shell Variables

The shell can store temporary variables, called *shell variables*, containing the values of text strings. Shell variables are very useful for keeping track of values in scripts, and some shell variables control the way the shell behaves. (For example, the bash shell reads the PS1 variable before displaying the prompt.)

To assign a value to a shell variable, use the equal sign (=). Here's a simple example:

```
$ STUFF=blah
```

The preceding example sets the value of the variable named STUFF to blah. To access this variable, use $STUFF (for example, try running echo $STUFF). You'll learn about the many uses of shell variables in Chapter 11.

An *environment variable* is like a shell variable, but it's not specific to the shell. All processes on Unix systems have environment variable storage. The main difference between environment and shell variables is that the operating system passes all of your shell's environment variables to programs that the shell runs, whereas shell variables cannot be accessed in the commands that you run.

Assign an environment variable with the shell's export command. For example, if you'd like to make the $STUFF shell variable into an environment variable, use the following:

```
$ STUFF=blah
$ export STUFF
```

Environment variables are useful because many programs read them for configuration and options. For example, you can put your favorite less command-line options in the LESS environment variable, and less will use those options when you run it. (Many manual pages contain a section marked ENVIRONMENT that describes these variables.)

2.9   The Command Path

PATH is a special environment variable that contains the *command path* (or *path* for short). A command path is a list of system directories that the shell searches when trying to locate a command. For example, when you run ls, the shell searches the directories listed in PATH for the ls program. If programs with the same name appear in several directories in the path, the shell runs the first matching program.

If you run echo $PATH, you'll see that the path components are separated by colons (:). For example:

```
$ echo $PATH
/usr/local/bin:/usr/bin:/bin
```

To tell the shell to look in more places for programs, change the PATH environment variable. For example, by using this command, you can add a directory *dir* to the beginning of the path so that the shell looks in *dir* before looking in any of the other PATH directories.

```
$ PATH=dir:$PATH
```

Or you can append a directory name to the end of the PATH variable, causing the shell to look in *dir* last:

```
$ PATH=$PATH:dir
```

NOTE   *Be careful when modifying the path because you can accidentally wipe out your entire path if you mistype $PATH. If this happens, don't panic! The damage isn't permanent; you can just start a new shell. (For a lasting effect, you need to mistype it when editing a certain configuration file, and even then it isn't difficult to rectify.) One of the easiest ways to return to normal is to close the current terminal window and start another.*

2.10   Special Characters

When discussing Linux with others, you should know a few names for some of the special characters that you'll encounter. If you're amused by this sort of thing, see the "Jargon File" (*http://www.catb.org/jargon/html/*) or its printed companion, *The New Hacker's Dictionary* (MIT Press, 1996).

Table 2-1 describes a select set of the special characters, many of which you've already seen in this chapter. Some utilities, such as the Perl programming language, use almost all of these special characters! (Keep in mind that these are the American names for the characters.)

Table 2-1: Special Characters

Character	Name(s)	Uses
*	asterisk, star	Regular expression, glob character
.	dot	Current directory, file/hostname delimiter
!	bang	Negation, command history
|	pipe	Command pipes
/	(forward) slash	Directory delimiter, search command
\	backslash	Literals, macros (*never* directories)
$	dollar	Variable denotation, end of line
'	tick, (single) quote	Literal strings
`	backtick, backquote	Command substitution
"	double quote	Semi-literal strings
^	caret	Negation, beginning of line
~	tilde, squiggle	Negation, directory shortcut
#	hash, sharp, pound	Comments, preprocessor, substitutions
[ ]	(square) brackets	Ranges
{ }	braces, (curly) brackets	Statement blocks, ranges
_	underscore, under	Cheap substitute for a space

You will often see control characters marked with a caret; for example, ^C for CTRL-C.

2.11 Command-Line Editing

As you play with the shell, notice that you can edit the command line using the left and right arrow keys, as well as page through previous commands using the up and down arrows. This is standard on most Linux systems.

However, it's a good idea to forget about the arrow keys and use control key sequences instead. If you learn the ones listed in Table 2-2, you'll find that you're better able to enter text in the many Unix programs that use these standard keystrokes.

Table 2-2: Command-Line Keystrokes

Keystroke	Action
CTRL-B	Move the cursor left
CTRL-F	Move the cursor right
CTRL-P	View the previous command (or move the cursor up)
CTRL-N	View the next command (or move the cursor down)
CTRL-A	Move the cursor to the beginning of the line
CTRL-E	Move the cursor to the end of the line
CTRL-W	Erase the preceding word
CTRL-U	Erase from cursor to beginning of line
CTRL-K	Erase from cursor to end of line
CTRL-Y	Paste erased text (for example, from CTRL-U)

2.12 Text Editors

Speaking of editing, it's time to learn an editor. To get serious with Unix, you must be able to edit text files without damaging them. Most parts of the system use plaintext configuration files (like the ones in */etc*). It's not difficult to edit files, but you will do it so often that you need a powerful tool for the job.

You should try to learn one of the two de facto standard Unix text editors, vi and Emacs. Most Unix wizards are religious about their choice of editor, but don't listen to them. Just choose for yourself. If you choose one that matches the way that you work, you'll find it easier to learn. Basically, the choice comes down to this:

- If you want an editor that can do almost anything and has extensive online help, and you don't mind doing some extra typing to get these features, try Emacs.
- If speed is everything, give vi a shot; it "plays" a bit like a video game.

Learning the vi and Vim Editors: Unix Text Processing, 7th edition (O'Reilly, 2008) can tell you everything you need to know about vi. For Emacs, use the online tutorial: Start Emacs, press CTRL-H, and then type T. Or read *GNU Emacs Manual* (Free Software Foundation, 2011).

You might be tempted to experiment with a friendlier editor when you first start out, such as Pico or one of the myriad GUI editors out there, but if you tend to make a habit out of the first thing that you use, you don't want to go down this route.

NOTE   *Editing text is where you'll first start to see a difference between the terminal and the GUI. Editors such as vi run inside the terminal window, using the standard terminal I/O interface. GUI editors start their own window and present their own interface, independent of terminals. Emacs runs in a GUI by default but will run in a terminal window as well.*

2.13   Getting Online Help

Linux systems come with a wealth of documentation. For basic commands, the *manual pages* (or *man pages*) will tell you what you need to know. For example, to see the manual page for the ls command, run man as follows:

```
$ man ls
```

Most manual pages concentrate primarily on reference information, perhaps with some examples and cross-references, but that's about it. Don't expect a tutorial, and don't expect an engaging literary style.

When programs have many options, the manual page often lists the options in some systematic way (for example, in alphabetical order), but it won't tell you what the important ones are. If you're patient, you can usually find what you need to know in the man page. If you're impatient, ask a friend—or pay someone to be your friend so that you can ask him or her.

To search for a manual page by keyword, use the -k option:

```
$ man -k keyword
```

This is helpful if you don't quite know the name of the command that you want. For example, if you're looking for a command to sort something, run:

```
$ man -k sort
--snip--
comm (1)            - compare two sorted files line by line
qsort (3)           - sorts an array
sort (1)            - sort lines of text files
sortm (1)           - sort messages
tsort (1)           - perform topological sort
--snip--
```

The output includes the manual page name, the manual section (see below), and a quick description of what the manual page contains.

NOTE *If you have any questions about the commands described in the previous sections, you may be able to find the answers by using the man command.*

Manual pages are referenced by numbered sections. When someone refers to a manual page, the section number appears in parentheses next to the name, like ping(8), for example. Table 2-3 lists the sections and their numbers.

Table 2-3: Online Manual Sections

Section	Description
1	User commands
2	System calls
3	Higher-level Unix programming library documentation
4	Device interface and driver information
5	File descriptions (system configuration files)
6	Games
7	File formats, conventions, and encodings (ASCII, suffixes, and so on)
8	System commands and servers

Sections 1, 5, 7, and 8 should be good supplements to this book. Section 4 may be of marginal use, and Section 6 would be great if only it were a little larger. You probably won't be able to use Section 3 if you aren't a programmer, but you may be able to understand some of the material in Section 2 once you've read more about system calls in this book.

You can select a manual page by section, which is sometimes important because man displays the first manual page that it finds when matching a particular search term. For example, to read the */etc/passwd* file description (as opposed to the passwd command), you can insert the section number before the page name:

```
$ man 5 passwd
```

Manual pages cover the essentials, but there are many more ways to get online help. If you're just looking for a certain option for a command, try entering a command name followed by --help or -h (the option varies from command to command). You may get a deluge (as in the case of ls --help), or you may find just what you're looking for.

Some time ago, the GNU Project decided that it didn't like manual pages very much and switched to another format called *info* (or *texinfo*). Often this documentation goes further than a typical manual page does, but it is sometimes more complex. To access an info manual, use `info` with the command name:

```
$ info command
```

Some packages dump their available documentation into */usr/share/doc* with no regard for online manual systems such as `man` or `info`. See this directory on your system if you find yourself searching for documentation. And of course, search the Internet.

2.14   Shell Input and Output

Now that you're familiar with basic Unix commands, files, and directories, you're ready to learn how to redirect standard input and output. Let's start with standard output.

To send the output of *command* to a file instead of the terminal, use the `>` redirection character:

```
$ command > file
```

The shell creates *file* if it does not already exist. If *file* exists, the shell erases (*clobbers*) the original file first. (Some shells have parameters that prevent clobbering. For example, enter `set -C` to avoid clobbering in `bash`.)

You can append the output to the file instead of overwriting it with the `>>` redirection syntax:

```
$ command >> file
```

This is a handy way to collect output in one place when executing sequences of related commands.

To send the standard output of a command to the standard input of another command, use the pipe character (`|`). To see how this works, try these two commands:

change letters to caps

```
$ head /proc/cpuinfo
$ head /proc/cpuinfo | tr a-z A-Z
```

You can send output through as many piped commands as you wish; just add another pipe before each additional command.

2.14.1   Standard Error

Occasionally, you may redirect standard output but find that the program still prints something to the terminal. This is called *standard error* (stderr); it's an additional output stream for diagnostics and debugging. For example, this command produces an error:

```
$ ls /fffffffff > f
```

After completion, *f* should be empty, but you still see the following error message on the terminal as standard error:

```
ls: cannot access /ffffffffff: No such file or directory
```

You can redirect the standard error if you like. For example, to send standard output to *f* and standard error to *e*, use the 2> syntax, like this:

```
$ ls /ffffffffff > f 2> e
```

The number 2 specifies the *stream ID* that the shell modifies. Stream ID 1 is standard output (the default), and 2 is standard error.

You can also send the standard error to the same place as stdout with the >& notation. For example, to send both standard output and standard error to the file named *f,* try this command:

```
$ ls /ffffffffff > f 2>&1
```

2.14.2   Standard Input Redirection

To channel a file to a program's standard input, use the < operator:

```
$ head < /proc/cpuinfo
```

You will occasionally run into a program that requires this type of redirection, but because most Unix commands accept filenames as arguments, this isn't very common. For example, the preceding command could have been written as head /proc/cpuinfo.

2.15   Understanding Error Messages

When you encounter a problem on a Unix-like system such as Linux, you *must* read the error message. Unlike messages from other operating systems, Unix errors usually tell you exactly what went wrong.

2.15.1   Anatomy of a UNIX Error Message

Most Unix programs generate and report the same basic error messages, but there can be subtle differences between the output of any two programs. Here's an example that you'll certainly encounter in some form or other:

```
$ ls /dsafsda
ls: cannot access /dsafsda: No such file or directory
```

There are three components to this message:

- The program name, ls. Some programs omit this identifying information, which can be annoying when writing shell scripts, but it's not really a big deal.
- The filename, /dsafsda, which is a more specific piece of information. There's a problem with this path.
- The error No such file or directory indicates the problem with the filename.

Putting it all together, you get something like "ls tried to open /dsafsda but couldn't because it doesn't exist." This may seem obvious, but these messages can get a little confusing when you run a shell script that includes an erroneous command under a different name.

When troubleshooting errors, always address the first error first. Some programs report that they can't do anything before reporting a host of other problems. For example, say you run a fictitious program called scumd and you see this error message:

```
scumd: cannot access /etc/scumd/config: No such file or directory
```

Following this is a huge list of other error messages that looks like a complete catastrophe. Don't let those other errors distract you. You probably just need to create */etc/scumd/config*.

NOTE   *Don't confuse error messages with warning messages. Warnings often look like errors, but they contain the word* warning. *A warning usually means something is wrong but the program will try to continue running anyway. To fix a problem noted in a warning message, you may have to hunt down a process and kill it before doing anything else. (You'll learn about listing and killing processes in Section 2.16.)*

2.15.2   Common Errors

Many errors that you'll encounter in Unix programs result from things that can go wrong with files and processes. Here's an error message hit parade:

No such file or directory

This is the number one error. You tried to access a file that doesn't exist. Because the Unix file I/O system doesn't discriminate between files and directories, this error message occurs everywhere. You get it when you try to read a file that does not exist, when you try to change to a directory that isn't there, when you try to write to a file in a directory that doesn't exist, and so on.

File exists

In this case, you probably tried to create a file that already exists. This is common when you try to create a directory with the same name as a file.

Not a directory, Is a directory

These messages pop up when you try to use a file as a directory or a directory as a file. For example:

```
$ touch a
$ touch a/b
touch: a/b: Not a directory
```

Notice that the error message only applies to the a part of a/b. When you encounter this problem, you may need to dig around a little to find the path component that is being treated like a directory.

No space left on device

You're out of disk space.

Permission denied

You get this error when you attempt to read or write to a file or directory that you're not allowed to access (you have insufficient privileges). This error also shows when you try to execute a file that does not have the execute bit set (even if you can read the file). You'll read more about permissions in Section 2.17.

Operation not permitted

This usually happens when you try to kill a process that you don't own.

Segmentation fault, Bus error

A *segmentation fault* essentially means that the person who wrote the program that you just ran screwed up somewhere. The program tried to access a part of memory that it was not allowed to touch, and the operating system killed it. Similarly, a *bus error* means that the program tried to access some memory in a particular way that it shouldn't. When you get one of these errors, you might be giving a program some input that it did not expect.

2.16 Listing and Manipulating Processes

Recall from Chapter 1 that a *process* is a running program. Each process on the system has a numeric *process ID* (PID). For a quick listing of running processes, just run ps on the command line. You should get a list like this one:

```
$ ps
  PID TTY STAT TIME COMMAND
  520 p0 S    0:00 -bash
  545 ?  S    3:59 /usr/X11R6/bin/ctwm -W
  548 ?  S    0:10 xclock -geometry -0-0
 2159 pd SW   0:00 /usr/bin/vi lib/addresses
 31956 p3 R   0:00 ps
```

The fields are as follows:

PID The process ID.

TTY The terminal device where the process is running. More about this later.

STAT The process status, that is, what the process is doing and where its memory resides. For example, S means sleeping and R means running. (See the ps(1) manual page for a description of all the symbols.)

TIME The amount of CPU time in minutes and seconds that the process has used so far. In other words, the total amount of time that the process has spent running instructions on the processor.

COMMAND This one might seem obvious, but be aware that a process can change this field from its original value.

2.16.1   Command Options

The ps command has many options. To make things more confusing, you can specify options in three different styles—Unix, BSD, and GNU. Many people find the BSD style to be the most comfortable (perhaps because it involves less typing), so we'll use the BSD style in this book. Here are some of the most useful option combinations:

ps x Show all of your running processes.

ps ax Show all processes on the system, not just the ones you own.

ps u Include more detailed information on processes.

ps w Show full command names, not just what fits on one line.

As with other programs, you can combine options, as in ps aux and ps auxw.

To check on a specific process, add its PID to the argument list of the ps command. For example, to inspect the current shell process, you could use ps u $$, because $$ is a shell variable that evaluates to the current shell's PID. (You'll find information on the administration commands top and lsof in Chapter 8. These can be useful for locating processes, even when doing something other than system maintenance.)

2.16.2   Killing Processes

To terminate a process, send it a *signal* with the kill command. A signal is a message to a process from the kernel. When you run kill, you're asking the kernel to send a signal to another process. In most cases, all you need to do is this:

```
$ kill pid
```

There are many types of signals. The default is TERM, or terminate. You can send different signals by adding an extra option to kill. For example, to freeze a process instead of terminating it, use the STOP signal:

```
$ kill -STOP pid
```

A stopped process is still in memory, ready to pick up where it left off. Use the CONT signal to continue running the process again:

```
$ kill -CONT pid
```

NOTE   *Using CTRL-C to terminate a process that is running in the current terminal is the same as using kill to end the process with the INT (interrupt) signal.*

The most brutal way to terminate a process is with the KILL signal. Other signals give the process a chance to clean up after itself, but KILL does not. The operating system terminates the process and forcibly removes it from memory. Use this as a last resort.

You should not kill processes indiscriminately, especially if you don't know what they're doing. You may be shooting yourself in the foot.

You may see other users entering numbers instead of names with kill; for example, kill -9 instead of kill -KILL. This is because the kernel uses numbers to denote the different signals; you can use kill this way if you know the number of the signal that you want to send.

2.16.3   Job Control

Shells also support *job control*, which is a way to send TSTP (similar to STOP) and CONT signals to programs by using various keystrokes and commands. For example, you can send a TSTP signal with CTRL-Z, then start the process again by entering fg (bring to foreground) or bg (move to background; see the next section). But despite its utility and the habits of many experienced users, job control is not necessary and can be confusing for beginners: It's common for users to press CTRL-Z instead of CTRL-C, forget about what they were running, and eventually end up with numerous suspended processes hanging around.

HINT: *To see if you've accidentally suspended any processes on your current terminal, run the jobs command.*

If you want to run multiple shells, run each program in a separate terminal window, put noninteractive processes in the background (as explained in the next section), or learn to use the screen program.

2.16.4   Background Processes

Normally, when you run a Unix command from the shell, you don't get the shell prompt back until the program finishes executing. However, you can detach a process from the shell and put it in the "background" with the ampersand (&); this gives you the prompt back. For example, if you have a large file that you need to decompress with gunzip (you'll see this in Section 2.18), and you want to do some other stuff while it's running, run a command like this one:

```
$ gunzip file.gz &
```

The shell should respond by printing the PID of the new background process, and the prompt should return immediately so that you can continue working. The process will continue to run after you log out, which comes in particularly handy if you have to run a program that does a lot of number crunching for a while. (Depending on your setup, the shell might notify you when the process completes.)

The dark side of running background processes is that they may expect to work with the standard input (or worse, read directly from the terminal). If a program tries to read something from the standard input when it's in the background, it can freeze (try fg to bring it back) or terminate. Also, if the program writes to the standard output or standard error, the output can appear in the terminal window with no regard for anything else running there, meaning that you can get unexpected output when you're working on something else.

The best way to make sure that a background process doesn't bother you is to redirect its output (and possibly input) as described in Section 2.14.

If spurious output from background processes gets in your way, learn how to redraw the content of your terminal window. The bash shell and most full-screen interactive programs support CTRL-L to redraw the entire screen. If a program is reading from the standard input, CTRL-R usually redraws the current line, but pressing the wrong sequence at the wrong time can leave you in an even worse situation than before. For example, entering CTRL-R at the bash prompt puts you in reverse isearch mode (press ESC to exit).

2.17   File Modes and Permissions

Every Unix file has a set of *permissions* that determine whether you can read, write, or run the file. Running ls -l displays the permissions. Here's an example of such a display:

```
-rw-r--r--❶ 1 juser  somegroup   7041 Mar 26 19:34 endnotes.html
```

The file's *mode* ❶ represents the file's permissions and some extra information. There are four parts to the mode, as illustrated in Figure 2-1.

The first character of the mode is the *file type*. A dash (-) in this position, as in the example, denotes a *regular* file, meaning that there's nothing special about the file. This is by far the most common kind of file. Directories are also common and are indicated by a d in the file type slot. (Section 3.1 lists the remaining file types.)

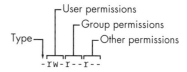

Figure 2-1: The pieces of a file mode

The rest of a file's mode contains the permissions, which break down into three sets: *user*, *group*, and *other*, in that order. For example, the rw- characters in the example are the user permissions, the r-- characters that follow are the group permissions, and the final r-- characters are the other permissions.

Each permission set can contain four basic representations:

r   Means that the file is readable.

w   Means that the file is writable.

x   Means that the file is executable (you can run it as a program).

-    Means nothing.

The user permissions (the first set) pertain to the user who owns the file. In the preceding example, that's juser. The second set, group permissions, are for the file's group (somegroup in the example). Any user in that group can take advantage of these permissions. (Use the groups command to see what group you're in, and see Section 7.3.5 for more information.)

Everyone else on the system has access according to the third set, the other permissions, which are sometimes called *world* permissions.

NOTE   *Each read, write, and execute permission slot is sometimes called a* permission bit. *Therefore, you may hear people refer to parts of the permissions as "the read bits."*

Some executable files have an s in the user permissions listing instead of an x. This indicates that the executable is *setuid*, meaning that when you execute the program, it runs as though the file owner is the user instead of you. Many programs use this setuid bit to run as root in order to get the privileges they need to change system files. One example is the passwd program, which needs to change the */etc/passwd* file.

2.17.1   Modifying Permissions

To change permissions, use the chmod command. First, pick the set of permissions that you want to change, and then pick the bit to change. For example, to add group (g) and world (o, for "other") read (r) permissions to *file*, you could run these two commands:

```
$ chmod g+r file
$ chmod o+r file
```

Or you could do it all in one shot:

```
$ chmod go+r file
```

To remove these permissions, use go-r instead of go+r.

NOTE   *Obviously, you shouldn't make files world-writable because doing so gives anyone on your system the ability to change them. But would this allow anyone connected to the Internet to change your files? Probably not, unless your system has a network security hole. In that case, file permissions won't help you anyway.*

You may sometimes see people changing permissions with numbers, for example:

```
$ chmod 644 file
```

This is called an *absolute* change because it sets all permission bits at once. To understand how this works, you need to know how to represent the permission bits in octal form (each numeral represents a number in base 8 and corresponds to a permission set). See the chmod(1) manual page or info manual for more.

You don't really need to know how to construct absolute modes; just memorize the modes that you use most often. Table 2-4 lists the most common ones.

Table 2-4: Absolute Permission Modes

Mode	Meaning	Used For
644	user: read/write; group, other: read	files
600	user: read/write; group, other: none	files
755	user: read/write/execute; group, other: read/execute	directories, programs
700	user: read/write/execute; group, other: none	directories, programs
711	user: read/write/execute; group, other: execute	directories

Directories also have permissions. You can list the contents of a directory if it's readable, but you can only access a file in a directory if the directory is executable. (One common mistake people make when setting the permissions of directories is to accidentally remove the execute permission when using absolute modes.)

Finally, you can specify a set of default permissions with the umask shell command, which applies a predefined set of permissions to any new file you create. In general, use umask 022 if you want everyone to be able to see all of the files and directories that you create, and use umask 077 if you don't. (You'll need to put the umask command with the desired mode in one of your startup files to make your new default permissions apply to later sessions, as discussed in Chapter 13.)

2.17.2   Symbolic Links

A *symbolic link* is a file that points to another file or a directory, effectively creating an alias (like a shortcut in Windows). Symbolic links offer quick access to obscure directory paths.

In a long directory listing, symbolic links look like this (notice the l as the file type in the file mode):

```
lrwxrwxrwx 1 ruser  users  11 Feb 27 13:52 somedir -> /home/origdir
```

If you try to access *somedir* in this directory, the system gives you */home/origdir* instead. Symbolic links are simply names that point to other names. Their names and the paths to which they point don't have to mean anything. For example, */home/origdir* doesn't even need to exist.

In fact, if */home/origdir* does not exist, any program that accesses *somedir* reports that *somedir* doesn't exist (except for `ls somedir`, a command that stupidly informs you that *somedir* is *somedir*). This can be baffling because you can see something named *somedir* right in front of your eyes.

This is not the only way that symbolic links can be confusing. Another problem is that you can't identify the characteristics of a link target just by looking at the name of the link; you must follow the link to see if it goes to a file or directory. Your system may also have links that point to other links, which are called *chained symbolic links*.

2.17.3   Creating Symbolic Links

To create a symbolic link from *target* to *linkname*, use `ln -s`:

```
$ ln -s target linkname
```

The `linkname` argument is the name of the symbolic link, the `target` argument is the path of the file or directory that the link *points* to, and the -s flag specifies a symbolic link (see the warning that follows).

When making a symbolic link, check the command twice before you run it because several things can go wrong. For example, if you reverse the order of the arguments (`ln -s linkname target`), you're in for some fun if *linkname* is a directory that already exists. If this is the case (and it quite often is), `ln` creates a link named *target* inside *linkname,* and the link will point to itself unless *linkname* is a full path. If something goes wrong when you create a symbolic link to a directory, check that directory for errant symbolic links and remove them.

Symbolic links can also cause headaches when you don't know that they exist. For example, you can easily edit what you think is a copy of a file but is actually a symbolic link to the original.

WARNING   *Don't forget the -s option when creating a symbolic link. Without it, ln creates a hard link, giving an additional real filename to a single file. The new filename has the status of the old one; it points (links) directly to the file data instead of to another filename as a symbolic link does. Hard links can be even more confusing than symbolic links. Unless you understand the material in Section 4.5, avoid using them.*

With all of these warnings regarding symbolic links, why would anyone bother to use them? Because they offer a convenient way to organize and share files, as well as patch up small problems.

2.18   Archiving and Compressing Files

Now that you've learned about files, permissions, and possible errors, you need to master gzip and tar.

2.18.1   gzip

The program gzip (GNU Zip) is one of the current standard Unix compression programs. A file that ends with *.gz* is a GNU Zip archive. Use gunzip *file*.gz to uncompress *<file>.gz* and remove the suffix; to compress it again, use gzip *file*.

2.18.2   tar

Unlike the zip programs for other operating systems, gzip does not create archives of files; that is, it doesn't pack multiple files and directories into one file. To create an archive, use tar instead:

```
$ tar cvf archive.tar file1 file2 ...
```

Archives created by tar usually have a *.tar* suffix (this is by convention; it isn't required). For example, in the command above, *file1*, *file2*, and so on are the names of the files and directories that you wish to archive in *<archive>.tar*. The c flag activates *create mode*. The r and f flags have more specific roles.

The v flag activates verbose diagnostic output, causing tar to print the names of the files and directories in the archive when it encounters them. Adding another v causes tar to print details such as file size and permissions. If you don't want tar to tell you what it's doing, omit the v flag.

The f flag denotes the file option. The next argument on the command line after the f flag must be the archive file for tar to create (in the preceding example, it is *<archive>.tar*). You *must* use this option followed by a filename at all times, except with tape drives. To use standard input or output, enter a dash (-) instead of the filename.

Unpacking tar files

To unpack a *.tar* file with tar use the x flag:

```
$ tar xvf archive.tar
```

In this command, the x flag puts tar into *extract* (*unpack*) *mode*. You can extract individual parts of the archive by entering the names of the parts at the end of the command line, but you must know their exact names. (To find out for sure, see the table-of-contents mode described shortly.)

NOTE   *When using extract mode, remember that* tar *does not remove the archived .tar file after extracting its contents.*

Table-of-Contents Mode

Before unpacking, it's usually a good idea to check the contents of a *.tar* file with the *table-of-contents mode* by using the t flag instead of the x flag. This mode verifies the archive's basic integrity and prints the names of all files inside. If you don't test an archive before unpacking it, you can end up dumping a huge mess of files into the current directory, which can be really difficult to clean up.

When you check an archive with the t mode, verify that everything is in a rational directory structure; that is, all file pathnames in the archive should start with the same directory. If you're unsure, create a temporary directory, change to it, and then extract. (You can always use mv * .. if the archive didn't create a mess.)

When unpacking, consider using the p option to preserve permissions. Use this in extract mode to override your umask and get the exact permissions specified in the archive. The p option is the default when working as the superuser. If you're having trouble with permissions and ownership when unpacking an archive as the superuser, make sure that you are waiting until the command terminates and you get the shell prompt back. Although you may only want to extract a small part of an archive, tar must run through the whole thing, and you must not interrupt the process because it sets the permissions only *after* checking the entire archive.

Commit *all* of the tar options and modes in this section to memory. If you're having trouble, make some flash cards. This may sound like grade-school, but it's very important to avoid careless mistakes with this command.

2.18.3   Compressed Archives (.tar.gz)

Many beginners find it confusing that archives are normally found compressed, with filenames ending in *.tar.gz*. To unpack a compressed archive, work from the right side to the left; get rid of the *.gz* first and then worry about the *.tar*. For example, these two commands decompress and unpack <*file*>*.tar.gz*:

```
$ gunzip file.tar.gz
$ tar xvf file.tar
```

When starting out, you can do this one step at a time, first running gunzip to decompress and then tar to verify and unpack. To create a compressed archive, do the reverse; run tar first and gzip second. Do this frequently enough, and you'll soon memorize how the archiving and compression process works. You'll also get tired of all of the typing and start to look for shortcuts. Let's take a look at those now.

2.18.4   zcat

The method shown above isn't the fastest or most efficient way to invoke `tar` on a compressed archive, and it wastes disk space and kernel I/O time. A better way is to combine archival and compression functions with a pipeline. For example, this command pipeline unpacks *<file>.tar.gz*:

```
$ zcat file.tar.gz | tar xvf -
```

The zcat command is the same as `gunzip -dc`. The `-d` option decompresses and the `-c` option sends the result to standard output (in this case, to the tar command).

Because it's so common to use zcat, the version of tar that comes with Linux has a shortcut. You can use z as an option to automatically invoke gzip on the archive; this works both for extracting an archive (with the x or t modes in tar) and creating one (with c). For example, use the following to verify a compressed archive:

```
$ tar ztvf file.tar.gz
```

However, you should try to master the longer form before taking the shortcut.

NOTE   *A .tgz file is the same as a .tar.gz file. The suffix is meant to fit into FAT (MS-DOS-based) filesystems.*

2.18.5   Other Compression Utilities

Another compression program in Unix is bzip2, whose compressed files end with *.bz2*. While marginally slower than gzip, bzip2 often compacts text files a little more, and it is therefore increasingly popular in the distribution of source code. The decompressing program to use is bunzip2, and the options of both components are close enough to those of gzip that you don't need to learn anything new. The bzip2 compression/decompression option for tar is j.

A new compression program named xz is also gaining popularity. The [1] corresponding decompression program is unxz, and the arguments are similar to those of gzip.

Most Linux distributions come with zip and unzip programs that are compatible with the zip archives on Windows systems. They work on the usual *.zip* files as well as self-extracting archives ending in *.exe*. But if you encounter a file that ends in *.Z*, you have found a relic created by the compress program, which was once the Unix standard. The gunzip program can unpack these files, but gzip won't create them.

1   Eg   cf   man   xZ

Unxz   -c   adafruit-arduino-1.6.1-linux32.tar.xz | tar xv

2.19 Linux Directory Hierarchy Essentials

Now that you know how to examine files, change directories, and read manual pages, you're ready to start exploring your system files. The details of the Linux directory structure are outlined in the Filesystem Hierarchy Standard, or FHS (*http://www.pathname.com/fhs/*), but a brief walkthrough should suffice for now.

Figure 2-2 offers a simplified overview of the hierarchy, showing some of the directories under /, */usr*, and */var*. Notice that the directory structure under */usr* contains some of the same directory names as /.

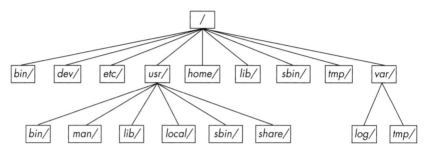

Figure 2-2: Linux directory hierarchy

Here are the most important subdirectories in root:

/bin Contains ready-to-run programs (also known as an executables), including most of the basic Unix commands such as ls and cp. Most of the programs in */bin* are in binary format, having been created by a C compiler, but some are shell scripts in modern systems.

/dev Contains device files. You'll learn more about these in Chapter 3.

/etc This core system configuration directory (pronounced *EHT-see*) contains the user password, boot, device, networking, and other setup files. Many items in */etc* are specific to the machine's hardware. For example, the */etc/X11* directory contains graphics card and window system configurations.

/home Holds personal directories for regular users. Most Unix installations conform to this standard.

/lib An abbreviation for library, this directory holds library files containing code that executables can use. There are two types of libraries: static and shared. The */lib* directory should contain only shared libraries, but other lib directories, such as */usr/lib*, contain both varieties as well as other auxiliary files. (We'll discuss shared libraries in more detail in Chapter 15.)

/proc Provides system statistics through a browsable directory-and-file interface. Much of the */proc* subdirectory structure on Linux is unique, but many other Unix variants have similar features. The */proc* directory contains information about currently running processes as well as some kernel parameters.

/sys This directory is similar to */proc* in that it provides a device and system interface. You'll read more about */sys* in Chapter 3.

/sbin The place for system executables. Programs in */sbin* directories relate to system management, so regular users usually do not have */sbin* components in their command paths. Many of the utilities found here will not work if you're not running them as root.

/tmp A storage area for smaller, temporary files that you don't care much about. Any user may read to and write from */tmp*, but the user may not have permission to access another user's files there. Many programs use this directory as a workspace. If something is extremely important, don't put it in */tmp* because most distributions clear */tmp* when the machine boots and some even remove its old files periodically. Also, don't let */tmp* fill up with garbage because its space is usually shared with something critical (like the rest of /, for example).

/usr Although pronounced "user," this subdirectory has no user files. Instead, it contains a large directory hierarchy, including the bulk of the Linux system. Many of the directory names in */usr* are the same as those in the root directory (like */usr/bin* and */usr/lib*), and they hold the same type of files. (The reason that the root directory does not contain the complete system is primarily historic—in the past, it was to keep space requirements low for the root.)

/var The variable subdirectory, where programs record runtime information. System logging, user tracking, caches, and other files that system programs create and manage are here. (You'll notice a */var/tmp* directory here, but the system doesn't wipe it on boot.)

2.19.1   Other Root Subdirectories

There are a few other interesting subdirectories in the root directory:

/boot Contains kernel boot loader files. These files pertain only to the very first stage of the Linux startup procedure; you won't find information about how Linux starts up its services in this directory. See Chapter 5 for more about this.

/media A base attachment point for removable media such as flash drives that is found in many distributions.

/opt This may contain additional third-party software. Many systems don't use */opt*.

2.19.2   The /usr Directory

The */usr* directory may look relatively clean at first glance, but a quick look at */usr/bin* and */usr/lib* reveals that there's a lot here; */usr* is where most of the user-space programs and data reside. In addition to */usr/bin*, */usr/sbin*, and */usr/lib*, */usr* contains the following:

/include Holds header files used by the C compiler.

/info Contains GNU info manuals (see Section 2.13).

/local   Is where administrators can install their own software. Its structure should look like that of / and */usr.*

/man   Contains manual pages.

/share   Contains files that should work on other kinds of Unix machines with no loss of functionality. In the past, networks of machines would share this directory, but a true */share* directory is becoming rare because there are no space issues on modern disks. Maintaining a */share* directory is often just a pain. In any case, */man*, */info*, and some other subdirectories are often found here.

2.19.3   Kernel Location

On Linux systems, the kernel is normally in */vmlinuz* or */boot/vmlinuz*. A *boot loader* loads this file into memory and sets it in motion when the system boots. (You'll find details on the boot loader in Chapter 5.)

Once the boot loader runs and sets the kernel in motion, the main kernel file is no longer used by the running system. However, you'll find many modules that the kernel can load and unload on demand during the course of normal system operation. Called *loadable kernel modules*, they are located under */lib/modules*.

2.20   Running Commands as the Superuser

Before going any further, you should learn how to run commands as the superuser. You probably already know that you can run the su command and enter the root password to start a root shell. This practice works, but it has certain disadvantages:

- You have no record of system-altering commands.
- You have no record of the users who performed system-altering commands.
- You don't have access to your normal shell environment.
- You have to enter the root password.

2.20.1   sudo

Most larger distributions use a package called sudo to allow administrators to run commands as root when they are logged in as themselves. For example, in Chapter 7, you'll learn about using vipw to edit the */etc/passwd* file. You could do it like this:

```
$ sudo vipw
```

When you run this command, sudo logs this action with the syslog service under the local2 facility. You'll also learn more about system logs in Chapter 7.

2.20.2 /etc/sudoers

Of course, the system doesn't let just *any* user run commands as the super-user; you must configure the privileged users in your */etc/sudoers* file. The sudo package has many options (that you'll probably never use), which makes the syntax in */etc/sudoers* somewhat complicated. For example, this file gives *user1* and *user2* the power to run any command as root without having to enter a password:

```
User_Alias ADMINS = user1, user2

ADMINS  ALL = NOPASSWD: ALL

root    ALL=(ALL) ALL
```

The first line defines an ADMINS user alias with the two users, and the second line grants the privileges. The ALL = NOPASSWD: ALL part means that the users in the ADMINS alias can use sudo to execute commands as root. The second ALL means "any command." The first ALL means "any host." (If you have more than one machine, you can set different kinds of access for each machine or group of machines, but we won't cover that feature.)

The root ALL=(ALL) ALL simply means that the superuser may also use sudo to run any command on any host. The extra (ALL) means that the super-user may also run commands as any other user. You can extend this privilege to the ADMINS users by adding (ALL) to the */etc/sudoers* line, as shown at ❶:

```
ADMINS  ALL = (ALL)❶ NOPASSWD: ALL
```

NOTE   *Use the* visudo *command to edit /etc/sudoers. This command checks for file syntax errors after you save the file.*

That's it for sudo for now. If you need to use its more advanced features, see the sudoers(5) and sudo(8) manual pages. (The actual mechanics of user switching are covered in Chapter 7.)

2.21   Looking Forward

You should now know how to do the following at the command line: run programs, redirect output, interact with files and directories, view process listings, view manual pages, and generally make your way around the user space of a Linux system. You should also be able to run commands as the superuser. You may not yet know much about the internal details of user-space components or what goes on in the kernel, but with the basics of files and processes under your belt, you're on your way. In the next few chapters, you'll be working with both kernel and user-space system components using the command-line tools that you just learned.

3

DEVICES

This chapter is a basic tour of the kernel-provided device infrastructure in a functioning Linux system. Throughout the history of Linux, there have been many changes to how the kernel presents devices to the user. We'll begin by looking at the traditional system of device files to see how the kernel provides device configuration information through sysfs. Our goal is to be able to extract information about the devices on a system in order to understand a few rudimentary operations. Later chapters will cover interacting with specific kinds of devices in greater detail.

It's important to understand how the kernel interacts with user space when presented with new devices. The udev system enables user-space programs to automatically configure and use new devices. You'll see the basic workings of how the kernel sends a message to a user-space process through udev, as well as what the process does with it.

3.1 Device Files

It is easy to manipulate most devices on a Unix system because the kernel presents many of the device I/O interfaces to user processes as files. These device files are sometimes called *device nodes*. Not only can a programmer use regular file operations to work with a device, but some devices are also accessible to standard programs like cat, so you don't have to be a programmer to use a device. However, there is a limit to what you can do with a file interface, so not all devices or device capabilities are accessible with standard file I/O.

Linux uses the same design for device files as do other Unix flavors. Device files are in the */dev* directory, and running ls /dev reveals more than a few files in */dev*. So how do you work with devices?

To get started, consider this command:

```
$ echo blah blah > /dev/null
```

As does any command with redirected output, this sends some stuff from the standard output to a file. However, the file is */dev/null*, a device, and the kernel decides what to do with any data written to this device. In the case of */dev/null*, the kernel simply ignores the input and throws away the data.

To identify a device and view its permissions, use ls -l:

```
$ ls -l
brw-rw----   1 root disk 8, 1 Sep  6 08:37 sda1
crw-rw-rw-   1 root root 1, 3 Sep  6 08:37 null
prw-r--r--   1 root root    0 Mar  3 19:17 fdata
srw-rw-rw-   1 root root    0 Dec 18 07:43 log
```

Listing 3-1: Device files

Note the first character of each line (the first character of the file's mode) in Listing 3-1. If this character is b, c, p, or s, the file is a device. These letters stand for *block, character, pipe,* and *socket,* respectively, as described in more detail below.

Block device

Programs access data from a *block device* in fixed chunks. The *sda1* in the preceding example is a *disk device,* a type of block device. Disks can be easily split up into blocks of data. Because a block device's total size is fixed and easy to index, processes have random access to any block in the device with the help of the kernel.

Character device

Character devices work with data streams. You can only read characters from or write characters to character devices, as previously demonstrated with */dev/null*. Character devices don't have a size; when you read from or write to one, the kernel usually performs a read or write operation on the device. Printers directly attached to your computer are represented by character devices. It's important to note that during character device interaction, the kernel cannot back up and reexamine the data stream after it has passed data to a device or process.

Pipe device

Named pipes are like character devices, with another process at the other end of the I/O stream instead of a kernel driver.

Socket device

Sockets are special-purpose interfaces that are frequently used for interprocess communication. They're often found outside of the */dev* directory. Socket files represent Unix domain sockets; you'll learn more about those in Chapter 10.

The numbers before the dates in the first two lines of Listing 3-1 are the *major* and *minor* device numbers that help the kernel identify the device. Similar devices usually have the same major number, such as *sda3* and *sdb1* (both of which are hard disk partitions).

NOTE   *Not all devices have device files because the block and character device I/O interfaces are not appropriate in all cases. For example, network interfaces don't have device files. It is theoretically possible to interact with a network interface using a single character device, but because it would be exceptionally difficult, the kernel uses other I/O interfaces.*

3.2   The sysfs Device Path

The traditional Unix */dev* directory is a convenient way for user processes to reference and interface with devices supported by the kernel, but it's also a very simplistic scheme. The name of the device in */dev* tells you a little about the device, but not a lot. Another problem is that the kernel assigns devices in the order in which they are found, so a device may have a different name between reboots.

To provide a uniform view for attached devices based on their actual hardware attributes, the Linux kernel offers the sysfs interface through a system of files and directories. The base path for devices is */sys/devices*. For example, the SATA hard disk at */dev/sda* might have the following path in sysfs:

```
/sys/devices/pci0000:00/0000:00:1f.2/host0/target0:0:0/0:0:0:0/block/sda
```

As you can see, this path is quite long compared with the */dev/sda* filename, which is also a directory. But you can't really compare the two paths because they have different purposes. The */dev* file is there so that user processes can use the device, whereas the */sys/devices* path is used to view information and manage the device. If you list the contents of a device path such as the preceding one, you'll see something like the following:

alignment_offset	discard_alignment	holders	removable	size	uevent
bdi	events	inflight	ro	slaves	
capability	events_async	power	sda1	stat	
dev	events_poll_msecs	queue	sda2	subsystem	
device	ext_range	range	sda5	trace	

The files and subdirectories here are meant to be read primarily by programs rather than humans, but you can get an idea of what they contain and represent by looking at an example such as the */dev* file. Running cat dev in this directory displays the numbers 8:0, which happen to be the major and minor device numbers of */dev/sda*.

There are a few shortcuts in the */sys* directory. For example, */sys/block* should contain all of the block devices available on a system. However, those are just symbolic links; run ls -l /sys/block to reveal the true sysfs paths.

It can be difficult to find the sysfs location of a device in */dev*. Use the udevadm command to show the path and other attributes:

```
$ udevadm info --query=all --name=/dev/sda
```

NOTE *The* udevadm *program is in* /sbin; *you can put this directory at the end of your path if it's not already there.*

You'll find more details about udevadm and the entire udev system in Section 3.5.

3.3 dd and Devices

The program dd is extremely useful when working with block and character devices. This program's sole function is to read from an input file or stream and write to an output file or stream, possibly doing some encoding conversion on the way.

dd copies data in blocks of a fixed size. Here's how to use dd with a character device and some common options:

```
$ dd if=/dev/zero of=new_file bs=1024 count=1
```

As you can see, the dd option format differs from the option formats of most other Unix commands; it's based on an old IBM Job Control Language (JCL) style. Rather than use the dash (-) character to signal an option, you name an option and set its value to something with the equals (=) sign. The preceding example copies a single 1024-byte block from */dev/zero* (a continuous stream of zero bytes) to *new_file*.

These are the important dd options:

if=*file*   The input file. The default is the standard input.

of=*file*   The output file. The default is the standard output.

bs=*size*   The block size. dd reads and writes this many bytes of data at a time. To abbreviate large chunks of data, you can use b and k to signify 512 and 1024 bytes, respectively. Therefore, the example above could read bs=1k instead of bs=1024.

ibs=*size*, obs=*size*   The input and output block sizes. If you can use the same block size for both input and output, use the bs option; if not, use ibs and obs for input and output, respectively.

count=*num*   The total number of blocks to copy. When working with a huge file—or with a device that supplies an endless stream of data, such as */dev/zero*—you want dd to stop at a fixed point or you could waste a lot of disk space, CPU time, or both. Use count with the skip parameter to copy a small piece from a large file or device.

skip=*num*   Skip past the first *num* blocks in the input file or stream and do not copy them to the output.

WARNING   *dd is very powerful, so make sure you know what you're doing when you run it. It's very easy to corrupt files and data on devices by making a careless mistake. It often helps to write the output to a new file if you're not sure what it will do.*

3.4   Device Name Summary

It can sometimes be difficult to find the name of a device (for example, when partitioning a disk). Here are a few ways to find out what it is:

- Query udevd using udevadm (see Section 3.5).

- Look for the device in the */sys* directory.

- Guess the name from the output of the dmesg command (which prints the last few kernel messages) or the kernel system log file (see Section 7.2). This output might contain a description of the devices on your system.

- For a disk device that is already visible to the system, you can check the output of the mount command.

- Run cat /proc/devices to see the block and character devices for which your system currently has drivers. Each line consists of a number and name. The number is the major number of the device as described in Section 3.1. If you can guess the device from the name, look in */dev* for the character or block devices with the corresponding major number, and you've found the device files.

Among these methods, only the first is reliable, but it does require udev. If you get into a situation where udev is not available, try the other methods but keep in mind that the kernel might not have a device file for your hardware.

The following sections list the most common Linux devices and their naming conventions.

3.4.1   Hard Disks: /dev/sd*

Most hard disks attached to current Linux systems correspond to device names with an *sd* prefix, such as */dev/sda*, */dev/sdb*, and so on. These devices represent entire disks; the kernel makes separate device files, such as */dev/sda1* and */dev/sda2*, for the partitions on a disk.

The naming convention requires a little explanation. The *sd* portion of the name stands for *SCSI disk*. *Small Computer System Interface (SCSI)* was originally developed as a hardware and protocol standard for communication between devices such as disks and other peripherals. Although traditional SCSI hardware isn't used in most modern machines, the SCSI protocol is everywhere due to its adaptability. For example, USB storage devices use it to communicate. The story on SATA disks is a little more complicated, but the Linux kernel still uses SCSI commands at a certain point when talking to them.

To list the SCSI devices on your system, use a utility that walks the device paths provided by sysfs. One of the most succinct tools is lsscsi. Here is what you can expect when you run it:

```
$ lsscsi
[0:0:0:0]❶  disk❷   ATA      WDC WD3200AAJS-2 01.0  /dev/sda❸
[1:0:0:0]   cd/dvd  Slimtype DVD A  DS8A5SH  XA15  /dev/sr0
[2:0:0:0]   disk    FLASH    Drive UT_USB20   0.00  /dev/sdb
```

The first column ❶ identifies the address of the device on the system, the second ❷ describes what kind of device it is, and the last ❸ indicates where to find the device file. Everything else is vendor information.

Linux assigns devices to device files in the order in which its drivers encounter devices. So in the previous example, the kernel found the disk first, the optical drive second, and the flash drive last.

Unfortunately, this device assignment scheme has traditionally caused problems when reconfiguring hardware. Say, for example, that you have a system with three disks: */dev/sda*, */dev/sdb*, and */dev/sdc*. If */dev/sdb* explodes and you must remove the disk so that the machine can work again, the former */dev/sdc* moves to */dev/sdb*, and there is no longer a */dev/sdc*. If you were referring to the device names directly in the *fstab* file (see Section 4.2.8), you'd have to make some changes to that file in order to get things (mostly) back to normal. To solve this problem, most modern Linux systems use the Universally Unique Identifier (UUID, see Section 4.2.4) for persistent disk device access.

This discussion has barely scratched the surface of how to use disks and other storage devices on Linux systems. See Chapter 4 for more information about using disks. Later in this chapter, we'll examine how SCSI support works in the Linux kernel.

3.4.2   CD and DVD Drives: /dev/sr*

Linux recognizes most optical storage drives as the SCSI devices */dev/sr0*, */dev/sr1*, and so on. However, if the drive uses an older interface, it might show up as a PATA device, as discussed below. The */dev/sr** devices are read only, and they are used only for reading from discs. For the write and rewrite capabilities of optical devices, you'll use the "generic" SCSI devices such as */dev/sg0*.

3.4.3   PATA Hard Disks: /dev/hd*

The Linux block devices */dev/hda*, */dev/hdb*, */dev/hdc*, and */dev/hdd* are common on older versions of the Linux kernel and with older hardware. These are fixed assignments based on the master and slave devices on interfaces 0 and 1. At times, you might find a SATA drive recognized as one of these disks. This means that the SATA drive is running in a compatibility mode, which hinders performance. Check your BIOS settings to see if you can switch the SATA controller to its native mode.

3.4.4   Terminals: /dev/tty*, /dev/pts/*, and /dev/tty

Terminals are devices for moving characters between a user process and an I/O device, usually for text output to a terminal screen. The terminal device interface goes back a long way, to the days when terminals were typewriter-based devices.

Pseudoterminal devices are emulated terminals that understand the I/O features of real terminals. But rather than talk to a real piece of hardware, the kernel presents the I/O interface to a piece of software, such as the shell terminal window that you probably type most of your commands into.

Two common terminal devices are */dev/tty1* (the first virtual console) and */dev/pts/0* (the first pseudoterminal device). The */dev/pts* directory itself is a dedicated filesystem.

The */dev/tty* device is the controlling terminal of the current process. If a program is currently reading from and writing to a terminal, this device is a synonym for that terminal. A process does not need to be attached to a terminal.

Display Modes and Virtual Consoles

Linux has two primary display modes: *text mode* and an *X Window System server* (graphics mode, usually via a display manager). Although Linux systems traditionally booted in text mode, most distributions now use kernel parameters and interim graphical display mechanisms (bootsplashes such as plymouth) to completely hide text mode as the system is booting. In such cases, the system switches over to full graphics mode near the end of the boot process.

Linux supports *virtual consoles* to multiplex the display. Each virtual console may run in graphics or text mode. When in text mode, you can switch between consoles with an ALT-Function key combination—for example, ALT-F1 takes you to */dev/tty1*, ALT-F2 goes to */dev/tty2*, and so on. Many of these may be occupied by a getty process running a login prompt, as described in Section 7.4.

A virtual console used by the X server in graphics mode is slightly different. Rather than getting a virtual console assignment from the init configuration, an X server takes over a free virtual console unless directed to use a specific virtual console. For example, if you have getty processes running on *tty1* and *tty2*, a new X server takes over *tty3*. In addition, after the X server puts a virtual console into graphics mode, you must normally press a CTRL-ALT-Function key combination to switch to another virtual console instead of the simpler ALT-Function key combination.

The upshot of all of this is that if you want to see your text console after your system boots, press CTRL-ALT-F1. To return to the X11 session, press ALT-F2, ALT-F3, and so on, until you get to the X session.

If you run into trouble switching consoles due to a malfunctioning input mechanism or some other circumstance, you can try to force the system to change consoles with the chvt command. For example, to switch to *tty1*, run the following as root:

```
# chvt 1
```

3.4.5   Serial Ports: /dev/ttyS*

Older RS-232 type and similar serial ports are special terminal devices. You can't do much on the command line with serial port devices because there are too many settings to worry about, such as baud rate and flow control.

The port known as COM1 on Windows is */dev/ttyS0*; COM2 is */dev/ttyS1*; and so on. Plug-in USB serial adapters show up with *USB* and *ACM* with the names */dev/ttyUSB0*, */dev/ttyACM0*, */dev/ttyUSB1*, */dev/ttyACM1*, and so on.

3.4.6   Parallel Ports: /dev/lp0 and /dev/lp1

Representing an interface type that has largely been replaced by USB, the unidirectional parallel port devices */dev/lp0* and */dev/lp1* correspond to LPT1: and LPT2: in Windows. You can send files (such as a file to be printed) directly to a parallel port with the cat command, but you might need to give the printer an extra form feed or reset afterward. A print server such as CUPS is much better at handling interaction with a printer.

The bidirectional parallel ports are */dev/parport0* and */dev/parport1*.

3.4.7 Audio Devices: /dev/snd/*, /dev/dsp, /dev/audio, and More

Linux has two sets of audio devices. There are separate devices for the *Advanced Linux Sound Architecture (ALSA)* system interface and the older *Open Sound System (OSS)*. The ALSA devices are in the */dev/snd* directory, but it's difficult to work with them directly. Linux systems that use ALSA support OSS backward-compatible devices if the OSS kernel support is currently loaded.

Some rudimentary operations are possible with the OSS *dsp* and *audio* devices. For example, the computer plays any WAV file that you send to */dev/dsp*. However, the hardware may not do what you expect due to frequency mismatches. Furthermore, on most systems, the device is often busy as soon as you log in.

NOTE *Linux sound is a messy subject due to the many layers involved. We've just talked about the kernel-level devices, but typically there are user-space servers such as pulse-audio that manage audio from different sources and act as intermediaries between the sound devices and other user-space processes.*

3.4.8 Creating Device Files

In modern Linux systems, you do not create your own device files; this is done with devtmpfs and udev (see Section 3.5). However, it is instructive to see how it was once done, and on a rare occasion, you might need to create a named pipe.

The mknod command creates one device. You must know the device name as well as its major and minor numbers. For example, creating */dev/sda1* is a matter of using the following command:

```
# mknod /dev/sda1 b 8 2
```

The b 8 2 specifies a block device with a major number 8 and a minor number 2. For character or named pipe devices, use c or p instead of b (omit the major and minor numbers for named pipes).

As mentioned earlier, the mknod command is useful only for creating the occasional named pipe. At one time, it was also sometimes useful for creating missing devices in single-user mode during system recovery.

In older versions of Unix and Linux, maintaining the */dev* directory was a challenge. With every significant kernel upgrade or driver addition, the kernel could support more kinds of devices, meaning that there would be a new set of major and minor numbers to be assigned to device filenames. Maintaining this was difficult, so each system had a MAKEDEV program in */dev* to create groups of devices. When you upgraded your system, you would try to find an update to MAKEDEV and then run it in order to create new devices.

This static system became ungainly, so a replacement was in order. The first attempt to fix it was devfs, a kernel-space implementation of */dev* that contained all of the devices that the current kernel supported. However, there were a number of limitations, which led to the development of udev and devtmpfs.

3.5   udev

We've already talked about how unnecessary complexity in the kernel is dangerous because you can too easily introduce system instability. Device file management is an example: You can create device files in user space, so why would you do this in the kernel? The Linux kernel can send notifications to a user-space process (called udevd) upon detecting a new device on the system (for example, when someone attaches a USB flash drive). The user-space process on the other end examines the new device's characteristics, creates a device file, and then performs any device initialization.

That was the theory. Unfortunately, in practice, there is a problem with this approach—device files are necessary early in the boot procedure, so udevd must start early. To create device files, udevd could not depend on any devices that it was supposed to create, and it would need to perform its initial startup very quickly so that the rest of the system wouldn't get held up waiting for udevd to start.

3.5.1   devtmpfs

The devtmpfs filesystem was developed in response to the problem of device availability during boot (see Section 4.2 for more details on filesystems). This filesystem is similar to the older devfs support, but it's simplified. The kernel creates device files as necessary, but it also notifies udev that a new device is available. Upon receiving this signal, udevd does not create the device files, but it does perform device initialization and process notification. Additionally, it creates a number of symbolic links in */dev* to further identify devices. You can find examples in the directory */dev/disk/by-id*, where each attached disk has one or more entries.

For example, consider this typical disk:

```
lrwxrwxrwx 1 root root  9 Jul 26 10:23 scsi-SATA_WDC_WD3200AAJS-_WD-WMAV2FU80671 -> ../../sda
lrwxrwxrwx 1 root root 10 Jul 26 10:23 scsi-SATA_WDC_WD3200AAJS-_WD-WMAV2FU80671-part1 ->
 ../../sda1
lrwxrwxrwx 1 root root 10 Jul 26 10:23 scsi-SATA_WDC_WD3200AAJS-_WD-WMAV2FU80671-part2 ->
 ../../sda2
lrwxrwxrwx 1 root root 10 Jul 26 10:23 scsi-SATA_WDC_WD3200AAJS-_WD-WMAV2FU80671-part5 ->
 ../../sda5
```

udevd names the links by interface type, and then by manufacturer and model information, serial number, and partition (if applicable).

But how does udevd know which symbolic links to create, and how does it create them? The next section describes how udevd does its work. However, you don't need to know that to continue on with the book. In fact, if this is your first time looking at Linux devices, you're encouraged to move to the next chapter to start learning about how to use disks.

3.5.2 udevd Operation and Configuration

The udevd daemon operates as follows:

1. The kernel sends udevd a notification event, called a *uevent*, through an internal network link.
2. udevd loads all of the attributes in the uevent.
3. udevd parses its rules, and it takes actions or sets more attributes based on those rules.

An incoming uevent that udevd receives from the kernel might look like this:

```
ACTION=change
DEVNAME=sde
DEVPATH=/devices/pci0000:00/0000:00:1a.0/usb1/1-1/1-1.2/1-1.2:1.0/host4/
    target4:0:0/4:0:0:3/block/sde
DEVTYPE=disk
DISK_MEDIA_CHANGE=1
MAJOR=8
MINOR=64
SEQNUM=2752
SUBSYSTEM=block
UDEV_LOG=3
```

You can see here that there is a change to a device. After receiving the uevent, udevd knows the sysfs device path and a number of other attributes associated with the properties, and it is now ready to start processing rules.

The rules files are in the */lib/udev/rules.d* and */etc/udev/rules.d* directories. The rules in */lib* are the defaults, and the rules in */etc* are overrides. A full explanation of the rules would be tedious, and you can learn much more from the udev(7) manual page, but let's look at the symbolic links from the */dev/sda* example in Section 3.5.1. Those links were defined by rules in */lib/udev/rules.d/60-persistent-storage.rules*. Inside, you'll see the following lines:

```
# ATA devices using the "scsi" subsystem
KERNEL=="sd*[!0-9]|sr*", ENV{ID_SERIAL}!="?*", SUBSYSTEMS=="scsi", ATTRS{vendor}=="ATA",
  IMPORT{program}="ata_id --export $tempnode"
# ATA/ATAPI devices (SPC-3 or later) using the "scsi" subsystem
KERNEL=="sd*[!0-9]|sr*", ENV{ID_SERIAL}!="?*", SUBSYSTEMS=="scsi", ATTRS{type}=="5",
  ATTRS{scsi_level}=="[6-9]*", IMPORT{program}="ata_id --export $tempnode"
```

These rules match ATA disks presented through the kernel's SCSI subsystem (see Section 3.6). You can see that there are a few rules to catch different ways that the devices may be represented, but the idea is that udevd will try to match a device starting with sd or sr but without a number (with the KERNEL=="sd*[!0-9]|sr*" expression), as well as a subsystem (SUBSYSTEMS=="scsi"), and finally, some other attributes. If all of those conditional expressions are true, udevd moves to the next expression:

```
IMPORT{program}="ata_id --export $tempnode"
```

This is not a conditional, but rather, a directive to import variables from the */lib/udev/ata_id* command. If you have such a disk, try it yourself on the command line:

```
$ sudo /lib/udev/ata_id --export /dev/sda
ID_ATA=1
ID_TYPE=disk
ID_BUS=ata
ID_MODEL=WDC_WD3200AAJS-22L7A0
ID_MODEL_ENC=WDC\x20WD3200AAJS22L7A0\x20\x20\x20\x20\x20\x20\x20\x20\x20\x20
  \x20\x20\x20\x20\x20\x20\x20\x20\x20
ID_REVISION=01.03E10
ID_SERIAL=WDC_WD3200AAJS-22L7A0_WD-WMAV2FU80671
--snip--
```

The import now sets the environment so that all of the variable names in this output are set to the values shown. For example, any rule that follows will now recognize ENV{ID_TYPE} as disk.

Of particular note is ID_SERIAL. In each of the rules, this conditional appears second:

```
ENV{ID_SERIAL}!="?*"
```

This means that *ID_SERIAL* is true only if is not set. Therefore, if it *is* set, the conditional is false, the entire current rule is false, and udevd moves to the next rule.

So what's the point? The object of these two rules (and many around them in the file) is to find the serial number of the disk device. With ENV{ID_SERIAL} set, udevd can now evaluate this rule:

```
KERNEL=="sd*|sr*|cciss*", ENV{DEVTYPE}=="disk", ENV{ID_SERIAL}=="?*",
  SYMLINK+="disk/by-id/$env{ID_BUS}-$env{ID_SERIAL}"
```

You can see that this rule requires ENV{ID_SERIAL} to be set, and it has one directive:

```
SYMLINK+="disk/by-id/$env{ID_BUS}-$env{ID_SERIAL}"
```

Upon encountering this directive, udevd adds a symbolic link for the incoming device. So now you know where the device symbolic links came from!

You may be wondering how to tell a conditional expression from a directive. Conditionals are denoted by two equal signs (==) or a bang equal (!=), and directives by a single equal sign (=), a plus equal (+=), or a colon equal (:=).

3.5.3   udevadm

The udevadm program is an administration tool for udevd. You can reload udevd rules and trigger events, but perhaps the most powerful features of udevadm are the ability to search for and explore system devices and the ability to monitor uevents as udevd receives them from the kernel. The only trick is that the command syntax can get a bit involved.

Let's start by examining a system device. Returning to the example in Section 3.5.2, in order to look at all of the udev attributes used and generated in conjunction with the rules for a device such as */dev/sda*, run the following command:

```
$ udevadm info --query=all --name=/dev/sda
```

The output looks like this:

```
P: /devices/pci0000:00/0000:00:1f.2/host0/target0:0:0/0:0:0:0/block/sda
N: sda
S: disk/by-id/ata-WDC_WD3200AAJS-22L7A0_WD-WMAV2FU80671
S: disk/by-id/scsi-SATA_WDC_WD3200AAJS-_WD-WMAV2FU80671
S: disk/by-id/wwn-0x50014ee057faef84
S: disk/by-path/pci-0000:00:1f.2-scsi-0:0:0:0
E: DEVLINKS=/dev/disk/by-id/ata-WDC_WD3200AAJS-22L7A0_WD-WMAV2FU80671 /dev/disk/by-id/scsi
  -SATA_WDC_WD3200AAJS-_WD-WMAV2FU80671 /dev/disk/by-id/wwn-0x50014ee057faef84 /dev/disk/by
  -path/pci-0000:00:1f.2-scsi-0:0:0:0
E: DEVNAME=/dev/sda
E: DEVPATH=/devices/pci0000:00/0000:00:1f.2/host0/target0:0:0/0:0:0:0/block/sda
E: DEVTYPE=disk
E: ID_ATA=1
E: ID_ATA_DOWNLOAD_MICROCODE=1
E: ID_ATA_FEATURE_SET_AAM=1
--snip--
```

The prefix in each line indicates an attribute or other characteristic of the device. In this case, the P: at the top is the sysfs device path, the N: is the device node (that is, the name given to the */dev* file), S: indicates a symbolic link to the device node that udevd placed in */dev* according to its rules, and E: is additional device information extracted in the udevd rules. (There was far more output in this example than was necessary to show here; try the command for yourself to get a feel for what it does.)

3.5.4   Monitoring Devices

To monitor uevents with udevadm, use the monitor command:

```
$ udevadm monitor
```

Output (for example, when you insert a flash media device) looks like this abbreviated sample:

```
KERNEL[658299.569485] add    /devices/pci0000:00/0000:00:1d.0/usb2/2-1/2-1.2 (usb)
KERNEL[658299.569667] add    /devices/pci0000:00/0000:00:1d.0/usb2/2-1/2-1.2/2-1.2:1.0 (usb)
KERNEL[658299.570614] add    /devices/pci0000:00/0000:00:1d.0/usb2/2-1/2-1.2/2-1.2:1.0/host15
  (scsi)
KERNEL[658299.570645] add    /devices/pci0000:00/0000:00:1d.0/usb2/2-1/2-1.2/2-1.2:1.0/
  host15/scsi_host/host15 (scsi_host)
UDEV   [658299.622579] add    /devices/pci0000:00/0000:00:1d.0/usb2/2-1/2-1.2 (usb)
UDEV   [658299.623014] add    /devices/pci0000:00/0000:00:1d.0/usb2/2-1/2-1.2/2-1.2:1.0 (usb)
UDEV   [658299.623673] add    /devices/pci0000:00/0000:00:1d.0/usb2/2-1/2-1.2/2-1.2:1.0/host15
  (scsi)
UDEV   [658299.623690] add    /devices/pci0000:00/0000:00:1d.0/usb2/2-1/2-1.2/2-1.2:1.0/
  host15/scsi_host/host15 (scsi_host)
--snip--
```

There are two copies of each message in this output because the default behavior is to print both the incoming message from the kernel (marked with KERNEL) and the message that udevd sends out to other programs when it's finished processing and filtering the event. To see only kernel events, add the --kernel option, and to see only outgoing events, use --udev. To see the whole incoming uevent, including the attributes as shown in Section 3.5.2, use the --property option.

You can also filter events by subsystem. For example, to see only kernel messages pertaining to changes in the SCSI subsystem, use this command:

```
$ udevadm monitor --kernel --subsystem-match=scsi
```

For more on udevadm, see the udevadm(8) manual page.

There's much more to udev. For example, the D-Bus system for interprocess communication has a daemon called udisks-daemon that listens to the outgoing udevd events in order to automatically attach disks and to further notify other desktop software that a new disk is now available.

3.6   In-Depth: SCSI and the Linux Kernel

In this section, we'll take a look at the SCSI support in the Linux kernel as a way to explore part of the Linux kernel architecture. You don't need to know any of this information in order to use disks, so if you're in a hurry to use one, move on to Chapter 4. In addition, the material here is more advanced and theoretical in nature that what you've seen so far, so if you want to stay hands-on, you should definitely skip to the next chapter.

Let's begin with a little background. The traditional SCSI hardware setup is a host adapter linked with a chain of devices over an SCSI bus, as shown in Figure 3-1. The host adapter is attached to a computer. The host adapter and devices each have an SCSI ID, and there can be 8 or 16 IDs per bus, depending on the SCSI version. You might hear the term *SCSI target* used to refer to a device and its SCSI ID.

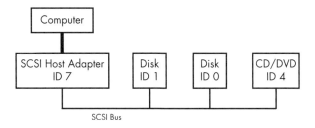

Figure 3-1: SCSI Bus with host adapter and devices

The host adapter communicates with the devices through the SCSI command set in a peer-to-peer relationship; the devices send responses back to the host adapter. The computer is not directly attached to the device chain, so it must go through the host adapter in order to communicate with disks and other devices. Typically, the computer sends SCSI commands to the host adapter to relay to the devices, and the devices relay responses back through the host adapter.

Newer versions of SCSI, such as *Serial Attached SCSI (SAS)*, offer exceptional performance, but you probably won't find true SCSI devices in most machines. You'll more often encounter USB storage devices that use SCSI commands. In addition, devices supporting ATAPI (such as CD/DVD-ROM drives) use a version of the SCSI command set.

SATA disks also appear on your system as SCSI devices by means of a translation layer in libata (see Section 3.6.2). Some SATA controllers (especially high-performance RAID controllers) perform this translation in hardware.

How does this all fit together? Consider the devices shown on the following system:

```
$ lsscsi
[0:0:0:0]    disk    ATA      WDC WD3200AAJS-2 01.0  /dev/sda
[1:0:0:0]    cd/dvd  Slimtype DVD A  DS8A5SH   XA15  /dev/sr0
[2:0:0:0]    disk    USB2.0   CardReader CF     0100  /dev/sdb
[2:0:0:1]    disk    USB2.0   CardReader SM XD 0100  /dev/sdc
[2:0:0:2]    disk    USB2.0   CardReader MS     0100  /dev/sdd
[2:0:0:3]    disk    USB2.0   CardReader SD     0100  /dev/sde
[3:0:0:0]    disk    FLASH    Drive UT_USB20   0.00  /dev/sdf
```

The numbers in brackets are, from left to right, the SCSI host adapter number, the SCSI bus number, the device SCSI ID, and the LUN (logical unit number, a further subdivision of a device). In this example, there are four attached adapters (scsi0, scsi1, scsi2, and scsi3), each of which has a single bus (all with bus number 0), and just one device on each bus (all with target 0). The USB card reader at 2:0:0 has four logical units, though—one for each kind of flash card that can be inserted. The kernel has assigned a different device file to each logical unit.

Figure 3-2 illustrates the driver and interface hierarchy inside the kernel for this particular system configuration, from the individual device drivers up to the block drivers. It does not include the SCSI generic (sg) drivers.

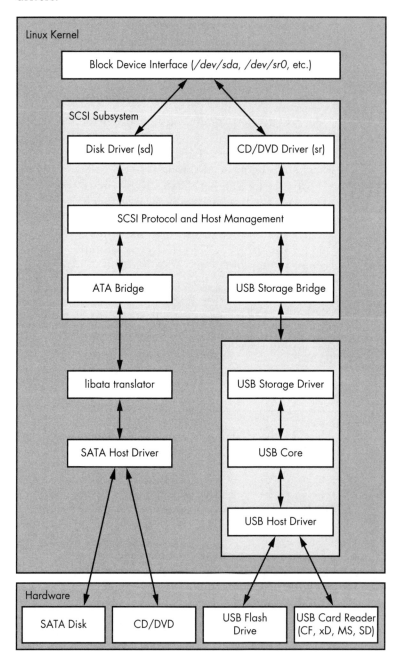

Figure 3-2: Linux SCSI subsystem schematic

Although this is a large structure and may look overwhelming at first, the data flow in the figure is very linear. Let's begin dissecting it by looking at the SCSI subsystem and its three layers of drivers:

- The top layer handles operations for a class of device. For example, the sd (SCSI disk) driver is at this layer; it knows how to translate requests from the kernel block device interface into disk-specific commands in the SCSI protocol, and vice versa.

- The middle layer moderates and routes the SCSI messages between the top and bottom layers, and keeps track of all of the SCSI buses and devices attached to the system.

- The bottom layer handles hardware-specific actions. The drivers here send outgoing SCSI protocol messages to specific host adapters or hardware, and they extract incoming messages from the hardware. The reason for this separation from the top layer is that although SCSI messages are uniform for a device class (such as the disk class), different kinds of host adapters have varying procedures for sending the same messages.

The top and bottom layers contain many different drivers, but it's important to remember that, for any given device file on your system, the kernel uses one top-layer driver and one lower-layer driver. For the disk at */dev/sda* in our example, the kernel uses the sd top-layer driver and the ATA bridge lower-layer driver.

There are times when you might use more than one upper-layer driver for one hardware device (see Section 3.6.3). For true hardware SCSI devices, such as a disk attached to an SCSI host adapter or a hardware RAID controller, the lower-layer drivers talk directly to the hardware below. However, for most hardware that you find attached to the SCSI subsystem, it's a different story.

3.6.1   USB Storage and SCSI

In order for the SCSI subsystem to talk to common USB storage hardware, as shown in Figure 3-2, the kernel needs more than just a lower-layer SCSI driver. The USB flash drive represented by */dev/sdf* understands SCSI commands, but to actually communicate with the drive, the kernel needs to know how to talk through the USB system.

In the abstract, USB is quite similar to SCSI—it has device classes, buses, and host controllers. Therefore, it should be no surprise that the Linux kernel includes a three-layer USB subsystem that closely resembles the SCSI subsystem, with device-class drivers at the top, a bus management core in the middle, and host controller drivers at the bottom. Much as the

SCSI subsystem passes SCSI commands between its components, the USB subsystem passes USB messages between its components. There's even an lsusb command that is similar to lsscsi.

The part we're really interested in here is the USB storage driver at the top. This driver acts as a translator. On one side, the driver speaks SCSI, and on the other, it speaks USB. Because the storage hardware includes SCSI commands inside its USB messages, the driver has a relatively easy job: It mostly repackages data.

With both the SCSI and USB subsystems in place, you have almost everything you need to talk to the flash drive. The final missing link is the lower-layer driver in the SCSI subsystem because the USB storage driver is a part of the USB subsystem, not the SCSI subsystem. (For organizational reasons, the two subsystems should not share a driver.) To get the subsystems to talk to one another, a simple, lower-layer SCSI bridge driver connects to the USB subsystem's storage driver.

3.6.2   SCSI and ATA

The SATA hard disk and optical drive shown in Figure 3-2 both use the same SATA interface. To connect the SATA-specific drivers of the kernel to the SCSI subsystem, the kernel employs a bridge driver, as with the USB drives, but with a different mechanism and additional complications. The optical drive speaks ATAPI, a version of SCSI commands encoded in the ATA protocol. However, the hard disk does not use ATAPI and does not encode any SCSI commands!

The Linux kernel uses part of a library called libata to reconcile SATA (and ATA) drives with the SCSI subsystem. For the ATAPI-speaking optical drives, this is a relatively simple task of packaging and extracting SCSI commands into and from the ATA protocol. But for the hard disk, the task is much more complicated because the library must do a full command translation.

The job of the optical drive is similar to typing an English book into a computer. You don't need to understand what the book is about in order to do this job, nor do you even need to understand English. But the task for the hard disk is more like reading a German book and typing it into the computer as an English translation. In this case, you need to understand both languages as well as the book's content.

Despite this difficulty, libata performs this task and makes it possible to attach the SCSI subsystem to ATA/SATA interfaces and devices. (There are typically more drivers involved than just the one SATA host driver shown in Figure 3-2, but they're not shown for the sake of simplicity.)

3.6.3 Generic SCSI Devices

When a user-space process communicates with the SCSI subsystem, it normally does so through the block device layer and/or another other kernel service that sits on top of an SCSI device class driver (like *sd* or *sr*). In other words, most user processes never need to know anything about SCSI devices or their commands.

However, user processes can bypass device class drivers and give SCSI protocol commands directly to devices through their *generic devices*. For example, consider the system described in Section 3.6, but this time, take a look at what happens when you add the -g option to lsscsi in order to show the generic devices:

```
$ lsscsi -g
[0:0:0:0]    disk    ATA        WDC WD3200AAJS-2 01.0  /dev/sda ❶/dev/sg0
[1:0:0:0]    cd/dvd  Slimtype DVD A  DS8A5SH   XA15  /dev/sr0  /dev/sg1
[2:0:0:0]    disk    USB2.0     CardReader CF    0100  /dev/sdb  /dev/sg2
[2:0:0:1]    disk    USB2.0     CardReader SM XD 0100  /dev/sdc  /dev/sg3
[2:0:0:2]    disk    USB2.0     CardReader MS    0100  /dev/sdd  /dev/sg4
[2:0:0:3]    disk    USB2.0     CardReader SD    0100  /dev/sde  /dev/sg5
[3:0:0:0]    disk    FLASH      Drive UT_USB20   0.00  /dev/sdf  /dev/sg6
```

In addition to the usual block device file, each entry lists an SCSI generic device file in the last column at ❶. For example, the generic device for the optical drive at */dev/sr0* is */dev/sg1*.

Why would you want to use an SCSI generic device? The answer has to do with the complexity of code in the kernel. As tasks get more complicated, it's better to leave them out of the kernel. Consider CD/DVD writing and reading. Not only is writing significantly more difficult than reading, but no critical system services depend on the action of writing. A user-space program might do the writing a little more inefficiently than a kernel service, but that program will be far easier to build and maintain than a kernel service, and bugs will not threaten kernel space. Therefore, to write to an optical disc in Linux, you run a program that talks to a generic SCSI device, such as */dev/sg1*. Due to the relative simplicity of reading compared to writing, however, you still read from the device using the specialized *sr* optical device driver in the kernel.

3.6.4 Multiple Access Methods for a Single Device

The two points of access (*sr* and *sg*) for an optical drive from user space are illustrated for the Linux SCSI subsystem in Figure 3-3 (any drivers below the SCSI lower layer have been omitted). Process A reads from the drive using the *sr* driver, and process B writes to the drive with the *sg* driver. However, processes such as these two would not normally run simultaneously to access the same device.

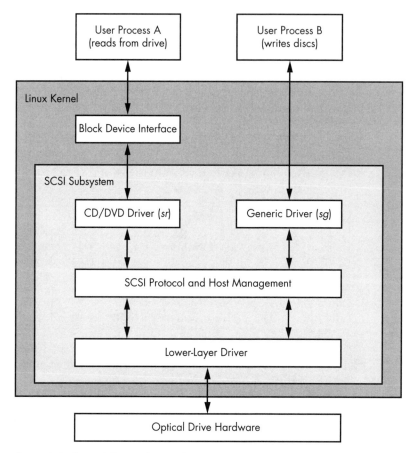

Figure 3-3: Optical device driver schematic

In Figure 3-3, process A reads from the block device. But do user processes really read data this way? Normally, the answer is no, not directly. There are more layers on top of the block devices and even more points of access for hard disks, as you'll learn in the next chapter.

4

DISKS AND FILESYSTEMS

In Chapter 3, we discussed some of the top-level disk devices that the kernel makes available. In this chapter, we'll discuss in detail how to work with disks on a Linux system. You'll learn how to partition disks, create and maintain the filesystems that go inside disk partitions, and work with swap space.

Recall that disk devices have names like */dev/sda*, the first SCSI subsystem disk. This kind of block device represents the entire disk, but there are many different components and layers inside a disk.

Figure 4-1 illustrates the schematic of a typical Linux disk (note that the figure is not to scale). As you progress through this chapter, you'll learn where each piece fits in.

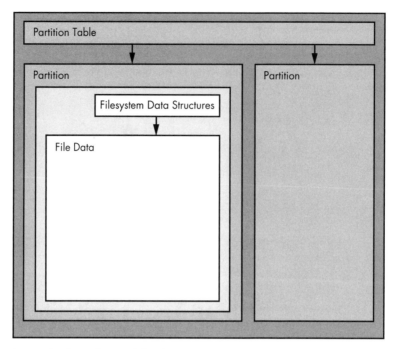

Figure 4-1: Typical Linux disk schematic

Partitions are subdivisions of the whole disk. On Linux, they're denoted with a number after the whole block device, and therefore have device names such as */dev/sda1* and */dev/sdb3*. The kernel presents each partition as a block device, just as it would an entire disk. Partitions are defined on a small area of the disk called a *partition table*.

NOTE   *Multiple data partitions were once common on systems with large disks because older PCs could boot only from certain parts of the disk. Also, administrators used partitions to reserve a certain amount of space for operating system areas; for example, they didn't want users to be able to fill up the entire system and prevent critical services from working. This practice is not unique to Unix; you'll still find many new Windows systems with several partitions on a single disk. In addition, most systems have a separate swap partition.*

Although the kernel makes it possible for you to access both an entire disk and one of its partitions at the same time, you would not normally do so, unless you were copying the entire disk.

The next layer after the partition is the *filesystem*, the database of files and directories that you're accustomed to interacting with in user space. We'll explore filesystems in Section 4.2.

As you can see in Figure 4-1, if you want to access the data in a file, you need to get the appropriate partition location from the partition table and then search the filesystem database on that partition for the desired file data.

To access data on a disk, the Linux kernel uses the system of layers shown in Figure 4-2. The SCSI subsystem and everything else described in Section 3.6 are represented by a single box. (Notice that you can work with the disk through the filesystem as well as directly through the disk devices. You'll do both in this chapter.)

To get a handle on how everything fits together, let's start at the bottom with partitions.

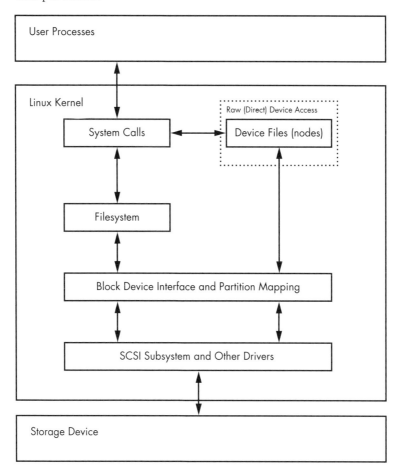

Figure 4-2: Kernel schematic for disk access

4.1   Partitioning Disk Devices

There are many kinds of partition tables. The traditional table is the one found inside the *Master Boot Record (MBR)*. A newer standard starting to gain traction is the *Globally Unique Identifier Partition Table (GPT)*.

Here is an overview of the many Linux partitioning tools available:

parted   A text-based tool that supports both MBR and GPT.

gparted   A graphical version of parted.

fdisk The traditional text-based Linux disk partitioning tool. fdisk does not support GPT.

gdisk A version of fdisk that supports GPT but not MBR.

Because it supports both MBR and GPT, we'll use parted in this book. However, many people prefer the fdisk interface, and there's nothing wrong with that.

NOTE *Although parted can create and resize filesystems, you shouldn't use it for filesystem manipulation because you can easily get confused. There is a critical difference between partitioning and filesystem manipulation. The partition table defines simple boundaries on the disk, whereas a filesystem is a much more involved data system. For this reason, we'll use parted for partitioning but use separate utilities for creating filesystems (see Section 4.2.2). Even the parted documentation encourages you to create filesystems separately.*

4.1.1 Viewing a Partition Table

You can view your system's partition table with **parted -l**. Here is sample output from two disk devices with two different kinds of partition tables:

```
# parted -l
Model: ATA WDC WD3200AAJS-2 (scsi)
Disk /dev/sda: 320GB
Sector size (logical/physical): 512B/512B
Partition Table: msdos

Number  Start    End    Size    Type      File system   Flags
1       1049kB   316GB  316GB   primary   ext4          boot
2       316GB    320GB  4235MB  extended
5       316GB    320GB  4235MB  logical   linux-swap(v1)

Model: FLASH Drive UT_USB20 (scsi)
Disk /dev/sdf: 4041MB
Sector size (logical/physical): 512B/512B
Partition Table: gpt

Number  Start    End     Size    File system  Name      Flags
1       17.4kB   1000MB  1000MB               myfirst
2       1000MB   4040MB  3040MB               mysecond
```

The first device, */dev/sda*, uses the traditional MBR partition table (called "msdos" by parted), and the second contains a GPT table. Notice that there are different parameters for each partition table, because the tables themselves are different. In particular, there is no Name column for the MBR table because names don't exist under that scheme. (I arbitrarily chose the names myfirst and mysecond in the GPT table.)

The MBR table in this example contains primary, extended, and logical partitions. A *primary partition* is a normal subdivision of the disk; partition 1 is such a partition. The basic MBR has a limit of four primary partitions, so if you want more than four, you designate one partition as an *extended partition*. Next, you subdivide the extended partition into *logical partitions* that the operating system can use as it would any other partition. In this example, partition 2 is an extended partition that contains logical partition 5.

NOTE *The filesystem that* parted *lists is not necessarily the system ID field defined in most MBR entries. The MBR system ID is just a number; for example, 83 is a Linux partition and 82 is Linux swap. Therefore,* parted *attempts to determine a filesystem on its own. If you absolutely must know the system ID for an MBR, use* fdisk -l.

Initial Kernel Read

When initially reading the MBR table, the Linux kernel produces the following debugging output (remember that you can view this with dmesg):

```
sda: sda1 sda2 < sda5 >
```

The sda2 < sda5 > output indicates that */dev/sda2* is an extended partition containing one logical partition, */dev/sda5*. You'll normally ignore extended partitions because you'll typically want to access only the logical partitions inside.

4.1.2 Changing Partition Tables

Viewing partition tables is a relatively simple and harmless operation. Altering partition tables is also relatively easy, but there are risks involved in making this kind of change to the disk. Keep the following in mind:

- Changing the partition table makes it quite difficult to recover any data on partitions that you delete because it changes the initial point of reference for a filesystem. Make sure that you have a backup if the disk you're partitioning contains critical data.

- Ensure that no partitions on your target disk are currently in use. This is a concern because most Linux distributions automatically mount any detected filesystem. (See Section 4.2.3 for more on mounting and unmounting.)

When you're ready, choose your partitioning program. If you'd like to use parted, you can use the command-line parted utility or a graphical interface such as gparted; for an fdisk-style interface, use gdisk if you're using GPT partitioning. These utilities all have online help and are easy to learn. (Try using them on a flash device or something similar if you don't have any spare disks.)

That said, there is a major difference in the way that fdisk and parted work. With fdisk, you design your new partition table before making the actual changes to the disk; fdisk only makes the changes as you exit the program. But with parted, partitions are created, modified, and removed *as you issue the commands*. You don't get the chance to review the partition table before you change it.

Disks and Filesystems   **69**

These differences are also important to understanding how these two utilities interact with the kernel. Both fdisk and parted modify the partitions entirely in user space; there is no need to provide kernel support for rewriting a partition table because user space can read and modify all of a block device.

Eventually, though, the kernel must read the partition table in order to present the partitions as block devices. The fdisk utility uses a relatively simple method: After modifying the partition table, fdisk issues a single system call on the disk to tell the kernel that it should reread the partition table. The kernel then generates debugging output that you can view with dmesg. For example, if you create two partitions on */dev/sdf*, you'll see this:

```
sdf: sdf1 sdf2
```

In comparison, the parted tools do not use this disk-wide system call. Instead, they signal the kernel when individual partitions are altered. After processing a single partition change, the kernel does not produce the preceding debugging output.

There are a few ways to see the partition changes:

- Use udevadm to watch the kernel event changes. For example, udevadm monitor --kernel will show the old partition devices being removed and the new ones being added.
- Check */proc/partitions* for full partition information.
- Check */sys/block/device/* for altered partition system interfaces or */dev* for altered partition devices.

If you absolutely must be sure that you have modified a partition table, you can perform the old-style system call that fdisk uses by using the blockdev command. For example, to force the kernel to reload the partition table on */dev/sdf*, run this:

```
# blockdev --rereadpt /dev/sdf
```

At this point, you have all you need to know about partitioning disks. However, if you're interested in learning a few more details about disks, read on. Otherwise, skip ahead to Section 4.2 to learn about putting a filesystem on the disk.

4.1.3   *Disk and Partition Geometry*

Any device with moving parts introduces complexity into a software system because there are physical elements that resist abstraction. A hard disk is no exception; even though you can think of a hard disk as a block device with random access to any block, there are serious performance consequences if you aren't careful about how you lay out data on the disk. Consider the physical properties of the simple single-platter disk illustrated in Figure 4-3.

The disk consists of a spinning platter on a spindle, with a head attached to a moving arm that can sweep across the radius of the disk. As the disk spins underneath the head, the head reads data. When the arm is in one position, the head can only read data from a fixed circle. This circle is called a *cylinder* because larger disks have more than one platter, all stacked and spinning around the same spindle. Each platter can have one or two heads, for the top and/or bottom of the platter, and all heads are attached to the same arm and move in concert. Because the arm moves, there are many cylinders on the disk, from small ones around the center to large ones around the periphery of the disk. Finally, you can divide a cylinder into slices called *sectors*. This way of thinking about the disk geometry is called *CHS*, for *cylinder-head-sector*.

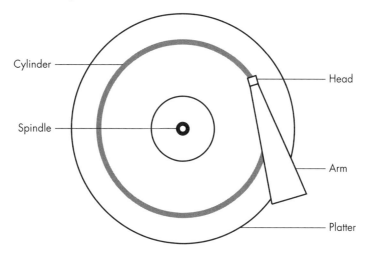

Figure 4-3: Top-down view of a hard disk

NOTE   *A track is a part of a cylinder that a single head accesses, so in Figure 4-3, a cylinder is also a track. You probably don't need to worry about tracks.*

The kernel and the various partitioning programs can tell you what a disk reports as its number of cylinders (and *sectors*, which are slices of cylinders). However, on a modern hard disk, *the reported values are fiction!* The traditional addressing scheme that uses CHS doesn't scale with modern disk hardware, nor does it account for the fact that you can put more data into outer cylinders than inner cylinders. Disk hardware supports *Logical Block Addressing (LBA)* to simply address a location on the disk by a block number, but remnants of CHS remain. For example, the MBR partition table contains CHS information as well as LBA equivalents, and some boot loaders are still dumb enough to believe the CHS values (don't worry—most Linux boot loaders use the LBA values).

Nevertheless, the idea of cylinders has been important to partitioning because cylinders are ideal boundaries for partitions. Reading a data stream from a cylinder is very fast because the head can continuously pick up data as the disk spins. A partition arranged as a set of adjacent cylinders also allows for fast continuous data access because the head doesn't need to move very far between cylinders.

Some partitioning programs complain if you don't place your partitions precisely on cylinder boundaries. Ignore this; there's little you can do because the reported CHS values of modern disks simply aren't true. The disk's LBA scheme ensures that your partitions are where they're supposed to be.

4.1.4   Solid-State Disks (SSDs)

Storage devices with no moving parts, such as *solid-state disks (SSDs)*, are radically different from spinning disks in terms of their access characteristics. For these, random access is not a problem because there's no head to sweep across a platter, but certain factors affect performance.

One of the most significant factors affecting the performance of SSDs is *partition alignment*. When you read data from an SSD, you read it in chunks—typically 4096 bytes at a time—and the read must begin at a multiple of that same size. So if your partition and its data do not lie on a 4096-byte boundary, you may have to do two reads instead of one for small, common operations, such as reading the contents of a directory.

Many partitioning utilities (parted and gparted, for example) include functionality to put newly created partitions at the proper offsets from the beginning of the disks, so you may never need to worry about improper partition alignment. However, if you're curious about where your partitions begin and just want to make sure that they begin on a boundary, you can easily find this information by looking in */sys/block*. Here's an example for a partition */dev/sdf2*:

```
$ cat /sys/block/sdf/sdf2/start
1953126
```

This partition starts at 1,953,126 bytes from the beginning of the disk. Because this number is not divisible by 4,096, the partition would not be attaining optimal performance if it were on SSD.

4.2   Filesystems

The last link between the kernel and user space for disks is typically the *filesystem*; this is what you're accustomed to interacting with when you run commands such as ls and cd. As previously mentioned, the filesystem is a form of database; it supplies the structure to transform a simple block device into the sophisticated hierarchy of files and subdirectories that users can understand.

At one time, filesystems resided on disks and other physical media used exclusively for data storage. However, the tree-like directory structure and I/O interface of filesystems are quite versatile, so filesystems now perform a variety of tasks, such as the system interfaces that you see in */sys* and */proc*.

Filesystems are also traditionally implemented in the kernel, but the innovation of 9P from Plan 9 (*http://plan9.bell-labs.com/sys/doc/9.html*) has inspired the development of user-space filesystems. The *File System in User Space (FUSE)* feature allows user-space filesystems in Linux.

The *Virtual File System (VFS)* abstraction layer completes the filesystem implementation. Much as the SCSI subsystem standardizes communication between different device types and kernel control commands, VFS ensures that all filesystem implementations support a standard interface so that user-space applications access files and directories in the same manner. VFS support has enabled Linux to support an extraordinarily large number of filesystems.

4.2.1 Filesystem Types

Linux filesystem support includes native designs optimized for Linux, foreign types such as the Windows FAT family, universal filesystems like ISO 9660, and many others. The following list includes the most common types of filesystems for data storage. The type names as recognized by Linux are in parentheses next to the filesystem names.

- The *Fourth Extended filesystem* (ext4) is the current iteration of a line of filesystems native to Linux. The *Second Extended filesystem* (ext2) was a longtime default for Linux systems inspired by traditional Unix filesystems such as the Unix File System (UFS) and the Fast File System (FFS). The *Third Extended filesystem* (ext3) added a journal feature (a small cache outside the normal filesystem data structure) to enhance data integrity and hasten booting. The ext4 filesystem is an incremental improvement with support for larger files than ext2 or ext3 support and a greater number of subdirectories.

   There is a certain amount of backward compatibility in the extended filesystem series. For example, you can mount ext2 and ext3 filesystems as each other, and you can mount ext2 and ext3 filesystems as ext4, but you *cannot* mount ext4 as ext2 or ext3.

- *ISO 9660* (iso9660) is a CD-ROM standard. Most CD-ROMs use some variety of the ISO 9660 standard.

- *FAT filesystems* (msdos, vfat, umsdos) pertain to Microsoft systems. The simple msdos type supports the very primitive monocase variety in MS-DOS systems. For most modern Windows filesystems, you should use the vfat filesystem in order to get full access from Linux. The rarely used umsdos filesystem is peculiar to Linux. It supports Unix features such as symbolic links on top of an MS-DOS filesystem.

- *HFS+* (hfsplus) is an Apple standard used on most Macintosh systems.

Although the Extended filesystem series has been perfectly acceptable to most casual users, many advances have been made in filesystem technology that even ext4 cannot utilize due to the backward compatibility requirement. The advances are primarily in scalability enhancements pertaining to very large numbers of files, large files, and similar scenarios. New Linux filesystems, such as Btrfs, are under development and may be poised to replace the Extended series.

4.2.2 Creating a Filesystem

Once you're done with the partitioning process described in Section 4.1, you're ready to create filesystems. As with partitioning, you'll do this in user space because a user-space process can directly access and manipulate a block device. The mkfs utility can create many kinds of filesystems. For example, you can create an ext4 partition on */dev/sdf2* with this command:

```
# mkfs -t ext4 /dev/sdf2
```

The mkfs program automatically determines the number of blocks in a device and sets some reasonable defaults. Unless you really know what you're doing and feel like reading the documentation in detail, don't change these.

When you create a filesystem, mkfs prints diagnostic output as it works, including output pertaining to the *superblock*. The superblock is a key component at the top level of the filesystem database, and it's so important that mkfs creates a number of backups in case the original is destroyed. Consider recording a few of the superblock backup numbers when mkfs runs, in case you need to recover the superblock in the event of a disk failure (see Section 4.2.11).

WARNING   *Filesystem creation is a task that you should only need to perform after adding a new disk or repartitioning an old one. You should create a filesystem just once for each new partition that has no preexisting data (or that has data that you want to remove). Creating a new filesystem on top of an existing filesystem will effectively destroy the old data.*

It turns out that mkfs is only a frontend for a series of filesystem creation programs, mkfs.*fs*, where *fs* is a filesystem type. So when you run mkfs -t ext4, mkfs in turn runs mkfs.ext4.

And there's even more indirection. Inspect the *mkfs.** files behind the commands and you'll see the following:

```
$ ls -l /sbin/mkfs.*
-rwxr-xr-x 1 root root 17896 Mar 29 21:49 /sbin/mkfs.bfs
-rwxr-xr-x 1 root root 30280 Mar 29 21:49 /sbin/mkfs.cramfs
lrwxrwxrwx 1 root root     6 Mar 30 13:25 /sbin/mkfs.ext2 -> mke2fs
lrwxrwxrwx 1 root root     6 Mar 30 13:25 /sbin/mkfs.ext3 -> mke2fs
lrwxrwxrwx 1 root root     6 Mar 30 13:25 /sbin/mkfs.ext4 -> mke2fs
lrwxrwxrwx 1 root root     6 Mar 30 13:25 /sbin/mkfs.ext4dev -> mke2fs
-rwxr-xr-x 1 root root 26200 Mar 29 21:49 /sbin/mkfs.minix
lrwxrwxrwx 1 root root     7 Dec 19  2011 /sbin/mkfs.msdos -> mkdosfs
lrwxrwxrwx 1 root root     6 Mar  5  2012 /sbin/mkfs.ntfs -> mkntfs
lrwxrwxrwx 1 root root     7 Dec 19  2011 /sbin/mkfs.vfat -> mkdosfs
```

As you can see, *mkfs.ext4* is just a symbolic link to *mke2fs*. This is important to remember if you run across a system without a specific `mkfs` command or when you're looking up the documentation for a particular filesystem. Each filesystem's creation utility has its own manual page, like mke2fs(8). This shouldn't be a problem on most systems, because accessing the mkfs.ext4(8) manual page should redirect you to the mke2fs(8) manual page, but keep it in mind.

4.2.3   Mounting a Filesystem

On Unix, the process of attaching a filesystem is called *mounting*. When the system boots, the kernel reads some configuration data and mounts root (/) bascd on the configuration data.

In order to mount a filesystem, you must know the following:

- The filesystem's device (such as a disk partition; where the actual filesystem data resides).

- The filesystem type.

- The *mount point*—that is, the place in the current system's directory hicrarchy where the filesystem will be attached. The mount point is always a normal directory. For instance, you could use */cdrom* as a mount point for CD-ROM devices. The mount point need not be directly below /; it may be anywhere on the system.

When mounting a filesystem, the common terminology is "mount a device *on* a mount point." To learn the current filesystem status of your system, run `mount`. The output should look like this:

```
$ mount
/dev/sda1 on / type ext4 (rw,errors=remount-ro)
proc on /proc type proc (rw,noexec,nosuid,nodev)
sysfs on /sys type sysfs (rw,noexec,nosuid,nodev)
none on /sys/fs/fuse/connections type fusectl (rw)
none on /sys/kernel/debug type debugfs (rw)
none on /sys/kernel/security type securityfs (rw)
udev on /dev type devtmpfs (rw,mode=0755)
devpts on /dev/pts type devpts (rw,noexec,nosuid,gid=5,mode=0620)
tmpfs on /run type tmpfs (rw,noexec,nosuid,size=10%,mode=0755)
--snip--
```

Each line corresponds to one currently mounted filesystem, with items in this order:

- The device, such as */dev/sda3*. Notice that some of these aren't real devices (proc, for example) but are stand-ins for real device names because these special-purpose filesystems do not need devices.

- The word on.

- The mount point.

- The word type.

- The filesystem type, usually in the form of a short identifier.
- Mount options (in parentheses). (See Section 4.2.6 for more details.)

To mount a filesystem, use the mount command as follows with the filesystem type, device, and desired mount point:

```
# mount -t type device mountpoint
```

For example, to mount the Fourth Extended filesystem */dev/sdf2* on */home/extra*, use this command:

```
# mount -t ext4 /dev/sdf2 /home/extra
```

You normally don't need to supply the -t *type* option because mount can usually figure it out for you. However, sometimes it's necessary to distinguish between two similar types, such as the various FAT-style filesystems.

See Section 4.2.6 for a few more long options to mount. To unmount (detach) a filesystem, use the umount command:

```
# umount mountpoint
```

You can also unmount a filesystem with its device instead of its mount point.

4.2.4   Filesystem UUID

The method of mounting filesystems discussed in the preceding section depends on device names. However, device names can change because they depend on the order in which the kernel finds the devices. To solve this problem, you can identify and mount filesystems by their Universally Unique Identifier (UUID), a software standard. The UUID is a type of serial number, and each one should be different. Filesystem creation programs like mke2fs generate a UUID identifier when initializing the filesystem data structure.

To view a list of devices and the corresponding filesystems and UUIDs on your system, use the blkid (block ID) program:

```
# blkid
/dev/sdf2: UUID="a9011c2b-1c03-4288-b3fe-8ba961ab0898" TYPE="ext4"
/dev/sda1: UUID="70ccd6e7-6ae6-44f6-812c-51aab8036d29" TYPE="ext4"
/dev/sda5: UUID="592dcfd1-58da-4769-9ea8-5f412a896980" TYPE="swap"
/dev/sde1: SEC_TYPE="msdos" UUID="3762-6138" TYPE="vfat"
```

In this example, blkid found four partitions with data: two with ext4 filesystems, one with a swap space signature (see Section 4.3), and one with a FAT-based filesystem. The Linux native partitions all have standard UUIDs, but the FAT partition doesn't have one. You can reference the FAT partition with its FAT volume serial number (in this case, 3762-6138).

To mount a filesystem by its UUID, use the UUID= syntax. For example, to mount the first filesystem from the preceding list on */home/extra*, enter:

```
# mount UUID=a9011c2b-1c03-4288-b3fe-8ba961ab0898 /home/extra
```

You will typically not manually mount filesystems by UUID as above, because you'll probably know the device, and it's much easier to mount a device by its name than by its crazy UUID number. Still, it's important to understand UUIDs. For one thing, they're the preferred way to automatically mount filesystems in */etc/fstab* at boot time (see Section 4.2.8). In addition, many distributions use the UUID as a mount point when you insert removable media. In the preceding example, the FAT filesystem is on a flash media card. An Ubuntu system with someone logged in will mount this partition at */media/3762-6138* upon insertion. The udevd daemon described in Chapter 3 handles the initial event for the device insertion.

You can change the UUID of a filesystem if necessary (for example, if you copied the complete filesystem from somewhere else and now need to distinguish it from the original). See the tune2fs(8) manual page for how to do this on an ext2/ext3/ext4 filesystem.

4.2.5   Disk Buffering, Caching, and Filesystems

Linux, like other versions of Unix, buffers writes to the disk. This means that the kernel usually doesn't immediately write changes to filesystems when processes request changes. Instead it stores the changes in RAM until the kernel can conveniently make the actual change to the disk. This buffering system is transparent to the user and improves performance.

When you unmount a filesystem with umount, the kernel automatically synchronizes with the disk. At any other time, you can force the kernel to write the changes in its buffer to the disk by running the sync command. If for some reason you can't unmount a filesystem before you turn off the system, be sure to run sync first.

In addition, the kernel has a series of mechanisms that use RAM to automatically cache blocks read from a disk. Therefore, if one or more processes repeatedly access a file, the kernel doesn't have to go to the disk again and again—it can simply read from the cache and save time and resources.

4.2.6   Filesystem Mount Options

There are many ways to change the mount command behavior, as is often necessary with removable media or when performing system maintenance. In fact, the total number of mount options is staggering. The extensive mount(8) manual page is a good reference, but it's hard to know where to start and what you can safely ignore. You'll see the most useful options in this section.

Options fall into two rough categories: general and filesystem-specific ones. General options include -t for specifying the filesystem type (as mentioned earlier). In contrast, a filesystem-specific option pertains only to certain filesystem types.

To activate a filesystem option, use the -o switch followed by the option. For example, -o norock turns off Rock Ridge extensions on an ISO 9660 filesystem, but it has no meaning for any other kind of filesystem.

Short Options

The most important general options are these:

-r The -r option mounts the filesystem in read-only mode. This has a number of uses, from write protection to bootstrapping. You don't need to specify this option when accessing a read-only device such as a CD-ROM; the system will do it for you (and will also tell you about the read-only status).

-n The -n option ensures that mount does not try to update the system runtime mount database, */etc/mtab*. The mount operation fails when it cannot write to this file, which is important at boot time because the root partition (and, therefore, the system mount database) is read-only at first. You'll also find this option handy when trying to fix a system problem in single-user mode, because the system mount database may not be available at the time.

-t The -t *type* option specifies the filesystem type.

Long Options

Short options like -r are too limited for the ever-increasing number of mount options; there are too few letters in the alphabet to accommodate all possible options. Short options are also troublesome because it is difficult to determine an option's meaning based on a single letter. Many general options and all filesystem-specific options use a longer, more flexible option format.

To use long options with mount on the command line, start with -o and supply some keywords. Here's a complete example, with the long options following -o:

```
# mount -t vfat /dev/hda1 /dos -o ro,conv=auto
```

The two long options here are ro and conv=auto. The ro option specifies read-only mode and is the same as the -r short option. The conv=auto option tells the kernel to automatically convert certain text files from the DOS newline format to the Unix style (you'll see more shortly).

The most useful long options are these:

exec, noexec Enables or disables execution of programs on the filesystem.

suid, nosuid Enables or disables setuid programs.

ro   Mounts the filesystem in read-only mode (as does the -r short option).

rw   Mounts the filesystem in read-write mode.

conv=*rule* (FAT-based filesystems) Converts the newline characters in files based on *rule*, which can be binary, text, or auto. The default is binary, which disables any character translation. To treat all files as text, use text. The auto setting converts files based on their extension. For example, a *.jpg* file gets no special treatment, but a *.txt* file does. Be careful with this option because it can damage files. Consider using it in read-only mode.

4.2.7   Remounting a Filesystem

There will be times when you may need to reattach a currently mounted filesystem at the same mount point when you need to change mount options. The most common such situation is when you need to make a read-only filesystem writable during crash recovery.

The following command remounts the root in read-write mode (you need the -n option because the mount command can't write to the system mount database when the root is read-only):

```
# mount -n -o remount /
```

This command assumes that the correct device listing for / is in */etc/fstab* (as discussed in the next section). If it is not, you must specify the device.

4.2.8   The /etc/fstab Filesystem Table

To mount filesystems at boot time and take the drudgery out of the mount command, Linux systems keep a permanent list of filesystems and options in */etc/fstab*. This is a plaintext file in a very simple format, as Listing 4-1 shows.

```
proc /proc proc nodev,noexec,nosuid 0 0
UUID=70ccd6e7-6ae6-44f6-812c-51aab8036d29 / ext4 errors=remount-ro 0 1
UUID=592dcfd1-58da-4769-9ea8-5f412a896980 none swap sw 0 0
/dev/sr0 /cdrom iso9660  ro,user,nosuid,noauto 0 0
```

Listing 4-1: List of filesystems and options in /etc/fstab

Each line corresponds to one filesystem, each of which is broken into six fields. These fields are as follows, in order from left to right:

The device or UUID   Most current Linux systems no longer use the device in */etc/fstab*, preferring the UUID. (Notice that the /proc entry has a stand-in device named proc.)

The mount point   Indicates where to attach the filesystem.

The filesystem type   You may not recognize swap in this list; this is a swap partition (see Section 4.3).

Options Use long options separated by commas.

Backup information for use by the dump command You should always use a 0 in this field.

The filesystem integrity test order To ensure that fsck always runs on the root first, always set this to 1 for the root filesystem and 2 for any other filesystems on a hard disk. Use 0 to disable the bootup check for everything else, including CD-ROM drives, swap, and the */proc* filesystem (see the fsck command in Section 4.2.11).

When using mount, you can take some shortcuts if the filesystem you want to work with is in */etc/fstab*. For example, if you were using Listing 4-1 and mounting a CD-ROM, you would simply run mount /cdrom.

You can also try to mount all entries at once in */etc/fstab* that do not contain the noauto option with this command:

```
# mount -a
```

Listing 4-1 contains some new options, namely errors, noauto, and user, because they don't apply outside the */etc/fstab* file. In addition, you'll often see the defaults option here. The meanings of these options are as follows:

defaults This uses the mount defaults: read-write mode, enable device files, executables, the setuid bit, and so on. Use this when you don't want to give the filesystem any special options but you do want to fill all fields in */etc/fstab*.

errors This ext2-specific parameter sets the kernel behavior when the system has trouble mounting a filesystem. The default is normally errors=continue, meaning that the kernel should return an error code and keep running. To have the kernel try the mount again in read-only mode, use errors=remount-ro. The errors=panic setting tells the kernel (and your system) to halt when there is a problem with the mount.

noauto This option tells a mount -a command to ignore the entry. Use this to prevent a boot-time mount of a removable-media device, such as a CD-ROM or floppy drive.

user This option allows unprivileged users to run mount on a particular entry, which can be handy for allowing access to CD-ROM drives. Because users can put a setuid-root file on removable media with another system, this option also sets nosuid, noexec, and nodev (to bar special device files).

4.2.9   Alternatives to /etc/fstab

Although the */etc/fstab* file has been the traditional way to represent filesystems and their mount points, two new alternatives have appeared. The first is an */etc/fstab.d* directory that contains individual filesystem configuration files (one file for each filesystem). The idea is very similar to many other configuration directories that you'll see throughout this book.

A second alternative is to configure systemd units for the filesystems. You'll learn more about systemd and its units in Chapter 6. However, the systemd unit configuration is often generated from (or based on) the */etc/fstab* file, so you may find some overlap on your system.

4.2.10   Filesystem Capacity

To view the size and utilization of your currently mounted filesystems, use the df command. The output should look like this:

```
$ df
Filesystem    1024-blocks     Used  Available Capacity Mounted on
/dev/sda1        1011928     71400     889124      7%  /
/dev/sda3       17710044   9485296    7325108     56%  /usr
```

Here's a brief description of the fields in the df output:

Filesystem   The filesystem device

1024-blocks   The total capacity of the filesystem in blocks of 1024 bytes

Used   The number of occupied blocks

Available   The number of free blocks

Capacity   The percentage of blocks in use

Mounted on   The mount point

It should be easy to see that the two filesystems here are roughly 1GB and 17.5GB in size. However, the capacity numbers may look a little strange because 71,400 plus 889,124 does not equal 1,011,928, and 9,485,296 does not constitute 56 percent of 17,710,044. In both cases, 5 percent of the total capacity is unaccounted for. In fact, the space is there, but it is hidden in *reserved* blocks. Therefore, only the superuser can use the full filesystem space if the rest of the partition fills up. This feature keeps system servers from immediately failing when they run out of disk space.

If your disk fills up and you need to know where all of those space-hogging media files are, use the du command. With no arguments, du prints the disk usage of every directory in the directory hierarchy, starting at the current working directory. (That's kind of a mouthful, so just run cd /; du to get the idea. Press CTRL-C when you get bored.) The du -s command turns on summary mode to print only the grand total. To evaluate a particular directory, change to that directory and run du -s *.

NOTE   *The POSIX standard defines a block size of 512 bytes. However, this size is harder to read, so by default, the df and du output in most Linux distributions is in 1024-byte blocks. If you insist on displaying the numbers in 512-byte blocks, set the POSIXLY_CORRECT environment variable. To explicitly specify 1024-byte blocks, use the -k option (both utilities support this). The df program also has a -m option to list capacities in 1MB blocks and a -h option to take a best guess at what a person can read.*

4.2.11 Checking and Repairing Filesystems

The optimizations that Unix filesystems offer are made possible by a sophisticated database mechanism. For filesystems to work seamlessly, the kernel has to trust that there are no errors in a mounted filesystem. If errors exist, data loss and system crashes may result.

Filesystem errors are usually due to a user shutting down the system in a rude way (for example, by pulling out the power cord). In such cases, the filesystem cache in memory may not match the data on the disk, and the system also may be in the process of altering the filesystem when you happen to give the computer a kick. Although a new generation of filesystems supports journals to make filesystem corruption far less common, you should always shut the system down properly. And regardless of the filesystem in use, filesystem checks are still necessary every now and to maintain sanity.

The tool to check a filesystem is fsck. As with the mkfs program, there is a different version of fsck for each filesystem type that Linux supports. For example, when you run fsck on an Extended filesystem series (ext2/ext3/ext4), fsck recognizes the filesystem type and starts the e2fsck utility. Therefore, you generally don't need to type e2fsck, unless fsck can't figure out the filesystem type or you're looking for the e2fsck manual page.

The information presented in this section is specific to the Extended filesystem series and e2fsck.

To run fsck in interactive manual mode, give the device or the mount point (as listed in */etc/fstab*) as the argument. For example:

```
# fsck /dev/sdb1
```

WARNING *You should never use fsck on a mounted filesystem because the kernel may alter the disk data as you run the check, causing runtime mismatches that can crash your system and corrupt files. There is only one exception: If you mount the root partition read-only in single-user mode, you may use fsck on it.*

In manual mode, fsck prints verbose status reports on its passes, which should look something like this when there are no problems:

```
Pass 1: Checking inodes, blocks, and sizes
Pass 2: Checking directory structure
Pass 3: Checking directory connectivity
Pass 4: Checking reference counts
Pass 5: Checking group summary information
/dev/sdb1: 11/1976 files (0.0% non-contiguous), 265/7891 blocks
```

If fsck finds a problem in manual mode, it stops and asks you a question relevant to fixing the problem. These questions deal with the internal structure of the filesystem, such as reconnecting loose inodes and clearing blocks (an inode is a building block of the filesystem; you'll see how inodes work in Section 4.5). When fsck asks you about reconnecting an inode, it has found a file that doesn't appear to have a name. When reconnecting such a file, fsck places the file in the *lost+found* directory in the filesystem, with a number as the filename. If this happens, you need to guess the name based on the content of the file; the original name is probably gone.

In general, it's pointless to sit through the fsck repair process if you've just uncleanly shut down the system, because fsck may have a lot of minor errors to fix. Fortunately, e2fsck has a -p option that automatically fixes ordinary problems without asking and aborts when there's a serious error. In fact, Linux distributions run some variant of fsck -p at boot time. (You may also see fsck -a, which just does the same thing.)

If you suspect a major disaster on your system, such as a hardware failure or device misconfiguration, you need to decide on a course of action because fsck can really mess up a filesystem that has larger problems. (One telltale sign that your system has a serious problem is that fsck asks a *lot* of questions in manual mode.)

If you think that something really bad has happened, try running fsck -n to check the filesystem without modifying anything. If there's a problem with the device configuration that you think you can fix (such as an incorrect number of blocks in the partition table or loose cables), fix it before running fsck for real, or you're likely to lose a lot of data.

If you suspect that only the superblock is corrupt (for example, because someone wrote to the beginning of the disk partition), you might be able to recover the filesystem with one of the superblock backups that mkfs creates. Use fsck -b *num* to replace the corrupted superblock with an alternate at block *num* and hope for the best.

If you don't know where to find a backup superblock, you may be able to run mkfs -n on the device to view a list of superblock backup numbers without destroying your data. (Again, *make sure* that you're using -n, or you'll *really* tear up the filesystem.)

Checking ext3 and ext4 Filesystems

You normally do not need to check ext3 and ext4 filesystems manually because the journal ensures data integrity. However, you may wish to mount a broken ext3 or ext4 filesystem in ext2 mode because the kernel will not mount an ext3 or ext4 filesystem with a nonempty journal. (If you don't shut your system down cleanly, you can expect the journal to contain some data.) To flush the journal in an ext3 or ext4 filesystem to the regular filesystem database, run e2fsck as follows:

```
# e2fsck -fy /dev/disk_device
```

The Worst Case

Disk problems that are worse in severity leave you with few choices:

* You can try to extract the entire filesystem image from the disk with dd and transfer it to a partition on another disk of the same size.

- You can try to patch the filesystem as much as possible, mount it in read-only mode, and salvage what you can.

- You can try debugfs.

In the first two cases, you still need to repair the filesystem before you mount it, unless you feel like picking through the raw data by hand. If you like, you can choose to answer y to all of the fsck questions by entering fsck -y, but do this as a last resort because issues may come up during the repair process that you would rather handle manually.

The debugfs tool allows you to look through the files on a filesystem and copy them elsewhere. By default, it opens filesystems in read-only mode. If you're recovering data, it's probably a good idea to keep your files intact to avoid messing things up further.

Now, if you're really desperate, say with a catastrophic disk failure on your hands and no backups, there isn't a lot you can do other than hope a professional service can "scrape the platters."

4.2.12 Special-Purpose Filesystems

Not all filesystems represent storage on physical media. Specifically, most versions of Unix have filesystems that serve as system interfaces. That is, rather than serving only as a means to store data on a device, a filesystem can represent system information such as process IDs and kernel diagnostics. This idea goes back to the /dev mechanism, which is an early model of using files for I/O interfaces. The /proc idea came from the eighth edition of research Unix, implemented by Tom J. Killian and accelerated when Bell Labs (including many of the original Unix designers) created Plan 9—a research operating system that took filesystem abstraction to a whole new level (*http://plan9.bell-labs.com/sys/doc/9.html*).

The special filesystem types in common use on Linux include the following:

proc Mounted on /proc. The name *proc* is actually an abbreviation for *process*. Each *numbered* directory inside /proc is actually the process ID of a current process on the system; the files in those directories represent various aspects of the processes. The file /proc/self represents the current process. The Linux proc filesystem includes a great deal of additional kernel and hardware information in files like /proc/cpuinfo. (There has been a push to move information unrelated to processes out of /proc and into /sys.)

sysfs Mounted on /sys. (You saw this in Chapter 3.)

tmpfs Mounted on /run and other locations. With tmpfs, you can use your physical memory and swap space as temporary storage. For example, you can mount tmpfs where you like, using the size and nr_blocks long options to control the maximum size. However, be careful not to constantly pour things into a tmpfs because your system will eventually run out of memory and programs will start to crash. (For years, Sun Microsystems used a version of tmpfs for /tmp that caused problems on long-running systems.)

4.3   Swap Space

Not every partition on a disk contains a filesystem. It's also possible to augment the RAM on a machine with disk space. If you run out of real memory,
the Linux virtual memory system can automatically move pieces of memory
to and from a disk storage. This is called *swapping* because pieces of idle programs are swapped to the disk in exchange for active pieces residing on the
disk. The disk area used to store memory pages is called *swap space* (or just
swap for short).

The free command's output includes the current swap usage in kilobytes as follows:

```
$ free
              total      used       free
--snip--
Swap:       514072    189804     324268
```

4.3.1   Using a Disk Partition as Swap Space

To use an entire disk partition as swap, follow these steps:

1.   Make sure the partition is empty.
2.   Run mkswap *dev*, where *dev* is the partition's device. This command puts
     a swap signature on the partition.
3.   Execute swapon *dev* to register the space with the kernel.

After creating a swap partition, you can put a new swap entry in your
/etc/fstab file to make the system use the swap space as soon as the machine
boots. Here is a sample entry that uses */dev/sda5* as a swap partition:

```
/dev/sda5 none swap sw 0 0
```

Keep in mind that many systems now use UUIDs instead of raw device
names.

4.3.2   Using a File as Swap Space

You can use a regular file as swap space if you're in a situation where you
would be forced to repartition a disk in order to create a swap partition.
You shouldn't notice any problems when doing this.

Use these commands to create an empty file, initialize it as swap, and
add it to the swap pool:

```
# dd if=/dev/zero of=swap_file bs=1024k count=num_mb
# mkswap swap_file
# swapon swap_file
```

Here, *swap_file* is the name of the new swap file, and *num_mb* is the
desired size, in megabytes.

To remove a swap partition or file from the kernel's active pool, use the
swapoff command.

4.3.3   How Much Swap Do You Need?

At one time, Unix conventional wisdom said you should always reserve at least twice as much swap as you have real memory. Today, not only do the enormous disk and memory capacities available cloud the issue, but so do the ways we use the system. On one hand, disk space is so plentiful that it's tempting to allocate more than double the memory size. On the other hand, you may never even dip into your swap space because you have so much real memory.

The "double the real memory" rule dated from a time when multiple users would be logged into one machine at a time. Not all of them would be active, though, so it was convenient to be able to swap out the memory of the inactive users when an active user needed more memory.

The same may still hold true for a single-user machine. If you're running many processes, it's generally fine to swap out parts of inactive processes or even inactive pieces of active processes. However, if you're constantly using the swap space because many active processes want to use the memory at once, you will suffer serious performance problems because disk I/O is just too slow to keep up with the rest of the system. The only solutions are to buy more memory, terminate some processes, or complain.

Sometimes, the Linux kernel may choose to swap out a process in favor of a little more disk cache. To prevent this behavior, some administrators configure certain systems with no swap space at all. For example, high-performance network servers should never dip into swap space and should avoid disk access if at all possible.

NOTE   *It's dangerous to do this on a general-purpose machine. If a machine completely runs out of both real memory and swap space, the Linux kernel invokes the out-of-memory (OOM) killer to kill a process in order to free up some memory. You obviously don't want this to happen to your desktop applications. On the other hand, high-performance servers include sophisticated monitoring and load-balancing systems to ensure that they never reach the danger zone.*

You'll learn much more about how the memory system works in Chapter 8.

4.4   Looking Forward: Disks and User Space

In disk-related components on a Unix system, the boundaries between user space and the kernel can be difficult to characterize. As you've seen, the kernel handles raw block I/O from the devices, and user-space tools can use the block I/O through device files. However, user space typically uses the block I/O only for initializing operations such as partitioning, filesystem creation, and swap space creation. In normal use, user space uses only the filesystem support that the kernel provides on top of the block I/O. Similarly, the kernel also handles most of the tedious details when dealing with swap space in the virtual memory system.

The remainder of this chapter briefly looks at the innards of a Linux filesystem. This is more advanced material, and you certainly don't need to know it to proceed with the book. If this is your first time through, skip to the next chapter and start learning about how Linux boots.

4.5   Inside a Traditional Filesystem

A traditional Unix filesystem has two primary components: a pool of data blocks where you can store data and a database system that manages the data pool. The database is centered around the inode data structure. An *inode* is a set of data that describes a particular file, including its type, permissions, and—perhaps most importantly—where in the data pool the file data resides. Inodes are identified by numbers listed in an inode table.

Filenames and directories are also implemented as inodes. A directory inode contains a list of filenames and corresponding links to other inodes.

To provide a real-life example, I created a new filesystem, mounted it, and changed the directory to the mount point. Then, I added some files and directories with these commands (feel free to do this yourself with a flash drive):

```
$ mkdir dir_1
$ mkdir dir_2
$ echo a > dir_1/file_1
$ echo b > dir_1/file_2
$ echo c > dir_1/file_3
$ echo d > dir_2/file_4
$ ln dir_1/file_3 dir_2/file_5
```

Note that I created *dir_2/file_5* as a hard link to *dir_1/file_3*, meaning that these two filenames actually represent the same file. (More on this shortly.)

If you were to explore the directories in this filesystem, its contents would appear to the user as shown in Figure 4-4. The actual layout of the filesystem, as shown in Figure 4-5, doesn't look nearly as clean as the user-level representation.

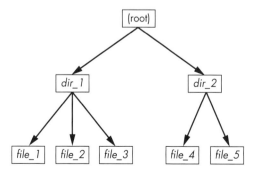

Figure 4-4: User-level representation of a filesystem

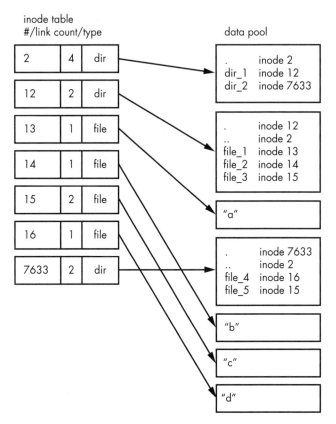

inode table
#/link count/type

2	4	dir
12	2	dir
13	1	file
14	1	file
15	2	file
16	1	file
7633	2	dir

data pool

.	inode 2
dir_1	inode 12
dir_2	inode 7633

.	inode 12
..	inode 2
file_1	inode 13
file_2	inode 14
file_3	inode 15

"a"

.	inode 7633
..	inode 2
file_4	inode 16
file_5	inode 15

"b"

"c"

"d"

Figure 4-5: Inode structure of the filesystem shown in Figure 4-4

How do we make sense of this? For any ext2/3/4 filesystem, you start at inode number 2—the *root inode*. From the inode table in Figure 4-5, you can see that this is a directory inode (dir), so you can follow the arrow over to the data pool, where you see the contents of the root directory: two entries named *dir_1* and *dir_2* corresponding to inodes 12 and 7633, respectively. To explore those entries, go back to the inode table and look at either of those inodes.

To examine *dir_1/file_2* in this filesystem, the kernel does the following:

1. Determines the path's components: a directory named *dir_1*, followed by a component named *file_2*.

2. Follows the root inode to its directory data.

3. Finds the name *dir_1* in inode 2's directory data, which points to inode number 12.

4. Looks up inode 12 in the inode table and verifies that it is a directory inode.

5. Follows inode 12's data link to its directory information (the second box down in the data pool).

6. Locates the second component of the path (*file_2*) in inode 12's directory data. This entry points to inode number 14.

7. Looks up inode 14 in the directory table. This is a file inode.

At this point, the kernel knows the properties of the file and can open it by following inode 14's data link.

This system, of inodes pointing to directory data structures and directory data structures pointing to inodes, allows you to create the filesystem hierarchy that you're used to. In addition, notice that the directory inodes contain entries for . (the current directory) and .. (the parent directory, except for the root directory). This makes it easy to get a point of reference and to navigate back down the directory structure.

4.5.1 Viewing Inode Details

To view the inode numbers for any directory, use the `ls -i` command. Here's what you'd get at the root of this example. (For more detailed inode information, use the `stat` command.)

```
$ ls -i
  12 dir_1   7633 dir_2
```

Now you're probably wondering about the link count. You've already seen the *link count* in the output of the common `ls -l` command, but you likely ignored it. How does the link count relate to the files in Figure 4-5, in particular the "hard-linked" *file_5*? The link count field is the number of total directory entries (across all directories) that point to an inode. Most of the files have a link count of 1 because they occur only once in the directory entries. This is expected: Most of the time when you create a file, you create a new directory entry and a new inode to go with it. However, inode 15 occurs twice: First it's created as *dir_1/file_3*, and then it's linked to as *dir_2/file_5*. A hard link is just a manually created entry in a directory to an inode that already exists. The `ln` command (without the -s option) allows you to manually create new links.

This is also why removing a file is sometimes called *unlinking*. If you run `rm dir_1/file_2`, the kernel searches for an entry named *file_2* in inode 12's directory entries. Upon finding that *file_2* corresponds to inode 14, the kernel removes the directory entry and then subtracts 1 from inode 14's link count. As a result, inode 14's link count will be 0, and the kernel will know that there are no longer any names linking to the inode. Therefore, it can now delete the inode and any data associated with it.

However, if you run `rm dir_1/file_3`, the end result is that the link count of inode 15 goes from 2 to 1 (because *dir_2/file_5* still points there), and the kernel knows not to remove the inode.

Link counts work much the same for directories. Observe that inode 12's link count is 2, because there are two inode links there: one for *dir_1* in the directory entries for inode 2 and the second a self-reference (.) in its own directory entries. If you create a new directory *dir_1/dir_3*, the link count for inode 12 would go to 3 because the new directory would include a parent (..) entry that links back to inode 12, much as inode 12's parent link points to inode 2.

There is one small exception. The root inode 2 has a link count of 4. However, Figure 4-5 shows only three directory entry links. The "fourth" link is in the filesystem's superblock because the superblock tells you where to find the root inode.

Don't be afraid to experiment on your system. Creating a directory structure and then using ls -i or stat to walk through the pieces is harmless. You don't need to be root (unless you mount and create a new filesystem).

But there's still one piece missing: When allocating data pool blocks for a new file, how does the filesystem know which blocks are in use and which are available? One of the most basic ways is with an additional management data structure called a *block bitmap*. In this scheme, the filesystem reserves a series of bytes, with each bit corresponding to one block in the data pool. A value of 0 means that the block is free, and a 1 means that it's in use. Thus, allocating and deallocating blocks is a matter of flipping bits.

Problems in a filesystem arise when the inode table data doesn't match the block allocation data or when the link counts are incorrect; this can happen when you don't cleanly shut down a system. Therefore, when you check a filesystem, as described in Section 4.2.11, the fsck program walks through the inode table and directory structure to generate new link counts and a new block allocation map (such as the block bitmap), and then it compares the newly generated data with the filesystem on the disk. If there are mismatches, fsck must fix the link counts and determine what to do with any inodes and/or data that didn't come up when it traversed the directory structure. Most fsck programs make these "orphans" new files in the filesystem's *lost+found* directory.

4.5.2   *Working with Filesystems in User Space*

When working with files and directories in user space, you shouldn't have to worry much about the implementation going on below them. You're expected to access the contents of files and directories of a mounted filesystem through kernel system calls. Curiously, though, you do have access to certain filesystem information that doesn't seem to fit in user space—in particular, the stat() system call returns inode numbers and link counts.

When not maintaining a filesystem, do you have to worry about inode numbers and link counts? Generally, no. This stuff is accessible to user mode programs primarily for backward compatibility. Furthermore, not all filesystems available in Linux have these filesystem internals. The *Virtual File System (VFS)* interface layer ensures that system calls always return inode numbers and link counts, but those numbers may not necessarily mean anything.

You may not be able to perform traditional Unix filesystem operations on nontraditional filesystems. For example, you can't use ln to create a hard link on a mounted VFAT filesystem because the directory entry structure is entirely different.

Fortunately, the system calls available to user space on Unix/Linux systems provide enough abstraction for painless file access—you don't need to know anything about the underlying implementation in order to access files. In addition, filenames are flexible in format and mixed-case names are supported, making it easy to support other hierarchical-style filesystems.

Remember, specific filesystem support does not necessarily need to be in the kernel. In user-space filesystems, the kernel only needs to act as a conduit for system calls.

4.5.3   The Evolution of Filesystems

As you can see, even the simple filesystem just described has many different components to maintain. At the same time, the demands placed on filesystems continuously increase with new tasks, technology, and storage capacity. Today's performance, data integrity, and security requirements are beyond the offerings of older filesystem implementations, so filesystem technology is constantly changing. We've already mentioned Btrfs as an example of a next-generation filesystem (see Section 4.2.1).

One example of how filesystems are changing is that new filesystems use separate data structures to represent directories and filenames, rather than the directory inodes described here. They reference data blocks differently. Also, filesystems that optimize for SSDs are still evolving. Continuous change in the development of filesystems is the norm, but keep in mind that the evolution of filesystems doesn't change their purpose.

5

HOW THE LINUX KERNEL BOOTS

You now know the physical and logical structure of a Linux system, what the kernel is, and how to work with processes. This chapter will teach you how the kernel starts— or boots. In other words, you'll learn how the kernel moves into memory up to the point where the first user process starts.

A simplified view of the boot process looks like this:

1. The machine's BIOS or boot firmware loads and runs a boot loader.
2. The boot loader finds the kernel image on disk, loads it into memory, and starts it.
3. The kernel initializes the devices and its drivers.
4. The kernel mounts the root filesystem.
5. The kernel starts a program called *init* with a process ID of 1. This point is the *user space start*.

6. init sets the rest of the system processes in motion.

7. At some point, init starts a process allowing you to log in, usually at the end or near the end of the boot.

This chapter covers the first four stages, focusing on the kernel and boot loaders. Chapter 6 continues with the user space start.

Your ability to identify each stage of the boot process will prove invaluable in fixing boot problems and understanding the system as a whole. However, the default behavior in many Linux distributions often makes it difficult, if not impossible, to identify the first few boot stages as they proceed, so you'll probably be able to get a good look only after they've completed and you log in.

5.1 Startup Messages

Traditional Unix systems produce many diagnostic messages upon boot that tell you about the boot process. The messages come first from the kernel and then from processes and initialization procedures that init starts. However, these messages aren't pretty or consistent, and in some cases they aren't even very informative. Most current Linux distributions do their best to hide them with splash screens, filler, and boot options. In addition, hardware improvements have caused the kernel to start much faster than before; the messages flash by so quickly, it can be difficult to see what is happening.

There are two ways to view the kernel's boot and runtime diagnostic messages. You can:

- Look at the kernel system log file. You'll often find this in */var/log/kern.log*, but depending on how your system is configured, it might also be lumped together with a lot of other system logs in */var/log/messages* or elsewhere.

- Use the dmesg command, but be sure to pipe the output to less because there will be much more than a screen's worth. The dmesg command uses the kernel ring buffer, which is of limited size, but most newer kernels have a large enough buffer to hold boot messages for a long time.

Here's a sample of what you can expect to see from the dmesg command:

```
$ dmesg
[    0.000000] Initializing cgroup subsys cpu
[    0.000000] Linux version 3.2.0-67-generic-pae (buildd@toyol) (gcc version 4.
6.3 (Ubuntu/Linaro 4.6.3-1ubuntu5) ) #101-Ubuntu SMP Tue Jul 15 18:04:54 UTC 2014
 (Ubuntu 3.2.0-67.101-generic-pae 3.2.60)
[    0.000000] KERNEL supported cpus:
--snip--
[    2.986148] sr0: scsi3-mmc drive: 24x/8x writer dvd-ram cd/rw xa/form2 cdda tray
[    2.986153] cdrom: Uniform CD-ROM driver Revision: 3.20
[    2.986316] sr 1:0:0:0: Attached scsi CD-ROM sr0
[    2.986416] sr 1:0:0:0: Attached scsi generic sg1 type 5
[    3.007862]  sda: sda1 sda2 < sda5 >
[    3.008658] sd 0:0:0:0: [sda] Attached SCSI disk
--snip--
```

After the kernel has started, the user-space startup procedure often generates messages. These messages will likely be more difficult to view and review because on most systems you won't find them in a single log file. Startup scripts usually print the messages to the console and they're erased after the boot process finishes. However, this usually isn't a problem because each script typically writes its own log. Some versions of init, such as Upstart and systemd, can capture diagnostic messages from startup and runtime that would normally go to the console.

5.2   Kernel Initialization and Boot Options

Upon startup, the Linux kernel initializes in this general order:

1. CPU inspection
2. Memory inspection
3. Device bus discovery
4. Device discovery
5. Auxiliary kernel subsystem setup (networking, and so on)
6. Root filesystem mount
7. User space start

The first steps aren't too remarkable, but when the kernel gets to devices, a question of dependencies arises. For example, the disk device drivers may depend on bus support and SCSI subsystem support.

Later in the initialization process, the kernel must mount a root file-system before starting init. In general, you won't have to worry about any of this, except that some necessary components may be loadable kernel modules rather than part of the main kernel. On some machines, you may need to load these kernel modules before the true root filesystem is mounted. We'll cover this problem and its initial RAM filesystem workaround solutions in Section 6.8.

As of this writing, the kernel does not emit specific messages when it's about to start its first user process. However, the following memory management messages are a good indication that the user-space handoff is about to happen because this is where the kernel protects its own memory from user-space processes:

```
Freeing unused kernel memory: 740k freed
Write protecting the kernel text: 5820k
Write protecting the kernel read-only data: 2376k
NX-protecting the kernel data: 4420k
```

You may also see a message about the root filesystem being mounted at this point.

NOTE *Feel free to skip ahead to Chapter 6 to learn the specifics of user space start and the init program that the kernel runs as its first process. The remainder of this chapter details how the kernel starts.*

5.3   Kernel Parameters

When running the Linux kernel, the boot loader passes in a set of text-based *kernel parameters* that tell the kernel how it should start. The parameters specify many different types of behavior, such as the amount of diagnostic output the kernel should produce and device driver–specific options.

You can view the kernel parameters from your system's boot by looking at the */proc/cmdline* file:

```
$ cat /proc/cmdline
BOOT_IMAGE=/boot/vmlinuz-3.2.0-67-generic-pae root=UUID=70ccd6e7-6ae6-44f6-
  812c-51aab8036d29 ro quiet splash vt.handoff=7
```

The parameters are either simple one-word flags, such as ro and quiet, or *key=value* pairs, such as vt.handoff=7. Many of the parameters are unimportant, such as the splash flag for displaying a splash screen, but one that is critical is the root parameter. This is the location of the root filesystem; without it, the kernel cannot find init and therefore cannot perform the user space start.

The root filesystem can be specified as a device file, such as in this example:

```
root=/dev/sda1
```

However, on most modern desktop systems, a UUID is more common (see Section 4.2.4):

```
root=UUID=70ccd6e7-6ae6-44f6-812c-51aab8036d29
```

The ro parameter is normal; it instructs the kernel to mount the root filesystem in read-only mode upon user space start. (Read-only mode ensures that fsck can check the root filesystem safely; after the check, the bootup process remounts the root filesystem in read-write mode.)

Upon encountering a parameter that it does not understand, the Linux kernel saves the parameter. The kernel later passes the parameter to init when performing the user space start. For example, if you add -s to the kernel parameters, the kernel passes the -s to the init program to indicate that it should start in single-user mode.

Now let's look at the mechanics of how boot loaders start the kernel.

5.4 Boot Loaders

At the start of the boot process, before the kernel and init start, a boot loader starts the kernel. The task of a boot loader sounds simple: It loads the kernel into memory, and then starts the kernel with a set of kernel parameters. But consider the questions that the boot loader must answer:

- Where is the kernel?
- What kernel parameters should be passed to the kernel when it starts?

The answers are (typically) that the kernel and its parameters are usually somewhere on the root filesystem. It sounds like the kernel parameters should be easy to find, except that the kernel is not yet running, so it can't traverse a filesystem to find the necessary files. Worse, the kernel device drivers normally used to access the disk are also unavailable. Think of this as a kind of "chicken or egg" problem.

Let's start with the driver concern. On PCs, boot loaders use the *Basic Input/Output System (BIOS)* or *Unified Extensible Firmware Interface (UEFI)* to access disks. Nearly all disk hardware has firmware that allows the BIOS to access attached storage hardware with *Linear Block Addressing (LBA)*. Although it exhibits poor performance, this mode of access does allow universal access to disks. Boot loaders are often the only programs to use the BIOS for disk access; the kernel uses its own high-performance drivers.

The filesystem question is trickier. Most modern boot loaders can read partition tables and have built-in support for read-only access to filesystems. Thus, they can find and read files. This capability makes it far easier to dynamically configure and enhance the boot loader. Linux boot loaders have not always had this capability; without it, configuring the boot loader was more difficult.

5.4.1 Boot Loader Tasks

A Linux boot loader's core functionality includes the ability to do the following:

- Select among multiple kernels.
- Switch between sets of kernel parameters.
- Allow the user to manually override and edit kernel image names and parameters (for example, to enter single-user mode).
- Provide support for booting other operating systems.

Boot loaders have become considerably more advanced since the inception of the Linux kernel, with features such as history and menu systems, but the basic need has always been flexibility in kernel image and parameter selection. One interesting phenomenon is that certain needs have diminished. For example, because you can now perform an emergency or recovery boot partially or entirely from a USB storage device, you probably won't have to worry about manually entering kernel parameters or going into single-user mode. But modern boot loaders offer more power than ever, which can be particularly handy if you're building custom kernels or just want to tweak parameters.

5.4.2   Boot Loader Overview

Here are the main boot loaders that you may encounter, in order of popularity:

GRUB   A near-universal standard on Linux systems

LILO   One of the first Linux boot loaders. ELILO is a UEFI version

SYSLINUX   Can be configured to run from many different kinds of filesystems

LOADLIN   Boots a kernel from MS-DOS

efilinux   A UEFI boot loader intended to serve as a model and reference for other UEFI boot loaders

coreboot (formerly LinuxBIOS)   A high-performance replacement for the PC BIOS that can include a kernel

Linux Kernel EFISTUB   A kernel plugin for loading the kernel directly from the EFI/UEFI System Partition (ESP) found on recent systems

This book deals exclusively with GRUB. The rationale behind using other boot loaders is either that they are simpler to configure than GRUB or that they are faster.

To enter a kernel name and parameters, you first need to know how to get to a boot prompt. Unfortunately, this can sometimes be difficult to figure out because Linux distributions customize boot loader behavior and appearance to their hearts' content.

The next sections tell you how to get to a boot prompt in order to enter a kernel name and parameters. Once you're comfortable with that, you'll see how to configure and install a boot loader.

5.5   GRUB Introduction

GRUB stands for *Grand Unified Boot Loader*. We'll cover GRUB 2; there is also an older version now called GRUB Legacy that is slowing falling out of use.

One of GRUB's most important capabilities is filesystem navigation that allows for much easier kernel image and configuration selection. One of the best ways to see this in action and to learn about GRUB in general is to look at its menu. The interface is easy to navigate, but there's a good chance that you've never seen it. Linux distributions often do their best to hide the boot loader from you.

To access the GRUB menu, press and hold SHIFT when your BIOS or firmware startup screen first appears. Otherwise, the boot loader configuration may not pause before loading the kernel. Figure 5-1 shows the GRUB menu. Press ESC to temporarily disable the automatic boot timeout after the GRUB menu appears.

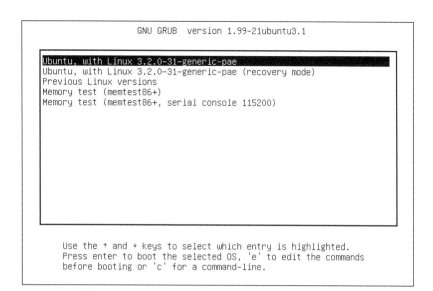

```
                    GNU GRUB   version 1.99-21ubuntu3.1

 ┌──────────────────────────────────────────────────────────────────────────┐
 │Ubuntu, with Linux 3.2.0-31-generic-pae                                     │
 │Ubuntu, with Linux 3.2.0-31-generic-pae (recovery mode)                     │
 │Previous Linux versions                                                     │
 │Memory test (memtest86+)                                                    │
 │Memory test (memtest86+, serial console 115200)                            │
 │                                                                            │
 │                                                                            │
 │                                                                            │
 │                                                                            │
 │                                                                            │
 │                                                                            │
 │                                                                            │
 └──────────────────────────────────────────────────────────────────────────┘

        Use the ↑ and ↓ keys to select which entry is highlighted.
        Press enter to boot the selected OS, 'e' to edit the commands
        before booting or 'c' for a command-line.
```

Figure 5-1: GRUB menu

Try the following to explore the boot loader:

1. Reboot or power on your Linux system.
2. Hold down SHIFT during the BIOS/Firmware self-test and/or splash screen to get the GRUB menu.
3. Press **e** to view the boot loader configuration commands for the default boot option. You should see something like Figure 5-2.

```
                    GNU GRUB   version 1.99-21ubuntu3.1

 ┌──────────────────────────────────────────────────────────────────────────┐
 │ setparams 'Ubuntu, with Linux 3.2.0-31-generic-pae'                        │
 │                                                                            │
 │ recordfail                                                                 │
 │ gfxmode $linux_gfx_mode                                                     │
 │ insmod gzio                                                                │
 │ insmod part_msdos                                                          │
 │ insmod ext2                                                                │
 │ set root='(hd0,msdos1)'                                                     │
 │ search --no-floppy --fs-uuid --set=root 4898e145-b064-45bd-b7b4-7326\      │
 │ b00273b7                                                                   │
 │ linux /boot/vmlinuz-3.2.0-31-generic-pae root=UUID=4898e145-b064-45b\      │
 │ d-b7b4-7326b00273b7 ro   quiet splash $vt_handoff                          │
 │ initrd /boot/initrd.img-3.2.0-31-generic-pae                               │
 │                                                                            │
 └──────────────────────────────────────────────────────────────────────────┘

     Minimum Emacs-like screen editing is supported. TAB lists
     completions. Press Ctrl-x or F10 to boot, Ctrl-c or F2 for
     a command-line or ESC to discard edits and return to the GRUB
     menu.
```

Figure 5-2: GRUB configuration editor

This screen tells us that for this configuration, the root is set with a UUID, the kernel image is */boot/vmlinuz-3.2.0-31-generic-pae*, and the kernel parameters include `ro`, `quiet`, and `splash`. The initial RAM filesystem is */boot/initrd.img-3.2.0-31-generic-pae*. But if you've never seen this sort of configuration before, you may find it somewhat confusing. Why are there multiple references to `root`, and why are they different? Why is `insmod` here? Isn't that a Linux kernel feature normally run by udevd?

The double-takes are warranted, because GRUB doesn't really *use* the Linux kernel—it *starts* it. The configuration you see consists wholly of GRUB internal commands. GRUB really is an entirely separate world.

The confusion stems from the fact that GRUB borrows terminology from many sources. GRUB has its own "kernel" and its own `insmod` command to dynamically load GRUB modules, completely independent of the Linux kernel. Many GRUB commands are similar to Unix shell commands; there's even an `ls` command to list files.

But the most confusion comes from the use of the word *root*. To clear it up, there is one simple rule to follow when you're looking for your system's root filesystem: *Only* the root *kernel* parameter will be the root filesystem when you boot your system.

In the GRUB configuration, that kernel parameter is somewhere after the image name of the `linux` command. Every other reference to `root` in the configuration is to the GRUB root, which exists only inside of GRUB. The GRUB "root" is the filesystem where GRUB searches for kernel and RAM filesystem image files.

In Figure 5-2, the GRUB root is first set to a GRUB-specific device (`hd0,msdos1`). Then in the following command, GRUB searches for a particular UUID on a partition. If it finds that UUID, it sets the GRUB root to that partition.

To wrap things up, the `linux` command's first argument (`/boot/vmlinuz-...`) is the location of the Linux kernel image file. GRUB loads this file from the GRUB root. The `initrd` command is similar, specifying the file for the initial RAM filesystem.

You can edit this configuration inside GRUB; doing so is usually the easiest way to temporarily fix an erroneous boot. To permanently fix a boot problem, you'll need to change the configuration (see Section 5.5.2), but for now, let's go one step deeper and examine some GRUB internals with the command-line interface.

5.5.1 Exploring Devices and Partitions with the GRUB Command Line

As you can see in Figure 5-2, GRUB has its own device-addressing scheme. For example, the first hard disk found is hd0, followed by hd1, and so on. But device assignments are subject to change. Fortunately, GRUB can search all partitions for a UUID in order to find the one where the kernel resides, as you just saw with the `search` command.

Listing Devices

To get a feel for how GRUB refers to the devices on your system, access the GRUB command line by pressing C at the boot menu or configuration editor. You should get the GRUB prompt:

```
grub>
```

You can enter any command here that you see in a configuration, but to get started, try a diagnostic command instead: **ls**. With no arguments, the output is a list of devices known to GRUB:

```
grub> ls
(hd0) (hd0,msdos1) (hd0,msdos5)
```

In this case, there is one main disk device denoted by (hd0) and the partitions (hd0,msdos1) and (hd0,msdos5). The *msdos* prefix on the partitions tells you that the disk contains an MBR partition table; it would begin with *gpt* for GPT. (You will find even deeper combinations with a third identifier, where a BSD disklabel map resides inside a partition, but you won't normally have to worry about this unless you're running multiple operating systems on one machine.)

To get more detailed information, use ls -l. This command can be particularly useful because it displays any UUIDs of the partitions on the disk. For example:

```
grub> ls -l
Device hd0: Not a known filesystem - Total size 426743808 sectors
        Partition hd0,msdos1: Filesystem type ext2 – Last modification time
            2015-09-18 20:45:00 Friday, UUID 4898e145-b064-45bd-b7b4-7326b00273b7 -
Partition start at 2048 - Total size 424644608 sectors
        Partition hd0,msdos5: Not a known filesystem - Partition start at
            424648704 - Total size 2093056 sectors
```

This particular disk has a Linux ext2/3/4 filesystem on the first MBR partition and a Linux swap signature on partition 5, which is a fairly common configuration. (You can't tell that (hd0,msdos5) is a swap partition from this output, though.)

File Navigation

Now let's look at GRUB's filesystem navigation capabilities. Determine the GRUB root with the echo command (recall that this is where GRUB expects to find the kernel):

```
grub> echo $root
hd0,msdos1
```

To use GRUB's ls command to list the files and directories in that root, you can append a forward slash to the end of the partition:

```
grub> ls (hd0,msdos1)/
```

But it's a pain to remember and type the actual root partition, so use the root variable to save yourself some time:

```
grub> ls ($root)/
```

The output is a short list of file and directory names on that partition's filesystem, such as *etc/*, *bin/*, and *dev/*. You should realize that this is now a completely different function of the GRUB ls: Before, you were listing devices, partition tables, and perhaps some filesystem header information. Now you're actually looking at the contents of filesystems.

You can take a deeper look into the files and directories on a partition in a similar manner. For example, to inspect the */boot* directory, start with the following:

```
grub> ls ($root)/boot
```

NOTE   *Use the up and down arrow keys to flip through GRUB command history and the left and right arrows to edit the current command line. The standard readline keys (CTRL-N, CTRL-P, and so on) also work.*

You can also view all currently set GRUB variables with the set command:

```
grub> set
?=0
color_highlight=black/white
color_normal=white/black
--snip--
prefix=(hd0,msdos1)/boot/grub
root=hd0,msdos1
```

One of the most important of these variables is $prefix, the filesystem and directory where GRUB expects to find its configuration and auxiliary support. We'll explore this in the next section.

Once you've finished with the GRUB command-line interface, enter the **boot** command to boot your current configuration or just press ESC to return to the GRUB menu. In any case, boot your system; we're going to explore the GRUB configuration, and that's best done when you have your full system available.

5.5.2   GRUB Configuration

The GRUB configuration directory contains the central configuration file (*grub.cfg*) and numerous loadable modules with a *.mod* suffix.

(As GRUB versions progress, these modules will move into subdirectories such as *i386-pc.*) The directory is usually */boot/grub* or */boot/grub2*. We won't modify *grub.cfg* directly; instead, we'll use the grub-mkconfig command (or grub2-mkconfig on Fedora).

Reviewing Grub.cfg

First, take a quick look at *grub.cfg* to see how GRUB initializes its menu and kernel options. You'll see that the *grub.cfg* file consists of GRUB commands, which usually begin with a number of initialization steps followed by a series of menu entries for different kernel and boot configurations. The initialization isn't complicated; it's a bunch of function definitions and video setup commands like this:

```
if loadfont /usr/share/grub/unicode.pf2 ; then
  set gfxmode=auto
  load_video
  insmod gfxterm
  --snip--
```

Later in this file you should see the available boot configurations, each beginning with the menuentry command. You should be able to read and understand this example based on what you learned in the preceding section:

```
menuentry 'Ubuntu, with Linux 3.2.0-34-generic-pae' --class ubuntu --class gnu-linux --class gnu
--class os {
        recordfail
        gfxmode $linux_gfx_mode
        insmod gzio
        insmod part_msdos
        insmod ext2
        set root='(hd0,msdos1)'
        search --no-floppy --fs-uuid --set=root 70ccd6e7-6ae6-44f6-812c-51aab8036d29
        linux   /boot/vmlinuz-3.2.0-34-generic-pae root=UUID=70ccd6e7-6ae6-44f6-812c-51aab8036d29
          ro   quiet splash $vt_handoff
        initrd  /boot/initrd.img-3.2.0-34-generic-pae
}
```

Watch for submenu commands. If your *grub.cfg* file contains numerous menuentry commands, most of them are probably wrapped up inside a submenu command for older versions of the kernel so that they don't crowd the GRUB menu.

Generating a New Configuration File

If you want to make changes to your GRUB configuration, you won't edit your *grub.cfg* file directly because it's automatically generated and the system occasionally overwrites it. You'll add your new configuration elsewhere, then run grub-mkconfig to generate the new configuration.

To see how the configuration generation works, look at the very beginning of *grub.cfg*. There should be comment lines such as this:

```
### BEGIN /etc/grub.d/00_header ###
```

Upon further inspection, you'll find that every file in */etc/grub.d* is a shell script that produces a piece of the *grub.cfg* file. The grub-mkconfig command itself is a shell script that runs everything in */etc/grub.d*.

Try it yourself as root. (Don't worry about overwriting your current configuration. This command by itself simply prints the configuration to the standard output.)

```
# grub-mkconfig
```

What if you want to add menu entries and other commands to the GRUB configuration? The short answer is that you should put your customizations into a new *custom.cfg* file in your GRUB configuration directory, such as */boot/grub/custom.cfg*.

The long answer is a little more complicated. The */etc/grub.d* configuration directory gives you two options: *40_custom* and *41_custom*. The first, *40_custom*, is a script that you can edit yourself, but it's probably the least stable; a package upgrade is likely to destroy any changes you make. The *41_custom* script is simpler; it's just a series of commands that load *custom.cfg* when GRUB starts. (Keep in mind that if you choose this second option, your changes won't appear when you generate your configuration file.)

The two options for custom configuration files aren't particularly extensive. You'll see additions in your particular distribution's */etc/grub.d* directory. For example, Ubuntu adds memory tester boot options (memtest86+) to the configuration.

To write and install a newly generated GRUB configuration file, you can write the configuration to your GRUB directory with the -o option to grub-mkconfig, like this:

```
# grub-mkconfig -o /boot/grub/grub.cfg
```

Or if you're an Ubuntu user, just run install-grub. In any case, back up your old configuration, make sure that you're installing to the correct directory, and so on.

Now we're going to get into some of the more technical details of GRUB and boot loaders. If you're tired of hearing about boot loaders and the kernel, feel free to skip to Chapter 6.

5.5.3 GRUB Installation

Installing GRUB is more involved than configuring it. Fortunately, you won't normally have to worry about installation because your distribution should handle it for you. However, if you're trying to duplicate or restore a bootable disk, or preparing your own boot sequence, you might need to install it on your own.

Before proceeding, read Section 5.8.3 to get an idea of how PCs boot and determine whether you're using MBR or EFI boot. Next, build the GRUB software set and determine where your GRUB directory will be; the default is */boot/grub*. You may not need to build GRUB if your distribution does it for you, but if you do, see Chapter 16 for how to build software from source code. Make sure that you build the correct target: It's different for MBR or UEFI boot (and there are even differences between 32-bit and 64-bit EFI).

Installing GRUB on Your System

Installing the boot loader requires that you or an installer determine the following:

- The target GRUB directory as seen by your currently running system. That's usually */boot/grub*, but it might be different if you're installing GRUB on another disk for use on another system.
- The current device of the GRUB target disk.
- For UEFI booting, the current mount point of the UEFI boot partition.

Remember that GRUB is a modular system, but in order to load modules, it must read the filesystem that contains the GRUB directory. Your task is to construct a version of GRUB capable of reading that filesystem so that it can load the rest of its configuration (*grub.cfg*) and any required modules. On Linux, this usually means building a version of GRUB with its *ext2.mod* module preloaded. Once you have this version, all you need to do is place it on the bootable part of the disk and place the rest of the required files into */boot/grub*.

Fortunately, GRUB comes with a utility called `grub-install` (not to be confused with Ubuntu's `install-grub`), which performs most of the work of installing the GRUB files and configuration for you. For example, if your current disk is at */dev/sda* and you want to install GRUB on that disk with your current */boot/grub* directory, use this command to install GRUB on the MBR:

```
# grub-install /dev/sda
```

 Incorrectly installing GRUB may break the bootup sequence on your system, so don't take this command lightly. If you're concerned, read up on how to back up your MBR with dd, back up any other currently installed GRUB directory, and make sure that you have an emergency bootup plan.

Installing GRUB on an External Storage Device

To install GRUB on a storage device outside the current system, you must manually specify the GRUB directory on that device as your current system now sees it. For example, say that you have a target device of */dev/sdc* and that device's root/boot filesystem (for example, */dev/sdc1*) is mounted on

/mnt of your current system. This implies that when you install GRUB, your current system will see the GRUB files in */mnt/boot/grub*. When running grub-install, tell it where those files should go as follows:

```
# grub-install --boot-directory=/mnt/boot /dev/sdc
```

Installing GRUB with UEFI

UEFI installation is supposed to be easier, because you all you need to do is copy the boot loader into place. But you also need to "announce" the boot loader to the firmware with the efibootmgr command. The grub-install command runs this if it's available, so in theory all you need to do to install on an UEFI partition is the following:

```
# grub-install --efi-directory=efi_dir --bootloader-id=name
```

Here, efi_dir is where the UEFI directory appears on your current system (usually */boot/efi/efi*, because the UEFI partition is often mounted at */boot/efi*) and name is an identifier for the boot loader, as described in Section 5.8.2.

Unfortunately, many problems can crop up when installing a UEFI boot loader. For example, if you're installing to a disk that will eventually end up in another system, you have to figure out how to announce that boot loader to the new system's firmware. And there are differences in the install procedure for removable media.

But one of the biggest problems is UEFI secure boot.

5.6   UEFI Secure Boot Problems

One of the newest problems affecting Linux installations is the secure boot feature found on recent PCs. When active, this mechanism in UEFI requires boot loaders to be digitally signed by a trusted authority in order to run. Microsoft has required vendors shipping Windows 8 to use secure boot. The result is that if you try to install an unsigned boot loader (which is most current Linux distributions), it will not load.

The easiest way around this for anyone with no interest in Windows is to disable secure boot in the EFI settings. However, this won't work cleanly for dual-boot systems and may not be an option for all users. Therefore, Linux distributions are offering signed boot loaders. Some solutions are just front-ends to GRUB, some offer a fully signed loading sequence (from the boot loader to the kernel), and others are entirely new boot loaders (some based on efilinux).

5.7   Chainloading Other Operating Systems

UEFI makes it relatively easy to support loading other operating systems because you can install multiple boot loaders in the EFI partition. However, the older MBR style doesn't support it, and even if you do have UEFI, you may still have an individual partition with an MBR-style boot loader that you want to use. You can get GRUB to load and run a different boot loader on a specific partition on your disk by *chainloading*.

To chainload, create a new menu entry in your GRUB configuration (using one of the methods on page 103). Here's an example for a Windows installation on the third partition of a disk:

```
menuentry "Windows" {
        insmod chain
        insmod ntfs
        set root=(hd0,3)
        chainloader +1
}
```

The +1 option to `chainloader` tells it to load whatever is at the first sector of a partition. You can also get it to directly load a file by using a line like this to load the *io.sys* MS-DOS loader:

```
menuentry "DOS" {
        insmod chain
        insmod fat
        set root=(hd0,3)
        chainloader /io.sys
}
```

5.8   Boot Loader Details

Now we'll look quickly at some boot loader internals. Feel free to skip to the next chapter if this material doesn't interest you.

To understand how boot loaders like GRUB work, let's first survey how a PC boots when you turn it on. Due to the repeated inadequacies of traditional PC boot mechanisms, there are several variations, but there are two main schemes: MBR and UEFI.

5.8.1   MBR Boot

In addition to the partition information described in Section 4.1, the *Master Boot Record (MBR)* includes a small area (441 bytes) that the PC BIOS loads and executes after its *Power-On Self-Test (POST)*. Unfortunately, this is too little storage to house almost any boot loader, so additional space is necessary, resulting in what is sometimes called a *multi-stage boot loader*. In this case the initial piece of code in the MBR does nothing other than load the rest of the boot loader code. The remaining pieces of the boot loader are usually stuffed into the space between the MBR and the first partition on the disk.

Of course, this isn't terribly secure because anything can overwrite the code there, but most boot loaders do it, including most GRUB installations. In addition, this scheme won't work with a GPT-partitioned disk using the BIOS to boot because the GPT table information resides in the area after the MBR. (GPT leaves the traditional MBR alone for backward compatibility.)

The workaround for GPT is to create a small partition called a *BIOS boot partition* with a special UUID to give the full boot loader code a place to reside. But GPT is normally used with UEFI, not the traditional BIOS, which leads us to the UEFI boot scheme.

5.8.2 UEFI Boot

PC manufacturers and software companies realized that the traditional PC BIOS is severely limited, so they decided to develop a replacement called *Extensible Firmware Interface (EFI)*. EFI took a while to catch on for most PCs, but now it's fairly common. The current standard is *Unified EFI (UEFI)*, which includes features such as a built-in shell and the ability to read partition tables and navigate filesystems. The GPT partitioning scheme is part of the UEFI standard.

Booting is radically different on UEFI systems and, for the most part, much easier to understand. Rather than executable boot code residing outside of a filesystem, there is always a special filesystem called the *EFI System Partition (ESP)*, which contains a directory named *efi*. Each boot loader has its own identifier and a corresponding subdirectory, such as *efi/microsoft*, *efi/apple*, or *efi/grub*. A boot loader file has an *.efi* extension and resides in one of these subdirectories, along with other supporting files.

NOTE *The ESP differs from the BIOS boot partition described in Section 5.8.1 and has a different UUID.*

There's a wrinkle, though: You can't just put old boot loader code into the ESP because that code was written for the BIOS interface. Instead, you must provide a boot loader written for UEFI. For example, when using GRUB, you have to install the UEFI version of GRUB rather than the BIOS version. In addition, you must "announce" new boot loaders to the firmware.

And, as mentioned in Section 5.6, we have the "secure boot" issue.

5.8.3 How GRUB Works

Let's wrap up our discussion of GRUB by looking at how it does its work:

1. The PC BIOS or firmware initializes the hardware and searches its boot-order storage devices for boot code.
2. Upon finding the boot code, the BIOS/firmware loads and executes it. This is where GRUB begins.
3. The GRUB core loads.
4. The core initializes. At this point, GRUB can now access disks and filesystems.

5. GRUB identifies its boot partition and loads a configuration there.

6. GRUB gives the user a chance to change the configuration.

7. After a timeout or user action, GRUB executes the configuration (the sequence of commands outlined in Section 5.5.2).

8. In the course of executing the configuration, GRUB may load additional code (*modules*) in the boot partition.

9. GRUB executes a `boot` command to load and execute the kernel as specified by the configuration's `linux` command.

Steps 3 and 4 of the preceding sequence, where the GRUB core loads, can be complicated due to the repeated inadequacies of traditional PC boot mechanisms. The biggest question is "Where *is* the GRUB core?" There are three basic possibilities:

- Partially stuffed between the MBR and the beginning of the first partition
- In a regular partition
- In a special boot partition: a GPT boot partition, EFI System Partition (ESP), or elsewhere

In all cases except where you have an ESP, the PC BIOS loads 512 bytes from the MBR, and that is where GRUB starts. This little piece (derived from *boot.img* in the GRUB directory) isn't yet the core, but it contains the start location of the core and loads the core from this point.

However, if you have an ESP, the GRUB core goes there as a file. The firmware can navigate the ESP and directly execute the GRUB core or any other operating system loader located there.

Still, on most systems, this is not the complete picture. The boot loader might also need to load an initial RAM filesystem image into memory before loading and executing the kernel. That's what the `initrd` configuration parameter in Section 6.8 specifies. But before you learn about the initial RAM filesystem, you should learn about the user space start—that's where the next chapter begins.

6

HOW USER SPACE STARTS

The point where the kernel starts its first user-space process, init, is significant—not just because that's where the memory and CPU are finally ready for normal system operation, but because that's where you can see how the rest of the system builds up as a whole. Prior to this point, the kernel executes a well-controlled path of execution defined by a relatively small number of software developers. User space is far more modular. It's much easier to see what goes into the user space startup and operation. For the adventurous, it's also relatively easy to change the user space startup because doing so requires no low-level programming.

User space starts in roughly this order:

1. init
2. Essential low-level services such as udevd and syslogd
3. Network configuration

4. Mid- and high-level services (cron, printing, and so on)

5. Login prompts, GUIs, and other high-level applications

6.1   Introduction to init

The init program is a user-space program like any other program on the Linux system, and you'll find it in */sbin* along with many of the other system binaries. Its main purpose is to start and stop the essential service processes on the system, but newer versions have more responsibilities.

There are three major implementations of init in Linux distributions:

System V init   A traditional sequenced init (Sys V, usually pronounced "sys-five"). Red Hat Enterprise Linux and several other distributions use this version.

systemd   The emerging standard for init. Many distributions have moved to systemd, and most that have not yet done so are planning to move to it.

Upstart   The init on Ubuntu installations. However, as of this writing, Ubuntu has also planned to migrate to systemd.

There are various other versions of init as well, especially on embedded platforms. For example, Android has its own init. The BSDs also have their version of init, but you are unlikely to see them on a modern Linux machine. (Some distributions have also modified the System V init configuration to resemble the BSD style.)

There are many different implementations of init because System V init and other older versions relied on a sequence that performed only one startup task at a time. Under this scheme, it is relatively easy to resolve dependencies. However, performance isn't terribly good, because two parts of the boot sequence cannot normally run at once. Another limitation is that you can only start a fixed set of services as defined by the boot sequence: When you plug in new hardware or need a service that isn't already running, there is no standardized way to coordinate the new components with init.

systemd and Upstart attempt to remedy the performance issue by allowing many services to start in parallel thereby speeding up the boot process. Their implementations are quite different, though:

- systemd is goal oriented. You define a target that you want to achieve, along with its dependencies, and when you want to reach the target. systemd satisfies the dependencies and resolves the target. systemd can also defer the start of a service until it is absolutely needed.

- Upstart is reactionary. It receives events and, based on those events, runs jobs that can in turn produce more events, causing Upstart to run more jobs, and so on.

The systemd and Upstart init systems also offer a more advanced way to start and track services. In traditional init systems, service daemons are expected to start themselves from scripts. A script runs a daemon program, which detaches itself from the script and runs autonomously. To find the PID of a service daemon, you need to use ps or some other mechanism specific to the service. In contrast, Upstart and systemd can manage individual service daemons from the beginning, giving the user more power and insight into exactly what is running on the system.

Because the new init systems are not script-centric, configuring services for them also tends to be easier. In particular, System V init scripts tend to contain many similar commands designed to start, stop, and restart services. You don't need all of this redundancy with systemd and Upstart, which allow you to concentrate on the services themselves, rather than their scripts.

Finally, systemd and Upstart both offer some level of on-demand services. Rather than trying to start all the services that may be necessary at boot time (as the System V init would do), they start some services only when needed. This idea is not really new; this was done with the traditional inetd daemon, but the new implementations are more sophisticated.

Both systemd and Upstart offer some System V backward compatibility. For example, both support the concept of runlevels.

6.2   System V Runlevels

At any given time on a Linux system, a certain base set of processes (such as crond and udevd) is running. In System V init, this state of the machine is called its *runlevel*, which is denoted by a number from 0 through 6. A system spends most of its time in a single runlevel, but when you shut the machine down, init switches to a different runlevel in order to terminate the system services in an orderly fashion and to tell the kernel to stop.

You can check your system's runlevel with the who -r command. A system running Upstart responds with something like this:

```
$ who -r
run-level 2  2015-09-06 08:37
```

This output tells us that the current runlevel is 2, as well as the date and time that the runlevel was established.

Runlevels serve various purposes, but the most common one is to distinguish between system startup, shutdown, single-user mode, and console mode states. For example, Fedora-based systems traditionally used runlevels 2 through 4 for the text console; a runlevel of 5 means that the system will start a GUI login.

But runlevels are becoming a thing of the past. Even though all three init versions in this book support them, systemd and Upstart consider runlevels obsolete as end states for the system. To systemd and Upstart, runlevels exist primarily to start services that support only the System V init scripts, and the implementations are so different that even if you're familiar with one type of init, you won't necessarily know what to do with another.

6.3   Identifying Your init

Before proceeding, you need to determine your system's version of init. If you're not sure, check your system as follows:

- If your system has */usr/lib/systemd* and */etc/systemd* directories, you have systemd. Go to Section 6.4.

- If you have an */etc/init* directory that contains several *.conf* files, you're probably running Upstart (unless you're running Debian 7, in which case you probably have System V init). Go to Section 6.5.

- If neither of the above is true, but you have an */etc/inittab* file, you're probably running System V init. Go to Section 6.6.

If your system has manual pages installed, viewing the init(8) manual page should help identify your version.

6.4   systemd

The systemd init is one of the newest init implementations on Linux. In addition to handling the regular boot process, systemd aims to incorporate a number of standard Unix services such as cron and inetd. As such, it takes some inspiration from Apple's launchd. One of its most significant features is its ability to defer the start of services and operating system features until they are necessary.

There are so many systemd features that it can be very difficult to know where to start learning the basics. Let's outline what happens when systemd runs at boot time:

1. systemd loads its configuration.
2. systemd determines its boot goal, which is usually named *default.target*.
3. systemd determines all of the dependencies of the default boot goal, dependencies of these dependencies, and so on.
4. systemd activates the dependencies and the boot goal.
5. After boot, systemd can react to system events (such as uevents) and activate additional components.

When starting services, systemd does not follow a rigid sequence. As with other modern init systems, there is a considerable amount of flexibility in the systemd bootup process. Most systemd configurations deliberately try to avoid any kind of startup sequence, preferring to use other methods to resolve strict dependencies.

6.4.1   Units and Unit Types

One of the most interesting things about systemd is that it does not just operate processes and services; it can also mount filesystems, monitor network sockets, run timers, and more. Each type of capability is called a *unit type*, and each specific capability is called a *unit*. When you turn on a unit, you *activate* it.

Rather than describe all of the unit types (you'll find them in the systemd(1) manual page), here's a look at a few of the unit types that perform the boot-time tasks required in any Unix system:

Service units   Control the traditional service daemons on a Unix system.

Mount units   Control the attachment of filesystems to the system.

Target units   Control other units, usually by grouping them.

The default boot goal is usually a target unit that groups together a number of service and mount units as dependencies. As a result, it's easy to get a partial picture of what's going to happen when you boot, and you can even create a dependency tree diagram with the systemctl dot command. You'll find the tree to be quite large on a typical system, because many units don't run by default.

Figure 6-1 shows a part of the dependency tree for the *default.target* unit found on a Fedora system. When you activate that unit, all of the units below it on the tree also activate.

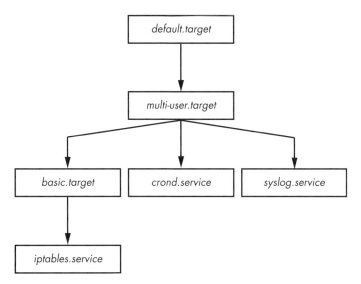

Figure 6-1: Unit dependency tree

6.4.2   *systemd Dependencies*

Boot-time and operational dependencies are more complicated than they may seem at first because strict dependencies are too inflexible. For example, imagine a scenario in which you want to display a login prompt after starting a database server, so you define a dependency from the login prompt to the database server. However, if the database server fails, the login prompt will also fail due to that dependency, and you won't even be able to log in to your machine to fix it.

Unix boot-time tasks are fairly fault tolerant and can often fail without causing serious problems for standard services. For example, if a data disk for a system was removed but its */etc/fstab* entry remained, the initial filesystem mount would fail. However, that failure typically wouldn't seriously affect standard operating system operation.

To accommodate the need for flexibility and fault tolerance, systemd offers a myriad of dependency types and styles. We'll label them by their keyword syntax, and but we won't go into details about configuration syntax until Section 6.4.3. Let's first look at the basic types:

Requires   Strict dependencies. When activating a unit with a Requires dependency unit, systemd attempts to activate the dependency unit. If the dependency unit fails, systemd deactivates the dependent unit.

Wants   Dependencies for activation only. Upon activating a unit, systemd activates the unit's Wants dependencies, but it doesn't care if those dependencies fail.

Requisite   Units that must already be active. Before activating a unit with a Requisite dependency, systemd first checks the status of the dependency. If the dependency has not been activated, systemd fails on activation of the unit with the dependency.

Conflicts   Negative dependencies. When activating a unit with a Conflict dependency, systemd automatically deactivates the dependency if it is active. Simultaneous activation of two conflicting units fails.

NOTE   *The Wants dependency type is especially significant because it does not propagate failures to other units. The systemd documentation states that this is the way you should specify dependencies if possible, and it's easy to see why. This behavior produces a much more robust system, similar to that of a traditional init.*

You can also attach dependencies "in reverse." For example, in order to add Unit A as a Wants dependency to Unit B, you don't have to add the Wants in Unit B's configuration. Instead, you can install it as a WantedBy in Unit A's configuration. The same is true of the RequiredBy dependency. The configuration for (and result of) a "By" dependency is slightly more involved than just editing a configuration file; see "Enabling Units and the [Install] Section" on page 119.

You can view a unit's dependencies with the systemctl command, as long as you specify a type of dependency, such as Wants or Requires:

```
# systemctl show -p type unit
```

Ordering

None of the dependency syntax that you've seen so far explicitly specifies order. By default, activating a unit with a Requires or Wants causes systemd to activate all of these dependencies at the same time as the first unit. This is optimal, because you want to start as many services as possible as quickly as possible to reduce boot time. However, there are situations when one unit must start after another. For instance, in the system that Figure 6-1 is based on, the *default.target* unit is set to start after *multi-user.service* (this order distinction is not shown in the figure).

To activate units in a particular order, you can use the following dependency modifiers:

Before   The current unit will activate before the listed unit(s). For example, if *Before=bar.target* appears in *foo.target*, systemd activates *foo.target* before *bar.target*.

After   The current unit activates after the listed unit(s).

Conditional Dependencies

Several dependency condition keywords operate on various operation system states rather than systemd units. For example:

ConditionPathExists=*p*:   True if the (file) path *p* exists in the system.

ConditionPathIsDirectory=*p*:   True if *p* is a directory.

ConditionFileNotEmpty=*p*:   True if *p* is a file and it's not zero-length.

If a conditional dependency in a unit is false when systemd tries to activate the unit, the unit does not activate, though this applies only to the unit in which it appears. Therefore, if you activate a unit that has a condition dependency as well as some other unit dependencies, systemd attempts to activate the unit dependencies regardless of whether the condition is true or false.

Other dependencies are primarily variations on the preceding. For example, the *RequiresOverridable* dependency is just like Requires when running normally, but it acts like a Wants dependency if a unit is manually activated. (For a full list, see the systemd.unit(5) manual page.)

Now that you've seen some of the a few pieces of the systemd configuration, let's look at some actual unit files and how to work with them.

6.4.3   systemd Configuration

The systemd configuration files are spread among many directories across the system, so you typically won't find the files for all of the units on a system in one place. That said, there are two main directories for systemd configuration: the *system unit* directory (globally configured, usually */usr/lib/systemd/system*) and a *system configuration* directory (local definitions, usually */etc/systemd/system*).

To prevent confusion, stick to this rule: Avoid making changes to the system unit directory because your distribution will maintain it for you. Make your local changes to the system configuration directory. So when given the choice between modifying something in */usr* and */etc*, always change */etc*.

NOTE *You can check the current systemd configuration search path (including precedence) with this command:*

```
# systemctl -p UnitPath show
```

However, this particular setting comes from a third source: pkg-config *settings. To see the system unit and configuration directories on your system, use the following commands:*

```
$ pkg-config systemd --variable=systemdsystemunitdir
$ pkg-config systemd --variable=systemdsystemconfdir
```

Unit Files

Unit files are derived from the XDG Desktop Entry Specification (for *.desktop* files, which are very similar to *.ini* files on Microsoft systems), with section names in brackets ([]) and variable and value assignments (options) in each section.

Consider the example unit file *media.mount* in */usr/lib/systemd/system*, which is standard on Fedora installations. This file represents the */media* tmpfs filesystem, which is a container directory for mounting removable media.

```
[Unit]
Description=Media Directory
Before=local-fs.target

[Mount]
What=tmpfs
Where=/media
Type=tmpfs
Options=mode=755,nosuid,nodev,noexec
```

There are two sections here. The [Unit] section gives some details about the unit and contains description and dependency information. In particular, this unit is set to activate before the *local-fs.target* unit.

The [Mount] section details the unit as being a mount unit, and it gives the details on the mount point, the type of filesystem, and the mount options as described in Section 4.2.6. The What= variable identifies the device or UUID of the device to mount. Here, it's set to tmpfs because this filesystem does not have a device. (For a full list of mount unit options, see the systemd.mount(5) manual page.)

Many other unit configuration files are similarly straightforward. For example, the service unit file *sshd.service* enables secure shell logins:

```
[Unit]
Description=OpenSSH server daemon
After=syslog.target network.target auditd.service

[Service]
EnvironmentFile=/etc/sysconfig/sshd
ExecStartPre=/usr/sbin/sshd-keygen
ExecStart=/usr/sbin/sshd -D $OPTIONS
ExecReload=/bin/kill -HUP $MAINPID

[Install]
WantedBy=multi-user.target
```

Because this is a service target, you'll find the details about the service in the [Service] section, including how to prepare, start, and reload the service. You'll find a complete listing in the systemd.service(5) manual page (and in systemd.exec(5)), as well as in the discussion of process tracking in Section 6.4.6.

Enabling Units and the [Install] Section

The [Install] section in the *sshd.service* unit file is important because it helps us to understand how to use systemd's WantedBy and RequiredBy dependency options. It's actually a mechanism for enabling units without modifying any configuration files. During normal operation, systemd ignores the [Install] section. However, consider the case when *sshd.service* is disabled on your system and you would like to turn it on. When you *enable* a unit, systemd reads the [Install] section; in this case, enabling the *sshd.service* unit causes systemd to see the WantedBy dependency for *multi-user.target*. In response, systemd creates a symbolic link to *sshd.service* in the system configuration directory as follows:

```
ln -s '/usr/lib/systemd/system/sshd.service' '/etc/systemd/system/multi-user.
target.wants/sshd.service'
```

Notice that the symbolic link is placed into a subdirectory corresponding to the dependent unit (*multi-user.target* in this case).

The [Install] section is usually responsible for the the *.wants* and *.requires* directories in the system configuration directory (*/etc/systemd/system*). However, there are also *.wants* directories in the unit configuration directory (*/usr/lib/systemd/system*), and you may also add links that don't correspond to [Install] sections in the unit files. These manual additions are a simple way to add a dependency without modifying a unit file that may be overwritten in the future (by a software upgrade, for instance).

NOTE *Enabling a unit is different from activating a unit. When you enable a unit, you are installing it into systemd's configuration, making semipermanent changes that will survive a reboot. But you don't always need to explicitly enable a unit. If the unit file has an [Install] section, you must enable it with* systemctl enable; *otherwise, the existence of the file is enough to enable it. When you activate a unit with* systemctl start, *you're just turning it on in the current runtime environment. In addition, enabling a unit does not activate it.*

Variables and Specifiers

The *sshd.service* unit file also shows use of variables—specifically, the $OPTIONS and $MAINPID environment variables that are passed in by systemd. $OPTIONS are options that you can pass to sshd when you activate the unit with systemctl, and $MAINPID is the tracked process of the service (see Section 6.4.6).

A *specifier* is another variable-like feature often found in unit files. Specifiers start with a percent (%). For example, the %n specifier is the current unit name, and the %H specifier is the current hostname.

NOTE *The unit name can contain some interesting specifiers. You can parameterize a single unit file in order to spawn multiple copies of a service, such as* getty *processes running on tty1, tty2, and so on. To use these specifiers, add the @ symbol to the end of the unit name. For* getty, *create a unit file named* getty@.service, *which allows you to refer to units such as* getty@tty1 *and* getty@tty2. *Anything after the @ is called the* instance, *and when processing the unit file, systemd expands the* %I *specifier to the instance. You can see this in action with the* getty@.service *unit files that come with most distributions running systemd.*

6.4.4   systemd Operation

You'll interact with systemd primarily through the systemctl command, which allows you to activate and deactivate services, list status, reload the configuration, and much more.

The most essential basic commands deal with obtaining unit information. For example, to view a list of active units on your system, issue a list-units command. (This is actually the default command for systemctl, so you don't really need the list-units part.):

```
$ systemctl list-units
```

The output format is typical of a Unix information-listing command. For example, the header and the line for *media.mount* would look like this:

UNIT	LOAD	ACTIVE	SUB	JOB DESCRIPTION
media.mount	loaded	active	mounted	Media Directory

This command produces a lot of output, because a typical system has numerous active units, but it will still be abridged because systemctl truncates any really large unit names. To see the full names of the units, use the `--full` option, and to see all units (not just active), use the `--all` option.

A particularly useful `systemctl` operation is getting the status of a unit. For example, here is a typical status command and its output:

```
$ systemctl status media.mount
media.mount - Media Directory
        Loaded: loaded (/usr/lib/systemd/system/media.mount; static)
        Active: active (mounted) since Wed, 13 May 2015 11:14:55 -0800;
37min ago
         Where: /media
          What: tmpfs
       Process: 331 ExecMount=/bin/mount tmpfs /media -t tmpfs -o
mode=755,nosuid,nodev,noexec (code=exited, status=0/SUCCESS)
        CGroup: name=systemd:/system/media.mount
```

Notice that there is much more information output here than you would see on any traditional init system. You get not only the state of the unit but also the exact command used to perform the mount, its PID, and its exit status.

One of the most interesting pieces of the output is the control group name. In the preceding example, the control group doesn't include any information other than the name `systemd:/system/media.mount` because the unit's processes have already terminated. However, if you get the status of a service unit such as *NetworkManager.service*, you'll also see the process tree of the control group. You can view control groups without the rest of the unit status with the `systemd-cgls` command. You'll learn more about control groups in Section 6.4.6.

The status command also displays recent information from the unit's journal (a log that records diagnostic information for each unit). You can view a unit's entire journal with this command:

```
$ journalctl _SYSTEMD_UNIT=unit
```

(This syntax is a bit odd because `journalctl` can access the logs of more than just a systemd unit.)

To activate, deactivate, and restart units, use the `systemd start`, `stop`, and `restart` commands. However, if you've changed a unit configuration file, you can tell systemd to reload the file in one of two ways:

systemctl reload *unit*   Reloads just the configuration for *unit*.

systemctl daemon-reload   Reloads all unit configurations.

Requests to activate, reactivate, and restart units are known as *jobs* in systemd, and they are essentially unit state changes. You can check the current jobs on a system with

```
$ systemctl list-jobs
```

If a system has been running for some time, you can reasonably expect there to be no active jobs on it because all of the activations should be complete. However, at boot time, you can sometimes log in fast enough to see some units start so slowly that they are not yet fully active. For example:

```
JOB UNIT                         TYPE    STATE
  1 graphical.target             start   waiting
  2 multi-user.target            start   waiting
 71 systemd-...nlevel.service    start   waiting
 75 sm-client.service            start   waiting
 76 sendmail.service             start   running
120 systemd-...ead-done.timer    start   waiting
```

In this case, job 76, the *sendmail.service* unit startup, is taking a really long time. The other listed jobs are in a waiting state, most likely because they're all waiting for job 76. When *sendmail.service* finishes starting and becomes fully active, job 76 will complete, the rest of the jobs will also complete, and the job list will be empty.

NOTE   *The term* job *can be confusing, especially because Upstart, another init system described in this chapter, uses the word* job *to (roughly) refer to what systemd calls a unit. It's important to remember that although a systemd job associated with a unit will terminate, the unit itself can be active and running afterwards, especially in the case of service units.*

See Section 6.7 for how to shut down and reboot the system.

6.4.5   Adding Units to systemd

Adding units to systemd is primarily a matter of creating, then activating and possibly enabling, unit files. You should normally put your own unit files in the system configuration directory */etc/systemd/system* so that you won't confuse them with anything that came with your distribution and so that the distribution won't overwrite them when you upgrade.

Because it's easy to create target units that don't do anything and don't interfere with anything, you should try it. Here's how to create two targets, one with a dependency on the other:

1. Create a unit file named *test1.target*:

```
[Unit]
Description=test 1
```

2. Create a *test2.target* file with a dependency on *test1.target*:

```
[Unit]
Description=test 2
Wants=test1.target
```

3. Activate the *test2.target* unit (remember that the dependency in *test2.target* causes systemd to activate *test1.target* when you do this):

```
# systemctl start test2.target
```

4. Verify that both units are active:

```
# systemctl status test1.target test2.target
test1.target - test 1
          Loaded: loaded (/etc/systemd/system/test1.target; static)
          Active: active since Thu, 12 Nov 2015 15:42:34 -0800; 10s ago

test2.target - test 2
          Loaded: loaded (/etc/systemd/system/test2.target; static)
          Active: active since Thu, 12 Nov 2015 15:42:34 -0800; 10s ago
```

NOTE   *If your unit file has an [Install] section, "enable" the unit before activating it:*

```
# systemctl enable unit
```

Try this with the preceding example. Remove the dependency from test2.target *and add an [Install] section to* test1.target *containing WantedBy=test2.target.*

Removing Units

To remove a unit, follow these steps:

1. Deactivate the unit if necessary:

```
# systemctl stop unit
```

2. If the unit has an [Install] section, disable the unit to remove any dependent symbolic links:

```
# systemctl disable unit
```

3. Remove the unit file, if you like.

6.4.6   systemd Process Tracking and Synchronization

systemd wants a reasonable amount of information and control over every process that it starts. The main problem that it faces is that a service can start in different ways; it may fork new instances of itself or even daemonize and detach itself from the original process.

To minimize the work that a package developer or administrator needs to do in order to create a working unit file, systemd uses *control groups* (cgroups), an optional Linux kernel feature that allows for finer tracking of a process hierarchy. If you've worked with Upstart before, you know that you have to do a little extra work to figure out what the main process is for a service. In systemd, you don't have to worry about how many times a process forks—just whether it forks. Use the `Type` option in your service unit file to indicate its startup behavior. There are two basic startup styles:

`Type=simple` The service process doesn't fork.

`Type=forking` The service forks, and systemd expects the original service process to terminate. Upon termination, systemd assumes that the service is ready.

The `Type=simple` option doesn't account for the fact that a service may take some time to set up, and systemd doesn't know when to start any dependencies that absolutely require such a service to be ready. One way to deal with this is to use delayed startup (see Section 6.4.7). However, some `Type` startup styles can indicate that the service itself will notify systemd when it is ready:

`Type=notify` The service sends a notification specific to systemd (with the `sd_notify()` function call) when it's ready.

`Type=dbus` The service registers itself on the D-bus (Desktop Bus) when it's ready.

Another service startup style is specified with `Type=oneshot`; here the service process actually terminates completely when it's finished. With such a service, you will almost certainly need to add a `RemainAfterExit=yes` option so that systemd will still regard the service as active even after its processes terminate.

Finally, there's one last style: `Type=idle`. This simply instructs systemd not to start the service until there are no active jobs. The idea here is just to delay a service start until other services have started to keep the system load down, or to keep services from stepping on one another's output. (Remember, once a service has started, the systemd job that started the service terminates.)

6.4.7   systemd On-Demand and Resource-Parallelized Startup

One of systemd's most significant features is its ability to delay a unit startup until it is absolutely needed. The setup typically works like this:

1. You create a systemd unit (call it Unit A) for the system service that you'd like to provide, as normal.

2. You identify a system resource such as a network port/socket, file, or device that Unit A uses to offer its services.

3. You create another systemd unit, Unit R, to represent that resource. These units have special types such as socket units, path units, and device units.

Operationally, it goes like this:

1. Upon activation of Unit R, systemd monitors the resource.
2. When anything tries to access the resource, systemd blocks the resource, and the input to the resource is buffered.
3. systemd activates Unit A.
4. When the service from Unit A is ready, it takes control of the resource, reads the buffered input, and runs normally.

There are a few concerns:

- You must make sure that your resource unit covers every resource that the service provides. This normally isn't a problem, as most services have just one point of access.
- You need to make sure your resource unit is tied to the service unit that it represents. This can be implicit or explicit, and in some cases, many options represent different ways for systemd to perform the handoff to the service unit.
- Not all servers know how to interface with the units that systemd can provide.

If you already know what utilities like inetd, xinetd, and automount do, you'll see that there are a lot of similarities. Indeed, the concept is nothing new (and in fact, systemd includes support for automount units). We'll go over an example of a socket unit on page 127. But let's first take a look at how these resource units help you at boot time.

Boot Optimization with Auxiliary Units

A common style of unit activation in systemd attempts to simplify dependency order and speed up boot time. It's similar to on-demand startup in that a service unit and an auxiliary unit represent the service unit's offered resource, except that in this case systemd starts the service unit as soon as it activates the auxiliary unit.

The reasoning behind this scheme is that essential boot-time service units such as *syslog* and *dbus* take some time to start, and many other units depend on them. However, systemd can offer a unit's essential resource (such as a socket unit) very quickly, and then it can immediately activate not only the essential unit but also any units that depend on the essential resource. Once the essential unit is ready, it takes control of the resource.

Figure 6-2 shows how this might work in a traditional system. In this boot timeline, Service E provides an essential Resource R. Services A, B, and C depend on this resource and must wait until Service E has started. When booting, the system takes quite a long time to get around to starting Service C.

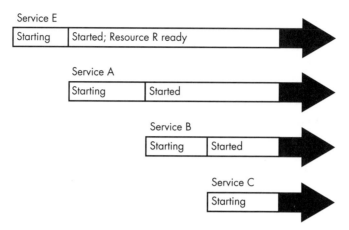

Figure 6-2: Sequential boot timeline with a resource dependency

Figure 6-3 shows an equivalent systemd boot configuration. The services are represented by Units A, B, C, and E, and a new Unit R represents the resource that Unit E provides. Because systemd can provide an interface for Unit R while Unit E starts, Units A, B, C, and E can all be started at the same time. Unit E takes over for Unit R when ready. (An interesting point here is that Units A, B, and C may not need to explicitly access Unit R before they finish their startup, as Unit B in the figure demonstrates.)

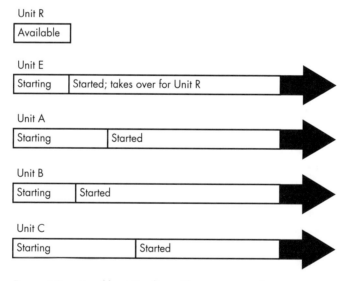

Figure 6-3: systemd boot timeline with a resource unit

NOTE *When parallelizing startup like this, there is a chance that your system may slow down temporarily due to a large number of units starting at once.*

The takeaway is that, although you're not creating an on-demand unit startup in this case, you're using the same features that make on-demand startup possible. For common real-life examples, see the syslog and D-Bus configuration units on a machine running systemd; they're very likely to be parallelized in this way.

An Example Socket Unit and Service

We'll now look at an example, a simple network echo service that uses a socket unit. This is somewhat advanced material, and you may not really understand it until you've read the discussion of TCP, ports, and listening in Chapter 9 and sockets in Chapter 10, so feel free to skip this and come back later.

The idea behind this service is that when a network client connects to the service, the service repeats anything that the client sends back to the client. The unit will listen on TCP port 22222. We'll call it the echo service and start with a socket unit, represented by the following *echo.socket* unit file:

```
[Unit]
Description=echo socket

[Socket]
ListenStream=22222
Accept=yes
```

Note that there's no mention of the service unit that this socket supports inside the unit file. So what is the corresponding service unit file?

Its name is *echo@.service*. The link is done by naming convention; if a service unit file has the same prefix as a *.socket* file (in this case, *echo*), systemd knows to activate that service unit when there's activity on the socket unit. In this case, systemd creates an instance of *echo@.service* when there's activity on *echo.socket*.

Here is the *echo@.service* unit file:

```
[Unit]
Description=echo service

[Service]
ExecStart=-/bin/cat
StandardInput=socket
```

NOTE   *If you don't like the implicit activation of units based on the prefixes, or you need to create an activation mechanism between two units with different prefixes, you can use an explicit option in the unit defining your resource. For example, use* Socket=bar.socket *inside* foo.service *to have* bar.socket *hand its socket to* foo.service.

To get this example service unit running, you need to start the *echo.socket* unit behind it, like this:

```
# systemctl start echo.socket
```

Now you can test the service by connecting to your local port 22222. When the following telnet command connects, type anything and press ENTER. The service repeats what you typed back to you:

```
$ telnet localhost 22222
Trying 127.0.0.1...
Connected to localhost.
Escape character is '^]'.
Hi there.
Hi there.
```

When you're bored with this, press CTRL-] on a line by itself, and then CTRL-D. To stop the service, stop the socket unit:

```
# systemctl stop echo.socket
```

Instances and Handoff

Because the *echo@.service* unit supports multiple simultaneous instances, there's an @ in the name (recall from page 120 that @ signifies parameterization). Why would you want multiple instances? The reason is that you may have more than one network client connecting to the service at the same time, and each connection should have its own instance.

In this case, the service unit *must* support multiple instances because of the Accept option in *echo.socket*. That option instructs systemd not only to listen on the port, but also to accept incoming connections and pass the incoming connections on to the service unit, with each connection a separate instance. Each instance reads data from the connection as standard input, but it doesn't necessarily need to know that the data is coming from a network connection.

NOTE *Most network connections require more flexibility than just a simple gateway to standard input and output, so don't expect to be able to create network services with a service unit file like the* echo@.service *unit file shown here.*

Although the service unit could do all of the work of accepting the connection, it wouldn't have the @ in its name if it did. In that case, it would take complete control of the socket, and systemd wouldn't attempt to listen on the network port again until the service unit has finished.

The many different resources and options for handoff to service units make it difficult to provide a categorical summary. Also, the documentation for the options is spread out over several manual pages. The ones to check for the resource-oriented units are systemd.socket(5), systemd.path(5), and systemd.device(5). One document that's often overlooked for service units is systemd.exec(5), which contains information about how the service unit can expect to receive a resource upon activation.

6.4.8   systemd System V Compatibility

One feature that sets systemd apart from other newer-generation init systems is that it tries to do a more complete job of tracking services started by System V–compatible init scripts. It works like this:

1. First, systemd activates *runlevel<N>.target*, where *N* is the runlevel.
2. For each symbolic link in */etc/rc<N>.d*, systemd identifies the script in */etc/init.d*.
3. systemd associates the script name with a service unit (for example, */etc/init.d/foo* would be *foo.service*).
4. systemd activates the service unit and runs the script with either a start or stop argument, based on its name in *rc<N>.d*.
5. systemd attempts to associate any processes from the script with the service unit.

Because systemd makes the association with a service unit name, you can use systemctl to restart the service or view its status. But don't expect any miracles from System V compatibility mode; it still must run the init scripts serially, for example.

6.4.9   systemd Auxiliary Programs

When starting out with systemd, you may notice the exceptionally large number of programs in */lib/systemd*. These are primarily support programs for units. For example, udevd is part of systemd, and you'll find it there as systemd-udevd. Another, the systemd-fsck program, works as a middleman between systemd and fsck.

Many of these programs exist because they contain notification mechanisms that the standard system utilities lack. Often, they simply run the standard system utilities and notify systemd of the results. (After all, it would be silly to try to reimplement all of fsck inside systemd.)

NOTE   *One other interesting aspect of these programs is that they are written in C, because one goal of systemd is to reduce the number of shell scripts on a system. There is some debate as to whether it's a good idea to do so (after all, many of these programs could probably be written as shell scripts), but as long as everything works and does so reliably, securely, and reasonably quickly, there's little reason to bother taking sides.*

When you see a program in */lib/systemd* that you can't identify, see the manual page. There's a good chance that the manual page will not only describe the utility but also describe the type of unit that it's meant to augment.

If you're not running (or interested in) Upstart, skip ahead to Section 6.6 for an overview of the System V init process.

6.5   Upstart

The Upstart version of init revolves around *jobs* and *events*. Jobs are startup and runtime actions for Upstart to perform (such as system services and configuration), and events are messages that Upstart receives from itself or other processes (such as udevd). Upstart works by starting jobs in response to events.

To get an idea of how this works, consider the *udev* job for starting the udevd daemon. Its configuration file is typically */etc/init/udev.conf*, which includes the following:

```
start on virtual-filesystems
stop on runlevel [06]
```

These lines mean that Upstart starts the *udev* job upon receiving the virtual-filesystems event, and it stops the job upon receiving a runlevel event with an argument of 0 or 6.

There are many variations on events and their arguments. For example, Upstart can react to events emitted in response to job status, such as the started udev event emitted by the *udev* job above. But before explaining jobs in detail, here's a high-level overview of how Upstart works.

6.5.1   Upstart Initialization Procedure

Upon startup, Upstart does the following:

1.   Loads its configuration and the job configuration files in */etc/init*.
2.   Emits the startup event.
3.   Runs jobs configured to start upon receiving the startup event.
4.   These initial jobs emit their own events, triggering more jobs and events.

Upon finishing all jobs associated with a normal startup, Upstart continues to monitor and react to events during the entire system uptime. Most Upstart installations run like this:

1.   The most significant job that Upstart runs in response to the startup event is *mountall*. This job attaches all necessary local and virtual filesystems to the currently running system so that everything else can run.
2.   The *mountall* job emits a number of events, including filesystem, virtual-filesystems, local-filesystems, remote-filesystems, and all-swaps, among others. These events indicate that the important filesystems on the system are now attached and ready.
3.   In response to these events, Upstart starts a number of essential service jobs. For example, *udev* starts in response to the virtual-filesystems event, and *dbus* starts in response to the local-filesystems event.

4. Among the essential service jobs, Upstart starts the *network-interfaces* job, usually in response to the local-filesystems event and udevd being ready.

5. The *network-interfaces* job emits the static-network-up event.

6. Upstart runs the *rc-sysinit* job in response to the filesystem and static-network-up events. This job is responsible for maintaining the system's current runlevel, and when started for the first time without a runlevel, it switches the system to the default runlevel by emitting a runlevel event.

7. Upstart runs most of the other startup jobs on the system in response to the runlevel event and the new runlevel.

The process can become complicated because it's not always clear where events originate. Upstart emits only a few events, and the rest come from jobs. Job configuration files usually declare the events that they will emit, but the details of how the job emits the events are usually not in the Upstart job configuration files.

To get to the bottom of things, you'll often have to dig. For example, consider the static-network-up event. The *network-interface.conf* job configuration file says that it emits this event, but it doesn't say where. It turns out that the event stems from the ifup command, which this job runs when initializing a network interface in the */etc/network/if-up.d/upstart* script.

NOTE *Though all of this is documented (the* ifup.d *directory is in the interfaces(5) manual page referenced by the ifup(8) manual page), it can be challenging to find out how this all works just by reading the documentation. It's usually faster to* grep *the event name in a lot of configuration files to see what comes up, then to try to piece everything back together from there.*

One issue with Upstart is that there's currently no clear way to view events. You can turn its log priority to debug, which will cause it to log everything that comes in (typically to */var/log/syslog*), but the copious amount of extraneous information in this file makes it difficult to determine an event's context.

6.5.2   Upstart Jobs

Each file in the Upstart */etc/init* configuration directory corresponds to a job, and the main configuration file for each job has a *.conf* extension. For example, */etc/init/mountall.conf* defines the *mountall* job.

There are two primary kinds of Upstart jobs:

Task jobs   These are jobs with a clear end. For example, *mountall* is a task job because it terminates when finished mounting filesystems.

Service jobs   These jobs have no defined stop. Servers (daemons) such as udevd, database servers, and web servers are all service jobs.

A third kind of job is an *abstract job*. Think of this as a kind of virtual service job. Abstract jobs exist only in Upstart and start nothing by themselves, but they are sometimes used as management tools for other jobs because other jobs can start and stop based on the events coming from an abstract job.

Viewing Jobs

You can view Upstart jobs and job status with the `initctl` command. To get an overview of what's happening on your system, run:

```
$ initctl list
```

You'll get a lot of output, so let's just look at two sample jobs that might appear in a typical listing. Here's a simple example of a task job status:

```
mountall stop/waiting
```

This indicates that the *mountall* task job has a status of stop/waiting, meaning that it's not running. (Unfortunately, as of this writing, you can't use the status to determine whether a job already ran or not because stop/waiting also applies to jobs that have never run.)

Service jobs that have associated processes appear in the status listing as follows:

```
tty1 start/running, process 1634
```

This line shows that the *tty1* job is running and that process ID 1634 is performing the job. (Not all service jobs have associated processes.)

NOTE *If you know a job's name, you can view its status directly with* `initctl status` *job.*

The status portion of the `initctl` output (e.g., stop/waiting) can be confusing. The left-hand side (before the /) is the *goal*, or what the job is supposed to be working toward, such as start or stop. The right-hand side is the current *job state*, or what the job is doing right now, such as waiting or running. For example, in the preceding listing, the *tty1* job has the status start/running, meaning that its goal is to start. The state of running indicates that it has started successfully. (For service jobs, the running state is nominal.)

The *mountall* case is a bit different because task jobs don't remain running. The stop/waiting status usually indicates that the job started and completed its task. Upon completing its task, it moved from a start to a stop goal, and it is now waiting for further commands from Upstart.

Unfortunately, as mentioned earlier, because jobs that have never started also have an Upstart stop/waiting status, you can't really tell whether a job has run or never started unless you enable debugging and look at the logs, as described in Section 6.5.5.

NOTE *You won't see jobs running on your system that were started with Upstart's System V compatibility feature.*

Job State Transitions

There are many job states, but there's a set way to move between them. For example, here's how a typical job starts:

1. All jobs begin in the stop/waiting status.
2. When a user or a system event starts a job, the job's goal changes from stop to start.
3. Upstart changes the job's state from waiting to starting, so the status is now start/starting.
4. Upstart emits a starting *job* event.
5. The job performs whatever it needs to do for the starting state.
6. Upstart changes the job's state from starting to pre-start and emits the pre-start *job* event.
7. The job works its way through several more states until it hits the running state.
8. Upstart emits a started job event.

Task termination involves a similar set of state changes and events. (See the upstart-events(7) manual page for details on all of the states and transitions in both goals.)

6.5.3 Upstart Configuration

Let's examine the two configuration files: one for the task job *mountall* and the other for the service job *tty1*. Like all Upstart configuration files, the configuration files are in */etc/init*, and they are named *mountall.conf* and *tty1.conf*. The configuration files are organized into smaller pieces called *stanzas*. Each stanza starts with a leading keyword, such as description or start.

To get started, open the *mountall.conf* file on your system. Look for a line like this in the first stanza:

```
description     "Mount filesystems on boot"
```

This stanza gives a short text description of the job.

Next you'll see a few stanzas describing how the *mountall* job starts:

```
start on startup
stop on starting rcS
```

Here, the first line tells Upstart to start the job upon receiving the startup event (the initial event that Upstart emits). The second line tells Upstart to terminate the job upon receiving the rcS event, when the system goes into single-user mode.

The next two lines tell Upstart how the *mountall* job behaves:

```
expect daemon
task
```

The task stanza tells Upstart that this is a task job, so the job should complete at some point. The expect stanza is tricky. It means that the *mountall* job will spawn a daemon that will operate independently of the original job script. Upstart needs to know this because it must know when the daemon terminates in order to correctly signal that the *mountall* job has terminated. (We'll discuss this in more detail in "Process Tracking and the Upstart expect Stanza" on page 136.)

The *mountall.conf* file continues with several emits stanzas, indicating events that the jobs produce:

```
emits virtual-filesystems
emits local-filesystems
emits remote-filesystems
emits all-swaps
emits filesystem
emits mounting
emits mounted
```

NOTE   *As mentioned in Section 6.5.1, even though these lines are present, this is not the actual source of the events. You'll need to hunt through the job script to find them.*

You may also see a console stanza stating where Upstart should send the output:

```
console output
```

With the output parameter, Upstart sends the *mountall* job's output to the system's console.

Now you'll see the details of the job itself—in this case, with a script stanza:

```
script
    . /etc/default/rcS
    [ -f /forcefsck ] && force_fsck="--force-fsck"
    [ "$FSCKFIX" = "yes" ] && fsck_fix="-fsck-fix"

    # set $LANG so that messages appearing in plymouth are translated
    if [ -r /etc/default/locale ]; then
        . /etc/default/locale
        export LANG LANGUAGE LC_MESSAGES LC_ALL
    fi

    exec mountall --daemon $force_fsck $fsck_fix
end script
```

This is a shell script (see Chapter 11), most of which is preparatory—setting locale and determining whether an fsck is necessary. The exec mountall command near the bottom of this script is where the real action happens. This command mounts the filesystems and emits the job's events when finished.

A Service Job: tty1

The service job *tty1* is much simpler; it controls a virtual console login prompt. Its entire configuration file, *tty1.conf*, looks like this:

```
start on stopped rc RUNLEVEL=[2345] and (
        not-container or
        container CONTAINER=lxc or
        container CONTAINER=lxc-libvirt)

stop on runlevel [!2345]

respawn
exec /sbin/getty -8 38400 tty1
```

The most complicated part of this job is actually when it starts, but for now, ignore the container lines and concentrate on this portion:

```
start on stopped rc RUNLEVEL=[2345]
```

This part tells Upstart to activate the job upon receiving a `stopped rc` event from Upstart when the *rc* task job has run and terminated. To make the condition true, the *rc* job must also set the `RUNLEVEL` environment variable to a value from 2 through 5 (see Section 6.5.6).

NOTE   *Other jobs that start on runlevels aren't so picky. For example, you might see this instead:*

```
start on runlevel [2345]
```

The only real difference between these last two start *stanzas is timing; this example activates the job as soon as the runlevel is set, while the prior one waits until the System V stuff finishes.*

The container configuration is there because Upstart not only runs directly on top of the Linux kernel on real hardware, but it can also run in virtual environments or containers. Some of these environments do not have virtual consoles, and you don't want to run getty on a console that doesn't exist.

Stopping the *tty1* job is straightforward:

```
stop on runlevel [!2345]
```

This stop stanza tells Upstart to terminate the job whenever the runlevel is not 2 through 5 (for example, during system shutdown).

The exec stanza at the bottom is the command to run:

```
exec /sbin/getty -8 38400 tty1
```

This stanza is much like the script stanza that you saw for the *mountall* job, except that the *tty1* job has no complicated setup to perform—it's easy to start with a single line. In this case, we're running the login prompt program getty on */dev/tty1*, which is the first virtual console (the one you get when you press CTRL-ALT-F1 in graphics mode).

The respawn stanza instructs Upstart to restart the *tty1* job if the job terminates. In this case, Upstart runs a new getty for a new login prompt when you log out of the virtual console.

Those are the basics of Upstart configuration. You'll find much more detail in the init(5) manual page and online resources, but one stanza requires special attention. The expect stanza is discussed next.

Process Tracking and the Upstart expect Stanza

Because Upstart tracks processes in jobs once they've started (so that it can terminate and restart them efficiently), it wants to know which processes are relevant to each job. This can be a difficult task, because in the traditional Unix startup scheme, processes fork from others during startup to become daemons, and the main process for a job may start after one or two forks. Without proper process tracking, Upstart won't be able to finalize its job startup, or it may track the incorrect PID for the job.

You tell Upstart how a job behaves with the expect stanza. There are four basic possibilities:

No expect stanza   The main job process does not fork. Track the main process.

expect fork   The process forks once. Track the forked process.

expect daemon   The process forks twice. Track the second fork.

expect stop   The job's main process will raise a SIGSTOP signal to indicate that it is ready. (This is rare.)

For Upstart and other modern versions of init, such as systemd, the ideal case is the first one (no expect stanza), because the main job process doesn't have to include any of its own startup and shutdown mechanics. In other words, it doesn't need to bother with forking or detaching itself from a current terminal—nuisances that Unix systems developers have had to deal with for years.

Many traditional service daemons already include debugging-style options that tell the main process to not fork. Examples include the Secure Shell daemon, sshd, and its -D option. A look at the */etc/init/ssh.conf* startup stanzas reveals a simple configuration to start sshd, prevent rapid respawning, and eliminate spurious output to stderr:

```
respawn
respawn limit 10 5
umask 022

# 'sshd -D' leaks stderr and confuses things in conjunction with 'console log'
console none
```

```
--snip--

exec /usr/sbin/sshd -D
```

Among jobs that require an expect stanza, expect fork is the most common. For example, here's the startup portion of the */etc/init/cron.conf* file:

```
expect fork
respawn

exec cron
```

A simple job startup like this usually indicates a well-behaved, stable daemon.

NOTE   *It's worth reading more about the* expect *stanza on the* upstart.ubuntu.com *site because it relates directly to process life span. For example, you can trace the life of a process and its system calls, including* fork()*, with the* strace *command.*

6.5.4   Upstart Operation

In addition to the list and status commands described in Section 6.5.2, you can also use the initctl utility to control Upstart and its jobs. You should read the initctl(8) manual page at some point, but for now let's look at the essentials.

To start an Upstart job, use initctl start:

```
# initctl start job
```

To stop a job, use initctl stop:

```
# initctl stop job
```

To restart a job:

```
# initctl restart job
```

If you need to emit an event to Upstart, you can do it manually with:

```
# initctl emit event
```

You can also add environment variables to the emitted event by adding *key=value* parameters after *event*.

NOTE   *You can't start and stop individual services that started via Upstart's System V compatibility feature. See Section 6.6.1 for more on how to do this in a System V init script.*

There are many ways to disable an Upstart job so that it will not start at boot time, but the most maintainable one is to determine the name of the job's configuration file (usually */etc/init/<job>.conf*) and then create a new file called */etc/init/<job>.override* containing only the line:

```
manual
```

Now the only way that the job will start is by running initctl start *job*.

The primary advantage to this method is that it's easily reversible. To reenable the job at boot, remove the *.override* file.

6.5.5 Upstart Logs

There are two basic kinds of logs in Upstart: service job logs, and diagnostic messages that Upstart itself produces. Service job logs record the standard output and standard error of the scripts and daemons that run the services. These messages, recorded in */var/log/upstart*, are in addition to the standard syslog messages that a service may produce. (You'll learn more about syslog in Chapter 7.) It's hard to categorize what goes into these logs because there are no standards, but the most common contents are startup and shutdown messages, as well as emergency error messages. Many services produce no messages at all because they send everything to syslog or their own logging facility.

Upstart's own diagnostic log can contain information about when it starts and reloads, as well as certain information about jobs and events. This diagnostic log goes to the kernel syslog utility. On Ubuntu, you'll usually find this log in the */var/log/kern.log* file and the catchall */var/log/syslog* file.

That said, by default, Upstart logs little to nothing, so to see anything at all in the logs, you must change the Upstart log priority. The name of the default priority is message. To log events and job changes on a running system, change the log priority to info:

```
# initctl log-priority info
```

Keep in mind that this won't be permanent and the priority will reset after a reboot. To have Upstart log everything when it starts, add a --verbose parameter as a boot parameter, as described in Section 5.5.

6.5.6 Upstart Runlevels and System V Compatibility

So far, we've touched upon a few places where Upstart supports the idea of System V runlevels and mentioned that it has the ability to run System V startup scripts as a job. Here's a more detailed overview of how it works on Ubuntu systems:

1. The *rc-sysinit* job runs, usually after getting the filesystem and static-network-up events. Before it runs, there is no runlevel.

2. The *rc-sysinit* job determines which runlevel to enter. Usually, the runlevel is the default, but it can also parse an older */etc/inittab* file or take the runlevel from a kernel parameter (in */proc/cmdline*).

3. The *rc-sysinit* job runs `telinit` to switch the runlevel. The command emits a `runlevel` event, specifying the runlevel in the `RUNLEVEL` environment variable.

4. Upstart receives the `runlevel` event. A number of jobs are configured to start on the `runlevel` event paired with a certain runlevel, and Upstart sets these in motion.

5. One of the runlevel-activated task jobs, *rc*, is responsible for running the System V start. In order to do so, the *rc* job runs */etc/init.d/rc*, just as System V init would (see Section 6.6).

6. Once the *rc* job terminates, Upstart can start a number of other jobs upon receiving the `stopped rc` event (such as the *tty1* job on page 135).

Notice that although Upstart treats the runlevel no differently than any other event, many of the job configuration files on most Upstart systems refer to the runlevel.

In any case, there is a critical point during boot when the filesystems are mounted and when most of the important system initialization is done. At this point, the system is ready to start higher-level system services such as graphical display managers and database servers. A `runlevel` event is handy for marking this point. You could configure Upstart to use any event as a trigger, though. One challenge comes when trying to determine which services start as Upstart jobs and which ones start in System V compatibility mode. The easiest way to find out is to look in your runlevel's System V link farm (see Section 6.6.2). For example, if your runlevel is 2, look in */etc/rc2.d*; anything there is likely running in System V compatibility mode.

NOTE *One stumbling block may be the presence of dummy scripts in* /etc/init.d. *For any Upstart service job, there may also be a System V–style script for that service in* /etc/init.d, *but that script won't do anything other than tell you that the service has been converted to an Upstart job. There also won't be a link to the script in the System V link directory. If you run into a dummy script, find out the Upstart job name, and use* initctl *to control the job.*

6.6   System V init

The System V init implementation on Linux dates to the early days of Linux; its core idea is to support an orderly bootup to different runlevels with a carefully sequenced process startup. Though System V is now uncommon on most desktop installations, you may encounter System V init in Red Hat Enterprise Linux, as well as in embedded Linux environments such as routers and phones.

There are two major components to a typical System V init installation: a central configuration file and a large set of boot scripts augmented by a symbolic link farm. The configuration file */etc/inittab* is where it all starts. If you have System V init, look for a line like the following in your *inittab* file:

```
id:5:initdefault:
```

This indicates that the default runlevel is 5.

All lines in *inittab* take the following form, with four fields separated by colons in this order:

- A unique identifier (a short string, such as id in the previous example)
- The applicable runlevel number(s)
- The action that init should take (default runlevel to 5 in the previous example)
- A command to execute (optional)

To see how commands work in an *inittab* file, consider this line:

```
l5:5:wait:/etc/rc.d/rc 5
```

This particular line is important because it triggers most of the system configuration and services. Here, the wait action determines when and how System V init runs the command: Run /etc/rc.d/rc 5 once when entering runlevel 5, then wait for this command to finish before doing anything else. To make a long story short, the rc 5 command executes anything in */etc/rc5.d* that starts with a number (in the order of the numbers).

S⟨n⟩ or K⟨n⟩   ?

The following are some of the most common *inittab* actions in addition to initdefault and wait.

respawn

The respawn action tells init to run the command that follows and, if the command finishes executing, to run it again. You're likely to see something like this in an *inittab* file:

```
1:2345:respawn:/sbin/mingetty tty1
```
└ run levels

The getty programs provide login prompts. The line above is used for the first virtual console (*/dev/tty1*), which is the one you see when you press ALT-F1 or CTRL-ALT-F1 (see Section 3.4.4). The respawn action brings the login prompt back after you log out.

ctrlaltdel

The ctrlaltdel action controls what the system does when you press CTRL-ALT-DEL on a virtual console. On most systems, this is some sort of reboot command, using the shutdown command (discussed in Section 6.7).

sysinit

The sysinit action is the first thing that init should run when starting, before entering any runlevels.

NOTE   *For more available actions, see the inittab(5) manual page.*

6.6.1 System V init: Startup Command Sequence

You are now ready to learn how System V init starts system services, just before it lets you log in. Recall this *inittab* line from earlier:

```
l5:5:wait:/etc/rc.d/rc 5
```

This small line triggers many other programs. In fact, rc stands for *run commands*, which many people refer to as scripts, programs, or services. But where are these commands?

The 5 in this line tells us that we're talking about runlevel 5. The commands are probably either in */etc/rc.d/rc5.d* or */etc/rc5.d*. (Runlevel 1 uses *rc1.d*, runlevel 2 uses *rc2.d*, and so on.) For example, you might find the following items in the *rc5.d* directory:

```
S10sysklogd      S20ppp           S99gpm
S12kerneld       S25netstd_nfs    S99httpd
S15netstd_init   S30netstd_misc   S99rmnologin
S18netbase       S45pcmcia        S99sshd
S20acct          S89atd
S20logoutd       S89cron
```

The rc 5 command starts programs in the *rc5.d* directory by executing the following commands in this sequence:

```
S10sysklogd start
S12kerneld start
S15netstd_init start
S18netbase start
--snip--
S99sshd start
```

Notice the start argument in each command. The capital *S* in a command name means that the command should run in *start* mode, and the number (00 through 99) determines where in the sequence rc starts the command. The *rc*.d* commands are usually shell scripts that start programs in */sbin* or */usr/sbin*.

Normally, you can figure out what a particular command does by viewing the script with less or another pager program.

NOTE *Some* rc*.d *directories contain commands that start with* K *(for "kill," or stop mode). In this case,* rc *runs the command with the* stop *argument instead of* start. *You will most likely encounter* K *commands in runlevels that shut down the system.*

You can run these commands by hand. However, you normally want to do so through the *init.d* directory instead of the *rc*.d* directories, which we'll now describe.

6.6.2 The System V init Link Farm

The contents of the *rc*.d* directories are actually symbolic links to files in yet another directory, *init.d*. If your goal is to interact with, add, delete, or modify services in the *rc*.d* directories, you need to understand these symbolic links. A long listing of a directory such as *rc5.d* reveals a structure like this:

```
lrwxrwxrwx . . . S10sysklogd -> ../init.d/sysklogd
lrwxrwxrwx . . . S12kerneld -> ../init.d/kerneld
lrwxrwxrwx . . . S15netstd_init -> ../init.d/netstd_init
lrwxrwxrwx . . . S18netbase -> ../init.d/netbase
--snip--
lrwxrwxrwx . . . S99httpd -> ../init.d/httpd
--snip--
```

A large number of symbolic links across several subdirectories such as this is called a *link farm*. Linux distributions contain these links so that they can use the same startup scripts for all runlevels. This convention is not a requirement, but it simplifies organization.

Starting and Stopping Services

To start and stop services by hand, use the script in the *init.d* directory. For example, one way to start the httpd web server program manually is to run init.d/httpd start. Similarly, to kill a running service, you can use the stop argument (httpd stop, for instance).

Modifying the Boot Sequence

Changing the boot sequence in System V init is normally done by modifying the link farm. The most common change is to prevent one of the commands in the *init.d* directory from running in a particular runlevel. You have to be careful about how you do this. For example, you might consider removing the symbolic link in the appropriate *rc*.d* directory. But beware: If you ever need to put the link back, you might have trouble remembering the exact name of the link. One of the best ways to do it is to add an underscore (_) at the beginning of the link name, like this:

```
# mv S99httpd _S99httpd
```

This change causes rc to ignore *_S99httpd* because the filename no longer starts with *S* or *K*, but the original name is still obvious.

To add a service, create a script like those in the *init.d* directory and then create a symbolic link in the correct *rc*.d* directory. The easiest way is to copy and modify one of the scripts already in *init.d* that you understand (see Chapter 11 for more information on shell scripts).

When adding a service, choose an appropriate place in the boot sequence to start it. If the service starts too soon, it may not work, due to a dependency on some other service. For nonessential services, most systems administrators prefer numbers in the 90s, which puts the services after most of the services that came with the system.

6.6.3　run-parts

The mechanism that System V init uses to run the *init.d* scripts has found its way into many Linux systems, regardless of whether they use System V init. It's a utility called run-parts, and the only thing it does is run a bunch of executable programs in a given directory, in some kind of predictable order. You can think of it as almost like a person who runs the ls command in some directory and then just runs whatever programs they see in the output.

The default behavior is to run all programs in a directory, but you often have the option to select certain programs and ignore others. In some distributions, you don't need much control over the programs that run. For example, Fedora ships with a very simple run-parts utility.

Other distributions, such as Debian and Ubuntu, have a more complicated run-parts program. Their features include the ability to run programs based on a regular expression (for example, using the S[0-9]{2} expression for running all "start" scripts in an */etc/init.d* runlevel directory) and to pass arguments to the programs. These capabilities allow you to start and stop System V runlevels with a single command.

You don't really need to understand the details of how to use run-parts; in fact, most people don't know that run-parts even exists. The main things to remember are that it shows up in scripts from time to time and that it exists solely to run the programs in a given directory.

6.6.4　Controlling System V init

Occasionally, you'll need to give init a little kick to tell it to switch runlevels, to reread its configuration, or to shut down the system. To control System V init, use telinit. For example, to switch to runlevel 3, enter:

```
# telinit 3
```

When switching runlevels, init tries to kill off any processes not in the *inittab* file for the new runlevel, so be careful when changing runlevels. *1*

When you need to add or remove jobs, or make any other change to the *inittab* file, you must tell init about the change and cause it to reload the file. The telinit command for this is:

```
# telinit q
```

You can also use telinit s to switch to single-user mode (see Section 6.9).

1 google : "unix-how-to-the-linux-etc-inittab-file."
↳ sys. admin guide
www.tldp.org / LDP/sag /html/config-init.html

6.7　Shutting Down Your System

init controls how the system shuts down and reboots. The commands to shut down the system are the same regardless of which version of init you run. The proper way to shut down a Linux machine is to use the shutdown command.

There are two basic ways to use shutdown. If you *halt* the system, it shuts the machine down and keeps it down. To make the machine halt immediately, run this: *or:* +3　(*in* 3 *min* , *etc*)

```
# shutdown -h now
```

On most machines and versions of Linux, a halt cuts the power to the machine. You can also *reboot* the machine. For a reboot, use -r instead of -h.

The shutdown process takes several seconds. You should never reset or power off a machine during this stage.

In the preceding example, now is the time to shut down. This argument is mandatory, but there are many ways to specify the time. For example, if you want the machine to shut down sometime in the future, you can use +*n*, where *n* is the number of minutes shutdown should wait before doing its work. (For other options, see the shutdown(8) manual page.)

To make the system reboot in 10 minutes, enter:

```
# shutdown -r +10
```

On Linux, shutdown notifies anyone logged on that the machine is going down, but it does little real work. If you specify a time other than now, the shutdown command creates a file called */etc/nologin*. When this file is present, the system prohibits logins by anyone except the superuser.

When system shutdown time finally arrives, shutdown tells init to begin the shutdown process. On systemd, it means activating the shutdown units; on Upstart, it means emitting the shutdown events; and on System V init, it means changing the runlevel to 0 or 6. Regardless of the init implementation or configuration, the procedure generally goes like this:

1.　init asks every process to shut down cleanly.

2.　If a process doesn't respond after a while, init kills it, first trying a TERM signal.

3.　If the TERM signal doesn't work, init uses the KILL signal on any stragglers.

4.　The system locks system files into place and makes other preparations for shutdown.

5.　The system unmounts all filesystems other than the root.

6.　The system remounts the root filesystem read-only.

7. The system writes all buffered data out to the filesystem with the `sync` program.

8. The final step is to tell the kernel to reboot or stop with the reboot(2) system call. This can be done by init or an auxiliary program such as `reboot`, `halt`, or `poweroff`.

The `reboot` and `halt` programs behave differently depending on how they're called, which may cause confusion. By default, these programs call `shutdown` with the `-r` or `-h` options. However, if the system is already at a halt or reboot runlevel, the programs tell the kernel to shut itself off immediately. If you really want to shut your machine down in a hurry, regardless of any potential damage from a disorderly shutdown, use the `-f` (force) option.

6.8   The Initial RAM Filesystem

The Linux boot process is, for the most part, fairly straightforward. However, one component has always been somewhat confounding: *initramfs*, or the *intitial RAM filesystem*. Think of this as a little user-space wedge that goes in front of the normal user mode start. But first, let's talk about why it exists.

The problem stems from the availability of many different kinds of storage hardware. Remember, the Linux kernel does not talk to the PC BIOS or EFI interfaces to get data from disks, so in order to mount its root filesystem, it needs driver support for the underlying storage mechanism. For example, if the root is on a RAID array connected to a third-party controller, the kernel needs the driver for that controller first. Unfortunately, there are so many storage controller drivers that distributions can't include all of them in their kernels, so many drivers are shipped as loadable modules. But loadable modules are files, and if your kernel doesn't have a filesystem mounted in the first place, it can't load the driver modules that it needs.

The workaround is to gather a small collection of kernel driver modules along with a few other utilities into an archive. The boot loader loads this archive into memory before running the kernel. Upon start, the kernel reads the contents of the archive into a temporary RAM filesystem (the initramfs), mounts it at /, and performs the user-mode handoff to the init on the initramfs. Then, the utilities included in the initramfs allow the kernel to load the necessary driver modules for the real root filesystem. Finally, the utilities mount the real root filesystem and start true init.

Implementations vary and are ever evolving. On some distributions, the init on the initramfs is a fairly simple shell script that starts a udevd to load drivers, then mounts the real root and executes the init there. On distributions that use systemd, you'll typically see an entire systemd installation there with no unit configuration files and just a few udevd configuration files.

One basic characteristic of the initial RAM filesystem that has (so far) remained unchanged since its inception is the ability to bypass it if you don't need it. That is, if your kernel has all the drivers it needs to mount your root filesystem, you can omit the initial RAM filesystem in your boot loader configuration. When successful, eliminating the initial RAM filesystem shortens boot time, usually by a couple of seconds. Try it yourself at boot time by using the GRUB menu editor to remove the initrd line. (It's best not to experiment by changing the GRUB configuration file, as you can make a mistake that will be difficult to repair.) Recently, it has been a little more difficult to bypass the initial RAM filesystem because features such as mount-by-UUID may not be available with generic distribution kernels.

It's easy to see the contents of your initial RAM filesystem because, on most modern systems, they are simple gzip-compressed cpio archives (see the cpio(1) manual page). First, find the archive file by looking at your boot loader configuration (for example, grep for initrd lines in your *grub.cfg* configuration file). Then use cpio to dump the contents of the archive into a temporary directory somewhere and peruse the results. For example:

```
$ mkdir /tmp/myinitrd
$ cd /tmp/myinitrd
$ zcat /boot/initrd.img-3.2.0-34 | cpio -i --no-absolute-filenames
--snip--
```

One particular piece of interest is the "pivot" near the very end of the init process on the initial RAM filesystem. This part is responsible for removing the contents of the temporary filesystem (to save memory) and permanently switch to the real root.

You won't typically create your own initial RAM filesystem, as this is a painstaking process. There are a number of utilities for creating initial RAM filesystem images, and your distribution likely comes with one. Two of the most common are dracut and mkinitramfs.

NOTE   *The term* initial RAM filesystem *(initramfs) refers to the implementation that uses the* cpio *archive as the source of the temporary filesystem. There is an older version called the initial RAM disk, or initrd, that uses a disk image as the basis of the temporary filesystem. This has fallen into disuse because it's much easier to maintain a* cpio *archive. However, you'll often see the term* initrd *used to refer to a* cpio-based *initial RAM filesystem. Often, as in the preceding example, the filenames and configuration files will still contain* initrd.

6.9   Emergency Booting and Single-User Mode

When something goes wrong with the system, the first recourse is usually to boot the system with a distribution's "live" image (most distributions' installation images double as live images) or with a dedicated rescue image such as SystemRescueCd that you can put on removable media. Common tasks for fixing a system include the following:

- Checking filesystems after a system crash
- Resetting a forgotten root password
- Fixing problems in critical files, such as */etc/fstab* and */etc/passwd*
- Restoring from backups after a system crash

Another option for booting quickly to a usable state is *single-user mode*. The idea is that the system quickly boots to a root shell instead of going through the whole mess of services. In the System V init, single-user mode is usually runlevel 1, and you can also enter the mode with an -s parameter to the boot loader. You may need to type the root password to enter single-user mode.

The biggest problem with single-user mode is that it doesn't offer many amenities. The network almost certainly won't be available (and if it is, it will be hard to use), you won't have a GUI, and your terminal may not even work correctly. For this reason, live images are nearly always considered preferable.

7

SYSTEM CONFIGURATION: LOGGING, SYSTEM TIME, BATCH JOBS, AND USERS

When you first look in the */etc* directory, you might feel a bit overwhelmed. Although most of the files that you see affect a system's operations to some extent, a few are fundamental. The subject material in this chapter covers the parts of the system that make the infrastructure discussed in Chapter 4 available to the user-level tools covered in Chapter 2. In particular, we're going to look at the following:

- Configuration files that the system libraries access to get server and user information
- Server programs (sometimes called *daemons*) that run when the system boots
- Configuration utilities that can be used to tweak the server programs and configuration files
- Administration utilities

As in previous chapters, there is virtually no networking material here because the network is a separate building block of the system. In Chapter 9, you'll see where the network fits in.

7.1 The Structure of /etc

Most system configuration files on a Linux system are found in */etc*. Historically, each program had one or more configuration files there, and because there are so many packages on a Unix system, */etc* would accumulate files quickly.

There were two problems with this approach: It was hard to find particular configuration files on a running system, and it was difficult to maintain a system configured this way. For example, if you wanted to change the system logger configuration, you'd have to edit */etc/syslog.conf*. But after your change, an upgrade to your distribution could wipe out your customizations.

The trend for many years now has been to place system configuration files into subdirectories under */etc*, as you've already seen for the boot directories (*/etc/init* for Upstart and */etc/systemd* for systemd). There are still a few individual configuration files in */etc*, but for the most part, if you run ls -F /etc, you'll see that most of the items there are now subdirectories.

To solve the problem of overwriting configuration files, you can now place customizations in separate files in the configuration subdirectories, such as the ones in */etc/grub.d*.

What kind of configuration files are found in */etc*? The basic guideline is that customizable configurations for a single machine, such as user information (*/etc/passwd*) and network details (*/etc/network*), go into */etc*. However, general application details, such as a distribution's defaults for a user interface, don't belong in */etc*. And you'll often find that noncustomizable system configuration files may be found elsewhere, as with the prepackaged systemd unit files in */usr/lib/systemd*.

You've already seen some of the configuration files that pertain to booting. Now we'll look at a typical system service and how to view and specify its configuration.

7.2 System Logging

Most system programs write their diagnostic output to the *syslog* service. The traditional syslogd daemon waits for messages and, depending on the type of message received, funnels the output to a file, the screen, users, or some combination of these, or just ignores it.

7.2.1 The System Logger

The system logger is one of the most important parts of the system. When something goes wrong and you don't know where to start, check the system log files first. Here is a sample log file message:

```
Aug 19 17:59:48 duplex sshd[484]: Server listening on 0.0.0.0 port 22.
```

Most Linux distributions run a new version of syslogd called rsyslogd that does much more than simply write log messages to files. For example, you can use it to load a module to send log messages to a database. But when starting out with system logs, it's easiest to start with the log files normally stored in */var/log*. Check out some log files—once you know what they look like, you'll be ready to find out how they got there.

Many of the files in */var/log* aren't maintained by the system logger. The only way to know for sure which ones belong to rsyslogd is to look at its configuration file.

7.2.2 Configuration Files

The base rsyslogd configuration file is */etc/rsyslog.conf*, but you'll find certain configurations in other directories, such as */etc/rsyslog.d*. The configuration format is a blend of traditional rules and rsyslog-specific extensions. One rule of thumb is that anything beginning with a dollar sign ($) is an extension.

A traditional rule has a *selector* and an *action* to show how to catch logs and where to send them, respectively. For example:

selector (facility.priority)   *action: where to send the log*

```
kern.*                  /dev/console
*.info;authpriv.none❶   /var/log/messages
authpriv.*              /var/log/secure,root
mail.*                  /var/log/maillog
cron.*                  /var/log/cron
*.emerg                 *❷
local7.*                /var/log/boot.log
```

Listing 7-1: syslog rules

The selector is on the left. It's the type of information to be logged. The list on the right is the action: where to send the log. Most actions in Listing 7-1 are normal files, with some exceptions. For example, /dev/console refers to a special device for the system console, root means send a message to the superuser if that user is logged in, and * means message all users currently on the system. You can also send messages to another network host with @*host*.

Facility and Priority

The selector is a pattern that matches the *facility* and *priority* of log messages. The facility is a general category of message. (See rsyslog.conf(5) for a list of all facilities.)

The function of most facilities will be fairly obvious from their name. For example, the configuration file in Listing 7-1 catches messages carrying the kern, authpriv, mail, cron, and local7 facilities. In this same listing, the asterisk at ❷ is a wildcard that catches output related to all facilities.

The *priority* follows the dot (.) after the facility. The order of priorities from lowest to highest is debug, info, notice, warning, err, crit, alert, or emerg.

> **NOTE** *To exclude log messages from a facility in* rsyslog.conf, *specify a priority of none, as shown at ❶ in Listing 7-1.*

When you put a specific priority in a selector, rsyslogd sends messages with that priority *and all higher priorities* to the destination on that line. Therefore, in Listing 7-1, the *.info for the line at ❶ actually catches most log messages and puts them into */var/log/messages* because info is a relatively low priority.

Extended Syntax

As previously mentioned, the syntax of rsyslogd extends the traditional syslogd syntax. The configuration extensions are called *directives* and usually begin with a $. One of the most common extensions allows you to load additional configuration files. Check your *rsyslog.conf* file for a directive like this, which causes rsyslogd to load all *.conf* files in */etc/rsyslog.d* into the configuration:

```
$IncludeConfig /etc/rsyslog.d/*.conf
```

Most of the other extended directives are fairly self-explanatory. For example, these directives deal with users and permissions:

```
$FileOwner syslog
$FileGroup adm
$FileCreateMode 0640
$DirCreateMode 0755
$Umask 0022
```

> **NOTE** *Additional* rsyslogd *configuration file extensions define output templates and channels. If you need to use them, the rsyslogd(5) manual page is fairly comprehensive, but the web-based documentation is more complete.*

Troubleshooting

One of the easiest ways to test the system logger is to send a log message manually with the `logger` command, as shown here:

```
$ logger -p daemon.info something bad just happened
```

Very little can go wrong with `rsyslogd`. The most common problems occur when a configuration doesn't catch a certain facility or priority or when log files fill their disk partitions. Most distributions automatically trim the files in */var/log* with automatic invocations of `logrotate` or a similar utility, but if too many messages arrive in a brief period, you can still fill the disk or end up with a high system load.

NOTE   *The logs caught by `rsyslogd` are not the only ones recorded by various pieces of the system. We discussed the startup log messages captured by systemd and Upstart in Chapter 6, but you'll find many other sources, such as the Apache Web server, which normally records its own access and error logs. To find those logs, see the server configuration.*

Logging: Past and Future

The syslog service has evolved over time. For example, there was once a daemon called `klogd` that trapped kernel diagnostic messages for `syslogd`. (These messages are the ones you see with the `dmesg` command.) This capability has been folded into `rsyslogd`.

It's a near certainty that Linux system logging will change in the future. Unix system logging has never had a true standard, but efforts are underway to change that.

7.3   User Management Files

Unix systems allow for multiple independent users. At the kernel level, users are simply numbers *(user IDs)*, but because it's much easier to remember a name than a number, you'll normally work with *usernames* (or *login names*) instead of user IDs when managing Linux. Usernames exist only in user space, so any program that works with a username generally needs to be able to map the username to a user ID if it wants to refer to a user when talking to the kernel.

7.3.1   The /etc/passwd File

The plaintext file */etc/passwd* maps usernames to user IDs. It looks something like this:

```
root:x:0:0:Superuser:/root:/bin/sh
daemon:*:1:1:daemon:/usr/sbin:/bin/sh
bin:*:2:2:bin:/bin:/bin/sh
```

```
sys:*:3:3:sys:/dev:/bin/sh
nobody:*:65534:65534:nobody:/home:/bin/false
juser:x:3119:1000:J. Random User:/home/juser:/bin/bash
beazley:x:143:1000:David Beazley:/home/beazley:/bin/bash
```

Listing 7-2: A list of users in /etc/passwd

Each line represents one user and has seven fields separated by colons. The fields are as follows:

- The username.

- The user's encrypted password. On most Linux systems, the password is not actually stored in the *passwd* file, but rather, in the *shadow* file (see Section 7.3.3). The *shadow* file format is similar to that of *passwd*, but normal users do not have read permission for *shadow*. The second field in *passwd* or *shadow* is the encrypted password, and it looks like a bunch of unreadable garbage, such as d1CVEWiB/oppc. (Unix passwords are never stored as clear text.)

  An x in the second *passwd* file field indicates that the encrypted password is stored in the *shadow* file. A star (*) indicates that the user cannot log in, and if the field is blank (that is, you see two colons in a row, like ::), no password is required to log in. (Beware of blank passwords. You should never have a user without a password.)

- The *user ID* (UID), which is the user's representation in the kernel. You can have two entries with the same user ID, but doing this will confuse you, and your software may mix them up as well. Keep the user ID unique.

- The *group ID* (GID). This should be one of the numbered entries in the */etc/group* file. Groups determine file permissions and little else. This group is also called the user's *primary group*.

- The user's real name (often called the *GECOS* field). You'll sometimes find commas in this field, denoting room and telephone numbers.

- The user's home directory.

- The user's shell (the program that runs when the user runs a terminal session).

Figure 7-1 identifies the various fields in one of the entries in Listing 7-2.

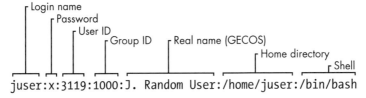

Figure 7-1: An entry in the password file

The *etc/passwd* file syntax is fairly strict, allowing for no comments or blank lines.

NOTE *A user in* /etc/passwd *and a corresponding home directory are collectively known as an* account.

7.3.2   Special Users

You will find a few special users in *etc/passwd*. The *superuser* (root) always has UID 0 and GID 0, as in Listing 7-2. Some users, such as *daemon*, have no login privileges. The *nobody* user is an underprivileged user. Some processes run as *nobody* because the *nobody* user cannot write to anything on the system.

The users that cannot log in are called *pseudo-users*. Although they can't log in, the system can start processes with their user IDs. Pseudo-users such as *nobody* are usually created for security reasons.

7.3.3   The /etc/shadow File

The shadow password file (*etc/shadow*) on a Linux system normally contains user authentication information, including the encrypted passwords and password expiration information that correspond to the users in *etc/passwd*.

The *shadow* file was introduced to provide a more flexible (and more secure) way of storing passwords. It included a suite of libraries and utilities, many of which were soon replaced by pieces of PAM (see Section 7.10). Rather than introduce an entirely new set of files for Linux, PAM uses *etc/shadow,* but not certain corresponding configuration files such as *etc/login.defs*.

7.3.4   Manipulating Users and Passwords

Regular users interact with *etc/passwd* using the passwd command. By default, passwd changes the user's password, but you can also use -f to change the user's real name or -s to change the user's shell to one listed in *etc/shells*. (You can also use the commands chfn and chsh to change the real name and shell.) The passwd command is an suid-root program, because only the superuser can change the *etc/passwd* file.

Changing /etc/passwd as the Superuser

Because *etc/passwd* is plaintext, the superuser may use any text editor to make changes. To add a user, simply add an appropriate line and create a home directory for the user; to delete, do the opposite. However, to edit the file, you'll most likely want to use the vipw program, which backs up and locks *etc/passwd* while you're editing it as an added precaution. To edit *etc/shadow* instead of *etc/passwd*, use vipw -s. (You'll likely never need to do this, though.)

Most organizations frown on editing *passwd* directly because it's too easy to make a mistake. It's much easier (and safer) to make changes to users using separate commands available from the terminal or through the GUI. For example, to set a user's password, run `passwd` *user* as the superuser. Use `adduser` and `userdel` to add and remove users.

7.3.5 Working with Groups

Groups in Unix offer a way to share files with certain users but deny access to all others. The idea is that you can set read or write permission bits for a particular group, excluding everyone else. This feature was once important because many users shared one machine, but it's become less significant in recent years as workstations are shared less often.

The */etc/group* file defines the group IDs (such as the ones found in the */etc/passwd* file). Listing 7-3 is an example.

```
root:*:0:juser
daemon:*:1:
bin:*:2:
sys:*:3:
adm:*:4:
disk:*:6:juser,beazley
nogroup:*:65534:
user:*:1000:
```

Listing 7-3: A sample /etc/group file

Like the */etc/passwd* file, each line in */etc/group* is a set of fields separated by colons. The fields in each entry are as follows, from left to right:

The group name   This appears when you run a command like `ls -l`.

The group password   This is hardly ever used, nor should you use it (use `sudo` instead). Use * or any other default value.

The group ID (a number)   The GID must be unique within the group file. This number goes into a user's group field in that user's */etc/passwd* entry.

An optional list of users that belong to the group   In addition to the users listed here, users with the corresponding group ID in their *passwd* file entries also belong to the group.

Figure 7-2 identifies the fields in a *group* file entry.

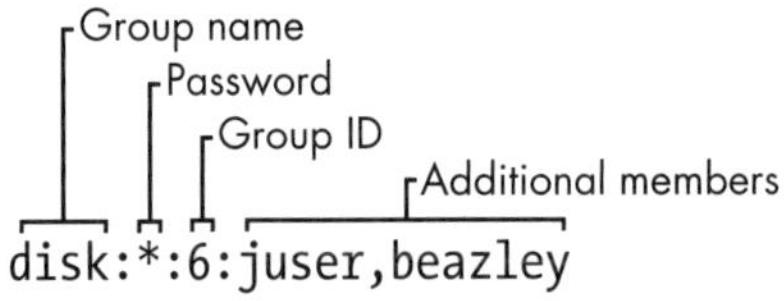

Figure 7-2: An entry in the group file

To see the groups you belong to, run `groups`.

Linux distributions often create a new group for each new user added, with the same name as the user.

7.4 getty and login

getty is a program that attaches to terminals and displays a login prompt. On most Linux systems, getty is uncomplicated because the system only uses it for logins on virtual terminals. In a process listing, it usually looks something like this (for example, when running on */dev/tty1*):

```
$ ps ao args | grep getty
/sbin/getty 38400 tty1
```

In this example, 38400 is the baud rate. Some getty programs don't need the baud rate setting. (Virtual terminals ignore the baud rate; it's only there for backward compatibility with software that connects to real serial lines.)

After you enter your login name, getty replaces itself with the login program, which asks for your password. If you enter the correct password, login replaces itself (using exec()) with your shell. Otherwise, you get a "Login incorrect" message.

You now know what getty and login do, but you'll probably never need to configure or change them. In fact, you'll rarely even use them, because most users now log in either through a graphical interface such as gdm or remotely with SSH, neither of which uses getty or login. Much of the login program's real authentication work is handled by PAM (see Section 7.10).

7.5 Setting the Time

Unix machines depend on accurate timekeeping. The kernel maintains the *system clock*, which is the clock that is consulted when you run commands like date. You can also set the system clock using the date command, but it's usually a bad idea to do so because you'll never get the time exactly right. Your system clock should be as close to the correct time as possible.

PC hardware has a battery-backed *real-time clock* (*RTC*). The RTC isn't the best clock in the world, but it's better than nothing. The kernel usually sets its time based on the RTC at boot time, and you can reset the system clock to the current hardware time with hwclock. Keep your hardware clock in Universal Coordinated Time (UTC) in order to avoid any trouble with time zone or daylight savings time corrections. You can set the RTC to your kernel's UTC clock using this command:

```
# hwclock --hctosys --utc
```

Unfortunately, the kernel is even worse at keeping time than the RTC, and because Unix machines often stay up for months or years on a single boot, they tend to develop time drift. *Time drift* is the current difference between the kernel time and the true time (as defined by an atomic clock or another very accurate clock).

You should not try to fix the drift with hwclock because time-based system events can get lost or mangled. You could run a utility like adjtimex to smoothly update the clock, but usually it's best to keep your system time correct with a network time daemon (see Section 7.5.2).

7.5.1   Kernel Time Representation and Time Zones

The kernel's system clock represents the current time as the number of seconds since 12:00 midnight on January 1, 1970, UTC. To see this number at the moment, run:

```
$ date +%s
```

To convert this number into something that humans can read, user-space programs change it to local time and compensate for daylight savings time and any other strange circumstances (such as living in Indiana). The local time zone is controlled by the file */etc/localtime*. (Don't bother trying to look at it; it's a binary file.)

The time zone files on your system are in */usr/share/zoneinfo*. You'll find that this directory contains a lot of time zones and a lot of aliases for time zones. To set your system's time zone manually, either copy one of the files in */usr/share/zoneinfo* to */etc/localtime* (or make a symbolic link) or change it with your distribution's time zone tool. (The command-line program tzselect may help you identify a time zone file.)

To use a time zone other than the system default for just one shell session, set the TZ environment variable to the name of a file in */usr/share/zoneinfo* and test the change, like this:

```
$ export TZ=US/Central
$ date
```

As with other environment variables, you can also set the time zone for the duration of a single command like this:

```
$ TZ=US/Central date
```

7.5.2   Network Time

If your machine is permanently connected to the Internet, you can run a Network Time Protocol (NTP) daemon to maintain the time using a remote server. Many distributions have built-in support for an NTP daemon, but it may not be enabled by default. You might need to install an ntpd package to get it to work.

If you need to do the configuration by hand, you'll find help on the main NTP web page at *http://www.ntp.org/*, but if you'd rather not read through the mounds of documentation there, do this:

1. Find the closest NTP time server from your ISP or from the *ntp.org* web page.
2. Put that time server in */etc/ntpd.conf.*
3. Run ntpdate *server* at boot time.
4. Run ntpd at boot time, after the ntpdate command.

If your machine doesn't have a permanent Internet connection, you can use a daemon like chronyd to maintain the time during disconnections.

You can also set your hardware clock based on the network time in order to help your system maintain time coherency when it reboots. (Many distributions do this automatically.) To do so, set your system time from the network with ntpdate (or ntpd), then run the command you saw back on page 157:

```
# hwclock --systohc --utc
```

7.6   Scheduling Recurring Tasks with cron

The Unix cron service runs programs repeatedly on a fixed schedule. Most experienced administrators consider cron to be vital to the system because it can perform automatic system maintenance. For example, cron runs log file rotation utilities to ensure that your hard drive doesn't fill up with old log files. You should know how to use cron because it's just plain useful.

You can run any program with cron at whatever times suit you. The program running through cron is called a *cron job*. To install a cron job, you'll create an entry line in your *crontab file*, usually by running the crontab command. For example, the crontab entry schedules the /home/juser/bin/spmake command daily at 9:15 AM:

```
15 09 * * * /home/juser/bin/spmake
```

The five fields at the beginning of this line, delimited by whitespace, specify the scheduled time (see also Figure 7-3). The fields are as follows, in order:

- Minute (0 through 59). The cron job above is set for minute 15.
- Hour (0 through 23). The job above is set for the ninth hour.
- Day of month (1 through 31).
- Month (1 through 12).
- Day of week (0 through 7). The numbers 0 and 7 are Sunday.

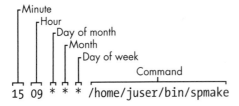

Figure 7-3: An entry in the crontab file

A star (*) in any field means to match every value. The preceding example runs spmake daily because the day of month, month, and day of week fields are all filled with stars, which cron reads as "run this job every day, of every month, of every week."

To run spmake only on the 14th day of each month, you would use this crontab line:

```
15 09 14 * * /home/juser/bin/spmake
```

You can select more than one time for each field. For example, to run the program on the 5th and the 14th day of each month, you could enter 5,14 in the third field:

```
15 09 5,14 * * /home/juser/bin/spmake
```

NOTE   *If the cron job generates standard output or an error or exits abnormally, cron should mail this information to you. Redirect the output to /dev/null or some other log file if you find the email annoying.*

The crontab(5) manual page provides complete information on the crontab format.

7.6.1   Installing Crontab Files

Each user can have his or her own crontab file, which means that every system may have multiple crontabs, usually found in */var/spool/cron/crontabs*. Normal users can't write to this directory; the crontab command installs, lists, edits, and removes a user's crontab.

The easiest way to install a crontab is to put your crontab entries into a file and then use **crontab** *file* to install *file* as your current crontab. The crontab command checks the file format to make sure that you haven't made any mistakes. To list your cron jobs, run crontab -l. To remove the crontab, use crontab -r.

However, after you've created your initial crontab, it can be a bit messy to use temporary files to make further edits. Instead, you can edit and install your crontab in one step with the crontab -e command. If you make a mistake, crontab should tell you where the mistake is and ask if you want to try editing again.

7.6.2   System Crontab Files

Rather than use the superuser's crontab to schedule recurring system tasks, Linux distributions normally have an */etc/crontab* file. Don't use crontab to edit this file, because this version has an additional field inserted before the command to run—the user that should run the job. For example, this cron job defined in */etc/crontab* runs at 6:42 AM as the superuser (root, shown at ❶):

```
42 6 * * * root❶ /usr/local/bin/cleansystem > /dev/null 2>&1
```

NOTE   *Some distributions store system crontab files in the* /etc/cron.d *directory. These files may have any name, but they have the same format as* /etc/crontab.

7.6.3   The Future of cron

The cron utility is one of the oldest components of a Linux system; it's been around for decades (predating Linux itself), and its configuration format hasn't changed much for many years. When something gets to be this old, it becomes fodder for replacement, and there are efforts underway to do exactly that.

The proposed replacements are actually just parts of the newer versions of init: For systemd, there are timer units, and for Upstart, the idea is to be able to create recurring events to trigger jobs. After all, both versions of init can run tasks as any user, and they offer certain advantages, such as custom logging.

However, the reality is that neither systemd nor Upstart currently has all of the capabilities of cron. Furthermore, when they do become capable, backward compatibility will be necessary to support everything that relies on cron. For these reasons, it's unlikely that the cron format will go away anytime soon.

7.7   Scheduling One-Time Tasks with at

To run a job once in the future without using cron, use the at service. For example, to run myjob at 10:30 PM, enter this command:

```
$ at 22:30            at 10:30 PM  run myjob
at> myjob
```

End the input with CTRL-D. (The at utility reads the commands from the standard input.)

To check that the job has been scheduled, use atq. To remove it, use atrm. You can also schedule jobs days into the future by adding the date in DD.MM.YY format, for example, at 22:30 30.09.15.

There isn't much else to the at command. Though at isn't used that often, it can be handy for that odd time when you need to tell the system to shut down in the future.

7.8 Understanding User IDs and User Switching

We've discussed how setuid programs such as sudo and su allow you to change users, and we've mentioned system components like login that control user access. Perhaps you're wondering how these pieces work and what role the kernel plays in user switching.

There are two ways to change a user ID, and the kernel handles both. The first is with a setuid executable, which is covered in Section 2.17. The second is through the setuid() family of system calls. There are a few different versions of this system call to accommodate the various user IDs associated with a process, as you'll learn in Section 7.8.1.

The kernel has basic rules about what a process can or can't do, but here are the three basics:

- A process running as root (userid 0) can use setuid() to become any other user.

- A process not running as root has severe restrictions on how it may use setuid(); in most cases, it cannot.

- Any process can execute a setuid program as long as it has adequate file permissions.

NOTE   *User switching has nothing to do with passwords or usernames. Those are strictly user-space concepts, as you first saw in the* /etc/passwd *file in Section 7.3.1. You'll learn more details about how this works in Section 7.9.1.*

7.8.1   Process Ownership, Effective UID, Real UID, and Saved UID

Our discussion of user IDs so far has been simplified. In reality, every process has more than one user ID. We've described the *effective user ID* (*euid*), which defines the access rights for a process. A second user ID, the *real user ID* (*ruid*), indicates who initiated a process. When you run a setuid program, Linux sets the effective user ID to the program's owner during execution, but it keeps your original user ID in the real user ID.

On modern systems, the difference between the effective and real user IDs is confusing, so much so that a lot of documentation regarding process ownership is incorrect.

Think of the effective user ID as the *actor* and the real user ID as the *owner*. The real user ID defines the user that can interact with the running process—most significantly, which user can kill and send signals to a process. For example, if user A starts a new process that runs as user B (based on setuid permissions), user A still owns the process and can kill it.

On normal Linux systems, most processes have the same effective user ID and real user ID. By default, ps and other system diagnostic programs show the effective user ID. To view both the effective and real user IDs on your system, try this, but don't be surprised if you find that the two user ID columns are identical for all processes on your system:

```
$ ps -eo pid,euser,ruser,comm
```

To create an exception just so that you can see different values in the columns, try experimenting by creating a setuid copy of the sleep command, running the copy for a few seconds, and then running the preceding ps command in another window before the copy terminates.

To add to the confusion, in addition to the real and effective user IDs, there is also a *saved user ID* (which is usually not abbreviated). A process can switch its effective user ID to the real or saved user ID during execution. (To make things even more complicated, Linux has yet another user ID: the *file system user ID* [*fsuid*], which defines the user accessing the filesystem but is rarely used.)

Typical Setuid Program Behavior

The idea of the real user ID might contradict your previous experience. Why don't you have to deal with the other user IDs very frequently? For example, after starting a process with sudo, if you want to kill it, you still use sudo; you can't kill it as your own regular user. Shouldn't your regular user be the real user ID in this case, giving you the correct permissions?

The cause of this behavior is that sudo and many other setuid programs explicitly change the effective *and* real user IDs with one of the setuid() system calls. These programs do so because there are often unintended side effects and access problems when all of the user IDs do not match.

NOTE *If you're interested in the details and rules regarding user ID switching, read the setuid(2) manual page and check the other manual pages listed in the SEE ALSO section. There are many different system calls for diverse situations.*

Some programs don't like to have a real user ID of root. To prevent sudo from changing the real user ID, add this line to your */etc/sudoers* file (and beware of side effects on other programs you want to run as root!):

```
Defaults        stay_setuid
```

Security Implications

Because the Linux kernel handles all user switches (and as a result, file access permissions) through setuid programs and subsequent system calls, systems developers and administrators must be extremely careful with two things:

- The programs that have setuid permissions
- What those programs do

If you make a copy of the bash shell that is setuid root, any local user can execute it and have complete run of the system. It's really that simple. Furthermore, even a special-purpose program that is setuid root can pose a danger if it has bugs. Exploiting weaknesses in programs running as root is a primary method of systems intrusion, and there are too many such exploits to count.

Because there are so many ways to break into a system, preventing intrusion is a multifaceted affair. One of the most essential ways to keep unwanted activity off your system is to enforce user authentication with usernames and passwords.

7.9   User Identification and Authentication

A multiuser system must provide basic support for user security in terms of identification and authentication. The *identification* portion of security answers the question of *who* users are. The *authentication* piece asks users to *prove* that they are who they say they are. Finally, *authorization* is used to define and limit what users are *allowed* to do.

When it comes to user identification, the Linux kernel knows only the numeric user IDs for process and file ownership. The kernel knows authorization rules for how to run setuid executables and how user IDs may run the setuid() family of system calls to change from one user to another. However, the kernel does not know anything about authentication: usernames, passwords, and so on. Practically everything related to authentication happens in user space.

We discussed the mapping between user IDs and passwords in Section 7.3.1; now we'll explain how user processes access this mapping. We'll begin with an oversimplified case, in which a user process wants to know its username (the name corresponding to the effective user ID). On a traditional Unix system, a process could do something like this to get its username:

1.   The process asks the kernel for its effective user ID with the geteuid() system call.
2.   The process opens the */etc/passwd* file and starts reading at the beginning.
3.   The process reads a line of the */etc/passwd* file. If there's nothing left to read, the process has failed to find the username.
4.   The process parses the line into fields (breaking out everything between the colons). The third field is the user ID for the current line.
5.   The process compares the ID from Step 4 to the ID from Step 1. If they're identical, the first field in Step 4 is the desired username, and the process can stop searching and use this name.
6.   The process moves on to the next line in */etc/passwd* and goes back to Step 3.

This is a long procedure that's usually much more complicated in reality.

7.9.1   Using Libraries for User Information

If every developer who needed to know the current username had to write all of the code you've just seen, the system would be a horrifyingly disjointed, buggy, bloated, and unmaintainable mess. Fortunately, we can use standard libraries to perform repetitive tasks, so all you'd normally need to do to get a username is call a function like `getpwuid()` in the standard library after you have the answer from `geteuid()`. (See the manual pages for these calls for more on how they work.)

When the standard library is shared, you can make significant changes to the implementation without changing any other program. For example, you can move away from using */etc/passwd* for your users and use a network service such as LDAP instead.

This approach has worked well for identifying usernames associated with user IDs, but passwords have proven more troublesome. Section 7.3.1 describes how, traditionally, the encrypted password was part of */etc/passwd*, so if you wanted to verify a password that a user entered, you'd encrypt whatever the user typed and compare it to the contents of the */etc/passwd* file.

This traditional implementation has the following limitations:

- It doesn't set a system-wide standard for the encryption protocol.
- It assumes that you have access to the encrypted password.
- It assumes that you want to prompt the user for a password every time the user wants to access something that requires authentication (which gets annoying).
- It assumes that you want to use passwords. If you want to use one-time tokens, smart cards, biometrics, or some other form of user authentication, you have to add that support yourself.

Some of these limitations contributed to the development of the shadow password package discussed in Section 7.3.3, which took the first step in allowing system-wide password configuration. But the solution to the bulk of the problems came with the design and implementation of PAM.

7.10 PAM

To accommodate flexibility in user authentication, in 1995 Sun Microsystems proposed a new standard called *Pluggable Authentication Modules (PAM)*, a system of shared libraries for authentication (Open Source Software Foundation RFC 86.0, October 1995). To authenticate a user, an application hands the user to PAM to determine whether the user can successfully identify itself. This way, it's relatively easy to add support for additional authentication techniques, such as two-factor and physical keys. In addition to authentication mechanism support, PAM also provides a limited amount of authorization control for services (for example, if you'd like to deny a service like cron to certain users).

Because there are many kinds of authentication scenarios, PAM employs a number of dynamically loadable *authentication modules*. Each module performs a specific task; for example, the *pam_unix.so* module can check a user's password.

This is tricky business, to say the least. The programming interface isn't easy, and it's not clear that PAM actually solves all of the existing problems. Nevertheless, PAM support is in nearly every program that requires authentication on a Linux system, and most distributions use PAM. And because it works on top of the existing Unix authentication API, integrating support into a client requires little, if any, extra work.

7.10.1   PAM Configuration

We'll explore the basics of how PAM works by examining its configuration. You'll normally find PAM's application configuration files in the */etc/pam.d* directory (older systems may use a single */etc/pam.conf* file). Most installations include many files, so you may not know where to start. Some filenames should correspond to parts of the system that you know already, such as *cron* and *passwd*.

Because the specific configuration in these files varies significantly between distributions, it can be difficult to find a common example. We'll look at an example configuration line that you might find for chsh (the change shell program):

```
auth        requisite   pam_shells.so
```

This line says that the user's shell must be in */etc/shells* in order for the user to successfully authenticate with the chsh program. Let's see how. Each configuration line has three fields: a function type, control argument, and module, in that order. Here's what they mean for this example:

Function type   The function that a user application asks PAM to perform. Here, it's auth, the task of authenticating the user.

Control argument   This setting controls what PAM does *after* success or failure of its action for the current line (requisite in this example). We'll get to this shortly.

Module   The authentication module that runs for this line, determining what the line actually does. Here, the *pam_shells.so* module checks to see whether the user's current shell is listed in */etc/shells*.

PAM configuration is detailed on the pam.conf(5) manual page. Let's look at a few of the essentials.

Function Types

A user application can ask PAM to perform one of the following four functions:

auth   Authenticate a user (see if the user is who they say they are).

account   Check user account status (whether the user is authorized to do something, for example).

session   Perform something only for the user's current session (such as displaying a message of the day).

password   Change a user's password or other credentials.

For any configuration line, the module and function together determine PAM's action. A module can have more than one function type, so when determining the purpose of a configuration line, always remember to consider the function and module as a pair. For example, the *pam_unix.so* module checks a password when performing the auth function, but it sets a password when performing the password function.

Control Arguments and Stacked Rules

One important feature of PAM is that the rules specified by its configuration lines *stack*, meaning that you can apply many rules when performing a function. This is why the control argument is important: The success or failure of an action in one line can impact following lines or cause the entire function to succeed or fail.

There are two kinds of control arguments: the simple syntax and a more advanced syntax. Here are the three major simple syntax control arguments that you'll find in a rule:

sufficient   If this rule succeeds, the authentication is successful, and PAM does not need to look at any more rules. If the rule fails, PAM proceeds to additional rules.

requisite   If this rule succeeds, PAM proceeds to additional rules. If the rule fails, the authentication is unsuccessful, and PAM does not need to look at any more rules.

required   If this rule succeeds, PAM proceeds to additional rules. If the rule fails, PAM proceeds to additional rules but will always return an unsuccessful authentication regardless of the end result of the additional rules.

Continuing with the preceding example, here is an example stack for the chsh authentication function:

```
auth       sufficient    pam_rootok.so
auth       requisite     pam_shells.so
auth       sufficient    pam_unix.so
auth       required      pam_deny.so
```

With this configuration, when the chsh command asks PAM to perform the authentication function, PAM does the following (see Figure 7-4 for a flowchart):

1. The *pam_rootok.so* module checks to see if the root user is the one trying to authenticate. If so, it immediately succeeds and attempts no further authentication. This works because the control argument is set to sufficient, meaning that success from this action is good enough for PAM to immediately report success back to chsh. Otherwise, it proceeds to Step 2.

2. The *pam_shells.so* module checks to see if the user's shell is in */etc/shells*. If the shell is not there, the module returns failure, and the requisite control argument indicates that PAM must immediately report this

failure back to chsh and attempt no further authentication. Otherwise, the shell is in */etc/shells*, so the module returns success and fulfills the control flag of required; proceed to Step 3.

3. The *pam_unix.so* module asks the user for the user's password and checks it. The control argument is set to sufficient, so success from this module (a correct password) is enough for PAM to report success to chsh. If the password is incorrect, PAM continues to Step 4.

4. The *pam_deny.so* module always fails, and because the required control argument is present, PAM reports failure back to chsh. This is a default for when there's nothing left to try. (Note that a required control argument does not cause PAM to fail its function immediately—it will run any lines left on its stack—but the report back to the application will always be of failure.)

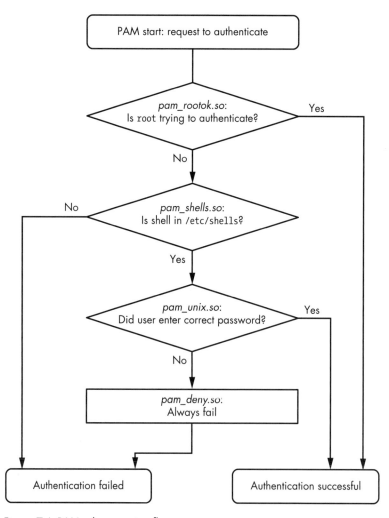

Figure 7-4: PAM rule execution flow

Don't confuse the terms function *and* action *when working with PAM. The function is the high-level goal: what the user application wants PAM to do (authenticate
a user, for example). An action is a specific step that PAM takes in order to reach that
goal. Just remember that the user application invokes the function first and that PAM
takes care of the particulars with actions.*

The advanced control argument syntax, denoted inside square brackets ([ ]), allows you to manually control a reaction based on the specific
return value of the module (not just success or failure). For details, see
the pam.conf(5) manual page; when you understand the simple syntax,
you'll have no trouble with the advanced syntax.

Module Arguments

PAM modules can take arguments after the module name. You'll often
encounter this example with the *pam_unix.so* module:

```
auth      sufficient   pam_unix.so   nullok
```

The `nullok` argument here says that the user can have no password (the
default would be fail if the user has no password).

7.10.2   Notes on PAM

Due to its control flow capability and module argument syntax, the PAM
configuration syntax has many features of a programming language and
a certain degree of power. We've only scratched the surface so far, but here
are a few more tips on PAM:

- To find out which PAM modules are present on your system, try
  `man -k pam_` (note the underscore). It can be difficult to track down
  the location of modules. Try the `locate unix_pam.so` command and see
  where that leads you.
- The manual pages contain the functions and arguments for each module.
- Many distributions automatically generate certain PAM configuration
  files, so it may not be wise to change them directly in */etc/pam.d*. Read
  the comments in your */etc/pam.d* files before editing them; if they're
  generated files, the comments will tell you where they came from.
- The */etc/pam.d/other* configuration file defines the default configuration
  for any application that lacks its own configuration file. The default is
  often to deny everything.
- There are different ways to include additional configuration files in a
  PAM configuration file. The `@include` syntax loads an entire configuration
  file, but you can also use a control argument to load only the configuration for a particular function. The usage varies among distributions.
- PAM configuration doesn't end with module arguments. Some modules
  can access additional files in */etc/security*, usually to configure per-user
  restrictions.

7.10.3   PAM and Passwords

Due to the evolution of Linux password verification over the years, a number of password configuration artifacts remain that can cause confusion at times. The first to be aware of is the file */etc/login.defs*. This is the configuration file for the original shadow password suite. It contains information about the encryption algorithm used for the shadow password file, but it's rarely used on a modern system with PAM installed, because the PAM configuration contains this information. This said, the encryption algorithm in */etc/login.defs* should match the PAM configuration in the rare case that you run into an application that doesn't support PAM.

Where does PAM get its information about the password encryption scheme? Recall that there are two ways for PAM to interact with passwords: the auth function (for verifying a password) and the password function (for setting a password). It's easiest to track down the password-setting parameter. The best way is probably just to grep it:

```
$ grep password.*unix /etc/pam.d/*
```

The matching lines should contain *pam_unix.so* and look something like this:

```
password        sufficient      pam_unix.so obscure sha512
```

The arguments obscure and sha512 tell PAM what to do when setting a password. First, PAM checks to see if the password is "obscure" enough (that is, the password isn't too similar to the old password, among other things), and then PAM uses the SHA512 algorithm to encrypt the new password.

But this happens *only* when a user *sets* a password, not when PAM is *verifying* a password. So how does PAM know which algorithm to use when authenticating? Unfortunately, the configuration won't tell you anything; there are no encryption arguments for *pam_unix.so* for the auth function. The manual pages also tell you nothing.

It turns out that (as of this writing) *pam_unix.so* simply tries to guess the algorithm, usually by asking the libcrypt library to do the dirty work of trying a whole bunch of things until something works or there's nothing left to try. Therefore, you normally don't have to worry about the verification encryption algorithm.

7.11   Looking Forward

We're now at about the midpoint in our progression through this book, having covered many of the vital building blocks of a Linux system. The discussion of logging and users on a Linux system has introduced you to what makes it possible to divide services and tasks into small, independent chunks that still know how to interact to a certain extent.

This chapter dealt almost exclusively with user space, and we now need to refine our view of user-space processes and the resources they consume. To do so, we'll go back into the kernel in Chapter 8.

8

A CLOSER LOOK AT PROCESSES AND RESOURCE UTILIZATION

This chapter takes you deeper into the relationships between processes, the kernel, and system resources. There are three basic kinds of hardware resources: CPU, memory, and I/O. Processes vie for these resources, and the kernel's job is to allocate resources fairly. The kernel itself is also a resource—a software resource that processes use to perform tasks such as creating new processes and communicating with other processes.

Many of the tools that you see in this chapter are often thought of as performance-monitoring tools. They're particularly helpful if your system is slowing to a crawl and you're trying to figure out why. However, you shouldn't get too distracted by performance; trying to optimize a system that's already working correctly is often a waste of time. Instead, concentrate on understanding what the tools actually measure, and you'll gain great insight into how the kernel works.

8.1 Tracking Processes

You learned how to use ps in Section 2.16 to list processes running on your system at a particular time. The ps command lists current processes, but it does little to tell you how processes change over time. Therefore, it won't really help you to determine which process is using too much CPU time or memory.

The top program is often more useful than ps because it displays the current system status as well as many of the fields in a ps listing, and it updates the display every second. Perhaps most important is that top shows the most active processes (that is, those currently taking up the most CPU time) at the top of its display.

You can send commands to top with keystrokes. These are some of the most important commands:

Spacebar   Updates the display immediately.

M   Sorts by current resident memory usage.

T   Sorts by total (cumulative) CPU usage.

P   Sorts by current CPU usage (the default).

u   Displays only one user's processes.

f   Selects different statistics to display.

?   Displays a usage summary for all top commands.

Two other utilities for Linux, similar to top, offer an enhanced set of views and features: atop and htop. Most of the extra features are available from other utilities. For example, htop has many of abilities of the lsof command described in the next section.

8.2 Finding Open Files with lsof

The lsof command lists open files and the processes using them. Because Unix places a lot of emphasis on files, lsof is among the most useful tools for finding trouble spots. But lsof doesn't stop at regular files—it can list network resources, dynamic libraries, pipes, and more.

8.2.1 *Reading the lsof Output*

Running lsof on the command line usually produces a tremendous amount of output. Below is a fragment of what you might see. This output includes open files from the init process as well as a running vi process:

```
$ lsof
COMMAND  PID   USER   FD   TYPE  DEVICE   SIZE    NODE NAME
init      1    root   cwd   DIR   8,1    4096       2 /
init      1    root   rtd   DIR   8,1    4096       2 /
init      1    root   mem   REG   8,    47040  9705817 /lib/i386-linux-gnu/libnss_files-2.15.so
init      1    root   mem   REG   8,1   42652  9705821 /lib/i386-linux-gnu/libnss_nis-2.15.so
init      1    root   mem   REG   8,1   92016  9705833 /lib/i386-linux-gnu/libnsl-2.15.so
--snip--
```

```
vi    22728  juser  cwd  DIR  8,1  4096  14945078  /home/juser/w/c
vi    22728  juser  4u   REG  8,1  1288  1056519   /home/juser/w/c/f
--snip--
```

The output shows the following fields (listed in the top row):

COMMAND   The command name for the process that holds the file descriptor.

PID   The process ID.

USER   The user running the process.

FD   This field can contain two kinds of elements. In the output above, the FD column shows the purpose of the file. The FD field can also list the *file descriptor* of the open file—a number that a process uses together with the system libraries and kernel to identify and manipulate a file.

TYPE   The file type (regular file, directory, socket, and so on).

DEVICE   The major and minor number of the device that holds the file.

SIZE   The file's size.

NODE   The file's inode number.

NAME   The filename.

The lsof(1) manual page contains a full list of what you might see for each field, but you should be able to figure out what you're looking at just by looking at the output. For example, look at the entries with cwd in the FD field as highlighted in bold. These lines indicate the current working directories of the processes. Another example is the very last line, which shows a file that the user is currently editing with vi.

8.2.2   Using lsof

There are two basic approaches to running lsof:

- List everything and pipe the output to a command like less, and then search for what you're looking for. This can take a while due to the amount of output generated.
- Narrow down the list that lsof provides with command-line options.

You can use command-line options to provide a filename as an argument and have lsof list only the entries that match the argument. For example, the following command displays entries for open files in */usr*:

```
$ lsof /usr
```

To list the open files for a particular process ID, run:

```
$ lsof -p pid
```

For a brief summary of lsof's many options, run lsof -h. Most options pertain to the output format. (See Chapter 10 for a discussion of the lsof network features.)

NOTE   *lsof is highly dependent on kernel information. If you upgrade your kernel and you're not routinely updating everything, you might need to upgrade lsof. In addition, if you perform a distribution update to both the kernel and lsof, the updated lsof might not work until you reboot with the new kernel.*

8.3 Tracing Program Execution and System Calls

The tools we've seen so far examine active processes. However, if you have no idea why a program dies almost immediately after starting up, even lsof won't help you. In fact, you'd have a difficult time even running lsof concurrently with a failed command.

The strace (system call trace) and ltrace (library trace) commands can help you discover what a program attempts to do. These tools produce extraordinarily large amounts of output, but once you know what to look for, you'll have more tools at your disposal for tracking down problems.

8.3.1 strace

Recall that a *system call* is a privileged operation that a user-space process asks the kernel to perform, such as opening and reading data from a file. The strace utility prints all the system calls that a process makes. To see it in action, run this command:

```
$ strace cat /dev/null
```

In Chapter 1, you learned that when one process wants to start another process, it invokes the fork() system call to spawn a copy of itself, and then the copy uses a member of the exec() family of system calls to start running a new program. The strace command begins working on the new process (the copy of the original process) just after the fork() call. Therefore, the first lines of the output from this command should show execve() in action, followed by a memory initialization call, brk(), as follows:

```
execve("/bin/cat", ["cat", "/dev/null"], [/* 58 vars */]) = 0
brk(0)                                    = 0x9b65000
```

The next part of the output deals primarily with loading shared libraries. You can ignore this unless you really want to know what the shared library system does.

```
access("/etc/ld.so.nohwcap", F_OK)      = -1 ENOENT (No such file or directory)
mmap2(NULL, 8192, PROT_READ|PROT_WRITE, MAP_PRIVATE|MAP_ANONYMOUS, -1, 0) = 0xb77b5000
access("/etc/ld.so.preload", R_OK)      = -1 ENOENT (No such file or directory)
open("/etc/ld.so.cache", O_RDONLY|O_CLOEXEC) = 3
--snip--
open("/lib/libc.so.6", O_RDONLY)        = 3
read(3, "\177ELF\1\1\1\0\0\0\0\0\0\0\0\0\3\0\3\0\1\0\0\0\200^\1"..., 1024) = 1024
```

In addition, skip past the mmap output until you get to the lines that look
like this:

```
fstat64(1, {st_mode=S_IFCHR|0620, st_rdev=makedev(136, 6), ...}) = 0
open("/dev/null", O_RDONLY|O_LARGEFILE) = 3
fstat64(3, {st_mode=S_IFCHR|0666, st_rdev=makedev(1, 3), ...}) = 0
fadvise64_64(3, 0, 0, POSTX_FADV_SEQUENTIAL) = 0
read(3, "", 32768)                      = 0
close(3)                                = 0
close(1)                                = 0
close(2)                                = 0
exit_group(0)                           = ?
```

This part of the output shows the command at work. First, look at the
open() call, which opens a file. The 3 is a result that means success (3 is the
file descriptor that the kernel returns after opening the file). Below that,
you see where cat reads from */dev/null* (the read() call, which also has 3 as
the file descriptor). Then there's nothing more to read, so the program
closes the file descriptor and exits with exit_group().

What happens when there's a problem? Try strace cat not_a_file instead
and examine the open() call in the resulting output:

```
open("not_a_file", O_RDONLY|O_LARGEFILE) = -1 ENOENT (No such file or directory)
```

Because open() couldn't open the file, it returned -1 to signal an error.
You can see that strace reports the exact error and gives you a small description of the error.

Missing files are the most common problems with Unix programs, so if
the system log and other log information aren't very helpful and you have
nowhere else to turn, strace can be of great use. You can even use it on daemons that detach themselves. For example:

```
$ strace -o crummyd_strace -ff crummyd
```

In this example, the -o option to strace logs the action of any child process that crummyd spawns into crummyd_strace.*pid*, where *pid* is the process ID
of the child process.

8.3.2   ltrace

The ltrace command tracks shared library calls. The output is similar to that of strace, which is why we're mentioning it here, but it doesn't track anything at the kernel level. Be warned that there are *many* more shared library calls than system calls. You'll definitely need to filter the output, and ltrace itself has many built-in options to assist you.

NOTE   *See Section 15.1.4 for more on shared libraries. The* ltrace *command doesn't work on statically linked binaries.*

8.4   Threads

In Linux, some processes are divided into pieces called *threads*. A thread is very similar to a process—it has an identifier (TID, or thread ID), and the kernel schedules and runs threads just like processes. However, unlike separate processes, which usually do not share system resources such as memory and I/O connections with other processes, all threads inside a single process share their system resources and some memory.

8.4.1   Single-Threaded and Multithreaded Processes

Many processes have only one thread. A process with one thread is *single-threaded*, and a process with more than one thread is *multithreaded*. All processes start out single-threaded. This starting thread is usually called the *main thread*. The main thread may then start new threads in order for the process to become multithreaded, similar to the way a process can call fork() to start a new process.

NOTE   *It's rare to refer to threads at all when a process is single-threaded. This book will not mention threads unless multithreaded processes make a difference in what you see or experience.*

The primary advantage of a multithreaded process is that when the process has a lot to do, threads can run simultaneously on multiple processors, potentially speeding up computation. Although you can also achieve simultaneous computation with multiple processes, threads start faster than processes, and it is often easier and/or more efficient for threads to intercommunicate using their shared memory than it is for processes to communicate over a channel such as a network connection or a pipe.

Some programs use threads to overcome problems managing multiple I/O resources. Traditionally, a process would sometimes use fork() to start a new subprocess in order to deal with a new input or output stream. Threads offer a similar mechanism without the overhead of starting a new process.

8.4.2 Viewing Threads

By default, the output from the ps and top commands shows only processes. To display the thread information in ps, add the m option. Here is some sample output:

```
$ ps m
  PID TTY      STAT  TIME COMMAND
 3587 pts/3    -     0:00 bash❶
  - -           Ss    0:00 -
 3592 pts/4    -     0:00 bash❷
  - -           Ss    0:00 -
12287 pts/8    -     0:54 /usr/bin/python /usr/bin/gm-notify❸
  - -           SLl   0:48 -
  - -           SLl   0:00 -
  - -           SLl   0:06 -
  - -           SLl   0:00 -
```

Listing 8-1: Viewing threads with ps m

Listing 8-1 shows processes along with threads. Each line with a number in the PID column (at ❶, ❷, and ❸) represents a process, as in the normal ps output. The lines with the dashes in the PID column represent the threads associated with the process. In this output, the processes at ❶ and ❷ have only one thread each, but process 12287 at ❸ is multithreaded with four threads.

If you would like to view the thread IDs with ps, you can use a custom output format. This example shows only the process IDs, thread IDs, and command:

```
$ ps m -o pid,tid,command
  PID   TID  COMMAND
 3587    -   bash
   -   3587  -
 3592    -   bash
   -   3592  -
12287    -   /usr/bin/python /usr/bin/gm-notify
   -  12287  -
   -  12288  -
   -  12289  -
   -  12295  -
```

Listing 8-2: Showing process IDs and thread IDs with ps m

The sample output in Listing 8-2 corresponds to the threads shown in Listing 8-1. Notice that the thread IDs of the single-threaded processes are identical to the process IDs; this is the main thread. For the multithreaded process 12287, thread 12287 is also the main thread.

NOTE   *Normally, you won't interact with individual threads as you would processes. You need to know a lot about how a multithreaded program was written in order to act on one thread at a time, and even then, doing so might not be a good idea.*

Threads can confuse things when it comes to resource monitoring because individual threads in a multithreaded process can consume resources simultaneously. For example, top doesn't show threads by default; you'll need to press H to turn it on. For most of the resource monitoring tools that you're about to see, you'll have to do a little extra work to turn on the thread display.

8.5   Introduction to Resource Monitoring

Now we'll discuss some topics in resource monitoring, including processor (CPU) time, memory, and disk I/O. We'll examine utilization on a system-wide scale, as well as on a per-process basis.

Many people touch the inner workings of the Linux kernel in the interest of improving performance. However, most Linux systems perform well under a distribution's default settings, and you can spend days trying to tune your machine's performance without meaningful results, especially if you don't know what to look for. So rather than think about performance as you experiment with the tools in this chapter, think about seeing the kernel in action as it divides resources among processes.

8.6   Measuring CPU Time

To monitor one or more specific processes over time, use the -p option to top, with this syntax:

```
$ top -p pid1 [-p pid2 ...]
```

To find out how much CPU time a command uses during its lifetime, use time. Most shells have a built-in time command that doesn't provide extensive statistics, so you'll probably need to run /usr/bin/time. For example, to measure the CPU time used by ls, run

```
$ /usr/bin/time ls
```

After ls terminates, time should print output like that below. The key fields are in boldface:

```
0.05user 0.09system 0:00.44elapsed 31%CPU (0avgtext+0avgdata 0maxresident)k
0inputs+0outputs (125major+51minor)pagefaults 0swaps
```

User time   The number of seconds that the CPU has spent running the program's *own* code. On modern processors, some commands run so quickly, and therefore the CPU time is so low, that time rounds down to zero.

System time   How much time the kernel spends doing the process's work (for example, reading files and directories).

Elapsed time The total time it took to run the process from start to finish, including the time that the CPU spent doing other tasks. This number is normally not very useful for performance measurement, but subtracting the user and system time from elapsed time can give you a general idea of how long a process spends waiting for system resources.

The remainder of the output primarily details memory and I/O usage. You'll learn more about the page fault output in Section 8.9.

8.7 Adjusting Process Priorities

You can change the way the kernel schedules a process in order to give the process more or less CPU time than other processes. The kernel runs each process according to its scheduling *priority*, which is a number between –20 and 20, with –20 being the foremost priority. (Yes, this can be confusing.)

The ps -l command lists the current priority of a process, but it's a little easier to see the priorities in action with the top command, as shown here:

```
$ top
Tasks: 244 total,   2 running, 242 sleeping,   0 stopped,   0 zombie
Cpu(s): 31.7%us,  2.8%sy,  0.0%ni, 65.4%id,  0.2%wa,  0.0%hi,  0.0%si,  0.0%st
Mem:   6137216k total,  5583560k used,   553656k free,    72008k buffers
Swap:  4135932k total,   694192k used,  3441740k free,   767640k cached

  PID USER      PR  NI  VIRT  RES  SHR S %CPU %MEM    TIME+  COMMAND
28883 bri       20   0 1280m 763m  32m S   58 12.7 213:00.65 chromium-browse
 1175 root      20   0  210m  43m  28m R   44  0.7  14292:35 Xorg
 4022 bri       20   0  413m 201m  28m S   29  3.4   3640:13 chromium-browse
 4029 bri       20   0  378m 206m  19m S    2  3.5  32:50.86 chromium-browse
 3971 bri       20   0  881m 359m  32m S    2  6.0 563:06.88 chromium-browse
 5378 bri       20   0  152m  10m 7064 S    1  0.2  24:30.21 compiz
 3821 bri       20   0  312m  37m  14m S    0  0.6  29:25.57 soffice.bin
 4117 bri       20   0  321m 105m  18m S    0  1.8  34:55.01 chromium-browse
 4138 bri       20   0  331m  99m  21m S    0  1.7 121:44.19 chromium-browse
 4274 bri       20   0  232m  60m  13m S    0  1.0  37:33.78 chromium-browse
 4267 bri       20   0 1102m 844m  11m S    0 14.1  29:59.27 chromium-browse
 2327 bri       20   0  301m  43m  16m S    0  0.7 109:55.65 unity-2d-shell
```

In the top output above, the PR (priority) column lists the kernel's current schedule priority for the process. The higher the number, the less likely the kernel is to schedule the process if others need CPU time. The schedule priority alone does not determine the kernel's decision to give CPU time to a process, and it changes frequently during program execution according to the amount of CPU time that the process consumes.

Next to the priority column is the *nice value* (NI) column, which gives a hint to the kernel's scheduler. This is what you care about when trying to influence the kernel's decision. The kernel adds the nice value to the current priority to determine the next time slot for the process.

By default, the nice value is 0. Now, say you're running a big computation in the background that you don't want to bog down your interactive session. To have that process take a backseat to other processes and run only when the other tasks have nothing to do, you could change the nice value to 20 with the renice command (where *pid* is the process ID of the process that you want to change):

```
$ renice 20 pid
```

If you're the superuser, you can set the nice value to a negative number, but doing so is almost always a bad idea because system processes may not get enough CPU time. In fact, you probably won't need to alter nice values much because many Linux systems have only a single user, and that user does not perform much real computation. (The nice value was much more important back when there were many users on a single machine.)

8.8   Load Averages

CPU performance is one of the easier metrics to measure. The *load average* is the average number of processes currently ready to run. That is, it is an estimate of the number of processes that are capable of using the CPU at any given time. When thinking about a load average, keep in mind that most processes on your system are usually waiting for input (from the keyboard, mouse, or network, for example), meaning that most processes are not ready to run and should contribute nothing to the load average. Only processes that are actually doing something affect the load average.

8.8.1   Using uptime

The uptime command tells you three load averages in addition to how long the kernel has been running:

```
$ uptime
... up 91 days, ... load average: 0.08, 0.03, 0.01
```

The three bolded numbers are the load averages for the past 1 minute, 5 minutes, and 15 minutes, respectively. As you can see, this system isn't very busy: An average of only 0.01 processes have been running across all processors for the past 15 minutes. In other words, if you had just one processor, it was only running user-space applications for 1 percent of the last 15 minutes. (Traditionally, most desktop systems would exhibit a load average of about 0 when you were doing anything *except* compiling a program or playing a game. A load average of 0 is usually a good sign, because it means that your processor isn't being challenged and you're saving power.)

NOTE *User interface components on current desktop systems tend to occupy more of the CPU than those in the past. For example, on Linux systems, a web browser's Flash plugin can be a particularly notorious resource hog, and Flash applications can easily occupy much of a system's CPU and memory due to poor all-around implementation.*

If a load average goes up to around 1, a single process is probably using the CPU nearly all of the time. To identify that process, use the top command; the process will usually rise to the the top of the display.

Most modern systems have more than one processor core or CPU, so multiple processes can easily run simultaneously. If you have two cores, a load average of 1 means that only one of the cores is likely active at any given time, and a load average of 2 means that both cores have just enough to do all of the time.

8.8.2 High Loads

A high load average does not necessarily mean that your system is having trouble. A system with enough memory and I/O resources can easily handle many running processes. If your load average is high and your system still responds well, don't panic: The system just has a lot of processes sharing the CPU. The processes have to compete with each other for processor time, and as a result they'll take longer to perform their computations than they would if they were each allowed to use the CPU all of the time. Another case where you might see a high load average as normal is a web server, where processes can start and terminate so quickly that the load average measurement mechanism can't function effectively.

However, if you sense that the system is slow and the load average is high, you might be running into memory performance problems. When the system is low on memory, the kernel can start to *thrash*, or rapidly swap memory for processes to and from the disk. When this happens, many processes will become ready to run, but their memory might not be available, so they will remain in the ready-to-run state (and contribute to the load average) for much longer than they normally would.

We'll now look at memory in much more detail.

8.9 Memory

One of the simplest ways to check your system's memory status as a whole is to run the free command or view */proc/meminfo* to see how much real memory is being used for caches and buffers. As we've just mentioned, performance problems can arise from memory shortages. If there isn't much cache/buffer memory being used (and the rest of the real memory is taken), you may need more memory. However, it's too easy to blame a shortage of memory for every performance problem on your machine.

8.9.1 How Memory Works

Recall from Chapter 1 that the CPU has a memory management unit (MMU) that translates the virtual memory addresses used by processes into real ones. The kernel assists the MMU by breaking the memory used by processes into smaller chunks called *pages*. The kernel maintains a data structure, called a *page table*, that contains a mapping of a processes' virtual page addresses to real page addresses in memory. As a process accesses memory, the MMU translates the virtual addresses used by the process into real addresses based on the kernel's page table.

A user process does not actually need all of its pages to be immediately available in order to run. The kernel generally loads and allocates pages as a process needs them; this system is known as *on-demand paging* or just *demand paging*. To see how this works, consider how a program starts and runs as a new process:

1. The kernel loads the beginning of the program's instruction code into memory pages.

2. The kernel may allocate some working-memory pages to the new process.

3. As the process runs, it might reach a point where the next instruction in its code isn't in any of the pages that the kernel initially loaded. At this point, the kernel takes over, loads the necessary pages into memory, and then lets the program resume execution.

4. Similarly, if the program requires more working memory than was initially allocated, the kernel handles it by finding free pages (or by making room) and assigning them to the process.

8.9.2 Page Faults

If a memory page is not ready when a process wants to use it, the process triggers a *page fault*. In the event of a page fault, the kernel takes control of the CPU from the process in order to get the page ready. There are two kinds of page faults: minor and major.

Minor Page Faults

A minor page fault occurs when the desired page is actually in main memory but the MMU doesn't know where it is. This can happen when the process requests more memory or when the MMU doesn't have enough space to store all of the page locations for a process. In this case, the kernel tells the MMU about the page and permits the process to continue. Minor page faults aren't such a big deal, and many occur as a process runs. Unless you need maximum performance from some memory-intensive program, you probably shouldn't worry about them.

Major Page Faults

A major page fault occurs when the desired memory page isn't in main memory at all, which means that the kernel must load it from the disk or some other slow storage mechanism. A lot of major page faults will bog the system down because the kernel must do a substantial amount of work to provide the pages, robbing normal processes of their chance to run.

Some major page faults are unavoidable, such as those that occur when you load the code from disk when running a program for the first time. The biggest problems happen when you start running out of memory and the kernel starts to *swap* pages of working memory out to the disk in order to make room for new pages.

Watching Page Faults

You can drill down to the page faults for individual processes with the ps, top, and time commands. The following command shows a simple example of how the time command displays page faults. (The output of the cal command doesn't matter, so we're discarding it by redirecting that to */dev/null*.)

```
$ /usr/bin/time cal > /dev/null
0.00user 0.00system 0:00.06elapsed 0%CPU (0avgtext+0avgdata 3328maxresident)k
648inputs+0outputs (2major+254minor)pagefaults 0swaps
```

As you can see from the bolded text, when this program ran, there were 2 major page faults and 254 minor ones. The major page faults occurred when the kernel needed to load the program from the disk for the first time. If you ran the command again, you probably wouldn't get any major page faults because the kernel would have cached the pages from the disk.

If you'd rather see the page faults of processes as they're running, use top or ps. When running top, use f to change the displayed fields and u to display the number of major page faults. (The results will show up in a new, nFLT column. You won't see the minor page faults.)

When using ps, you can use a custom output format to view the page faults for a particular process. Here's an example for process ID 20365:

```
$ ps -o pid,min_flt,maj_flt 20365
  PID  MINFL  MAJFL
20365 834182     23
```

The MINFL and MAJFL columns show the numbers of minor and major page faults. Of course, you can combine this with any other process selection options, as described in the ps(1) manual page.

Viewing page faults by process can help you zero in on certain problematic components. However, if you're interested in your system performance as a whole, you need a tool to summarize CPU and memory action across all processes.

8.10   Monitoring CPU and Memory Performance with vmstat

Among the many tools available to monitor system performance, the vmstat command is one of the oldest, with minimal overhead. You'll find it handy for getting a high-level view of how often the kernel is swapping pages in and out, how busy the CPU is, and IO utilization.

The trick to unlocking the power of vmstat is to understand its output. For example, here's some output from vmstat 2, which reports statistics every 2 seconds:

```
$ vmstat 2
procs -----------memory---------- ---swap-- -----io---- -system-- ----cpu----
 r  b   swpd   free   buff  cache   si   so    bi    bo   in   cs us sy id wa
 2  0 320416 3027696 198636 1072568   0    0     1     1    2    0 15  2 83  0
 2  0 320416 3027288 198636 1072564   0    0     0  1182  407  636  1  0 99  0
 1  0 320416 3026792 198640 1072572   0    0     0    58  281  537  1  0 99  0
 0  0 320416 3024932 198648 1074924   0    0     0   308  318  541  0  0 99  1
 0  0 320416 3024932 198648 1074968   0    0     0     0  208  416  0  0 99  0
 0  0 320416 3026800 198648 1072616   0    0     0     0  207  389  0  0 100 0
```

The output falls into categories: procs for processes, memory for memory usage, swap for the pages pulled in and out of swap, io for disk usage, system for the number of times the kernel switches into kernel code, and cpu for the time used by different parts of the system.

The preceding output is typical for a system that isn't doing much. You'll usually start looking at the second line of output—the first one is an average for the entire uptime of the system. For example, here the system has 320416KB of memory swapped out to the disk (swpd) and around 3025000KB (3 GB) of real memory free. Even though some swap space is in use, the zero-valued si (swap-in) and so (swap-out) columns report that the kernel is not currently swapping anything in or out from the disk. The buff column indicates the amount of memory that the kernel is using for disk buffers (see Section 4.2.5).

On the far right, under the CPU heading, you see the distribution of CPU time in the us, sy, id, and wa columns. These list (in order) the percentage of time that the CPU is spending on user tasks, system (kernel) tasks, idle time, and waiting for I/O. In the preceding example, there aren't too many user processes running (they're using a maximum of 1 percent of the CPU); the kernel is doing practically nothing, while the CPU is sitting around doing nothing 99 percent of the time.

Now, watch what happens when a big program starts up sometime later (the first two lines occur right before the program runs):

```
procs -----------memory---------- ---swap-- -----io---- -system-- ----cpu----
 r  b   swpd   free   buff  cache   si   so    bi    bo   in   cs us sy id wa
 1  0 320412 2861252 198920 1106804   0    0     0     0 2477 4481 25  2 72  0❶
 1  0 320412 2861748 198924 1105624   0    0     0    40 2206 3966 26  2 72  0
 1  0 320412 2860508 199320 1106504   0    0   210    18 2201 3904 26  2 71  1
 1  1 320412 2817860 199332 1146052   0    0 19912     0 2446 4223 26  3 63  8
 2  2 320284 2791608 200612 1157752 202    0  4960   854 3371 5714 27  3 51 18❷
 1  1 320252 2772076 201076 1166656  10    0  2142  1190 4188 7537 30  3 53 14
 0  3 320244 2727632 202104 1175420  20    0  1890   216 4631 8706 36  4 46 14
```

Listing 8-3: Memory activity

As you can see at ❶ in Listing 8-3, the CPU starts to see some usage for an extended period, especially from user processes. Because there is enough free memory, the amount of cache and buffer space used starts to increase as the kernel starts to use the disk more.

Later on, we see something interesting: Notice at ❷ that the kernel pulls some pages into memory that were once swapped out (the si column). This means that the program that just ran probably accessed some pages shared by another process. This is common; many processes use the code in certain shared libraries only when starting up.

Also notice from the b column that a few processes are *blocked* (prevented from running) while waiting for memory pages. Overall, the amount of free memory is decreasing, but it's nowhere near being depleted. There's also a fair amount of disk activity, as seen by the increasing numbers in the bi (blocks in) and bo (blocks out) columns.

The output is quite different when you run out of memory. As the free space depletes, both the buffer and cache sizes decrease because the kernel increasingly needs the space for user processes. Once there is nothing left, you'll start to see activity in the so (swapped out) column as the kernel starts moving pages onto the disk, at which point nearly all of the other output columns change to reflect the amount of work that the kernel is doing. You see more system time, more data going in and out of the disk, and more processes blocked because the memory they want to use is not available (it has been swapped out).

We haven't explained all of the vmstat output columns. You can dig deeper into them in the vmstat(8) manual page, but you might have to learn more about kernel memory management first from a class or a book like *Operating System Concepts*, 9th edition (Wiley, 2012) in order to understand them.

8.11 I/O Monitoring

By default, vmstat shows you some general I/O statistics. Although you can get very detailed per-partition resource usage with vmstat -d, you'll get a lot of output from this option, which might be overwhelming. Instead, try starting out with a tool just for I/O called iostat.

8.11.1 *Using iostat*

Like vmstat, when run without any options, iostat shows the statistics for your machine's current uptime:

```
$ iostat
[kernel information]
avg-cpu:  %user   %nice %system %iowait  %steal   %idle
           4.46    0.01    0.67    0.31    0.00   94.55

Device:            tps    kB_read/s    kB_wrtn/s    kB_read    kB_wrtn
sda               4.67         7.28        49.86    9493727   65011716
sde               0.00         0.00         0.00       1230          0
```

The `avg-cpu` part at the top reports the same CPU utilization information as other utilities that you've seen in this chapter, so skip down to the bottom, which shows you the following for each device:

tps   Average number of data transfers per second

kB_read/s   Average number of kilobytes read per second

kB_wrtn/s   Average number of kilobytes written per second

kB_read   Total number of kilobytes read

kB_wrtn   Total number of kilobytes written

Another similarity to `vmstat` is that you can give an interval argument, such as iostat 2, to give an update every 2 seconds. When using an interval, you might want to display only the device report by using the -d option (such as iostat -d 2).

By default, the `iostat` output omits partition information. To show all of the partition information, use the -p ALL option. Because there are many partitions on a typical system, you'll get a lot of output. Here's part of what you might see:

```
$ iostat -p ALL
--snip--
Device:           tps    kB_read/s    kB_wrtn/s    kB_read    kB_wrtn
--snip--
sda              4.67         7.27        49.83    9496139   65051472
sda1             4.38         7.16        49.51    9352969   64635440
sda2             0.00         0.00         0.00          6          0
sda5             0.01         0.11         0.32     141884     416032
scd0             0.00         0.00         0.00          0          0
--snip--
sde              0.00         0.00         0.00       1230          0
```

In this example, sda1, sda2, and sda5 are all partitions of the sda disk, so there will be some overlap between the read and written columns. However, the sum of the partition columns won't necessarily add up to the disk column. Although a read from sda1 also counts as a read from sda, keep in mind that you can read from sda directly, such as when reading the partition table.

8.11.2   Per-Process I/O Utilization and Monitoring: iotop

If you need to dig even deeper to see I/O resources used by individual processes, the iotop tool can help. Using iotop is similar to using top. There is a continuously updating display that shows the processes using the most I/O, with a general summary at the top:

```
# iotop
Total DISK READ:      4.76 K/s | Total DISK WRITE:       333.31 K/s
   TID  PRIO  USER    DISK READ  DISK WRITE  SWAPIN      IO>    COMMAND
   260 be/3 root      0.00 B/s    38.09 K/s  0.00 %   6.98 % [jbd2/sda1-8]
  2611 be/4 juser     4.76 K/s    10.32 K/s  0.00 %   0.21 % zeitgeist-daemon
  2636 be/4 juser     0.00 B/s    84.12 K/s  0.00 %   0.20 % zeitgeist-fts
  1329 be/4 juser     0.00 B/s    65.87 K/s  0.00 %   0.03 % soffice.b~ash-pipe=6
```

```
 6845 be/4 juser        0.00 B/s  812.63 B/s  0.00 %  0.00 % chromium-browser
19069 be/4 juser        0.00 B/s  812.63 B/s  0.00 %  0.00 % rhythmbox
```

Along with the user, command, and read/write columns, notice that there is a TID column (thread ID) instead of a process ID. The iotop tool is one of the few utilities that displays threads instead of processes.

The PRIO (priority) column indicates the I/O priority. It's similar to the CPU priority that you've already seen, but it affects how quickly the kernel schedules I/O reads and writes for the process. In a priority such as be/4, the be part is the *scheduling class*, and the number is the priority level. As with CPU priorities, lower numbers are more important; for example, the kernel allows more time for I/O for a process with be/3 than onc with be/4.

The kernel uses the scheduling class to add more control for I/O scheduling. You'll see three scheduling classes from iotop:

be Best-effort. The kernel does its best to fairly schedule I/O for this class. Most processes run under this I/O scheduling class.

rt Real-time. The kernel schedules any real-time I/O before any other class of I/O, no matter what.

idle Idle. The kernel performs I/O for this class only when there is no other I/O to be done. There is no priority level for the idle scheduling class.

You can check and change the I/O priority for a process with the ionice utility; see the ionice(1) manual page for details. You probably will never need to worry about the I/O priority, though.

8.12 Per-Process Monitoring with pidstat

You've seen how you can monitor specific processes with utilities such as top and iotop. However, this display refreshes over time, and each update erases the previous output. The pidstat utility allows you to see the resource consumption of a process over time in the style of vmstat. Here's a simple example for monitoring process 1329, updating every second:

```
$ pidstat -p 1329 1
Linux 3.2.0-44-generic-pae (duplex)      07/01/2015      _i686_  (4 CPU)

09:26:55 PM      PID   %usr %system  %guest    %CPU   CPU  Command
09:27:03 PM     1329   8.00    0.00    0.00    8.00     1  myprocess
09:27:04 PM     1329   0.00    0.00    0.00    0.00     3  myprocess
09:27:05 PM     1329   3.00    0.00    0.00    3.00     1  myprocess
09:27:06 PM     1329   8.00    0.00    0.00    8.00     3  myprocess
09:27:07 PM     1329   2.00    0.00    0.00    2.00     3  myprocess
09:27:08 PM     1329   6.00    0.00    0.00    6.00     2  myprocess
```

The default output shows the percentages of user and system time and the overall percentage of CPU time, and it even tells you which CPU the process was running on. (The %guest column here is somewhat odd—it's the percentage of time that the process spent running something inside a virtual machine. Unless you're running a virtual machine, don't worry about this.)

Although pidstat shows CPU utilization by default, it can do much more. For example, you can use the -r option to monitor memory and -d to turn on disk monitoring. Try them out, and then look at the pidstat(1) manual page to see even more options for threads, context switching, or just about anything else that we've talked about in this chapter.

8.13   Further Topics

One reason there are so many tools to measure resource utilization is that a wide array of resource types are consumed in many different ways. In this chapter, you've seen CPU, memory, and I/O as system resources being consumed by processes, threads inside processes, and the kernel.

The other reason that the tools exist is that the resources are *limited* and, for a system to perform well, its components must strive to consume fewer resources. In the past, many users shared a machine, so it was necessary to make sure that each user had a fair share of resources. Now, although a modern desktop computer may not have multiple users, it still has many processes competing for resources. Likewise, high-performance network servers require intense system resource monitoring.

Further topics in resource monitoring and performance analysis include the following:

sar (System Activity Reporter)   The sar package has many of the continuous monitoring capabilities of vmstat, but it also records resource utilization over time. With sar, you can look back at a particular time to see what your system was doing. This is handy when you have a past system event that you want to analyze.

acct (Process accounting)   The acct package can record the processes and their resource utilization.

Quotas   You can limit many system resources on a per-process or per-user basis. See */etc/security/limits.conf* for some of the CPU and memory options; there's also a limits.conf(5) manual page. This is a PAM feature, so processes are subject to this only if they've been started from something that uses PAM (such as a login shell). You can also limit the amount of disk space that a user can use with the quota system.

If you're interested in systems tuning and performance in particular, *Systems Performance: Enterprise and the Cloud* by Brendan Gregg (Prentice Hall, 2013) goes into much more detail.

We also haven't yet touched on the many, many tools that can be used to monitor network resource utilization. To use those, you first have to understand how the network works. That's where we're headed next.

9

UNDERSTANDING YOUR NETWORK AND ITS CONFIGURATION

Networking is the practice of connecting computers and sending data between them. That sounds simple enough, but to understand how it works, you need to ask two fundamental questions:

- How does the computer sending the data know *where* to send its data?
- When the destination computer receives the data, how does it know *what* it just received?

A computer answers these questions by using a series of components, with each one responsible for a certain aspect of sending, receiving, and identifying data. The components are arranged in groups that form *network layers*, which stack on top of each other in order to form a complete system. The Linux kernel handles networking in a similar way to the SCSI subsystem described in Chapter 3.

Because each layer tends to be independent, it's possible to build networks with many different combinations of components. This is where network configuration can become very complicated. For this reason, we'll begin this chapter by looking at the layers in very simple networks. You'll learn how to view your own network settings, and when you understand the basic workings of each layer, you'll be ready to learn how to configure those layers by yourself. Finally, you'll move on to more advanced topics like building your own networks and configuring firewalls. (Skip over that material if your eyes start to glaze over; you can always come back.)

9.1   Network Basics

Before getting into the theory of network layers, take a look at the simple network shown in Figure 9-1.

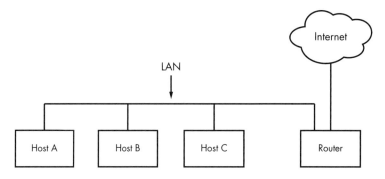

Figure 9-1: A typical local area network with a router that provides Internet access

This type of network is ubiquitous; most home and small office networks are configured this way. Each machine connected to the network is called a *host*. The hosts are connected to a *router*, which is a host that can move data from one network to another. These machines (here, Hosts A, B, and C) and the router form a local area network (LAN). The connections on the LAN can be wired or wireless.

The router is also connected to the Internet—the cloud in the figure. Because the router is connected to both the LAN and the Internet, all machines on the LAN also have access to the Internet through the router. One of the goals of this chapter is to see how the router provides this access.

Your initial point of view will be from a Linux-based machine such as Host A on the LAN in Figure 9-1.

9.1.1   Packets

A computer transmits data over a network in small chunks called *packets*, which consist of two parts: a *header* and a *payload*. The header contains identifying information such as the origin/destination hosts and basic protocol. The payload, on the other hand, is the actual application data that the computer wants to send (for example, HTML or image data).

Packets allow a host to communicate with others "simultaneously," because hosts can send, receive, and process packets in any order, regardless of where they came from or where they're going. Breaking messages into smaller units also makes it easier to detect and compensate for errors in transmission.

For the most part, you don't have to worry about translating between packets and the data that your application uses, because the operating system has facilities that do this for you. However, it is helpful to know the role of packets in the network layers that you're about to see.

9.2 Network Layers

A fully functioning network includes a full set of network layers called a *network stack*. Any functional network has a stack. The typical Internet stack, from the top to bottom layer, looks like this:

Application layer   Contains the "language" that applications and servers use to communicate; usually a high-level protocol of some sort. Common application layer protocols include Hypertext Transfer Protocol (HTTP, used for the Web), Secure Socket Layer (SSL), and File Transfer Protocol (FTP). Application layer protocols can often be combined. For example, SSL is commonly used in conjunction with HTTP.

Transport layer   Defines the data transmission characteristics of the application layer. This layer includes data integrity checking, source and destination ports, and specifications for breaking application data into packets (if the application layer has not already done so). Transmission Control Protocol (TCP) and User Datagram Protocol (UDP) are the most common transport layer protocols. The transport layer is also sometimes called the *protocol layer*.

Network or Internet layer   Defines how to move packets from a source host to a destination host. The particular packet transit rule set for the Internet is known as Internet Protocol (IP). Because we'll only talk about Internet networks in this book, we'll really only be talking about the Internet layer. However, because network layers are meant to be hardware independent, you can simultaneously configure several independent network layers (such as IP, IPv6, IPX, and AppleTalk) on a single host.

Physical layer   Defines how to send raw data across a physical medium, such as Ethernet or a modem. This is sometimes called the *link layer* or *host-to-network layer*.

It's important to understand the structure of a network stack because your data must travel through these layers at least twice before it reaches a program at its destination. For example, if you're sending data from Host A to Host B, as shown in Figure 9-1, your bytes leave the application layer on Host A and travel through the transport and network layers on Host A; then they go down to the physical medium, across the medium, and up again through the various lower levels to the application layer on Host B in much the same way. If you're sending something to a host on the Internet through the router, it will go through some (but usually not all) of the layers on the router and anything else in between.

The layers sometimes bleed into each other in strange ways because it can be inefficient to process all of them in order. For example, devices that historically dealt with only the physical layer now sometimes look at the transport and Internet layer data to filter and route data quickly. (Don't worry about this when you're learning the basics.)

We'll begin by looking at how your Linux machine connects to the network in order to answer the *where* question at the beginning of the chapter. This is the lower part of the stack—the physical and network layers. Later, we'll look at the upper two layers that answer the *what* question.

NOTE   *You might have heard of another set of layers known as the Open Systems Interconnection (OSI) Reference Model. This is a seven-layer network model often used in teaching and designing networks, but we won't cover the OSI model because you'll be working directly with the four layers described here. To learn a lot more about layers (and networks in general), see Andrew S. Tanenbaum and David J. Wetherall's* Computer Networks, *5th edition (Prentice Hall, 2010).*

9.3   The Internet Layer

Rather than start at the very bottom of the network stack with the physical layer, we'll start at the network layer because it can be easier to understand. The Internet as we currently know it is based on the Internet Protocol, version 4 (IPv4), though version 6 (IPv6) is gaining adoption. One of the most important aspects of the Internet layer is that it's meant to be a software network that places no particular requirements on hardware or operating systems. The idea is that you can send and receive Internet packets over any kind of hardware, using any operating system.

The Internet's topology is decentralized; it's made up of smaller networks called *subnets*. The idea is that all subnets are interconnected in some way. For example, in Figure 9-1, the LAN is normally a single subnet.

A host can be attached to more than one subnet. As you saw in Section 9.1, that kind of host is called a router if it can transmit data from one subnet to another (another term for router is *gateway*). Figure 9-2 refines Figure 9-1 by identifying the LAN as a subnet, as well as Internet addresses for each host and the router. The router in the figure has two addresses, the local subnet 10.23.2.1 and the link to the Internet (but this Internet link's address is not important right now so it's just marked "Uplink Address"). We'll look first at the addresses and then the subnet notation.

Each Internet host has at least one numeric *IP address* in the form of *a.b.c.d*, such as 10.23.2.37. An address in this notation is called a *dotted-quad* sequence. If a host is connected to multiple subnets, it has at least one IP address per subnet. Each host's IP address should be unique across the entire Internet, but as you'll see later, private networks and NAT can make this a little confusing.

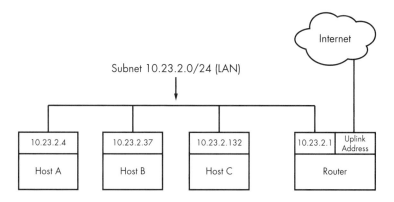

Figure 9-2: Network with IP addresses

NOTE   *Technically, an IP address consists of 4 bytes (or 32 bits),* abcd. *Bytes* a *and* d *are numbers from 1 to 254, and* b *and* c *are numbers from 0 to 255. A computer processes IP addresses as raw bytes. However, it's much easier for a human to read and write a dotted-quad address, such as 10.23.2.37, instead of something ugly like the hexadecimal 0x0A170225.*

IP addresses are like postal addresses in some ways. To communicate with another host, your machine must know that other host's IP address.

Let's take a look at the address on your machine.

9.3.1   Viewing Your Computer's IP Addresses

One host can have many IP addresses. To see the addresses that are active on your Linux machine, run

```
$ ifconfig
```

There will probably be a lot of output, but it should include something like this:

```
eth0      Link encap:Ethernet   HWaddr 10:78:d2:eb:76:97
          inet addr:10.23.2.4  Bcast:10.23.2.255  Mask:255.255.255.0
          inet6 addr: fe80::1278:d2ff:feeb:7697/64 Scope:Link
          UP BROADCAST RUNNING MULTICAST   MTU:1500  Metric:1
          RX packets:85076006 errors:0 dropped:0 overruns:0 frame:0
          TX packets:68347795 errors:0 dropped:0 overruns:0 carrier:0
          collisions:0 txqueuelen:1000
          RX bytes:86427623613 (86.4 GB)  TX bytes:23437688605 (23.4 GB)
          Interrupt:20 Memory:fe500000-fe520000
```

The ifconfig command's output includes many details from both the Internet layer and the physical layer. (Sometimes it doesn't even include an Internet address at all!) We'll discuss the output in more detail later, but for now, concentrate on the second line, which reports that the host is configured to have an IPv4 address (inet addr) of 10.23.2.4. On the same line, a Mask is reported as being 255.255.255.0. This is a *subnet mask*, which defines the subnet that an IP address belongs to. Let's see how that works.

NOTE   *The* ifconfig *command, as well some of the others you'll see later in this chapter (such as* route *and* arp*), has been technically supplanted with the newer* ip *command. The* ip *command can do more than the old commands, and it is preferable when writing scripts. However, most people still use the old commands when manually working with the network, and these commands can also be used on other versions of Unix. For this reason, we'll use the old-style commands.*

9.3.2 Subnets

A *subnet* is a connected group of hosts with IP addresses in some sort of order. Usually, the hosts are on the same physical network, as shown in Figure 9-2. For example, the hosts between 10.23.2.1 and 10.23.2.254 could comprise a subnet, as could all hosts between 10.23.1.1 and 10.23.255.254.

You define a subnet with two pieces: a *network prefix* and a subnet mask (such as the one in the output of ifconfig in the previous section). Let's say you want to create a subnet containing the IP addresses between 10.23.2.1 and 10.23.2.254. The network prefix is the part that is *common* to all addresses in the subnet; in this example, it's 10.23.2.0, and the subnet mask is 255.255.255.0. Let's see why those are the right numbers.

It's not immediately clear how the prefix and mask work together to give you all possible IP addresses on a subnet. Looking at the numbers in binary form helps clear it up. The mask marks the bit locations in an IP address that are common to the subnet. For example, here are the binary forms of 10.23.2.0 and 255.255.255.0:

10.23.2.0:	00001010 00010111 00000010 00000000
255.255.255.0:	11111111 11111111 11111111 00000000

Now, let's use boldface to mark the bit locations in 10.23.2.0 that are 1s in 255.255.255.0:

10.23.2.0:	**00001010 00010111 00000010** 00000000

Look at the bits that are *not* in bold. You can set any number of these bits to 1 to get a valid IP address in this subnet, with the exception of all 0s or all 1s.

Putting it all together, you can see how a host with an IP address of 10.23.2.1 and a subnet mask of 255.255.255.0 is on the same subnet as any other computers that have IP addresses beginning with 10.23.2. You can denote this entire subnet as 10.23.2.0/255.255.255.0.

9.3.3 Common Subnet Masks and CIDR Notation

If you're lucky, you'll only deal with easy subnet masks like 255.255.255.0 or 255.255.0.0, but you may be unfortunate and encounter stuff like 255.255.255.192, where it isn't quite so simple to determine the set of addresses that belong to the subnet. Furthermore, it's likely that you'll also encounter a different form of subnet representation called *Classless Inter-Domain Routing (CIDR)* notation, where a subnet such as 10.23.2.0/255.255.255.0 is written as 10.23.2.0/24.

To understand what this means, look at the mask in binary form (as in the example you saw in the preceding section). You'll find that nearly all subnet masks are just a bunch of 1s followed by a bunch of 0s. For example, you just saw that 255.255.255.0 in binary form is 24 1-bits followed by 8 0-bits. The CIDR notation identifies the subnet mask by the number of *leading* 1s in the subnet mask. Therefore, a combination such as 10.23.2.0/24 includes both the subnet prefix and its subnet mask.

Table 9-1 shows several example subnet masks and their CIDR forms.

Table 9-1: Subnet Masks

Long Form	CIDR Form
255.0.0.0	8
255.255.0.0	16
255.240.0.0	12
255.255.255.0	24
255.255.255.192	26

NOTE *If you aren't familiar with conversion between decimal, binary, and hexadecimal formats, you can use a calculator utility such as* bc *or* dc *to convert between different radix representations. For example, in* bc*, you can run the command* obase=2; 240 *to print the number 240 in binary (base 2) form.*

Identifying subnets and their hosts is the first building block to understanding how the Internet works. However, you still need to connect the subnets.

9.4 Routes and the Kernel Routing Table

Connecting Internet subnets is mostly a process of identifying the hosts connected to more than one subnet. Returning to Figure 9-2, think about Host A at IP address 10.23.2.4. This host is connected to a local network of 10.23.2.0/24 and can directly reach hosts on that network. To reach hosts on the rest of the Internet, it must communicate through the router at 10.23.2.1.

How does the Linux kernel distinguish between these two different kinds of destinations? It uses a destination configuration called a *routing table* to determine its routing behavior. To show the routing table, use the route -n command. Here's what you might see for a simple host such as 10.23.2.4:

```
$ route -n
Kernel IP routing table
Destination     Gateway          Genmask          Flags Metric Ref    Use Iface
0.0.0.0         10.23.2.1        0.0.0.0          UG    0      0        0 eth0
10.23.2.0       0.0.0.0          255.255.255.0    U     1      0        0 eth0
```

The last two lines here contain the routing information. The Destination column tells you a network prefix, and the Genmask column is the netmask corresponding to that network. There are two networks defined in this output: 0.0.0.0/0 (which matches every address on the Internet) and 10.23.2.0/24. Each network has a U under its Flags column, indicating that the route is active ("up").

Where the destinations differ is in the combination of their Gateway and Flags columns. For 0.0.0.0/0, there is a G in the Flags column, meaning that communication for this network must be sent through the gateway in the Gateway column (10.23.2.1, in this case). However, for 10.23.2.0/24, there is no G in Flags, indicating that the network is directly connected in some way. Here, 0.0.0.0 is used as a stand-in under Gateway. Ignore the other columns of output for now.

There's one tricky detail: Say the host wants to send something to 10.23.2.132, which matches both rules in the routing table, 0.0.0.0/0 and 10.23.2.0/24. How does the kernel know to use the second one? It chooses the longest destination prefix that matches. This is where CIDR network form comes in particularly handy: 10.23.2.0/24 matches, and its prefix is 24 bits long; 0.0.0.0/0 also matches, but its prefix is 0 bits long (that is, it has no prefix), so the rule for 10.23.2.0/24 takes priority.

NOTE *The -n option tells route to show IP addresses instead of showing hosts and networks by name. This is an important option to remember because you'll be able to use it in other network-related commands such as netstat.*

9.4.1 The Default Gateway

An entry for 0.0.0.0/0 in the routing table has special significance because it matches any address on the Internet. This is the *default route*, and the address configured under the Gateway column (in the route -n output) in the default route is the *default gateway*. When no other rules match, the default route always does, and the default gateway is where you send messages when there is no other choice. You can configure a host without a default gateway, but it won't be able to reach hosts outside the destinations in the routing table.

On most networks with a netmask of 255.255.255.0, the router is usually at address 1 of the subnet (for example, 10.23.2.1 in 10.23.2.0/24). Because this is simply a convention, there can be exceptions.

9.5   Basic ICMP and DNS Tools

Now it's time to look at some basic practical utilities to help you interact with hosts. These tools use two protocols of particular interest: Internet Control Message Protocol (ICMP), which can help you root out problems with connectivity and routing, and the Domain Name Service (DNS) system, which maps names to IP addresses so that you don't have to remember a bunch of numbers.

9.5.1   ping

ping (see *http://ftp.arl.mil/~mike/ping.html*) is one of the most basic network debugging tools. It sends ICMP echo request packets to a host that ask a recipient host to return the packet to the sender. If the recipient host gets the packet and is configured to reply, it sends an ICMP echo response packet in return.

For example, say that you run **ping 10.23.2.1** and get this output:

```
$ ping 10.23.2.1
PING 10.23.2.1 (10.23.2.1) 56(84) bytes of data.
64 bytes from 10.23.2.1: icmp_req=1 ttl=64 time=1.76 ms
64 bytes from 10.23.2.1: icmp_req=2 ttl=64 time=2.35 ms
64 bytes from 10.23.2.1: icmp_req=4 ttl=64 time=1.69 ms
64 bytes from 10.23.2.1: icmp_req=5 ttl=64 time=1.61 ms
```

The first line says that you're sending 56-byte packets (84 bytes, if you include the headers) to 10.23.2.1 (by default, one packet per second), and the remaining lines indicate responses from 10.23.2.1. The most important parts of the output are the sequence number (icmp_req) and the round-trip time (time). The number of bytes returned is the size of the packet sent plus 8. (The content of the packets isn't important to you.)

A gap in the sequence numbers, such as the one between 2 and 4, usually means there's some kind of connectivity problem. It's possible for packets to arrive out of order, and if they do, there's some kind of problem because ping sends only one packet a second. If a response takes more than a second (1000ms) to arrive, the connection is extremely slow.

The round-trip time is the total elapsed time between the moment that the request packet leaves and moment that the response packet arrives. If there's no way to reach the destination, the final router to see the packet returns an ICMP "host unreachable" packet to ping.

On a wired LAN, you should expect absolutely no packet loss and very low numbers for the round-trip time. (The preceding example output is from a wireless network.) You should also expect no packet loss from your network to and from your ISP and reasonably steady round-trip times.

For security reasons, not all hosts on the Internet respond to ICMP echo request pack-ets, so you might find that you can connect to a website on a host but not get a ping *response.*

9.5.2   traceroute

The ICMP-based program traceroute will come in handy when you reach the material on routing later in this chapter. Use traceroute *host* to see the path your packets take to a remote host. (traceroute -n *host* will disable hostname lookups.)

One of the best things about traceroute is that it reports return trip times at each step in the route, as demonstrated in this output fragment:

```
 4  206.220.243.106  1.163 ms   0.997 ms   1.182 ms
 5  4.24.203.65      1.312 ms   1.12 ms    1.463 ms
 6  64.159.1.225     1.421 ms   1.37 ms    1.347 ms
 7  64.159.1.38      55.642 ms  55.625 ms  55.663 ms
 8  209.247.10.230   55.89 ms   55.617 ms  55.964 ms
 9  209.244.14.226   55.851 ms  55.726 ms  55.832 ms
10  209.246.29.174   56.419 ms  56.44 ms   56.423 ms
```

Because this output shows a big latency jump between hops 6 and 7, that part of the route is probably some sort of long-distance link.

The output from traceroute can be inconsistent. For example, the replies may time out at a certain step, only to "reappear" in later steps. The reason is usually that the router at that step refused to return the debugging out-put that traceroute wants but routers in later steps were happy to return the output. In addition, a router might choose to assign a lower priority to the debugging traffic than it does to normal traffic.

9.5.3   DNS and host

IP addresses are difficult to remember and subject to change, which is why we normally use names such as *www.example.com* instead. The DNS library on your system normally handles this translation automatically, but some-times you'll want to manually translate between a name and an IP address. To find the IP address behind a domain name, use the host command:

```
$ host www.example.com
www.example.com has address 93.184.216.119
www.example.com has IPv6 address 2606:2800:220:6d:26bf:1447:1097:aa7
```

Notice how this example has both the IPv4 address 93.184.216.119 and the much larger IPv6 address. This means that this host also has an address on the next-generation version of the Internet.

You can also use host in reverse: Enter an IP address instead of a host-name to try to discover the hostname behind the IP address. But don't expect this to work reliably. Many hostnames can represent a single IP address, and DNS doesn't know how to determine which hostname should correspond to an IP address. The domain administrator must manually set up this reverse lookup, and often the administrator does not. (There is a lot more to DNS than the host command. We'll cover basic client configuration later in Section 9.12.)

9.6   The Physical Layer and Ethernet

One of the key things to understand about the Internet is that it's a *software* network. Nothing we've discussed so far is hardware specific, and indeed, one reason for the Internet's success is that it works on almost any kind of computer, operating system, and physical network. However, you still have to put a network layer on top of some kind of hardware, and that interface is called the physical layer.

In this book, we'll look at the most common kind of physical layer: an Ethernet network. The IEEE 802 family of standards documents defines many different kinds of Ethernet networks, from wired to wireless, but they all have a few things in common, in particular, the following:

- All devices on an Ethernet network have a *Media Access Control (MAC) address*, sometimes called a *hardware address*. This address is independent of a host's IP address, and it is unique to the host's Ethernet network (but not necessarily a larger software network such as the Internet). A sample MAC address is 10:78:d2:eb:76:97.

- Devices on an Ethernet network send messages in *frames*, which are wrappers around the data sent. A frame contains the origin and destination MAC addresses.

Ethernet doesn't really attempt to go beyond hardware on a single network. For example, if you have two different Ethernet networks with one host attached to both networks (and two different network interface devices), you can't directly transmit a frame from one Ethernet network to the other unless you set up a special Ethernet bridge. And this is where higher network layers (such as the Internet layer) come in. By convention, each Ethernet network is also usually an Internet subnet. Even though a frame can't leave one physical network, a router can take the data out of a frame, repackage it, and send it to a host on a different physical network, which is exactly what happens on the Internet.

9.7   Understanding Kernel Network Interfaces

The physical and the Internet layers must be connected in a way that allows the Internet layer to retain its hardware-independent flexibility. The Linux kernel maintains its own division between the two layers and provides communication standards for linking them called a *(kernel) network interface*. When you configure a network interface, you link the IP address settings from the Internet side with the hardware identification on the physical dcvice side. Network interfaces have names that usually indicate the kind of hardware underneath, such as *eth0* (the first Ethernet card in the computer) and *wlan0* (a wireless interface).

In Section 9.3.1, you learned the most important command for viewing or manually configuring the network interface settings: ifconfig. Recall this output:

```
eth0      Link encap:Ethernet  HWaddr 10:78:d2:eb:76:97
          inet addr:10.23.2.4  Bcast:10.23.2.255  Mask:255.255.255.0
          inet6 addr: fe80::1278:d2ff:feeb:7697/64 Scope:Link
          UP BROADCAST RUNNING MULTICAST  MTU:1500  Metric:1
          RX packets:85076006 errors:0 dropped:0 overruns:0 frame:0
          TX packets:68347795 errors:0 dropped:0 overruns:0 carrier:0
          collisions:0 txqueuelen:1000
          RX bytes:86427623613 (86.4 GB)  TX bytes:23437688605 (23.4 GB)
          Interrupt:20 Memory:fe500000-fe520000
```

For each network interface, the left side of the output shows the interface name, and the right side contains settings and statistics for the interface. In addition to the Internet layer pieces that we've already covered, you also see the MAC address on the physical layer (HWaddr). The lines containing UP and RUNNING tell you that the interface is working.

Although ifconfig shows some hardware information (in this case, even some low-level device settings such as the interrupt and memory used), it's designed primarily for viewing and configuring the software layers attached to the interfaces. To dig deeper into the hardware and physical layer behind a network interface, use something like the ethtool command to display or change the settings on Ethernet cards. (We'll look briefly at wireless networks in Section 9.23.)

9.8   Introduction to Network Interface Configuration

You've now seen all of the basic elements that go into the lower levels of a network stack: the physical layer, the network (Internet) layer, and the Linux kernel's network interfaces. In order to combine these pieces to connect a Linux machine to the Internet, you or a piece of software must do the following:

1. Connect the network hardware and ensure that the kernel has a driver for it. If the driver is present, ifconfig -a displays a kernel network interface corresponding to the hardware.
2. Perform any additional physical layer setup, such as choosing a network name or password.
3. Bind an IP address and netmask to the kernel network interface so that the kernel's device drivers (physical layer) and Internet subsystems (Internet layer) can talk to each other.
4. Add any additional necessary routes, including the default gateway.

When all machines were big stationary boxes wired together, this was relatively straightforward: The kernel did step 1, you didn't need step 2, and you'd do step 3 with the `ifconfig` command and step 4 with the `route` command.

To manually set the IP address and netmask for a kernel network interface, you'd do this:

```
# ifconfig interface address netmask mask
```

Here, *interface* is the name of the interface, such as eth0. When the interface was up, you'd be ready to add routes, which was typically just a matter of setting the default gateway, like this:

```
# route add default gw gw-address
```

The *gw-address* parameter is the IP address of your default gateway; it *must* be an address in a locally connected subnet defined by the *address* and *mask* settings of one of your network interfaces.

9.8.1   Manually Adding and Deleting Routes

To remove a default gateway, run

```
# route del -net default
```

You can easily override the default gateway with other routes. For example, say your machine is on subnet 10.23.2.0/24, you want to reach a subnet at 192.168.45.0/24, and you know that 10.23.2.44 can act as a router for that subnet. Run this command to send traffic bound for 192.168.45.0 to that router:

```
# route add -net 192.168.45.0/24 gw 10.23.2.44
```

You don't need to specify the router in order to delete a route:

```
# route del -net 192.168.45.0/24
```

Now, before you go crazy with routes, you should know that messing with routes is often more complicated than it appears. For this particular example, you also have to make sure that the routing for all hosts on 192.163.45.0/24 can lead back to 10.23.2.0/24, or the first route you add is basically useless.

Normally, you should keep things as simple as possible for your clients, setting up networks so that their hosts need only a default route. If you need multiple subnets and the ability to route between them, it's usually best to configure the routers acting as the default gateways to do all of the work of routing between different local subnets. (You'll see an example in Section 9.17.)

9.9 Boot-Activated Network Configuration

We've discussed ways to manually configure a network, and the traditional way to ensure the correctness of a machine's network configuration was to have init run a script to run the manual configuration at boot time. This boils down to running tools like ifconfig and route somewhere in the chain of boot events. Many servers still do it this way.

There have been many attempts in Linux to standardize configuration files for boot-time networking. The tools ifup and ifdown do so—for example, a boot script can (in theory) run ifup eth0 to run the correct ifconfig and route commands for the *eth0* interface. Unfortunately, different distributions have completely different implementations of ifup and ifdown, and as a result, their configuration files are also completely different. Ubuntu, for example, uses the ifupdown suite with configuration files in */etc/network*, and Fedora uses its own set of scripts with configuration in */etc/sysconfig/network-scripts*.

You don't need to know the details of these configuration files, and if you insist on doing it all by hand and bypass your distribution's configuration tools, you can just look up the formats in manual pages such as ifup(8) and interfaces(5). But it is important to know that this type of boot-activated configuration is often not even used. You'll most often see it for the local-host (or *lo*; see Section 9.13) network interface but nothing else because it's too inflexible to meet the needs of modern systems.

9.10 Problems with Manual and Boot-Activated Network Configuration

Although most systems used to configure the network in their boot mecha-nisms—and many servers still do—the dynamic nature of modern networks means that most machines don't have static (unchanging) IP addresses. Rather than storing the IP address and other network information on your machine, your machine gets this information from somewhere on the local physical network when it first attaches to that network. Most normal network client applications don't particularly care what IP address your machine uses, as long as it works. Dynamic Host Configuration Protocol (DHCP, described in Section 9.16) tools do the basic network layer configuration on typical clients.

There's more to the story, though. For example, wireless networks add additional dimensions to interface configuration, such as network names, authentication, and encryption techniques. When you step back to look at the bigger picture, you see that your system needs a way to answer the fol-lowing questions:

- If the machine has multiple physical network interfaces (such as a notebook with wired and wireless Ethernet), how do you choose which one(s) to use?
- How should the machine set up the physical interface? For wireless net-works, this includes scanning for network names, choosing a name, and negotiating authentication.

- Once the physical network interface is connected, how should the machine set up the software network layers, such as the Internet layer?
- How can you let a user choose connectivity options? For example, how do you let a user choose a wireless network?
- What should the machine do if it loses connectivity on a network interface?

Answering these questions is usually more than simple boot scripts can handle, and it's a real hassle to do it all by hand. The answer is to use a system service that can monitor physical networks and choose (and automatically configure) the kernel network interfaces based on a set of rules that makes sense to the user. The service should also be able to respond to requests from users, who should be able to change the wireless network they're on without having to become root just to fiddle around with network settings every time something changes.

9.11   Network Configuration Managers

There are several ways to automatically configure networks in Linux-based systems. The most widely used option on desktops and notebooks is NetworkManager. Other network configuration management systems are mainly targeted for smaller embedded systems, such as OpenWRT's `netifd`, Android's ConnectivityManager service, ConnMan, and Wicd. We'll briefly discuss NetworkManager because it's the one you're most likely to encounter. We won't go into a tremendous amount of detail, though, because after you see the big picture, NetworkManager and other configuration systems will be more transparent.

9.11.1   NetworkManager Operation

NetworkManager is a daemon that the system starts upon boot. Like all daemons, it does not depend on a running desktop component. Its job is to listen to events from the system and users and to change the network configuration based on a bunch of rules.

When running, NetworkManager maintains two basic levels of configuration. The first is a collection of information about available hardware devices, which it normally collects from the kernel and maintains by monitoring udev over the Desktop Bus (D-Bus). The second configuration level is a more specific list of *connections:* hardware devices and additional physical and network layer configuration parameters. For example, a wireless network can be represented as a connection.

To activate a connection, NetworkManager often delegates the tasks to other specialized network tools and daemons such as `dhclient` to get Internet layer configuration from a locally attached physical network. Because network configuration tools and schemes vary among distributions, NetworkManager uses plugins to interface with them, rather than imposing its own standard. There are plugins for the both the Debian/Ubuntu and Red Hat–style interface configuration, for example.

Upon startup, NetworkManager gathers all available network device information, searches its list of connections, and then decides to try to activate one. Here's how it makes that decision for Ethernet interfaces:

1. If a wired connection is available, try to connect using it. Otherwise, try the wireless connections.
2. Scan the list of available wireless networks. If a network is available that you've previously connected to, NetworkManager will try it again.
3. If more than one previously connected wireless networks are available, select the most recently connected.

After establishing a connection, NetworkManager maintains it until the connection is lost, a better network becomes available (for example, you plug in a network cable while connected over wireless), or the user forces a change.

9.11.2   Interacting with NetworkManager

Most users interact with NetworkManager through an applet on the desktop—it's usually an icon in the upper or lower right that indicates the connection status (wired, wireless, or not connected). When you click on the icon, you get a number of connectivity options, such as a choice of wireless networks and an option to disconnect from your current network. Each desktop environment has its own version of this applet, so it looks a little different on each one.

In addition to the applet, there are a few tools that you can use to query and control NetworkManager from your shell. For a very quick summary of your current connection status, use the nm-tool command with no arguments. You'll get a list of interfaces and configuration parameters. In some ways, this is like ifconfig except that there's more detail, especially when viewing wireless connections.

To control NetworkManager from the command line, use the nmcli command. This is a somewhat extensive command. See the nmcli(1) manual page for more information.

Finally, the utility nm-online will tell you whether the network is up or down. If the network is up, the command returns zero as its exit code; it's nonzero otherwise. (For more on how to use an exit code in a shell script, see Chapter 11.)

9.11.3   NetworkManager Configuration

The general configuration directory for NetworkManager is usually */etc/NetworkManager*, and there are several different kinds of configuration. The general configuration file is *NetworkManager.conf*. The format is similar to the XDG-style *.desktop* and Microsoft *.ini* files, with key-value parameters falling into different sections. You'll find that nearly every configuration file has a [main] section that defines the plugins to use. Here's a simple example that activates the ifupdown plugin used by Ubuntu and Debian:

```
[main]
plugins=ifupdown,keyfile
```

Other distribution-specific plugins are ifcfg-rh (for Red Hat–style distributions) and ifcfg-suse (for SuSE). The keyfile plugin that you also see here supports NetworkManager's native configuration file support. When using the plugin, you can see the system's known connections in */etc/NetworkManager/system-connections.*

For the most part, you won't need to change *NetworkManager.conf* because the more specific configuration options are found in other files.

Unmanaged Interfaces

Although you may want NetworkManager to manage most of your network interfaces, there will be times when you want it to ignore interfaces. For example, there's no reason why most users would need any kind of dynamic configuration on the localhost (*lo*) interface because the configuration never changes. You also want to configure this interface early in the boot process because basic system services often depend on it. Most distributions keep NetworkManager away from localhost.

You can tell NetworkManager to disregard an interface by using plugins. If you're using the ifupdown plugin (for example, in Ubuntu and Debian), add the interface configuration to your */etc/network/interfaces* file and then set the value of managed to false in the ifupdown section of the *NetworkManager.conf* file:

```
[ifupdown]
managed=false
```

For the ifcfg-rh plugin that Fedora and Red Hat use, look for a line like this in the */etc/sysconfig/network-scripts* directory that contains the *ifcfg-** configuration files:

```
NM_CONTROLLED=yes
```

If this line is not present or the value is set to no, NetworkManager ignores the interface. For example, you'll find it deactivated in the *ifcfg-lo* file. You can also specify a hardware address to ignore, like this:

```
HWADDR=10:78:d2:eb:76:97
```

If you don't use either of these network configuration schemes, you can still use the keyfile plugin to specify the unmanaged device directly inside your *NetworkManager.conf* file using the MAC address. Here's how that might look:

```
[keyfile]
unmanaged-devices=mac:10:78:d2:eb:76:97;mac:1c:65:9d:cc:ff:b9
```

Dispatching

One final detail of NetworkManager configuration relates to specifiying additional system actions for when a network interface goes up or down. For example, some network daemons need to know when to start or stop listening on an interface in order to work correctly (such as the secure shell daemon discussed in the next chapter).

When the network interface status on a system changes, NetworkManager runs everything in */etc/NetworkManager/dispatcher.d* with an argument such as up or down. This is relatively straightforward, but many distributions have their own network control scripts so they don't place the individual dispatcher scripts in this directory. Ubuntu, for example, has just one script named 01ifupdown that runs everything in an appropriate subdirectory of */etc/network*, such as */etc/network/if-up.d*.

As with the rest of the NetworkManager configuration, the details of these scripts are relatively unimportant; all you need to know is how to track down the appropriate location if you need to make an addition or change. As ever, don't be shy about looking at scripts on your system.

9.12   Resolving Hostnames

One of the final basic tasks in any network configuration is hostname resolution with DNS. You've already seen the host resolution tool that translates a name such as *www.example.com* to an IP address such as 10.23.2.132.

DNS differs from the network elements we've looked at so far because it's in the application layer, entirely in user space. Technically, it is slightly out of place in this chapter alongside the Internet and physical layer discussion, but without proper DNS configuration, your Internet connection is practically worthless. No one in their right mind advertises IP addresses for websites and email addresses because a host's IP address is subject to change and it's not easy to remember a bunch of numbers. Automatic network configuration services such as DHCP nearly always include DNS configuration.

Nearly all network applications on a Linux system perform DNS lookups. The resolution process typically unfolds like this:

1. The application calls a function to look up the IP address behind a hostname. This function is in the system's shared library, so the application doesn't need to know the details of how it works or whether the implementation will change.

2. When the function in the shared library runs, it acts according to a set of rules (found in */etc/nsswitch.conf*) to determine a plan of action on lookups. For example, the rules usually say that even before going to DNS, check for a manual override in the */etc/hosts* file.

3. When the function decides to use DNS for the name lookup, it consults an additional configuration file to find a DNS name server. The name server is given as an IP address.

4. The function sends a DNS lookup request (over the network) to the name server.

5. The name server replies with the IP address for the hostname, and the function returns this IP address to the application.

This is the simplified version. In a typical modern system, there are more actors attempting to speed up the transaction and/or add flexibility. Let's ignore that for now and take a closer look at the basic pieces.

9.12.1   /etc/hosts

On most systems, you can override hostname lookups with the */etc/hosts* file. It usually looks like this:

```
127.0.0.1      localhost
10.23.2.3      atlantic.aem7.net      atlantic
10.23.2.4      pacific.aem7.net       pacific
```

You'll nearly always see the entry for localhost here (see Section 9.13).

NOTE   *In the bad old days, there was one central hosts file that everyone copied to their own machine in order to stay up-to-date (see RFCs 606, 608, 623, and 625), but as the ARPANET/Internet grew, this quickly got out of hand.*

9.12.2   resolv.conf

The traditional configuration file for DNS servers is */etc/resolv.conf*. When things were simpler, a typical example might have looked like this, where the ISP's name server addresses are 10.32.45.23 and 10.3.2.3:

```
search mydomain.example.com example.com
nameserver 10.32.45.23
nameserver 10.3.2.3
```

The search line defines rules for incomplete hostnames (just the first part of the hostname; for example, `myserver` instead of `myserver.example.com`). Here, the resolver library would try to look up `host.mydomain.example.com` and `host.example.com`. But things are usually no longer this straightforward. Many enhancements and modifications have been made to the DNS configuration.

9.12.3 Caching and Zero-Configuration DNS

There are two main problems with the traditional DNS configuration. First, the local machine does not cache name server replies, so frequent repeated network access may be unnecessarily slow due to name server requests. To solve this problem, many machines (and routers, if acting as name servers) run an intermediate daemon to intercept name server requests and return a cached answer to name service requests if possible; otherwise, requests go to a real name server. Two of the most common such daemons for Linux are dnsmasq and nscd. You can also set up BIND (the standard Unix name server daemon) as a cache. You can often tell if you're running a name server caching daemon when you see 127.0.0.1 (localhost) in your */etc/resolv.conf* file or when you see 127.0.0.1 show up as the server if you run nslookup -debug *host*.

It can be a tricky to track down your configuration if you're running a name server–caching daemon. By default, dnsmasq has the configuration file */etc/dnsmasq.conf*, but your distribution may override that. For example, in Ubuntu, if you've manually set up an interface that's set up by NetworkManager, you'll find it in the appropriate file in */etc/NetworkManager/system-connections* because when NetworkManager activates a connection, it also starts dnsmasq with that configuration. (You can override all of this by uncommenting the dnsmasq part of your *NetworkManager.conf.*)

The other problem with the traditional name server setup is that it can be particularly inflexible if you want to be able to look up names on your local network without messing around with a lot of network configuration. For example, if you set up a network appliance on your network, you'll want to be able to call it by name immediately. This is part of the idea behind zero-configuration name service systems such as Multicast DNS (mDNS) and Simple Service Discovery Protocol (SSDP). If you want to find a host by name on the local network, you just broadcast a request over the network; if the host is there, it replies with its address. These protocols go beyond hostname resolution by also providing information about available services.

The most widely used Linux implementation of mDNS is called Avahi. You'll often see mdns as a resolver option in */etc/nsswitch.conf*, which we'll now look at in more detail.

9.12.4 /etc/nsswitch.conf

The */etc/nsswitch.conf* file controls several name-related precedence settings on your system, such as user and password information, but we'll only talk about the DNS settings in this chapter. The file on your system should have a line like this:

```
hosts:          files dns
```

Putting files ahead of dns here ensures that your system checks the */etc/hosts* file for the hostname of your requested IP address before asking the DNS server. This is usually a good idea (especially for looking up localhost, as discussed below), but your */etc/hosts* file should be as *short* as possible. Don't put anything in there to boost performance; doing so will burn you later. You can put all the hosts within a small private LAN in */etc/hosts*, but the general rule of thumb is that if a particular host has a DNS entry, it has no place in */etc/hosts*. (The */etc/hosts* file is also useful for resolving hostnames in the early stages of booting, when the network may not be available.)

NOTE   *DNS is a broad topic. If you have any responsibility for domain names, read* DNS and BIND, *5th edition, by Cricket Liu and Paul Albitz (O'Reilly, 2006).*

9.13   Localhost

When running `ifconfig`, you'll notice the *lo* interface:

```
lo          Link encap:Local Loopback
            inet addr:127.0.0.1  Mask:255.0.0.0
            inet6 addr: ::1/128 Scope:Host
            UP LOOPBACK RUNNING  MTU:16436  Metric:1
```

The *lo* interface is a virtual network interface called the *loopback* because it "loops back" to itself. The effect is that connecting to 127.0.0.1 is connecting to the machine that you're currently using. When outgoing data to localhost reaches the kernel network interface for *lo*, the kernel just repackages it as incoming data and sends it back through *lo*.

The *lo* loopback interface is often the only place you'll see static network configuration in boot-time scripts. For example, Ubuntu's `ifup` command reads */etc/network/interfaces* and Fedora uses */etc/sysconfig/network-interfaces/ifcfg-lo*. You can often find the loopback device configuration by digging around in */etc* with grep.

9.14   The Transport Layer: TCP, UDP, and Services

So far, we've only seen how packets move from host to host on the Internet—in other words, the *where* question from the beginning of the chapter. Now let's start to answer the *what* question. It's important to know how your computer presents the packet data it receives from other hosts to its running processes. It's difficult and inconvenient for user-space programs to deal with a bunch of raw packets the way that the kernel can. Flexibility is especially important: More than one application should be able to talk to the network at the same time (for example, you might have email and several web clients running).

Transport layer protocols bridge the gap between the raw packets of the Internet layer and the refined needs of applications. The two most popular transport protocols are the Transmission Control Protocol (TCP) and the User Datagram Protocol (UDP). We'll concentrate on TCP because it's by far the most common protocol in use, but we'll also take a quick look at UDP.

9.14.1 TCP Ports and Connections

TCP provides for multiple network applications on one machine by means of network *ports*. A port is just a number. If an IP address is like the postal address of an apartment building, a port is like a mailbox number—it's a further subdivision.

When using TCP, an application opens a *connection* (not to be confused with NetworkManager connections) between one port on its own machine and a port on a remote host. For example, an application such as a web browser could open a connection between port 36406 on its own machine and port 80 on a remote host. From the application's point of view, port 36406 is the local port and port 80 is the remote port.

You can identify a connection by using the pair of IP addresses and port numbers. To view the connections currently open on your machine, use netstat. Here's an example that shows TCP connections: The -n option disables hostname (DNS) resolution, and -t limits the output to TCP.

```
$ netstat -nt
Active Internet connections (w/o servers)
Proto Recv-Q Send-Q Local Address        Foreign Address        State
tcp        0      0 10.23.2.4:47626      10.194.79.125:5222     ESTABLISHED
tcp        0      0 10.23.2.4:41475      172.19.52.144:6667     ESTABLISHED
tcp        0      0 10.23.2.4:57132      192.168.231.135:22     ESTABLISHED
```

The Local Address and Foreign Address fields show connections from your machine's point of view, so the machine here has an interface configured at 10.23.2.4, and ports 47626, 41475, and 57132 on the local side are all connected. The first connection here shows port 47626 connected to port 5222 of 10.194.79.125.

9.14.2 Establishing TCP Connections

To establish a transport layer connection, a process on one host initiates the connection from one of its local ports to a port on a second host with a special series of packets. In order to recognize the incoming connection and respond, the second host must have a process *listening* on the correct port. Usually, the connecting process is called the *client*, and the listener is the called the *server* (more about this in Chapter 10).

The important thing to know about the ports is that the client picks a port on its side that isn't currently in use, but it nearly always connects to some well-known port on the server side. Recall this output from the netstat command in the preceding section:

```
Proto Recv-Q Send-Q Local Address        Foreign Address        State
tcp        0      0 10.23.2.4:47626      10.194.79.125:5222     ESTABLISHED
```

With a little help, you can see that this connection was probably initiated by a local client to a remote server because the port on the local side (47626) looks like a dynamically assigned number, whereas the remote port (5222) is a well-known service (the Jabber or XMPP messaging service, to be specific).

A dynamically assigned port is called an ephemeral port.

However, if the local port in the output is well-known, a remote host probably initiated the connection. In this example, remote host 172.24.54.234 has connected to port 80 (the default web port) on the local host.

```
Proto Recv-Q Send-Q Local Address          Foreign Address       State
tcp       0      0 10.23.2.4:80            172.24.54.234:43035   ESTABLISHED
```

A remote host connecting to your machine on a well-known port implies that a server on your local machine is listening on this port. To confirm this, list all TCP ports that your machine is listening on with netstat:

```
$ netstat -ntl
Active Internet connections (only servers)
Proto Recv-Q Send-Q Local Address          Foreign Address       State
tcp       0      0 0.0.0.0:80              0.0.0.0:*             LISTEN
tcp       0      0 127.0.0.1:53            0.0.0.0:*             LISTEN
--snip--
```

The line with 0.0.0.0:80 as the local address shows that the local machine is listening on port 80 for connections from any remote machine. (A server can restrict the access to certain interfaces, as shown in the last line, where something is listening for connections only on the localhost interface.) To learn even more, use lsof to identify the specific process that's listening (as discussed in Section 10.5.1).

9.14.3   Port Numbers and /etc/services

How do you know if a port is a well-known port? There's no single way to tell, but one good place to start is to look in */etc/services*, which translates well-known port numbers into names. This is a plaintext file. You should see entries like this:

```
ssh             22/tcp             # SSH Remote Login Protocol
smtp            25/tcp
domain          53/udp
```

The first column is a name and the second column indicates the port number and the specific transport layer protocol (which can be other than TCP).

NOTE   *In addition to* /etc/services, *an online registry for ports at* http://www.iana.org/ *is governed by the RFC6335 network standards document.*

On Linux, only processes running as the superuser can use ports 1 through 1023. All user processes may listen on and create connections from ports 1024 and up.

9.14.4   Characteristics of TCP

TCP is popular as a transport layer protocol because it requires relatively little from the application side. An application process only needs to know how to open (or listen for), read from, write to, and close a connection. To the application, it seems as if there are incoming and outgoing streams of data; the process is nearly as simple as working with a file.

However, there's a lot of work to do behind the scenes. For one, the TCP implementation needs to know how to break an outgoing data stream from a process into packets. However, the hard part is knowing how to convert a series of incoming packets into an input data stream for processes to read, especially when incoming packets don't necessarily arrive in the correct order. In addition, a host using TCP must check for errors: Packets can get lost or mangled when sent across the Internet, and a TCP implementation must detect and correct these situations. Figure 9-3 shows a simplification of how a host might use TCP to send a message.

Luckily, you need to know next to nothing about this mess other than that the Linux TCP implementation is primarily in the kernel and that utilities that work with the transport layer tend to manipulate kernel data structures. One example is the IP Tables packet-filtering system discussed in Section 9.21.

9.14.5   UDP

UDP is a far simpler transport layer than TCP. It defines a transport only for single messages; there is no data stream. At the same time, unlike TCP, UDP won't correct for lost or out-of-order packets. In fact, although UDP has ports, it doesn't even have connections! One host simply sends a message from one of its ports to a port on a server, and the server sends something back if it wants to. However, UDP *does* have error detection for data inside a packet; a host can detect if a packet gets mangled, but it doesn't have to do anything about it.

Where TCP is like having a telephone conversation, UDP is like sending a letter, telegram, or instant message (except that instant messages are more reliable). Applications that use UDP are often concerned with speed—sending a message as quickly as possible. They don't want the overhead of TCP because they assume the network between two hosts is generally reliable. They don't need TCP's error correction because they either have their own error detection systems or simply don't care about errors.

One example of an application that uses UDP is the *Network Time Protocol (NTP)*. A client sends a short and simple request to a server to get the current time, and the response from the server is equally brief. Because the client wants the response as quickly as possible, UDP suits the application; if the response from the server gets lost somewhere in the network, the client can just resend a request or give up. Another example is video chat—in this case, pictures are sent with UDP—and if some pieces get lost along the way, the client on the receiving end compensates the best it can.

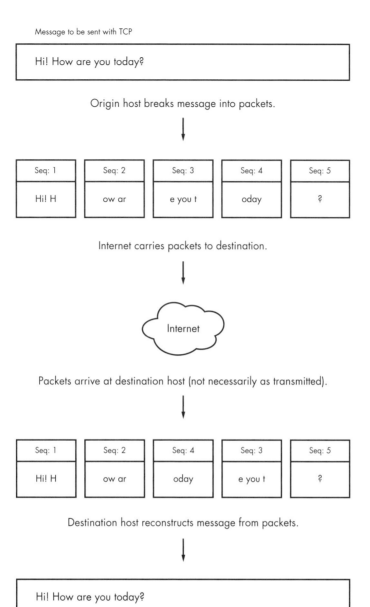

Figure 9-3: Sending a message with TCP

NOTE *The rest of this chapter deals with more advanced networking topics, such as network filtering and routers, as they relate to the lower network layers that we've already seen: physical, network, and transport. If you like, feel free to skip ahead to the next chapter to see the application layer where everything comes together in user space. You'll see processes that actually* use *the network rather than just throwing around a bunch of addresses and packets.*

9.15 Revisiting a Simple Local Network

We're now going to look at additional components of the simple network introduced in Section 9.3. Recall that this network consists of one local area network as one subnet and a router that connects the subnet to the rest of the Internet. You'll learn the following:

- How a host on the subnet automatically gets its network configuration
- How to set up routing
- What a router really is
- How to know which IP addresses to use for the subnet
- How to set up firewalls to filter out unwanted traffic from the Internet

Let's start by learning how a host on the subnet automatically gets its network configuration.

9.16 Understanding DHCP

When you set a network host to get its configuration automatically from the network, you're telling it to use the Dynamic Host Configuration Protocol (DHCP) to get an IP address, subnet mask, default gateway, and DNS servers. Aside from not having to enter these parameters by hand, DHCP has other advantages for a network administrator, such as preventing IP address clashes and minimizing the impact of network changes. It's very rare to see a modern network that doesn't use DHCP.

For a host to get its configuration with DHCP, it must be able to send messages to a DHCP server on its connected network. Therefore, each physical network should have its own DHCP server, and on a simple network (such as the one in Section 9.3), the router usually acts as the DHCP server.

NOTE *When making an initial DHCP request, a host doesn't even know the address of a DHCP server, so it broadcasts the request to all hosts (usually all hosts on its physical network).*

When a machine asks a DHCP server for an IP address, it's really asking for a *lease* on an address for a certain amount of time. When the lease is up, a client can ask to renew the lease.

9.16.1 The Linux DHCP Client

Although there are many different kinds of network manager systems, nearly all use the Internet Software Consortium (ISC) dhclient program to do the actual work. You can test dhclient by hand on the command line, but before doing so you *must* remove any default gateway route. To run the test, simply specify the network interface name (here, it's *eth0*):

```
# dhclient eth0
```

Upon startup, dhclient stores its process ID in */var/run/dhclient.pid* and its lease information in */var/state/dhclient.leases*.

9.16.2   Linux DHCP Servers

You can task a Linux machine with running a DHCP server, which provides a good amount of control over the addresses that it gives out. However, unless you're administering a large network with many subnets, you're probably better off using specialized router hardware that includes built-in DHCP servers.

Probably the most important thing to know about DHCP servers is that you want only one running on the same subnet in order to avoid problems with clashing IP addresses or incorrect configurations.

9.17   Configuring Linux as a Router

Routers are essentially just computers with more than one physical network interface. You can easily configure a Linux machine as a router.

For example, say you have two LAN subnets, 10.23.2.0/24 and 192.168.45.0/24. To connect them, you have a Linux router machine with three network interfaces: two for the LAN subnets and one for an Internet uplink, as shown in Figure 9-4. As you can see, this doesn't look very different from the simple network example that we've used in the rest of this chapter.

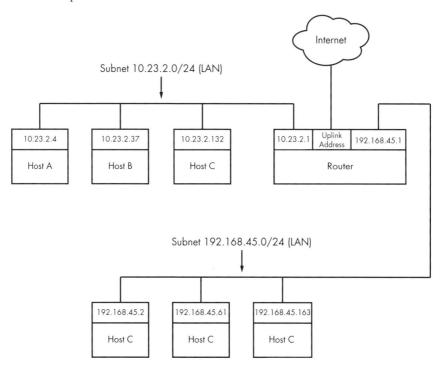

Figure 9-4: Two subnets joined with a router

The router's IP addresses for the LAN subnets are 10.23.2.1 and 192.168.45.1. When those addresses are configured, the routing table looks something like this (the interface names might vary in practice; ignore the Internet uplink for now):

Destination	Gateway	Genmask	Flags	Metric	Ref	Use	Iface
10.23.2.0	0.0.0.0	255.255.255.0	U	0	0	0	eth0
192.168.45.0	0.0.0.0	255.255.255.0	U	0	0	0	eth1

Now let's say that the hosts on each subnet have the router as their default gateway (10.23.2.1 for 10.23.2.0/24 and 192.168.45.1 for 192.168.45.0/24). If 10.23.2.4 wants to send a packet to anything outside of 10.23.2.0/24, it passes the packet to 10.23.2.1. For example, to send a packet from 10.23.2.4 (Host A) to 192.168.45.61 (Host E), the packet goes to 10.23.2.1 (the router) via its *eth0* interface, then back out through the router's *eth1* interface.

However, by default, the Linux kernel does not automatically move packets from one subnet to another. To enable this basic routing function, you need to enable *IP forwarding* in the router's kernel with this command:

```
# sysctl -w net.ipv4.ip_forward
```

As soon as you enter this command, the machine should start routing packets between the two subnets, assuming that the hosts on those subnets know to send their packets to the router you just created.

To make this change permanent upon reboot, you can add it to your */etc/sysctl.conf* file. Depending on your distribution, you may have the option to put it into a file in */etc/sysctl.d* so that distribution updates won't overwrite your changes.

9.17.1 Internet Uplinks

When the router also has the third network interface with an Internet uplink, this same setup allows Internet access for all hosts on both subnets because they're configured to use the router as the default gateway. But that's where things get more complicated. The problem is that certain IP addresses such as 10.23.2.4 are not actually visible to the whole Internet; they're on so-called *private networks*. To provide for Internet connectivity, you must set up a feature called *Network Address Translation (NAT)* on the router. The software on nearly all specialized routers does this, so there's nothing out of the ordinary here, but let's examine the problem of private networks in a bit more detail.

9.18   Private Networks

Say you decide to build your own network. You have your machines, router, and network hardware ready. Given what you know about a simple network so far, your next question is "What IP subnet should I use?"

If you want a block of Internet addresses that every host on the Internet can see, you can buy one from your ISP. However, because the range of IPv4 addresses is very limited, this costs a a lot and isn't useful for much more than running a server that the rest of the Internet can see. Most people don't really need this kind of service because they access the Internet as a client.

The conventional, inexpensive alternative is to pick a private subnet from the addresses in the RFC 1918/6761 Internet standards documents, shown in Table 9-2.

Table 9-2: Private Networks Defined by RFC 1918 and 6761

Network	Subnet Mask	CIDR Form
10.0.0.0	255.0.0.0	10.0.0.0/8
192.168.0.0	255.255.0.0	192.168.0.0/16
172.16.0.0	255.240.0.0	172.16.0.0/12

You can carve up private subnets as you wish. Unless you plan to have more than 254 hosts on a single network, pick a small subnet like 10.23.2.0/24, as we've been using throughout this chapter. (Networks with this netmask are sometimes called *class C* subnets. Although the term is technically somewhat obsolete, it's still useful.)

What's the catch? Hosts on the real Internet know nothing about private subnets and will not send packets to them, so without some help, hosts on private subnets cannot talk to the outside world. A router connected to the Internet (with a true, nonprivate address) needs to have some way to fill in the gap between that connection and the hosts on a private network.

9.19   Network Address Translation (IP Masquerading)

NAT is the most commonly used way to share a single IP address with a private network, and it's nearly universal in home and small office networks. In Linux, the variant of NAT that most people use is known as *IP masquerading*.

The basic idea behind NAT is that the router doesn't just move packets from one subnet to another; it transforms them as it moves them. Hosts on the Internet know how to connect to the router, but they know nothing about the private network behind it. The hosts on the private network need no special configuration; the router is their default gateway.

The system works roughly like this:

1.   A host on the internal private network wants to make a connection to the outside world, so it sends its connection request packets through the router.

2.   The router intercepts the connection request packet rather than passing it out to the Internet (where it would get lost because the public Internet knows nothing about private networks).

3.   The router determines the destination of the connection request packet and opens its own connection to the destination.

4. When the router obtains the connection, it fakes a "connection established" message back to the original internal host.

5. The router is now the middleman between the internal host and the destination. The destination knows nothing about the internal host; the connection on the remote host looks like it came from the router.

This isn't quite as simple as it sounds. Normal IP routing knows only source and destination IP addresses in the Internet layer. However, if the router dealt only with the Internet layer, each host on the internal network could establish only one connection to a single destination at one time (among other limitations), because there is no information in the Internet layer part of a packet to distinguish multiple requests from the same host to the same destination. Therefore, NAT must go beyond the Internet layer and dissect packets to pull out more identifying information, particularly the UDP and TCP port numbers from the transport layers. UDP is fairly easy because there are ports but no connections, but the TCP transport layer is complex.

In order to set up a Linux machine to perform as a NAT router, you must activate all of the following inside the kernel configuration: network packet filtering ("firewall support"), connection tracking, IP tables support, full NAT, and MASQUERADE target support. Most distribution kernels come with this support.

Next you need to run some complex-looking `iptables` commands to make the router perform NAT for its private subnet. Here's an example that applies to an internal Ethernet network on *eth1* sharing an external connection at *eth0* (you'll learn more about the `iptables` syntax in Section 9.21):

```
# sysctl -w net.ipv4.ip_forward
# iptables -P FORWARD DROP
# iptables -t nat -A POSTROUTING -o eth0 -j MASQUERADE
# iptables -A FORWARD -i eth0 -o eth1 -m state --state ESTABLISHED,RELATED -j ACCEPT
# iptables -A FORWARD -i eth1 -o eth0 -j ACCEPT
```

NOTE *Although NAT works well in practice, remember that it's essentially a hack used to extend the lifetime of the IPv4 address space. In a perfect world, we would all be using IPv6 (the next-generation Internet) and using its larger and more sophisticated address space without any pain.*

You likely won't ever need to use the commands above unless you're developing your own software, especially with so much special-purpose router hardware available. But the role of Linux in a network doesn't end here.

9.20 Routers and Linux

In the early days of broadband, users with less demanding needs simply connected their machine directly to the Internet. But it didn't take long for many users to want to share a single broadband connection with their own networks, and Linux users in particular would often set up an extra machine to use as a router running NAT.

Manufacturers responded to this new market by offering specialized router hardware consisting of an efficient processor, some flash memory, and several network ports—with enough power to manage a typical simple network, run important software such as a DHCP server, and use NAT. When it came to software, many manufacturers turned to Linux to power their routers. They added the necessary kernel features, stripped down the user-space software, and created GUI-based administration interfaces.

Almost as soon as the first of these routers appeared, many people became interested in digging deeper into the hardware. One manufacturer, Linksys, was required to release the source code for its software under the terms of the license of one its components, and soon specialized Linux distributions such as OpenWRT appeared for routers. (The "WRT" in these names came from the Linksys model number.)

Aside from the hobbyist aspect, there are good reasons to use these distributions: They're often more stable than the manufacturer firmware, especially on older router hardware, and they typically offer additional features. For example, to bridge a network with a wireless connection, many manufacturers require you to buy matching hardware, but with OpenWRT installed, the manufacturer and age of the hardware don't really matter. This is because you're using a truly open operating system on the router that doesn't care what hardware you use as long as your hardware is supported.

You can use much of the knowledge in this book to examine the internals of custom Linux firmware, though you'll encounter differences, especially when logging in. As with many embedded systems, open firmware tends to use BusyBox to provide many shell features. BusyBox is a single executable program that offers limited functionality for many Unix commands such as the shell, ls, grep, cat, and more. (This saves a significant amount of memory.) In addition, the boot-time init tends to be very simple on embedded systems. However, you typically won't find these limitations to be a problem, because custom Linux firmware often includes a web administration interface similar to what you'd see from a manufacturer.

9.21   Firewalls

Routers in particular should always include some kind of firewall to keep undesirable traffic out of your network. A *firewall* is a software and/or hardware configuration that usually sits on a router between the Internet and a smaller network, attempting to ensure that nothing "bad" from the Internet harms the smaller network. You can also set up firewall features for each machine where the machine screens all of its incoming and outgoing data at the packet level (as opposed to the application layer, where server programs usually try to perform some access control of their own). Firewalling on individual machines is sometimes called *IP filtering*.

A system can filter packets when it

- receives a packet,
- sends a packet, or
- forwards (routes) a packet to another host or gateway.

With no firewalling in place, a system just processes packets and sends them on their way. Firewalls put checkpoints for packets at the points of data transfer identified above. The checkpoints drop, reject, or accept packets, usually based on some of these criteria:

- The source or destination IP address or subnet
- The source or destination port (in the transport layer information)
- The firewall's network interface

Firewalls provide an opportunity to work with the subsystem of the Linux kernel that processes IP packets. Let's look at that now.

9.21.1   Linux Firewall Basics

In Linux, you create firewall rules in a series known as a *chain*. A set of chains makes up a *table*. As a packet moves through the various parts of the Linux networking subsystem, the kernel applies the rules in certain chains to the packets. For example, after receiving a new packet from the physical layer, the kernel activates rules in chains corresponding to input.

All of these data structures are maintained by the kernel. The whole system is called *iptables*, with an iptables user-space command to create and manipulate the rules.

NOTE   *There is a newer system called nftables that has a goal of replacing iptables, but as of this writing, iptables is the dominant system for firewalls.*

Because there can be many tables—each with their own sets of chains, each of which can contain many rules—packet flow can become quite complicated. However, you'll normally work primarily with a single table named *filter* that controls basic packet flow. There are three basic chains in the *filter* table: INPUT for incoming packets, OUTPUT for outgoing packets, and FORWARD for routed packets.

Figures 9-5 and 9-6 show simplified flowcharts for where rules are applied to packets in the *filter* table. There are two figures because packets can either come into the system from a network interface (Figure 9-5) or be generated by a local process (Figure 9-6). As you can see, an incoming packet from the network can be consumed by a user process and may not reach the FORWARD chain or the OUTPUT chain. Packets generated by user processes won't reach the INPUT or FORWARD chains.

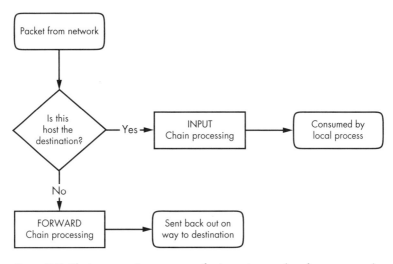

Figure 9-5: Chain-processing sequence for incoming packets from a network

Figure 9-6: Chain-processing sequence for incoming packets from a local process

This gets more complicated because there are many steps along the way other than just these three chains. For example, packets are subject to PREROUTING and POSTROUTING chains, and chain processing can also occur at any of the three lower network levels. For a big diagram for everything that's going on, search the Internet for "Linux netfilter packet flow," but remember that these diagrams try to include every possible scenario for packet input and flow. It often helps to break the diagrams down by packet source, as in Figures 9-5 and 9-6.

9.21.2 Setting Firewall Rules

Let's look at how the IP tables system works in practice. Start by viewing the current configuration with this command:

```
# iptables -L
```

The output is usually an empty set of chains, as follows:

```
Chain INPUT (policy ACCEPT)
target     prot opt source               destination

Chain FORWARD (policy ACCEPT)
target     prot opt source               destination

Chain OUTPUT (policy ACCEPT)
target     prot opt source               destination
```

Each firewall chain has a default *policy* that specifies what to do with a packet if no rule matches the packet. The policy for all three chains in this example is ACCEPT, meaning that the kernel allows the packet to pass through the packet-filtering system. The DROP policy tells the kernel to discard the packet. To set the policy on a chain, use iptables -P like this:

```
# iptables -P FORWARD DROP
```

WARNING *Don't do anything rash with the policies on your machine until you've read through the rest of this section.*

Say that someone at 192.168.34.63 is annoying you. To prevent them from talking to your machine, run this command:

```
# iptables -A INPUT -s 192.168.34.63 -j DROP
```

The -A INPUT parameter appends a rule to the INPUT chain. The -s 192.168.34.63 part specifies the source IP address in the rule, and -j DROP tells the kernel to discard any packet matching the rule. Therefore, your machine will throw out any packet coming from 192.168.34.63.

To see the rule in place, run iptables -L:

```
Chain INPUT (policy ACCEPT)
target     prot opt source               destination
DROP       all  --  192.168.34.63        anywhere
```

Unfortunately, your friend at 192.168.34.63 has told everyone on his subnet to open connections to your SMTP port (TCP port 25). To get rid of that traffic as well, run

```
# iptables -A INPUT -s 192.168.34.0/24 -p tcp --destination-port 25 -j DROP
```

This example adds a netmask qualifier to the source address as well as -p tcp to specify TCP packets only. A further restriction, --destination-port 25, says that the rule should only apply to traffic to port 25. The IP table list for INPUT now looks like this:

```
Chain INPUT (policy ACCEPT)
target     prot opt source               destination
DROP       all  --  192.168.34.63        anywhere
DROP       tcp  --  192.168.34.0/24      anywhere            tcp dpt:smtp
```

All is well until you hear from someone you know at 192.168.34.37 saying that they can't send you email because you blocked their machine. Thinking that this is a quick fix, you run this command:

```
# iptables -A INPUT -s 192.168.34.37 -j ACCEPT
```

However, it doesn't work. To see why, look at the new chain:

```
Chain INPUT (policy ACCEPT)
target     prot opt source             destination
DROP       all  --  192.168.34.63      anywhere
DROP       tcp  --  192.168.34.0/24    anywhere            tcp dpt:smtp
ACCEPT     all  --  192.168.34.37      anywhere
```

The kernel reads the chain from top to bottom, using the first rule that matches.

The first rule does not match 192.168.34.37, but the second does, because it applies to all hosts from 192.168.34.1 to 192.168.34.254 and this second rule says to drop packets. When a rule matches, the kernel carries out the action and looks no further down in the chain. (You might notice that 192.168.34.37 can send packets to any port on your machine *except* port 25 because the second rule *only* applies to port 25.)

The solution is to move the third rule to the top. First, delete the third rule with this command:

```
# iptables -D INPUT 3
```

Then *insert* that rule at the top of the chain with `iptables -I`:

```
# iptables -I INPUT -s 192.168.34.37 -j ACCEPT
```

To insert a rule elsewhere in a chain, put the rule number after the chain name (for example, `iptables -I INPUT 4 ...`).

9.21.3   Firewall Strategies

Although the tutorial above showed you how to insert rules and how the kernel processes IP chains, we haven't seen firewall strategies that actually work. Let's talk about that now.

There are two basic kinds of firewall scenarios: one for protecting individual machines (where you set rules in each machine's INPUT chain) and one for protecting a network of machines (where you set rules in the router's FORWARD chain). In both cases, you can't have serious security if you use a default policy of ACCEPT and continuously insert rules to drop packets from sources that start to send bad stuff. You must allow only the packets that you trust and deny everything else.

For example, say your machine has an SSH server on TCP port 22. There's no reason for any random host to initiate a connection to any other port on your machine, and you shouldn't give any such host a chance. To set that up, first set the INPUT chain policy to DROP:

```
# iptables -P INPUT DROP
```

To enable ICMP traffic (for ping and other utilities), use this line:

```
# iptables -A INPUT -p icmp -j ACCEPT
```

Make sure that you can receive packets you send to both your own network IP address and 127.0.0.1 (localhost). Assuming your host's IP address is *my_addr*, do this:

```
# iptables -A INPUT -s 127.0.0.1 -j ACCEPT
# iptables -A INPUT -s my_addr -j ACCEPT
```

If you control your entire subnet (and trust everything on it), you can replace *my_addr* with your subnet address and subnet mask, for example, 10.23.2.0/24.

Now, although you still want to deny incoming TCP connections, you still need to make sure that your host can make TCP connections to the outside world. Because all TCP connections start with a SYN (connection request) packet, if you let all TCP packets through that aren't SYN packets, you're still okay:

```
# iptables -A INPUT -p tcp '!' --syn -j ACCEPT
```

Next, if you're using remote UDP-based DNS, you must accept traffic from your name server so that your machine can look up names with DNS. Do this for *all* DNS servers in */etc/resolv.conf.* Use this command (where the name server's address is *ns_addr*):

```
# iptables -A INPUT -p udp --source-port 53 -s ns_addr -j ACCEPT
```

And finally, allow SSH connections from anywhere:

```
# iptables -A INPUT -p tcp --destination-port 22 -j ACCEPT
```

The preceding iptables settings work for many situations, including any direct connection (especially broadband) where an intruder is much more likely to port-scan your machine. You could also adapt these settings for a firewalling router by using the FORWARD chain instead of INPUT and using source and destination subnets where appropriate. For more advanced configurations, you may find a configuration tool such as Shorewall to be helpful.

This discussion has only touched on security policy. Remember that the key idea is to permit only the things that you find acceptable, not to try to find and execute the bad stuff. Furthermore, IP firewalling is only one piece of the security picture. (You'll see more in the next chapter.)

9.22 Ethernet, IP, and ARP

There is one interesting basic detail in the implementation of IP over Ethernet that we have yet to cover. Recall that a host must place an IP packet inside an Ethernet frame in order to transmit the packet across the physical layer to another host. Recall, too, that frames themselves do not include IP address information; they use MAC (hardware) addresses. The question is this: When constructing the Ethernet frame for an IP packet, how does the host know which MAC address corresponds to the destination IP address?

We don't normally think about this question much because networking software includes an automatic system of looking up MAC addresses called *Address Resolution Protocol (ARP)*. A host using Ethernet as its physical layer and IP as the network layer maintains a small table called an *ARP cache* that maps IP addresses to MAC addresses. In Linux, the ARP cache is in the kernel. To view your machine's ARP cache, use the arp command. (As with many other network commands, the -n option here disables reverse DNS lookups.)

```
$ arp -n
Address          Hwtype  Hwaddr             Flags Mask      Iface
10.1.2.141       ether   00:11:32:0d:ca:82  C               eth0
10.1.2.1         ether   00:24:a5:b5:a0:11  C               eth0
10.1.2.50        ether   00:0c:41:f6:1c:99  C               eth0
```

When a machine boots, its ARP cache is empty. So how do these MAC addresses get in the cache? It all starts when the machine wants to send a packet to another host. If a target IP address is not in an ARP cache, the following steps occur:

1. The origin host creates a special Ethernet frame containing an ARP request packet for the MAC address that corresponds to the target IP address.

2. The origin host broadcasts this frame to the entire physical network for the target's subnet.

3. If one of the other hosts on the subnet knows the correct MAC address, it creates a reply packet and frame containing the address and sends it back to the origin. Often, the host that replies *is* the target host and is simply replying with its own MAC address.

4. The origin host adds the IP-MAC address pair to the ARP cache and can proceed.

NOTE   *Remember that ARP only applies to machines on local subnets (refer to Section 9.4 to see your local subnets). To reach destinations outside your subnet, your host sends the packet to the router, and it's someone else's problem after that. Of course, your host still needs to know the MAC address for the router, and it can use ARP to find it.*

The only real problem you can have with ARP is that your system's cache can get out-of-date if you're moving an IP address from one network interface card to another because the cards have different MAC addresses (for example, when testing a machine). Unix systems invalidate ARP cache entries if there's no activity after a while, so there shouldn't be any trouble other than a small delay for invalidated data, but you can delete an ARP cache entry immediately with this command:

```
# arp -d host
```

You can also view the ARP cache for a single network interface with

```
$ arp -i interface
```

The arp(8) manual page explains how to manually set ARP cache entries, but you shouldn't need to do this.

NOTE *Don't confuse ARP with Reverse Address Resolution Protocol (RARP). RARP transforms a MAC address back to a hostname or IP address. Before DHCP became popular, some diskless workstations and other devices used RARP to get their configuration, but RARP is rare today.*

9.23 Wireless Ethernet

In principle, wireless Ethernet ("WiFi") networks aren't much different from wired networks. Much like any wired hardware, they have MAC addresses and use Ethernet frames to transmit and receive data, and as a result the Linux kernel can talk to a wireless network interface much as it would a wired network interface. Everything at the network layer and above is the same; the main differences are additional components in the physical layer such as frequencies, network IDs, security, and so on.

Unlike wired network hardware, which is very good at automatically adjusting to nuances in the physical setup without much fuss, wireless network configuration is much more open-ended. To get a wireless interface working properly, Linux needs additional configuration tools.

Let's take a quick look at the additional components of wireless networks.

Transmission details These are physical characteristics, such as the radio frequency.

Network identification Because more than one wireless network can share the same basic medium, you have to be able to distinguish between them. The SSID (Service Set Identifier, also known as the "network name") is the wireless network identifier.

Management Although it's possible to configure wireless networking to have hosts talk directly to each other, most wireless networks are managed by one or more *access points* that all traffic goes through. Access points often bridge a wireless network with a wired network, making both appear as one single network.

Authentication You may want to restrict access to a wireless network. To do so, you can configure access points to require a password or other authentication key before they'll even talk to a client.

Encryption In addition to restricting the initial access to a wireless network, you normally want to encrypt all traffic that goes out across radio waves.

The Linux configuration and utilities that handle these components are spread out over a number of areas. Some are in the kernel: Linux features a set of wireless extensions that standardize user-space access to hardware. As far as user space goes, wireless configuration can get complicated, so most people prefer to use GUI frontends, such as the desktop applet for NetworkManager, to get things working. Still, it's worth looking at a few of the things happening behind the scenes.

9.23.1 iw

You can view and change kernel space device and network configuration with a utility called iw. To use iw, you normally need to know the network interface name for the device, such as *wlan0*. Here's an example that dumps a scan of available wireless networks. (Expect a lot of output if you're in an urban area.)

```
# iw dev wlan0 scan
```

NOTE *The network interface must be up for this command to work (if it's not, run* ifconfig *wlan0 up), but you don't need to configure any network layer parameters, such as an IP address.*

If the network interface has joined a wireless network, you can view the network details like this:

```
# iw dev wlan0 link
```

The MAC address in the output of this command is from the access point that you're currently talking to.

NOTE *The* iw *command distinguishes between physical device names such as* phy0 *and network interface names such as* wlan0 *and allows you to change various settings for each. You can even create more than one network interface for a single physical device. However, in nearly all basic cases, you'll just use the network interface name.*

Use iw to connect a network interface to an unsecured wireless network as follows:

```
# iw wlan0 connect network_name
```

Connecting to secured networks is a different story. For the rather insecure Wired Equivalent Privacy (WEP) system, you can use the keys parameter with the `iw connect` command. However, you shouldn't use WEP if you're serious about security.

9.23.2 Wireless Security

For most wireless security setups, Linux relies on a daemon called wpa_supplicant to manage both authentication and encryption for a wireless network interface. This daemon can handle both WPA (WiFi Protected Access) and WPA2 schemes of authentication, as well as nearly any kind of encryption technique used on wireless networks. When the daemon first starts, it reads a configuration file (by default, */etc/wpa_supplicant.conf*) and attempts to identify itself to an access point and establish communication based on a given network name. The system is well documented; in particular, the wpa_supplicant(1) and wpa_supplicant.conf(5) manual pages are very detailed.

Running the daemon by hand every time you want to establish a connection is a lot of work. In fact, just creating the configuration file is tedious due to the number of possible options. To make matters worse, all of the work of running iw and wpa_supplicant simply allows your system to join a wireless physical network; it doesn't even set up the network layer. And that's where automatic network configuration managers such as NetworkManager take a lot of pain out of the process. Although they don't do any of the work on their own, they know the correct sequence and required configuration for each step toward getting a wireless network operational.

9.24 Summary

You can now see that understanding the positions and roles of the various network layers is critical to understanding how Linux networking operates and how to perform network configuration. Although we've covered only the basics, more advanced topics in the physical, network, and transport layers bear similarities to what you've seen. Layers themselves are often subdivided, as you just saw with the various pieces of the physical layer in a wireless network.

A substantial amount of action that you've seen in this chapter happens in the kernel, with some basic user-space control utilities to manipulate the kernel's internal data structures (such as routing tables). This is the traditional way of working with the network. However, as with many of the topics discussed in this book, some tasks aren't suitable for the kernel due to their complexity and need for flexibility, and that's where user-space utilities take over. In particular, NetworkManager monitors and queries the kernel and then manipulates the kernel configuration. Another example is support for dynamic routing protocols such as Border Gateway Protocol (BGP), which is used in large Internet routers.

But you're probably a little bit bored with network configuration by now. Let's turn to *using* the network—the application layer.

10

NETWORK APPLICATIONS AND SERVICES

This chapter explores basic network applications—the clients and servers running in user space that reside at the application layer. Because this layer is at the top of the stack, close to end users, you may find this material more accessible than the material in Chapter 9. Indeed, you interact with network client applications such as web browsers and email readers every day.

To do their work, network clients connect to corresponding network servers. Unix network servers come in many forms. A server program can listen to a port on its own or through a secondary server. In addition, servers have no common configuration database and a wide variety of features. Most servers have a configuration file to control their behavior (though with no common format), and most use the operating system's syslog service for message logging. We'll look at some common servers as well as some tools that will help you understand and debug server operation.

Network clients use the operating system's transport layer protocols and interfaces, so understanding the basics of the TCP and UDP transport layers is important. Let's start looking at network applications by experimenting with a network client that uses TCP.

10.1   The Basics of Services

TCP services are among the easiest to understand because they are built upon simple, uninterrupted two-way data streams. Perhaps the best way to see how they work is to talk directly to a web server on TCP port 80 to get an idea of how data moves across the connection. For example, run the following command to connect to a web server:

```
$ telnet www.wikipedia.org 80
```

You should get a response like this:

```
Trying some address...
Connected to www.wikipedia.org.
Escape character is '^]'.
```

Now enter

```
GET / HTTP/1.0
```

Press ENTER twice. The server should send a bunch of HTML text as a response and then terminate the connection.

This exercise tells us that

- the remote host has a web server process listening on TCP port 80; and
- telnet was the client that initiated the connection.

NOTE   *telnet is a program originally meant to enable logins to remote hosts. Although the non-Kerberos telnet remote login server is completely insecure (as you will learn later), the telnet client can be useful for debugging remote services. telnet does not work with UDP or any transport layer other than TCP. If you're looking for a general-purpose network client, consider netcat, described in Section 10.5.3.*

10.1.1   A Closer Look

In the example above, you manually interacted with a web server on the network with telnet, using the Hypertext Transfer Protocol (HTTP) application layer protocol. Although you'd normally use a web browser to make this sort of connection, let's take just one step up from telnet and use a command-line program that knows how to speak to the HTTP application layer. We'll use the curl utility with a special option to record details about its communication:

```
$ curl --trace-ascii trace_file http://www.wikipedia.org/
```

Your distribution may not have the curl package preinstalled, but you should have no trouble installing it if necessary.

You'll get a lot of HTML output. Ignore it (or redirect it to */dev/null*) and instead look at the newly created file *trace_file*. Assuming that the connection was successful, the first part of the file should look something like the following, at the point where curl attempts to establish the TCP connection to the server:

```
== Info: About to connect() to www.wikipedia.org port 80 (#0)
== Info:    Trying 10.80.154.224... == Info: connected
```

Everything you've seen so far happens in the transport layer or below. However, if this connection succeeds, curl tries to send the request (the "header"); this is where the application layer starts:

```
=> Send header, 167 bytes (0xa7)
0000: GET / HTTP/1.1
0010: User-Agent: curl/7.22.0 (i686-pc-linux-gnu) libcurl/7.22.0 OpenS
0050: SL/1.0.1 zlib/1.2.3.4 libidn/1.23 librtmp/2.3
007f: Host: www.wikipedia.org
0098: Accept: */*
00a5:
```

The first line here is curl debugging output telling you what it will do next. The remaining lines show what curl sends to the server. The text in bold is what goes to the server; the hexadecimal numbers at the beginning are just debugging offsets from curl to help you keep track of how much data was sent or received.

You can see that curl starts by issuing a GET command to the server (as you did with telnet), followed by some extra information for the server and an empty line. Next, the server sends a reply, first with its own header, shown here in bold:

```
<= Recv header, 17 bytes (0x11)
0000: HTTP/1.1 200 OK
<= Recv header, 16 bytes (0x10)
0000: Server: Apache
<= Recv header, 42 bytes (0x2a)
0000: X-Powered-By: PHP/5.3.10-1ubuntu3.9+wmf1
--snip--
```

Much like the previous output, the <= lines are debugging output, and 0000: precedes the lines of output to tell you offsets.

The header in the server's reply can be fairly long, but at some point the server transitions from transmitting headers to sending the actual requested document, like this:

```
<= Recv header, 55 bytes (0x37)
0000: X-Cache: cp1055 hit (16), cp1054 frontend hit (22384)
```

```
<= Recv header, 2 bytes (0x2)
0000:
<= Recv data, 877 bytes (0x36d)
0000: 008000
0008: <!DOCTYPE html>.<html lang="mul" dir="ltr">.<head>.<!-- Sysops:
--snip--
```

This output also illustrates an important property of the application layer. Even though the debugging output says Recv header and Recv data, implying that those are two different kinds of messages from the server, there's no difference in the way that curl talked to the operating system to retrieve the two kinds of messages, nor any difference in how the operating system handled them, nor any difference in the way that the network handled the packets underneath. The difference is entirely within the user-space curl application itself. curl knew that until this point it had been getting headers, but when it received a blank line (the 2-byte chunk in the middle) signifying the end of headers in HTTP, it knew to interpret anything that followed as the requested document.

The same is true of the server sending this data. When sending the reply, the server didn't differentiate between header and document data sent to the operating system; the distinctions happen inside the user-space server program.

10.2   Network Servers

Most network servers are like other server daemons on your system such as cron, except that they interact with network ports. In fact, recall syslogd discussed in Chapter 7; it accepts UDP packets on port 514 when started with the -r option.

These are some other common network servers that you might find running on your system:

httpd, apache, apache2   Web servers

sshd   Secure shell daemon (see Section 10.3)

postfix, qmail, sendmail   Mail servers

cupsd   Print server

nfsd, mountd   Network filesystem (file-sharing) daemons

smbd, nmbd   Windows file-sharing daemons (see Chapter 12)

rpcbind   Remote procedure call (RPC) portmap service daemon

One feature common to most network servers is that they usually operate as multiple processes. At least one process listens on a network port, and when a new incoming connection is received, the listening process uses fork() to create a new child process, which is then responsible for the new connection. The child, often called a *worker* process, terminates when the connection is closed. Meanwhile, the original listening process continues to listen on the network port. This process allows a server to easily handle many connections without much trouble.

There are some exceptions to this model, however. Calling fork() adds a significant amount of system overhead. In comparison, high-performance TCP servers such as the Apache web server can create a number of worker processes upon startup so that they are already there to handle connections as needed. Servers that accept UDP packets simply receive data and react to it; they don't have connections to listen for.

10.3   Secure Shell (SSH)

Every server works a bit differently. Let's take a close look at one—the standalone SSH server. One of the most common network service applications is the secure shell (SSH), the de facto standard for remote access to a Unix machine. When configured, SSH allows secure shell logins, remote program execution, simple file sharing, and more—replacing the old, insecure telnet and rlogin remote-access systems with public-key cryptography for authentication and simpler ciphers for session data. Most ISPs and cloud providers require SSH for shell access to their services, and many Linux-based network appliances (such as NAS devices) allow access via SSH as well. OpenSSH (*http://www.openssh.com/*) is a popular free SSH implementation for Unix, and nearly all Linux distributions come with it preinstalled. The OpenSSH client is ssh, and the server is sshd. There are two main SSH protocol versions: 1 and 2. OpenSSH supports both, but version 1 is rarely used.

Among its many useful capabilities and features, SSH does the following:

- Encrypts your password and all other session data, protecting you from snoopers.
- Tunnels other network connections, including those from X Window System clients. You'll learn more about X in Chapter 14.
- Offers clients for nearly any operating system.
- Uses keys for host authentication.

NOTE   *Tunneling is the process of packaging and transporting one network connection using another one. The advantages of using SSH to tunnel X Window System connections are that SSH sets up the display environment for you and encrypts the X data inside the tunnel.*

SSH does have its disadvantages. For one, in order to set up an SSH connection, you need the remote host's public key, and you don't necessarily get it in a secure way (though you can check it manually to make sure you're not being spoofed). For an overview of how several methods of cryptography work, get your hands on the book *Applied Cryptography: Protocols, Algorithms, and Source Code in C*, 2nd edition, by Bruce Schneier (Wiley, 1996).

Two in-depth books on SSH are *SSH Mastery: OpenSSH, PuTTY, Tunnels and Keys* by Michael W. Lucas (Tilted Windmill Press, 2012) and *SSH, The Secure Shell*, 2nd edition, by Daniel J. Barrett, Richard E. Silverman, and Robert G. Byrnes (O'Reilly, 2005).

10.3.1 The SSHD Server

Running sshd requires a configuration file and host keys. Most distributions keep configurations in the */etc/ssh* configuration directory and try to configure everything properly for you if you install their sshd package. (The configuration filename *sshd_config* is easy to confuse with the client's *ssh_config* setup file, so be careful.)

You shouldn't need to change anything in *sshd_config*, but it never hurts to check. The file consists of keyword-value pairs, as shown in this fragment:

```
Port 22
#Protocol 2,1
#ListenAddress 0.0.0.0
#ListenAddress ::
HostKey /etc/ssh/ssh_host_key
HostKey /etc/ssh/ssh_host_rsa_key
HostKey /etc/ssh/ssh_host_dsa_key
```

Lines beginning with # are comments, and many comments in your *sshd_config* might indicate default values. The sshd_config(5) manual page contains descriptions of all possible values, but these are the most important ones:

HostKey *file* Uses *file* as a host key. (Host keys are described shortly.)

LogLevel *level* Logs messages with syslog level *level*.

PermitRootLogin *value* Permits the superuser to log in with SSH if *value* is set to yes. Set *value* to no to prevent this.

SyslogFacility *name* Logs messages with syslog facility *name*.

X11Forwarding *value* Enables X Window System client tunneling if *value* is set to yes.

XAuthLocation *path* Provides a path for xauth. X11 tunneling will not work without this path. If xauth isn't in */usr/bin*, set *path* to the full pathname for xauth.

Host Keys

OpenSSH has three host key sets: one for protocol version 1 and two for protocol 2. Each set has a *public key* (with a *.pub* file extension) and a *private key* (with no extension). Do not let anyone see your private key, even on your own system, because if someone obtains it, you're at risk from intruders.

SSH version 1 has RSA keys only, and SSH version 2 has RSA and DSA keys. RSA and DSA are public key cryptography algorithms. The key filenames are given in Table 10-1.

Table 10-1: OpenSSH Key Files

Filename	Key Type
ssh_host_rsa_key	Private RSA key (version 2)
ssh_host_rsa_key.pub	Public RSA key (version 2)
ssh_host_dsa_key	Private DSA key (version 2)
ssh_host_dsa_key.pub	Public DSA key (version 2)
ssh_host_key	Private RSA key (version 1)
ssh_host_key.pub	Public RSA key (version 1)

Normally you won't need to build the keys because the OpenSSH installation program or your distribution's installation script will do it for you, but you do need to know how to create keys if you plan to use programs like ssh-agent. To create SSH protocol version 2 keys, use the ssh-keygen program that comes with OpenSSH:

```
# ssh-keygen -t rsa -N '' -f /etc/ssh/ssh_host_rsa_key
# ssh-keygen -t dsa -N '' -f /etc/ssh/ssh_host_dsa_key
```

For the version 1 keys, use

```
# ssh-keygen -t rsa1 -N '' -f /etc/ssh/ssh_host_key
```

The SSH server and clients also use a key file called *ssh_known_hosts*, which contains public keys from other hosts. If you intend to use host-based authentication, the server's *ssh_known_hosts* file must contain the public host keys of all trusted clients. Knowing about the key files is handy if you're replacing a machine. When installing a new machine from scratch, you can import the key files from the old machine to ensure that users don't get key mismatches when connecting to the new one.

Starting the SSH Server

Although most distributions ship with SSH, they usually don't start the sshd server by default. On Ubuntu and Debian, installing the SSH server package creates the keys, starts the server, and adds the startup to the bootup configuration. On Fedora, sshd is installed by default but turned off. To start sshd at boot, use chkconfig like this (this won't start the server immediately; use service sshd start for that):

```
# chkconfig sshd on
```

Fedora normally creates any missing host key files upon the first sshd startup.

If you don't have any init support installed yet, running sshd as root starts the server, and upon startup, sshd writes its PID to */var/run/sshd.pid*.

You can also start sshd as a socket unit in systemd or with inetd, but it's usually not a good idea to do so because the server occasionally needs to generate key files, a process that can take a long time.

10.3.2 The SSH Client

To log in to a remote host, run

```
$ ssh remote_username@host
```

You may omit *remote_username@* if your local username is the same as on *host*. You can also run pipelines to and from an ssh command as shown in the following example, which copies a directory *dir* to another host:

```
$ tar zcvf - dir | ssh remote_host tar zxvf -
```

The global SSH client configuration file *ssh_config* should be in */etc/ssh* with your *sshd_config* file. As with the server configuration file, the client configuration file has key-value pairs, but you shouldn't need to change them.

The most frequent problem with using SSH clients occurs when an SSH public key in your local *ssh_known_hosts* or *.ssh/known_hosts* file does not match the key on the remote host. Bad keys cause errors or warnings like this:

```
@@@@@@@@@@@@@@@@@@@@@@@@@@@@@@@@@@@@@@@@@@@@@@@@@@@@@@@@@@@
@    WARNING: REMOTE HOST IDENTIFICATION HAS CHANGED!     @
@@@@@@@@@@@@@@@@@@@@@@@@@@@@@@@@@@@@@@@@@@@@@@@@@@@@@@@@@@@
IT IS POSSIBLE THAT SOMEONE IS DOING SOMETHING NASTY!
Someone could be eavesdropping on you right now (man-in-the-middle attack)!
It is also possible that the RSA host key has just been changed.
The fingerprint for the RSA key sent by the remote host is
38:c2:f6:0d:0d:49:d4:05:55:68:54:2a:2f:83:06:11.
Please contact your system administrator.
Add correct host key in /home/user/.ssh/known_hosts to get rid of this
message.
Offending key in /home/user/.ssh/known_hosts:12❶
RSA host key for host has changed and you have requested
strict checking.
Host key verification failed.
```

This usually just means that the remote host's administrator changed the keys (this often happens when replacing hardware), but it never hurts to check with the administrator if you're not sure. In any case, the preceding message tells you that the bad key is in line 12 of a user's *known_hosts* file, as shown at ❶.

If you don't suspect foul play, just remove the offending line or replace it with the correct public key.

SSH File Transfer Clients

OpenSSH includes the file transfer programs scp and sftp, which are intended as replacements for the older, insecure programs rcp and ftp.

You can use scp to transfer files to or from a remote machine to your machine or from one host to another. It works like the cp command. Here are a few examples:

```
$ scp user@host:file .
$ scp file user@host:dir
$ scp user1@host1:file user2@host2:dir
```

The sftp program works like the command-line ftp client, using get and put commands. The remote host must have an sftp-server program installed, which you can expect if the remote host also uses OpenSSH.

NOTE *If you need more features and flexibility than the offerings of scp and sftp (for example, if you're transferring large numbers of files often), have a look at rsync, described in Chapter 12.*

SSH Clients for Non-Unix Platforms

There are SSH clients for all popular operating systems, as listed on the OpenSSH web page (*http://www.openssh.com/*). Which one should you choose? PuTTY is a good, basic Windows client that includes a secure file-copy program. MacSSH works well for Mac OS 9.*x* and lower. Mac OS X is based on Unix and includes OpenSSH.

10.4 The inetd and xinetd Daemons

Implementing standalone servers for every service can be somewhat inefficient. Each server must be separately configured to handle port listening, access control, and port configuration. These actions are performed in the same way for most services; only when a server accepts a connection is there any difference in the way communication is handled.

One traditional way to simplify the use of servers is with the inetd daemon, a kind of *superserver* designed to standardize network port access and interfaces between server programs and network ports. After you start inetd, it reads its configuration file and then listens on the network ports defined in that file. As new network connections come in, inetd attaches a newly started process to the connection.

A newer version of inetd called xinetd offers easier configuration and better access control, but xinetd itself is being phased out in favor of systemd, which can provide the same functionality through socket units, as described in Section 6.4.7.

Although inetd is no longer commonly used, its configuration shows everything necessary to set up a service. As it turns out, sshd can also be invoked by inetd rather than as a standalone server, as shown in this */etc/inetd.conf* configuration file:

```
ident      stream   tcp   nowait   root   /usr/sbin/sshd   sshd -i
```

The seven fields here are, from left to right:

Service name   The service name from */etc/services* (see Section 9.14.3).

Socket type   This is usually `stream` for TCP and `dgram` for UDP.

Protocol   The transport protocol, usually `tcp` or `udp`.

Datagram server behavior   For UDP, this is `wait` or `nowait`. Services using any other transport protocol should use `nowait`.

User   The username to run the service. Add *.group* to set a group.

Executable   The program that `inetd` should connect to the service.

Arguments   The arguments for the executable. The first argument should be the name of the program.

10.4.1   TCP Wrappers: tcpd, /etc/hosts.allow, and /etc/hosts.deny

Before lower-level firewalls became popular, many administrators used the *TCP wrapper* library and daemon for host control over network services. In these implementations, `inetd` runs the `tcpd` program, which first looks at the incoming connection as well as the access control lists in the */etc/hosts.allow* and */etc/hosts.deny* files. The `tcpd` program logs the connection, and if it decides that the incoming connection is okay, it hands it to the final service program. (Although you may find a system that still uses the TCP wrapper system, we won't cover it in detail because it has largely fallen into disuse.)

10.5   Diagnostic Tools

Let's look at a few diagnostic tools that are useful for poking around the application layer. Some dig into the transport and network layers, because everything in the application layer eventually maps down to something in those lower layers.

As discussed in Chapter 9, `netstat` is a basic network service debugging tool that can display a number of transport and network layer statistics. Table 10-2 reviews a few useful options for viewing connections.

Table 10-2: Useful Connection-Reporting Options for netstat

Option	Description
-t	Prints TCP port information
-u	Prints UDP port information
-l	Prints listening ports
-a	Prints every active port
-n	Disables name lookups (speeds things up; also useful if DNS isn't working)

10.5.1   lsof

In Chapter 8, you learned that lsof can track open files, but it can also list the programs currently using or listening to ports. For a complete list of programs using or listening to ports, run

```
# lsof -i
```

When run as a regular user, this command only shows that user's processes. When run as root, the output should look something like this, displaying a variety of processes and users:

```
COMMAND      PID     USER    FD    TYPE   DEVICE SIZE/OFF NODE NAME
rpcbind      700     root    6u    IPv4    10492      0t0  UDP *:sunrpc
rpcbind      700     root    8u    IPv4    10508      0t0  TCP *:sunrpc (LISTEN)
avahi-dae    872    avahi   13u    IPv4 21736375      0t0  UDP *:mdns
cupsd       1010     root    9u    IPv6 42321174      0t0  TCP ip6-localhost:ipp (LISTEN)
ssh        14366    juser    3u    IPv4 38995911      0t0  TCP thishost.local:55457->
    somehost.example.com:ssh (ESTABLISHED)
chromium-  26534    juser    8r    IPv4 42525253      0t0  TCP thishost.local:41551->
    anotherhost.example.com:https (ESTABLISHED)
```

This example output shows users and process IDs for server and client programs, from the old-style RPC services at the top, to the multicast DNS service provided by avahi, and even an IPv6-ready printer service (cupsd). The last two entries show client connections: an SSH connection and a secure web connection from the Chromium web browser. Because the output can be extensive, it's usually best to apply a filter (as discussed in the following section).

The lsof program is like netstat in that it tries to reverse-resolve every IP address that it finds into a hostname, which slows down the output. Use the -n option to disable name resolution:

```
# lsof -n -i
```

You can also specify -P to disable */etc/services* port name lookups.

Filtering by Protocol and Port

If you're looking for a particular port (say, you know that a process is using a particular port and you want to know what that process is), use this command:

```
# lsof -i:port
```

The full syntax is as follows:

```
# lsof -iprotocol@host:port
```

The *protocol*, *@host*, and *:port* parameters are all optional and will filter the lsof output accordingly. As with most network utilities, *host* and *port* can be either names or numbers. For example, if you only want to see connections on TCP port 80 (the HTTP port), use

```
# lsof -iTCP:80
```

Filtering by Connection Status

One particularly handy lsof filter is connection status. For example, to show only the processes listening on TCP ports, enter

```
# lsof -iTCP -sTCP:LISTEN
```

This command gives you a good overview of the network server processes currently running on your system. However, because UDP servers don't listen and don't have connections, you'll have to use -iUDP to view running clients as well as servers. This usually isn't a problem, because you probably won't have many UDP servers on your system.

10.5.2   tcpdump

If you need to see exactly what's crossing your network, tcpdump puts your network interface card into *promiscuous mode* and reports on every packet that crosses the wire. Entering tcpdump with no arguments produces output like the following, which includes an ARP request and web connection:

```
# tcpdump
tcpdump: listening on eth0
20:36:25.771304 arp who-has mikado.example.com tell duplex.example.com
20:36:25.774729 arp reply mikado.example.com is-at 0:2:2d:b:ee:4e
20:36:25.774796 duplex.example.com.48455 > mikado.example.com.www: S
3200063165:3200063165(0) win 5840 <mss 1460,sackOK,timestamp 38815804[|tcp]>
(DF)
20:36:25.779283 mikado.example.com.www > duplex.example.com.48455: S
3494716463:3494716463(0) ack 3200063166 win 5792 <mss 1460,sackOK,timestamp
4620[|tcp]> (DF)
20:36:25.779409 duplex.example.com.48455 > mikado.example.com.www: . ack 1 win
5840 <nop,nop,timestamp 38815805 4620> (DF)
20:36:25.779787 duplex.example.com.48455 > mikado.example.com.www: P 1:427(426)
ack 1 win 5840 <nop,nop,timestamp 38815805 4620> (DF)
20:36:25.784012 mikado.example.com.www > duplex.example.com.48455: . ack 427
win 6432 <nop,nop,timestamp 4620 38815805> (DF)
20:36:25.845645 mikado.example.com.www > duplex.example.com.48455: P 1:773(772)
ack 427 win 6432 <nop,nop,timestamp 4626 38815805> (DF)
20:36:25.845732 duplex.example.com.48455 > mikado.example.com.www: . ack 773
win 6948 <nop,nop,timestamp 38815812 4626> (DF)

9 packets received by filter
0 packets dropped by kernel
```

You can tell tcpdump to be more specific by adding filters. You can filter based on source and destination hosts, networks, Ethernet addresses, protocols at many different layers in the network model, and much more. Among the many packet protocols that tcpdump recognizes are ARP, RARP, ICMP, TCP, UDP, IP, IPv6, AppleTalk, and IPX packets. For example, to tell tcpdump to output only TCP packets, run

```
# tcpdump tcp
```

To see web packets and UDP packets, enter

```
# tcpdump udp or port 80
```

NOTE *If you need to do a lot of packet sniffing, consider using a GUI alternative to tcpdump such as Wireshark.*

Primitives

In the preceding examples, tcp, udp, and port 80 are called *primitives*. The most important primitives are in Table 10-3:

Table 10-3: tcpdump Primitives

Primitive	Packet Specification
tcp	TCP packets
udp	UDP packets
port *port*	TCP and/or UDP packets to/from port *port*
host *host*	Packets to or from *host*
net *network*	Packets to or from *network*

Operators

The or used in the previous example is an *operator*. tcpdump can use multiple operators (such as and and !), and you can group operators in parentheses. If you plan to do any serious work with tcpdump, make sure to read the manual page, especially the section that describes the primitives.

When Not to Use tcpdump

Be very careful when using tcpdump. The tcpdump output shown earlier in this section includes only packet TCP (transport layer) and IP (Internet layer) header information, but you can also make tcpdump print the entire packet contents. Even though many network operators make it far too easy to look at their network packets, you shouldn't snoop around on networks unless you own them.

10.5.3   *netcat*

If you need more flexibility in connecting to a remote host than a command like telnet *host port* allows, use netcat (or nc). netcat can connect to remote

TCP/UDP ports, specify a local port, listen on ports, scan ports, redirect standard I/O to and from network connections, and more. To open a TCP connection to a port with netcat, run

```
$ netcat host port
```

netcat only terminates when the other side of the connection ends the connection, which can confuse things if you redirect standard input to netcat. You can end the connection at any time by pressing CTRL-C. (If you'd like the program and network connection to terminate based on the standard input stream, try the sock program instead.)

To listen on a particular port, run

```
$ netcat -l -p port_number
```

10.5.4   Port Scanning

Sometimes you don't even know what services the machines on your networks are offering or even which IP addresses are in use. The Network Mapper (Nmap) program scans all ports on a machine or network of machines looking for open ports, and it lists the ports it finds. Most distributions have an Nmap package, or you can get it at *http://www.insecure.org/*. (See the Nmap manual page and online resources for all that Nmap can do.)

When listing ports on your own machine, it often helps to run the Nmap scan from at least two points: from your own machine and from another one (possibly outside your local network). Doing so will give you an overview of what your firewall is blocking.

WARNING *If someone else controls the network that you want to scan with Nmap, ask for permission. Network administrators watch for port scans and usually disable access to machines that run them.*

Run **nmap** *host* to run a generic scan on a host. For example:

```
$ nmap 10.1.2.2
Starting Nmap 5.21 ( http://nmap.org ) at 2015-09-21 16:51 PST
Nmap scan report for 10.1.2.2
Host is up (0.00027s latency).
Not shown: 993 closed ports
PORT      STATE SERVICE
22/tcp    open  ssh
25/tcp    open  smtp
80/tcp    open  http
111/tcp   open  rpcbind
8800/tcp  open  unknown
9000/tcp  open  cslistener
9090/tcp  open  zeus-admin

Nmap done: 1 IP address (1 host up) scanned in 0.12 seconds
```

As you can see, a number of services are open here, many of which are not enabled by default on most distributions. In fact, the only one here that's usually on by default is port 111, the rpcbind port.

10.6   Remote Procedure Call (RPC)

What about the rpcbind service that you just saw in the scan in the preceding section? RPC stands for *remote procedure call*, a system residing in the lower parts of the application layer. It's designed to make it easier for programmers to access network applications by leveraging the fact that programs call functions on remote programs (identified by program numbers) and the remote programs return a result code or message.

RPC implementations use transport protocols such as TCP and UDP, and they require a special intermediary service to map program numbers to TCP and UDP ports. The server is called rpcbind, and it must be running on any machine that wants to use RPC services.

To see what RPC services your computer has, run

```
$ rpcinfo -p localhost
```

RPC is one of those protocols that just doesn't want to die. The Network File System (NFS) and Network Information Service (NIS) systems use RPC, but they are completely unnecessary on standalone machines. But whenever you think that you've eliminated all need for rpcbind, something else comes up, such as File Access Monitor (FAM) support in GNOME.

10.7   Network Security

Because Linux is a very popular Unix flavor on the PC platform, and especially because it is widely used for web servers, it attracts many unpleasant characters who try to break into computer systems. Section 9.21 discussed firewalls, but that's not really the whole story on security.

Network security attracts extremists—those who *really* like to break into systems (whether for fun or money) and those who come up with elaborate protection schemes who *really* like to swat away people trying to break into their systems. (This, too, can be very profitable.) Fortunately, you don't need to know very much to keep your system safe. Here are a few basic rules of thumb:

Run as few services as possible   Intruders can't break into services that don't exist on your system. If you know what a service is and you're not using it, don't turn it on for the sole reason that you might want to use it "at some later point."

Block as much as possible with a firewall   Unix systems have a number of internal services that you may not know about (such as TCP port 111 for the RPC port-mapping server), and no other system in the world *should* know about them. It can be very difficult to track and regulate the services on your system because many different kinds of programs listen on various ports. To keep intruders from discovering internal services on your system, use effective firewall rules, and install a firewall at your router.

Track the services that you offer to the Internet   If you run an SSH server, Postfix, or similar services, keep your software up-to-date and get appropriate security alerts. (See Section 10.7.2 for some online resources.)

Use "long-term support" distribution releases for servers   Security teams normally concentrate their work on stable, supported distribution releases. Development and testing releases such Debian Unstable and Fedora Rawhide receive much less attention.

Don't give an account on your system to anyone who doesn't need one   It's much easier to gain superuser access from a local account than it is to break in remotely. In fact, given the huge base of software (and the resulting bugs and design flaws) available on most systems, it can be easy to gain superuser access to a system after you get to a shell prompt. Don't assume that your friends know how to protect their passwords (or choose good passwords in the first place).

Avoid installing dubious binary packages   They can contain Trojan horses.

That's the practical end of protecting yourself. But why is it important to do so? There are three basic kinds of network attacks:

Full compromise   This means getting superuser access (full control) of a machine. An intruder can accomplish this by trying a service attack, such as a buffer overflow exploit, or by taking over a poorly protected user account and then trying to exploit a poorly written setuid program.

Denial-of-service (DoS) attack   This prevents a machine from carrying out its network services or forces a computer to malfunction in some other way without the use of any special access. These attacks are harder to prevent, but they are easier to respond to.

Malware   Linux users are mostly immune to malware such as email worms and viruses, simply because their email clients aren't stupid enough to actually run programs that they get in message attachments. But Linux malware does exist. Avoid downloading and installing binary software from places that you've never heard of.

10.7.1   Typical Vulnerabilities

There are two important kinds of vulnerabilities to worry about: direct attacks and clear-text password sniffing. Direct attacks try to take over a machine without being terribly subtle. The most common is a buffer overflow exploit, where a careless programmer doesn't check the bounds of a buffer array. The attacker fabricates a stack frame inside a huge chunk of data, dumps it to the remote server, and then hopes that the server overwrites its program data and eventually executes the new stack frame. Although a somewhat complicated attack, it's easy to replicate.

A second attack to worry about is one that captures passwords sent across the wire as clear text. As soon as an attacker gets your password, it's game over. From there, the assailant will inevitably try to gain superuser access locally (which is much easier than making a remote attack), try to use the machine as an intermediary for attacking other hosts, or both.

NOTE *If you have a service that offers no native support for encryption, try Stunnel (*http://www.stunnel.org/*), an encryption wrapper package much like TCP wrappers. Like* tcpd, *Stunnel is especially good at wrapping* inetd *services.*

Some services are chronic attack targets due to poor implementation and design. You should always deactivate the following services (they're rarely activated by default on most systems):

ftpd For whatever reason, all FTP servers seem plagued with vulnerabilities. In addition, most FTP servers use clear-text passwords. If you have to move files from one machine to another, consider an SSH-based solution or an rsync server.

telnetd, rlogind, rexecd All of these pass remote session data (including passwords) in clear-text form. Avoid them unless you happen to have a Kerberos-enabled version.

fingerd Intruders can get user lists and other information with the finger service.

10.7.2   Security Resources

Here are three good security sites:

http://www.sans.org/   Offers training, services, a free weekly newsletter listing the top current vulnerabilities, sample security policies, and more.

http://www.cert.org/   A place to look for the most severe problems.

http://www.insecure.org/   This is the place to go for Nmap and pointers to all sorts of network exploit-testing tools. It's much more open and specific about exploits than are many other sites.

If you're interested in network security, you should learn all about Transport Layer Security (TLS) and its predecessor, Secure Socket Layer (SSL). These user-space network levels are typically added to networking clients and servers to support network transactions through the use of public-key encryption and certificates. A good guide is Davies's *Implementing SSL/TLS Using Cryptography and PKI* (Wiley, 2011).

10.8   Looking Forward

If you're interested in getting your hands dirty with some complicated network servers, two very common ones are the Apache web server and the Postfix email server. In particular, Apache is easy to install and most distributions supply a package. If your machine is behind a firewall or NAT-enabled router, you can experiment with the configuration as much as you'd like without worrying about security.

Throughout the last few chapters, we've been gradually moving from kernel space into user space. Only a few utilities discussed in this chapter, such as tcpdump, interact with the kernel. The remainder of this chapter describes how sockets bridge the gap between the kernel's transport layer and the user-space application layer. It's more advanced material, of particular interest to programmers, so feel free to skip to the next chapter if you like.

10.9 Sockets: How Processes Communicate with the Network

We're now going to shift gears a little and look at how processes do the work of reading data from and writing data to the network. It's easy enough for processes to read from and write to network connections that are already set up: All you need are some system calls, which you can read about in the recv(2) and send(2) manual pages. From the point of view of a process, perhaps the most important thing to know is how to refer to the network when using these system calls. On Unix systems, a process uses a *socket* to identify when and how it's talking to the network. Sockets are the interface that processes use to access the network through the kernel; they represent the boundary between user space and kernel space. They're often also used for interprocess communication (IPC).

There are different types of sockets because processes need to access the network in different ways. For example, TCP connections are represented by stream sockets (SOCK_STREAM, from a programmer's point of view), and UDP connections are represented by datagram sockets (SOCK_DGRAM).

Setting up a network socket can be somewhat complicated because you need to account for socket type, IP addresses, ports, and transport protocol at particular times. However, after all of the initial details are sorted out, servers use certain standard methods to deal with incoming traffic from the network.

The flowchart in Figure 10-1 shows how many servers handle connections for incoming stream sockets. Notice that this type of server involves two kinds of sockets: a listening socket and a socket for reading and writing. The master process uses the listening socket to look for connections from the network. When a new connection comes in, the master process uses the accept() system call to accept the connection, which creates the read/write socket dedicated to that one connection. Next, the master process uses fork() to create a new child process to deal with the connection. Finally, the original socket remains the listener and continues to look for more connections on behalf of the master process.

After a process has set up a socket of a particular type, it can interact with it in a way that fits the socket type. This is what makes sockets flexible: If you need to change the underlying transport layer, you don't have to rewrite all of the parts that send and receive data; you mostly need to modify the initialization code.

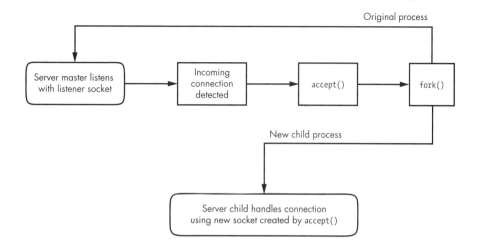

Figure 10-1: One method for accepting and processing incoming connections

If you're a programmer and you'd like to learn how to use the socket interface, *Unix Network Programming, Volume 1*, 3rd edition, by W. Richard Stephens, Bill Fenner, and Andrew M. Rudoff (Addison-Wesley Professional, 2003) is the classic guide. Volume 2 also covers interprocess communication.

10.10   Unix Domain Sockets

Applications that use network facilities don't have to involve two separate hosts. Many applications are built as client-server or peer-to-peer mechanisms, where processes running the same machine use interprocess communication (IPC) to negotiate what work needs to be done and who does it. For example, recall that daemons such as systemd and NetworkManager use D-Bus to monitor and react to system events.

Processes can use regular IP networking over localhost (127.0.0.1) to communicate, but instead, typically use a special kind of socket, which we briefly touched upon in Chapter 3, called a *Unix domain socket*. When a process connects to a Unix domain socket, it behaves almost exactly like a network socket: It can listen for and accept connections on the socket, and you can even choose between different kinds of socket types to make it behave like TCP or UDP.

NOTE   *It's important to remember that a Unix domain socket is not a network socket, and there's no network behind one. You don't even need networking to be configured to use one. And Unix domain sockets don't have to be bound to socket files. A process can create an unnamed Unix domain socket and share the address with another process.*

10.10.1   *Advantages for Developers*

Developers like Unix domain sockets for IPC for two reasons. First, they allow developers the option to use special socket files in the filesystem to control access, so any process that doesn't have access to a socket file can't use it. And because there's no interaction with the network, it's simpler and less prone to conventional network intrusion. For example, you'll usually find the socket file for D-Bus in */var/run/dbus*:

```
$ ls -l /var/run/dbus/system_bus_socket
srwxrwxrwx 1 root root 0 Nov  9 08:52 /var/run/dbus/system_bus_socket
```

Second, because the Linux kernel does not have to go through the many layers of its networking subsystem when working with Unix domain sockets, performance tends to be much better.

Writing code for Unix domain sockets is not much different from supporting normal network sockets. Because the benefits can be significant, some network servers offer communication through both network and Unix domain sockets. For example, the MySQL database server mysqld can accept client connections from remote hosts, but it usually also offers a Unix domain socket at */var/run/mysqld/mysqld.sock*.

10.10.2   Listing Unix Domain Sockets

You can view a list of Unix domain sockets currently in use on your system with lsof -U: *eg   lsof -U | grep python3   or 1*

```
# lsof -U
COMMAND      PID     USER   FD   TYPE     DEVICE SIZE/OFF     NODE NAME
mysqld     19701    mysql   12u  unix 0xe4defcc0      0t0 35201227 /var/run/mysqld/mysqld.sock
chromium-  26534    juser    5u  unix 0xeeac9b00      0t0 42445141 socket
tlsmgr     30480  postfix    5u  unix 0xc3384240      0t0 17009106 socket
tlsmgr     30480  postfix    6u  unix 0xe20161c0      0t0    10965 private/tlsmgr
--snip--
```

The listing will be quite long because many modern applications make extensive use of unnamed sockets. You can identify the unnamed ones because you'll see socket in the NAME output column.

1   lsof -U | cut -f1 -d'u' | sort -u | less

11

INTRODUCTION TO SHELL SCRIPTS

If you can enter commands into the shell, you can write shell scripts (also known as Bourne shell scripts). A *shell script* is a series of commands written in a file; the shell reads the commands from the file just as it would if you typed them into a terminal.

11.1 Shell Script Basics

Bourne shell scripts generally start with the following line, which indicates that the /bin/sh program should execute the commands in the script file. (Make sure that no whitespace appears at the beginning of the script file.)

```
#!/bin/sh
```

The #! part is called a *shebang*; you'll see it in other scripts in this book. You can list any commands that you want the shell to execute following the #!/bin/sh line. For example:

```
#!/bin/sh
#
# Print something, then run ls

echo About to run the ls command.
ls
```

NOTE   *A # character at the beginning of a line indicates that the line is a comment; that is, the shell ignores anything on a line after a #. Use comments to explain parts of your scripts that are difficult to understand.*

After creating a shell script and setting its permissions, you can run it by placing the script file in one of the directories in your command path and then running the script name on the command line. You can also run ./script if the script is located in your current working directory, or you can use the full pathname.

As with any program on Unix systems, you need to set the executable bit for a shell script file, but you must also set the read bit in order for the shell to read the file. The easiest way to do this is as follows:

```
$ chmod +rx script
```

This chmod command allows other users to read and execute *script*. If you don't want that, use the absolute mode 700 instead (and refer to Section 2.17 for a refresher on permissions).

With the basics behind us, let's look at some of the limitations of shell scripts.

11.1.1   Limitations of Shell Scripts

The Bourne shell manipulates commands and files with relative ease. In Section 2.14, you saw the way the shell can redirect output, one of the important elements of shell script programming. However, the shell script is only one tool for Unix programming, and although scripts have considerable power, they also have limitations.

One of the main strengths of shell scripts is that they can simplify and automate tasks that you can otherwise perform at the shell prompt, like manipulating batches of files. But if you're trying to pick apart strings, perform repeated arithmetic computations, or access complex databases, or if you want functions and complex control structures, you're better off using a scripting language like Python, Perl, or awk, or perhaps even a compiled language like C. (This is important, so we'll repeat it throughout the chapter.)

Finally, be aware of your shell script sizes. Keep your shell scripts short. Bourne shell scripts aren't meant to be big (though you will undoubtedly encounter some monstrosities)

11.2 Quoting and Literals

One of the most confusing elements of working with the shell and scripts is when to use quotation marks (or *quotes*) and other punctuation, and why it's sometimes necessary to do so. Let's say you want to print the string $100 and you do the following:

```
$ echo $100
00
```

Why did this print 00? Because the shell saw $1, which is a shell variable (we'll cover it soon). So you might think that if you surround it with double quotes, the shell will leave the $1 alone. But it still doesn't work:

```
$ echo "$100"
00
```

Then you ask a friend, who says that you need to use single quotes instead:

```
$ echo '$100'
$100
```

Why did this particular incantation work?

11.2.1   Literals

When you use quotes, you're often trying to create a *literal,* a string that you want the shell to pass to the command line untouched. In addition to the $ in the example that you just saw, other similar circumstances include when you want to pass a * character to a command such as grep instead of having the shell expand it, and when you need to need to use a semicolon (;) in a command.

When writing scripts and working on the command line, just remember what happens whenever the shell runs a command:

1. Before running the command, the shell looks for variables, globs, and other substitutions and performs the substitutions if they appear.

2. The shell passes the results of the substitutions to the command.

Problems involving literals can be subtle. Let's say you're looking for all entries in */etc/passwd* that match the regular expression r.*t (that is, a line that contains an r followed by a t later in the line, which would enable you to search for usernames such as root and ruth and robot). You can run this command:

```
$ grep r.*t /etc/passwd
```

It works most of the time, but sometimes it mysteriously fails. Why? The answer is probably in your current directory. If that directory contains files with names such as *r.input* and *r.output*, then the shell expands r.*t to r.input r.output and creates this command:

```
$ grep r.input r.output /etc/passwd
```

The key to avoiding problems like this is to first recognize the characters that can get you in trouble and then apply the correct kind of quotes to protect the characters.

11.2.2   Single Quotes

The easiest way to create a literal and make the shell leave a string alone is to enclose the entire string in single quotes, as in this example with grep and the * character:

```
$ grep 'r.*t' /etc/passwd
```

As far as the shell is concerned, all characters between the two single quotes, including spaces, make up a single parameter. Therefore, the following command does *not* work, because it asks the grep command to search for the string r.*t /etc/passwd in the standard input (because there's only one parameter to grep):

```
$ grep 'r.*t /etc/passwd'
```

When you need to use a literal, you should always turn to single quotes first, because you're guaranteed that the shell won't try *any* substitutions. As a result, it's a generally clean syntax. However, sometimes you need a little more flexibility, so you can turn to double quotes.

11.2.3   Double Quotes

Double quotes (") work just like single quotes, except that the shell expands any variables that appear within double quotes. You can see the difference by running the following command and then replacing the double quotes with single quotes and running it again.

```
$ echo "There is no * in my path: $PATH"
```

When you run the command, notice that the shell substitutes for $PATH but does not substitute for the *.

NOTE   *If you're using double quotes when printing large amounts of text, consider using a here document, as described in Section 11.9.*

11.2.4   Passing a Literal Single Quote

One tricky part to using literals with the Bourne shell comes when passing a literal single quote to a command. One way to do this is to place a backslash before the single quote character:

```
$ echo I don\'t like contractions inside shell scripts.
```

The backslash and quote *must* appear outside any pair of single quotes, and a string such as 'don\'t results in a syntax error. Oddly enough, you can enclose the single quote inside double quotes, as shown in the following example (the output is identical to that of the preceding command):

```
$ echo "I don't like contractions inside shell scripts."
```

If you're in a bind and you need a general rule to quote an entire string with no substitutions, follow this procedure:

1. Change all instances of ' (single quote) to '\'' (single quote, backslash, single quote, single quote).
2. Enclose the entire string in single quotes.

Therefore, you can quote an awkward string such as this isn't a forward slash: \ as follows:

```
$ echo 'this isn'\''t a forward slash: \'
```

NOTE   *It's worth repeating that when you quote a string, the shell treats everything inside the quotes as a single parameter. Therefore, a b c counts as three parameters, but a "b c" is only two.*

11.3   Special Variables

Most shell scripts understand command-line parameters and interact with the commands that they run. To take your scripts from being just a simple list of commands to becoming more flexible shell script programs, you need to know how to use the special Bourne shell variables. These special variables are like any other shell variable as described in Section 2.8, except that you cannot change the values of certain ones.

NOTE   *After reading the next few sections, you'll understand why shell scripts accumulate many special characters as they are written. If you're trying to understand a shell script and you come across a line that looks completely incomprehensible, pick it apart piece by piece.*

11.3.1 Individual Arguments: $1, $2, ...

$1, $2, and all variables named as positive nonzero integers contain the values of the script parameters, or arguments. For example, say the name of the following script is *pshow*:

```
#!/bin/sh
echo First argument: $1
echo Third argument: $3
```

Try running the script as follows to see how it prints the arguments:

```
$ ./pshow one two three
First argument: one
Third argument: three
```

The built-in shell command `shift` can be used with argument variables to remove the first argument ($1) and advance the rest of the arguments forward. Specifically, $2 becomes $1, $3 becomes $2, and so on. For example, assume that the name of the following script is *shiftex*:

```
#!/bin/sh
echo Argument: $1
shift
echo Argument: $1
shift
echo Argument: $1
```

Run it like this to see it work:

```
$ ./shiftex one two three
Argument: one
Argument: two
Argument: three
```

As you can see, `shiftex` prints all three arguments by printing the first, shifting the remaining arguments, and repeating.

11.3.2 Number of Arguments: $#

The $# variable holds the number of arguments passed to a script and is especially important when running `shift` in a loop to pick through arguments. When $# is 0, no arguments remain, so $1 is empty. (See Section 11.6 for a description of loops.)

11.3.3 All Arguments: $@

The $@ variable represents all of a script's arguments, and it is very useful for passing them to a command inside the script. For example, Ghostscript commands (gs) are usually long and complicated. Suppose you want a shortcut for rasterizing a PostScript file at 150 dpi, using the standard output stream, while also leaving the door open for passing other options to gs. You could write a script like this to allow for additional command-line options:

```
#!/bin/sh
gs -q -dBATCH -dNOPAUSE -dSAFER -sOutputFile=- -sDEVICE=pnmraw $@
```

NOTE   *If a line in your shell script gets too long for your text editor, you can split it up with a backslash (\). For example, you can alter the preceding script as follows:*

```
#!/bin/sh
gs -q -dBATCH -dNOPAUSE -dSAFER \
    -sOutputFile=- -sDEVICE=pnmraw $@
```

11.3.4   Script Name: $0

The $0 variable holds the name of the script, and it is useful for generating diagnostic messages. For example, say your script needs to report an invalid argument that is stored in the $BADPARM variable. You can print the diagnostic message with the following line so that the script name appears in the error message:

```
echo $0: bad option $BADPARM
```

All diagnostic error messages should go to the standard error. Recall from Section 2.14.1 that 2>&1 redirects the standard error to the standard output. For writing to the standard error, you can reverse the process with 1>&2. To do this for the preceding example, use this:

```
echo $0: bad option $BADPARM 1>&2
```

11.3.5   Process ID: $$

The $$ variable holds the process ID of the shell.

11.3.6   Exit Code: $?

The $? variable holds the exit code of the last command that the shell executed. Exit codes, which are critical to mastering shell scripts, are discussed next.

11.4   Exit Codes

When a Unix program finishes, it leaves an *exit code* for the parent process that started the program. The exit code is a number and is sometimes called an *error code* or *exit value*. When the exit code is zero (0), it typically means that the program ran without a problem. However, if the program has an error, it usually exits with a number other than 0 (but not always, as you'll see next).

The shell holds the exit code of the last command in the $? special variable, so you can check it out at your shell prompt:

```
$ ls / > /dev/null
$ echo $?
0
$ ls /asdfasdf > /dev/null
ls: /asdfasdf: No such file or directory
$ echo $?
1
```

You can see that the successful command returned 0 and the unsuccessful command returned 1 (assuming, of course, that you don't have a directory named */asdfasdf* on your system).

If you intend to use the exit code of a command, you *must* use or store the code immediately after running the command. For example, if you run echo $? twice in a row, the output of the second command is always 0 because the first echo command completes successfully.

When writing shell code that aborts a script abnormally, use something like exit 1 to pass an exit code of 1 back to whatever parent process ran the script. (You may want to use different numbers for different conditions.)

One thing to note is that some programs like diff and grep use nonzero exit codes to indicate normal conditions. For example, grep returns 0 if it finds something matching a pattern and 1 if it doesn't. For these programs, an exit code of 1 is not an error; grep and diff use the exit code 2 for real problems. If you think a program is using a nonzero exit code to indicate success, read its manual page. The exit codes are usually explained in the EXIT VALUE or DIAGNOSTICS section.

11.5 Conditionals

The Bourne shell has special constructs for conditionals, such as if/then/ else and case statements. For example, this simple script with an if conditional checks to see whether the script's first argument is hi:

```
#!/bin/sh
if [ $1 = hi ]; then
    echo 'The first argument was "hi"'
else
    echo -n 'The first argument was not "hi" -- '
    echo It was '"'"$1'"'
fi
```

The words if, then, else, and fi in the preceding script are shell keywords; everything else is a command. This distinction is extremely important because one of the commands is [$1 = "hi"] and the [character is an actual program on a Unix system, *not* special shell syntax. (This is actually not quite true, as you'll soon learn, but treat it as a separate command in your head for now.) All Unix systems have a command called [that performs tests for shell script conditionals. This program is also known as test and careful examination of [and test should reveal that they share an inode, or that one is a symbolic link to the other.

Understanding the exit codes in Section 11.4 is vital, because this is how the whole process works:

1. The shell runs the command after the if keyword and collects the exit code of that command.

2. If the exit code is 0, the shell executes the commands that follow the then keyword, stopping when it reaches an else or fi keyword.

3. If the exit code is not 0 and there is an else clause, the shell runs the commands after the else keyword.

4. The conditional ends at fi.

11.5.1   Getting Around Empty Parameter Lists

There is a slight problem with the conditional in the preceding example due to a very common mistake: $1 could be empty, because the user might not enter a parameter. Without a parameter, the test reads [= hi], and the [command aborts with an error. You can fix this by enclosing the parameter in quotes in one of two ways (both of which are common):

```
if [ "$1" = hi ]; then
if [ x"$1" = x"hi" ]; then
```

11.5.2   Using Other Commands for Tests

The stuff following if is always a command. Therefore, if you want to put the then keyword on the same line, you need a semicolon (;) after the test command. If you skip the semicolon, the shell passes then as a parameter to the test command. (If you don't like the semicolon, you can put the then keyword on a separate line.)

There are many possibilities for using other commands instead of the [command. Here's an example that uses grep:

```
#!/bin/sh
if grep -q daemon /etc/passwd; then
    echo The daemon user is in the passwd file.
else
    echo There is a big problem. daemon is not in the passwd file.
fi
```

11.5.3 elif

There is also an elif keyword that lets you string if conditionals together, as shown below. But don't get too carried away with elif, because the case construct that you'll see in Section 11.5.6 is often more appropriate.

```
#!/bin/sh
if [ "$1" = "hi" ]; then
    echo 'The first argument was "hi"'
elif [ "$2" = "bye" ]; then
    echo 'The second argument was "bye"'
else
    echo -n 'The first argument was not "hi" and the second was not "bye"-- '
    echo They were '"'"$1'"'"' and '"'"$2'"'"'
fi
```

11.5.4 && and || Logical Constructs

There are two quick one-line conditional constructs that you may see from time to time: && ("and") and || ("or"). The && construct works like this:

```
command1 && command2
```

Here, the shell runs *command1*, and if the exit code is 0, the shell also runs *command2*. The || construct is similar; if the command before a || returns a nonzero exit code, the shell runs the second command.

The constructs && and || often find their way into use in if tests, and in both cases, the exit code of the last command run determines how the shell processes the conditional. In the case of the && construct, if the first command fails, the shell uses its exit code for the if statement, but if the first command succeeds, the shell uses the exit code of the second command for the conditional. In the case of the || construct, the shell uses the exit code of the first command if successful, or the exit code of the second if the first is unsuccessful.

For example:

```
#!/bin/sh
if [ "$1" = hi ] || [ "$1" = bye ]; then
    echo 'The first argument was "'$1'"'
fi
```

If your conditionals include the test ([) command, as shown here, you can use -a and -o instead of && and ||, as described in the next section.

11.5.5 Testing Conditions

You've seen how [works: The exit code is 0 if the test is true and nonzero when the test fails. You also know how to test string equality with [*str1* = *str2*]. However, remember that shell scripts are well suited to operations on entire files because the most useful [tests involve file properties. For example, the following line checks whether *file* is a regular file (not a directory or special file):

```
[ -f file ]
```

In a script, you might see the -f test in a loop similar to this next one, which tests all of the items in the current working directory (you'll learn more about loops in general shortly):

```
for filename in *; do
    if [ -f $filename ]; then
        ls -l $filename
        file $filename
    else
        echo $filename is not a regular file.
    fi
done
```

You can invert a test by placing the ! operator before the test arguments. For example, [! -f *file*] returns true if *file* is not a regular file. Furthermore, the -a and -o flags are the logical "and" and "or" operators (for example, [-f *file1* -a *file2*]).

NOTE   *Because the* test *command is so widely used in scripts, many versions of the Bourne shell (including bash) incorporate the* test *command as a built-in. This can speed up scripts because the shell doesn't have to run a separate command for each test.*

There are dozens of test operations, all of which fall into three general categories: file tests, string tests, and arithmetic tests. The info manual contains complete online documentation, but the test(1) manual page is a fast reference. The following sections outline the main tests. (I've omitted some of the less common ones.)

File Tests

Most file tests, like -f, are called *unary* operations because they require only one argument: the file to test. For example, here are two important file tests:

-e   Returns true if a file exists

-s   Returns true if a file is not empty

Several operations inspect a file's type, meaning that they can determine whether something is a regular file, a directory, or some kind of special device, as listed in Table 11-1. There are also a number of unary operations that check a file's permissions, as listed in Table 11-2. (See Section 2.17 for an overview of permissions.)

Table 11-1: File Type Operators

Operator	Tests For
-f	Regular file
-d	Directory
-h	Symbolic link
-b	Block device
-c	Character device
-p	Named pipe
-S	Socket

NOTE *The* test *command follows symbolic links (except for the -h test). That is, if* link *is a symbolic link to a regular file,* [-f link] *returns an exit code of true (0).*

Table 11-2: File Permissions Operators

Operator	Operator
-r	Readable
-w	Writable
-x	Executable
-u	Setuid
-g	Setgid
-k	"Sticky"

Finally, three *binary* operators (tests that need two files as arguments) are used in file tests, but they're not terribly common. Consider this command that includes -nt (newer than):

```
[ file1 -nt file2 ]
```

This exits true if *file1* has a newer modification date than *file2*. The -ot (older than) operator does the opposite. And if you need to detect identical hard links, -ef compares two files and returns true if they share inode numbers and devices.

String Tests

You've seen the binary string operator = that returns true if its operands are equal. The != operator returns true if its operands are not equal. And there are two unary string operations:

-z Returns true if its argument is empty ([-z ""] returns 0)

-n Returns true if its argument is not empty ([-n ""] returns 1)

Arithmetic Tests

It's important to recognize that the equal sign (=) looks for *string* equality, not *numeric* equality. Therefore, [1 = 1] returns 0 (true), but [01 = 1] returns false. When working with numbers, use -eq instead of the equal sign: [01 -eq 1] returns true. Table 11-3 provides the full list of numeric comparison operators.

Table 11-3: Arithmetic Comparison Operators

Operator	Returns True When the First Argument Is . . . the Second
-eq	Equal to
-ne	Not equal to
-lt	Less than
-gt	Greater than
-le	Less than or equal to
-ge	Greater than or equal to

11.5.6   Matching Strings with case

The case keyword forms another conditional construct that is exceptionally useful for matching strings. The case conditional does not execute any test commands and therefore does not evaluate exit codes. However, it can do pattern matching. This example should tell most of the story:

```
#!/bin/sh
case $1 in
    bye)
        echo Fine, bye.
        ;;
    hi|hello)
        echo Nice to see you.
        ;;
    what*)
        echo Whatever.
        ;;
    *)
        echo 'Huh?'
        ;;
esac
```

The shell executes this as follows:

1. The script matches $1 against each case value demarcated with the) character.

2. If a case value matches $1, the shell executes the commands below the case until it encounters ;;, at which point it skips to the esac keyword.

3. The conditional ends with esac.

For each case value, you can match a single string (like bye in the preceding example) or multiple strings with | (hi|hello returns true if $1 equals hi or hello), or you can use the * or ? patterns (what*). To make a default case that catches all possible values other than the case values specified, use a single * as shown by the final case in the preceding example.

NOTE *Each case must end with a double semicolon (;;) or you risk a syntax error.*

11.6   Loops

There are two kinds of loops in the Bourne shell: for and while loops.

11.6.1   *for Loops*

The for loop (which is a "for each" loop) is the most common. Here's an example:

```
#!/bin/sh
for str in one two three four; do
    echo $str
done
```

In this listing, for, in, do, and done are all shell keywords. The shell does the following:

1. Sets the variable str to the first of the four space-delimited values following the in keyword (one).
2. Runs the echo command between the do and done.
3. Goes back to the for line, setting str to the next value (two), runs the commands between do and done, and repeats the process until it's through with the values following the in keyword.

The output of this script looks like this:

```
one
two
three
four
```

11.6.2   *while Loops*

The Bourne shell's while loop uses exit codes, like the if conditional. For example, this script does 10 iterations:

```
#!/bin/sh
FILE=/tmp/whiletest.$$;
echo firstline > $FILE
```

```
while tail -10 $FILE | grep -q firstline; do
    # add lines to $FILE until tail -10 $FILE no longer prints "firstline"
    echo -n Number of lines in $FILE:' '
    wc -l $FILE | awk '{print $1}'
    echo newline >> $FILE
done

rm -f $FILE
```

Here, the exit code of grep -q firstline is the test. As soon as the exit code is nonzero (in this case, when the string firstline no longer appears in the last 10 lines in $FILE), the loop exits.

You can break out of a while loop with the break statement. The Bourne shell also has an until loop that works just like while, except that it breaks the loop when it encounters a zero exit code rather than a nonzero exit code. This said, you shouldn't need to use the while and until loops very often. In fact, if you find that you need to use while, you should probably be using a language like awk or Python instead.

11.7 Command Substitution

The Bourne shell can redirect a command's standard output back to the shell's own command line. That is, you can use a command's output as an argument to another command, or you can store the command output in a shell variable by enclosing a command in $().

This example stores a command inside the FLAGS variable. The bold in the second line shows the command substitution.

```
#!/bin/sh
FLAGS=$(grep ^flags /proc/cpuinfo | sed 's/.*://' | head -1)
echo Your processor supports:
for f in $FLAGS; do
    case $f in
        fpu)    MSG="floating point unit"
                ;;
        3dnow)  MSG="3DNOW graphics extensions"
                ;;
        mtrr)   MSG="memory type range register"
                ;;
        *)      MSG="unknown"
                ;;
    esac
    echo $f: $MSG
done
```

This example is somewhat complicated because it demonstrates that you can use both single quotes and pipelines inside the command substitution. The result of the grep command is sent to the sed command (more about sed in Section 11.10.3), which removes anything matching the expression .*:, and the result of sed is passed to head.

It's easy to go overboard with command substitution. For example, don't use $(ls) in a script because using the shell to expand * is faster. Also, if you want to invoke a command on several filenames that you get as a result of a find command, consider using a pipeline to xargs rather than command substitution, or use the -exec option (see Section 11.10.4).

NOTE   *The traditional syntax for command substitution is to enclose the command in back-ticks (`` `` ``), and you'll see this in many shell scripts. The $() syntax is a newer form, but it is a POSIX standard and is generally easier to read and write.*

11.8   Temporary File Management

It's sometimes necessary to create a temporary file to collect output for use by a later command. When making such a file, make sure that the filename is distinct enough that no other programs will accidentally write to it.

Here's how to use the mktemp command to create temporary filenames. This script shows you the device interrupts that have occurred in the last two seconds:

```
#!/bin/sh
TMPFILE1=$(mktemp /tmp/im1.XXXXXX)
TMPFILE2=$(mktemp /tmp/im2.XXXXXX)

cat /proc/interrupts > $TMPFILE1
sleep 2
cat /proc/interrupts > $TMPFILE2
diff $TMPFILE1 $TMPFILE2
rm -f $TMPFILE1 $TMPFILE2
```

The argument to mktemp is a template. The mktemp command converts the XXXXXX to a unique set of characters and creates an empty file with that name. Notice that this script uses variable names to store the filenames so that you only have to change one line if you want to change a filename.

NOTE   *Not all Unix flavors come with mktemp. If you're having portability problems, it's best to install the GNU coreutils package for your operating system.*

Another problem with scripts that employ temporary files is that if the script is aborted, the temporary files could be left behind. In the preceding example, pressing CTRL-C before the second cat command leaves a temporary file in */tmp*. Avoid this if possible. Instead, use the trap command to create a signal handler to catch the signal that CTRL-C generates and remove the temporary files, as in this handler:

```
#!/bin/sh
TMPFILE1=$(mktemp /tmp/im1.XXXXXX)
TMPFILE2=$(mktemp /tmp/im2.XXXXXX)
trap "rm -f $TMPFILE1 $TMPFILE2; exit 1" INT
    --snip--
```

You must use exit in the handler to explicitly end script execution, or the shell will continue running as usual after running the signal handler.

NOTE   *You don't need to supply an argument to* mktemp; *if you don't, the template will begin with a* /tmp/tmp. *prefix.*

11.9   Here Documents

Say you want to print a large section of text or feed a lot of text to another command. Rather than use several echo commands, you can use the shell's *here document* feature, as shown in the following script:

```
#!/bin/sh
DATE=$(date)
cat <<EOF
Date: $DATE

The output above is from the Unix date command.
It's not a very interesting command.
EOF
```

The items in bold control the here document. The <<EOF tells the shell to redirect all lines that follow the standard input of the command that precedes <<EOF, which in this case is cat. The redirection stops as soon as the EOF marker occurs on a line by itself. The marker can actually be any string, but remember to use the same marker at the beginning and end of the here document. Also, convention dictates that the marker be in all uppercase letters.

Notice the shell variable $DATE in the here document. The shell expands shell variables inside here documents, which is especially useful when you're printing out reports that contain many variables.

11.10   Important Shell Script Utilities

Several programs are particularly useful in shell scripts. Certain utilities such as basename are really only practical when used with other programs, and therefore don't often find a place outside shell scripts. However, others such as awk can be quite useful on the command line, too.

11.10.1   *basename*

If you need to strip the extension from a filename or get rid of the directories in a full pathname, use the basename command. Try these examples on the command line to see how the command works:

```
$ basename example.html .html
$ basename /usr/local/bin/example
```

In both cases, basename returns example. The first command strips the *.html* suffix from *example.html*, and the second removes the directories from the full pathname.

This example shows how you can use basename in a script to convert GIF image files to the PNG format:

```
#!/bin/sh
for file in *.gif; do
    # exit if there are no files
    if [ ! -f $file ]; then
        exit
    fi
    b=$(basename $file .gif)
    echo Converting $b.gif to $b.png...
    giftopnm $b.gif | pnmtopng > $b.png
done
```

11.10.2   awk

The awk command is not a simple single-purpose command; it's actually a powerful programming language. Unfortunately, awk usage is now something of a lost art, having been replaced by larger languages such as Python.

The are entire books on the subject of awk, including *The AWK Programming Language* by Alfred V. Aho, Brian W. Kernighan, and Peter J. Weinberger (Addison-Wesley, 1988). This said, many, many people use awk to do one thing—to pick a single field out of an input stream like this:

```
$ ls -l | awk '{print $5}'
```

This command prints the fifth field of the ls output (the file size). The result is a list of file sizes.

11.10.3   sed

The sed program (sed stands for stream editor) is an automatic text editor that takes an input stream (a file or the standard input), alters it according to some expression, and prints the results to standard output. In many respects, sed is like ed, the original Unix text editor. It has dozens of operations, matching tools, and addressing capabilities. As with awk, entire books have been written about sed including a quick reference covering both, *sed & awk Pocket Reference*, 2nd edition, by Arnold Robbins (O'Reilly, 2002).

Although sed is a big program, and an in-depth analysis is beyond the scope of this book, it's easy to see how it works. In general, sed takes an address and an operation as one argument. The address is a set of lines, and the command determines what to do with the lines.

A very common task for sed is to substitute some text for a regular expression (see Section 2.5.1), like this:

```
$ sed 's/exp/text/'
```

So if you wanted to replace the first colon in */etc/passwd* with a % and send the result to the standard output, you'd do it like this:

```
$ sed 's/:/%/' /etc/passwd
```

To substitute *all* colons in */etc/passwd*, add a g modifier to the end of the operation, like this:

```
$ sed 's/:/%/g' /etc/passwd
```

Here's a command that operates on a per-line basis; it reads */etc/passwd* and deletes lines three through six and sends the result to the standard output:

```
$ sed 3,6d /etc/passwd
```

In this example, 3,6 is the address (a range of lines), and d is the operation (delete). If you omit the address, sed operates on all lines in its input stream. The two most common sed operations are probably s (search and replace) and d.

You can also use a regular expression as the address. This command deletes any line that matches the regular expression *exp*:

```
$ sed '/exp/d'
```

11.10.4   *xargs*

When you have to run one command on a huge number of files, the command or shell may respond that it can't fit all of the arguments in its buffer. Use xargs to get around this problem by running a command on each filename in its standard input stream.

Many people use xargs with the find command. For example, the script below can help you verify that every file in the current directory tree that ends with *.gif* is actually a GIF (Graphic Interchange Format) image:

```
$ find . -name '*.gif' -print | xargs file
```

In the example above, xargs runs the file command. However, this invocation can cause errors or leave your system open to security problems, because filenames can include spaces and newlines. When writing a script, use the following form instead, which changes the find output separator and the xargs argument delimiter from a newline to a NULL character:

```
$ find . -name '*.gif' -print0 | xargs -0 file
```

xargs starts a *lot* of processes, so don't expect great performance if you have a large list of files.

You may need to add two dashes (--) to the end of your xargs command if there is a chance that any of the target files start with a single dash (-). The double dash (--) can be used to tell a program that any arguments that follow the double dash are filenames, not options. However, keep in mind that not all programs support the use of a double dash.

There's an alternative to xargs when using find: the -exec option. However, the syntax is somewhat tricky because you need to supply a {} to substitute the filename and a literal ; to indicate the end of the command. Here's how to perform the preceding task using only find:

```
$ find . -name '*.gif' -exec file {} \;
```

11.10.5   expr

If you need to use arithmetic operations in your shell scripts, the expr command can help (and even do some string operations). For example, the command expr 1 + 2 prints 3. (Run expr --help for a full list of operations.)

The expr command is a clumsy, slow way of doing math. If you find yourself using it frequently, you should probably be using a language like Python instead of a shell script.

11.10.6   exec

The exec command is a built-in shell feature that replaces the current shell process with the program you name after exec. It carries out the exec() system call that you learned about in Chapter 1. This feature is designed for saving system resources, but remember that there's no return; when you run exec in a shell script, the script and shell running the script are gone, replaced by the new command.

To test this in a shell window, try running exec cat. After you press CTRL-D or CTRL-C to terminate the cat program, your window should disappear because its child process no longer exists.

11.11   Subshells

Say you need to alter the environment in a shell slightly but don't want a permanent change. You can change and restore a part of the environment (such as the path or working directory) using shell variables, but that's a clumsy way to go about things. The easy way around these kinds of problems is to use a *subshell*, an entirely new shell process that you can create just to run a command or two. The new shell has a copy of the original shell's environment, and when the new shell exits, any changes you made to its shell environment disappear, leaving the initial shell to run as normal.

To use a subshell, put the commands to be executed by the subshell in parentheses. For example, the following line executes the command uglyprogram in *uglydir* and leaves the original shell intact:

```
$ (cd uglydir; uglyprogram)
```

This example shows how to add a component to the path that might cause problems as a permanent change:

```
$ (PATH=/usr/confusing:$PATH; uglyprogram)
```

Using a subshell to make a single-use alteration to an environment variable is such a common task that there is even a built-in syntax that avoids the subshell:

```
$ PATH=/usr/confusing:$PATH uglyprogram
```

Pipes and background processes work with subshells, too. The following example uses tar to archive the entire directory tree within *orig* and then unpacks the archive into the new directory *target*, which effectively duplicates the files and folders in *orig* (this is useful because it preserves ownership and permissions, and it's generally faster than using a command such as cp -r):

```
$ tar cf - orig | (cd target; tar xvf -)
```

WARNING   *Double-check this sort of command before you run it to make sure that the* target *directory exists and is completely separate from the* orig *directory.*

11.12 Including Other Files in Scripts

If you need to include another file in your shell script, use the dot (.) operator. For example, this runs the commands in the file *config.sh*:

```
. config.sh
```

This "include" file syntax does not start a subshell, and it can be useful for a group of scripts that need to use a single configuration file.

11.13 Reading User Input

The read command reads a line of text from the standard input and stores the text in a variable. For example, the following command stores the input in $*var*:

```
$ read var
```

This is a built-in shell command that can be useful in conjunction with other shell features not mentioned in this book.

11.14 When (Not) to Use Shell Scripts

The shell is so feature-rich that it's difficult to condense its important elements into a single chapter. If you're interested in what else the shell can do, have a look at some of the books on shell programming, such as *Unix Shell Programming*, 3rd edition, by Stephen G. Kochan and Patrick Wood (SAMS Publishing, 2003), or the shell script discussion in *The UNIX Programming Environment* by Bran W. Kernighan and Rob Pike (Prentice Hall, 1984).

However, at a certain point (especially when you start using the read built-in), you have to ask yourself if you're still using the right tool for the job. Remember what shell scripts do best: manipulate simple files and commands. As stated earlier, if you find yourself writing something that looks convoluted, especially if it involves complicated string or arithmetic operations, you should probably look to a scripting language like Python, Perl, or awk.

12

MOVING FILES
ACROSS THE NETWORK

This chapter surveys options for moving and sharing files between machines on a network. We'll start by looking at some ways to copy files other than the scp and sftp utilities that you've already seen. Then we'll briefly look at true file sharing, where you attach a directory on one machine to another machine.

This chapter describes some alternative ways to transfer files because not every file transfer problem is the same. Sometimes you need to provide quick, temporary access to machines that you don't know much about, sometimes you need to efficiently maintain copies of large directory structures, and sometimes you need more constant access.

12.1 Quick Copy

Let's say you want to copy a file (or files) from your machine to another one on your network, and you don't care about copying it back or need to do anything fancy. You just want to do it quickly. There's a convenient way to do this with Python. Just go to the directory containing the file(s) and run

```
$ python -m SimpleHTTPServer
```

This starts a basic web server that makes the directory available to any browser on the network. It usually runs on port 8000, so if the machine you run this on is at 10.1.2.4, go to *http://10.1.2.4:8000* on the destination and you'll be able to grab what you need.

12.2 rsync

If you want to move an entire directory structure around, you can do so with scp -r—or if you need a little more performance, tar in a pipeline:

```
$ tar cBvf - directory | ssh remote_host tar xBvpf -
```

These methods get the job done but are not very flexible. In particular, after the transfer completes, the remote host may not have an exact copy of the directory. If *directory* already exists on the remote machine and contains some extraneous files, those files persist after the transfer.

If you need to do this sort of thing regularly (and especially if you plan to automate the process), use a dedicated synchronizer system. On Linux, rsync is the standard synchronizer, offering good performance and many useful ways to perform transfers. We'll cover some of the essential rsync operation modes and look at some of its peculiarities.

12.2.1 rsync Basics

To get rsync working between two hosts, the rsync program must be installed on both the source and destination, and you'll need a way to access one machine from the other. The easiest way to transfer files is to use a remote shell account, and we'll assume that you want to transfer files using SSH access. However, remember that rsync can be handy even for copying files and directories between locations on a single machine, such as from one filesystem to another.

On the surface, the rsync command is not much different from scp. In fact, you can run rsync with the same arguments. For example, to copy a group of files to your home directory on *host*, enter

```
$ rsync file1 file2 ... host:
```

On any modern system, rsync assumes that you're using SSH to connect to the remote host.

Beware of this error message:

```
rsync not found
rsync: connection unexpectedly closed (0 bytes read so far)
rsync error: error in rsync protocol data stream (code 12) at io.c(165)
```

This notice says that your remote shell can't find rsync on its system. If rsync isn't in the remote path but is on the system, use --rsync-path=*path* to manually specify its location.

If your username is different on the remote host, add *user@* to the hostname, where *user* is your username on *host*:

```
$ rsync file1 file2 ... user@host:
```

Unless you supply extra options, rsync copies only files. In fact, if you specify just the options described so far and you supply a directory *dir* as an argument, you'll see this message:

```
skipping directory dir
```

To transfer entire directory hierarchies—complete with symbolic links, permissions, modes, and devices—use the -a option. Furthermore, if you want to copy to some place other than your home directory on the remote host, place this destination after the remote host, like this:

```
$ rsync -a dir host:destination_dir
```

Copying directories can be tricky, so if you're not exactly sure what will happen when you transfer the files, use the -nv option combination. The -n option tells rsync to operate in "dry run" mode—that is, to run a trial without actually copying any files. The -v option is for verbose mode, which shows details about the transfer and the files involved:

```
$ rsync -nva dir host:destination_dir
```

The output looks like this:

```
building file list ... done
ml/nftrans/nftrans.html
[more files]
wrote 2183 bytes read 24 bytes 401.27 bytes/sec
```

12.2.2   Making Exact Copies of a Directory Structure

By default, rsync copies files and directories without considering the previous contents of the destination directory. For example, if you transferred the directory *d* containing the files *a* and *b* to a machine that already had a file named *d/c*, the destination would contain *d/a*, *d/b*, and *d/c* after the rsync.

To make an exact replica of the source directory, you must delete files in the destination directory that do not exist in the source directory, such as *d/c* in this example. Use the --delete option to do that:

```
$ rsync -a --delete dir host:destination_dir
```

WARNING *This can be dangerous, because you should typically inspect the destination directory to see if there's anything that you'll inadvertently delete. Remember, if you're not certain about your transfer, use the -n option to perform a dry run so that you'll know exactly when rsync wants to delete a file.*

12.2.3   Using the Trailing Slash

Be particularly careful when specifying a directory as the source in an rsync command line. Consider the basic command that we've been working with so far:

```
$ rsync -a dir host:dest_dir
```

Upon completion, you'll have a directory *dir* inside *dest_dir* on *host*. Figure 12-1 shows an example of how rsync normally handles a directory with files named *a* and *b*. However, adding a slash (/) significantly changes the behavior:

```
$ rsync -a dir/ host:dest_dir
```

Here, rsync copies everything *inside dir* to *dest_dir* on *host* without actually creating *dir* on the destination host. Therefore, you can think of a transfer of *dir/* as an operation similar to cp dir/* dest_dir on the local filesystem.

For example, say you have a directory *dir* containing the files *a* and *b* (*dir/a* and *dir/b*). You run the trailing-slash version of the command to transfer them to the *dest_dir* directory on *host*:

```
$ rsync -a dir/ host:dest_dir
```

When the transfer completes, *dest_dir* contains copies of *a* and *b* but *not dir*. If, however, you had omitted the trailing / on *dir*, *dest_dir* would have gotten a copy of *dir* with *a* and *b* inside. Then, as a result of the transfer, you'd have files and directories named *dest_dir/dir/a* and *dest_dir/dir/b* on the remote host. Figure 12-2 illustrates how rsync handles the directory structure from Figure 12-1 when using a trailing slash.

When transferring files and directories to a remote host, accidentally adding a / after a path would normally be nothing more than a nuisance; you could go to the remote *host*, add the *dir* directory, and put all of the transferred items back in *dir*. Unfortunately, you must be careful to avoid disaster when combining the trailing / with the --delete option, because you can easily remove unrelated files this way.

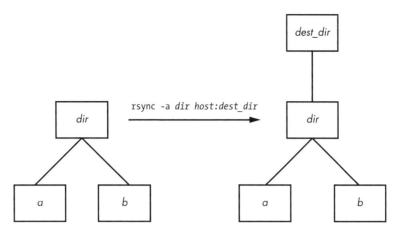

Figure 12-1: Normal rsync copy

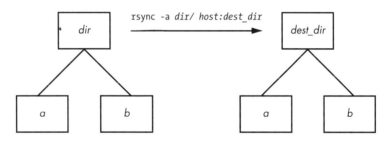

Figure 12-2: Effect of trailing slash in rsync

NOTE   *Be wary of your shell's automatic filename completion feature. GNU readline and many other completion libraries tack trailing slashes onto completed directory names.*

12.2.4   Excluding Files and Directories

One very important feature of rsync is its ability to exclude files and directories from a transfer operation. For example, say you'd like to transfer a local directory called *src* to *host*, but you want to exclude anything named *.git*. You can do it like this:

```
$ rsync -a --exclude=.git src host:
```

Note that this command excludes *all* files and directories named *.git* because --exclude takes a pattern, not an absolute filename. To exclude one specific item, specify an absolute path that starts with /, as shown here:

```
$ rsync -a --exclude=/src/.git src host:
```

NOTE *The first / in /src/.git in this command is not the root directory of your system but rather the base directory of the transfer.*

Here are a few more tips on how to exclude patterns:

- You can have as many --exclude parameters as you like.
- If you use the same patterns repeatedly, place them in a plaintext file (one pattern per line) and use --exclude-from=*file*.
- To exclude directories named *item* but include files with this name, use a trailing slash: --exclude=*item*/.
- The exclude pattern is based on a full file or directory name component and may contain simple globs (wildcards). For example, t*s matches *this*, but it does not match *ethers*.
- If you exclude a directory or filename but find that your pattern is too restrictive, use --include to specifically include another file or directory.

12.2.5   Transfer Integrity, Safeguards, and Verbose Modes

To speed operation, rsync uses a quick check to determine whether any files on the transfer source are already on the destination. The quick check uses a combination of the file size and its last-modified date. The first time you transfer an entire directory hierarchy to a remote host, rsync sees that none of the files already exist at the destination, and it transfers everything. Testing your transfer with rsync -n verifies this for you.

After running rsync once, run it again using rsync -v. This time you should see that no files show up in the transfer list because the file set exists on both ends, with the same modification dates.

When the files on the source side are not identical to the files on the destination side, rsync transfers the source files and overwrites any files that exist on the remote side. The default behavior may be inadequate, though, because you may need additional reassurance that files are indeed the same before skipping over them in transfers, or you may want to put in some extra safeguards. Here are some options that come in handy:

--checksum (abbreviation: -c)   Compute checksums (mostly unique signatures) of the files to see if they're the same. This consumes additional I/O and CPU resources during transfers, but if you're dealing with sensitive data or files that often have uniform sizes, this option is a must.

--ignore-existing   Doesn't clobber files already on the target side.

--backup (abbreviation: -b)   Doesn't clobber files already on the target but rather renames these existing files by adding a ~ suffix to their names before transferring the new files.

--suffix=s   Changes the suffix used with --backup from ~ to s.

--update (abbreviation: -u)   Doesn't clobber any file on the target that has a later date than the corresponding file on the source.

With no special options, rsync operates quietly, only producing output when there is a problem. However, you can use `rsync -v` for verbose mode or `rsync -vv` for even more details. (You can tack on as many v options as you like, but two is probably more than you need.) For a comprehensive summary after the transfer, use `rsync --stats`.

12.2.6   Compression

Many users like the `-z` option in conjunction with `-a` to compress the data before transmission:

```
$ rsync -az dir host:destination_dir
```

Compression can improve performance in certain situations, such as when uploading a large amount of data across a slow connection (like the slow upstream link on many DSL connections) or when the latency between the two hosts is high. However, across a fast local area network, the two endpoint machines can be constrained by the CPU time that it takes to compress and decompress data, so uncompressed transfer may be faster.

12.2.7   Limiting Bandwidth

It's easy to clog the uplink of Internet connections when uploading a large amount of data to a remote host. Even though you won't be using your (normally large) downlink capacity during such a transfer, your connection will still seem quite slow if you let rsync go as fast as it can, because outgoing TCP packets such as HTTP requests will have to compete with your transfers for bandwidth on your uplink.

To get around this, use `--bwlimit` to give your uplink a little breathing room. For example, to limit the bandwidth to 10,000 Kpbs you might do something like this:

```
$ rsync --bwlimit=10000 -a dir host:destination_dir
```

12.2.8   Transferring Files to Your Computer

The rsync command isn't just for copying files from your local machine to a remote host. You can also transfer files from a remote machine to your local host by placing the remote host and remote source path as the first argument on the command line. Therefore, to transfer *src_dir* on the host to *dest_dir* on the local host, run this command:

```
$ rsync -a host:src_dir dest_dir
```

NOTE   *As mentioned before, you can use* rsync *to duplicate directories on your local machines if you omit* host: *entirely.*

12.2.9   *Further rsync Topics*

Whenever you need to copy numerous files, rsync should be one of the first utilities that comes to mind. Running rsync in batch mode is particularly useful, and you'll find a number of options to employ auxiliary files related to command options, logging, and transfer state. In particular, the state files make long transfers faster and easier to resume when interrupted.

You'll also find rsync useful for making backups. For example, you can attach Internet storage, such as Amazon's S3, to your Linux system and then use rsync --delete to periodically synchronize a filesystem with the network storage to create a very effective backup system.

There are many more command-line options than those described here. For a rough overview, run rsync --help. You'll find more detailed information in the rsync(1) manual page as well as at the rsync home page: *http://rsync.samba.org/*.

12.3   Introduction to File Sharing

Your Linux machine probably doesn't live alone on your network, and when you have multiple machines on a network, there's nearly always a reason to share files between them. For the remainder of this chapter, we'll primarily be concerned with file sharing between Windows and Mac OS X machines, because it's interesting to see how Linux adapts to completely foreign environments. For the purpose of sharing files between Linux machines, or for accessing files from a Network Area Storage (NAS) device, we'll briefly talk about using Network File System (NFS) as a client.

12.4   Sharing Files with Samba

If you have machines running Windows, you'll probably want to permit access to your Linux system's files and printers from those Windows machines using the standard Windows network protocol, Server Message Block (SMB). Mac OS X also supports SMB file sharing.

The standard file-sharing software suite for Unix is called Samba. Not only does Samba allow your network's Windows computers to get to your Linux system, but it works the other way around: You can print and access files on Windows servers from your Linux machine with the Samba client software.

To set up a Samba server, perform these steps:

1.   Create an *smb.conf* file.
2.   Add file-sharing sections to *smb.conf*.
3.   Add printer-sharing sections to *smb.conf*.
4.   Start the Samba daemons nmbd and smbd.

When you install Samba from a distribution package, your system should perform the steps listed above using some reasonable defaults for the server. However, it probably won't be able to determine which particular *shares* (resources) on your Linux machine you offer to clients.

NOTE *The discussion of Samba in this chapter is brief and limited to getting Windows machines on a single subnet to see a standalone Linux machine through the Windows Network Places browser. There are countless ways to configure Samba, because there are many possibilities for access control and network topology. For the gory details on how to configure a large-scale server, see* Using Samba, *3rd edition (O'Reilly, 2007), a much more extensive guide, and visit the Samba website,* http://www.samba.org/.

12.4.1   Configuring the Server

The central Samba configuration file is *smb.conf*, which most distributions place in an *etc* directory such as */etc/samba*. However, you may have to hunt around to find this file, as it may also be in a *lib* directory such as */usr/local/ samba/lib*.

The *smb.conf* file is similar to the XDG style that you've seen elsewhere (such as the systemd configuration format) and breaks down into several sections denoted with square brackets (such as [global] and [printers]). The [global] section in *smb.conf* contains general options that apply to the entire server and all shares. These options primarily pertain to network configuration and access control. The sample [global] section below shows how to set the server name, description, and workgroup:

```
[global]
# server name
netbios name = name
# server description
server string = My server via Samba
# workgroup
workgroup = MYNETWORK
```

These parameters work like this:

`netbios name`   The server name. If you omit this parameter, Samba uses the Unix hostname.

`server string`   A short description of the server. The default is the Samba version number.

`workgroup`   The SMB workgroup name. If you're on a Windows domain, set this parameter to the name of your domain.

12.4.2   Server Access Control

You can add options to your *smb.conf* file to limit the machines and users that can access your Samba server. The following list includes many options that you can set in your [global] section and in the sections that control individual shares (as described later in the chapter):

interfaces Set this to have Samba listen on the given networks or interfaces. For example:

```
interfaces = 10.23.2.0/255.255.255.0
interfaces = eth0
```

bind interfaces only Set this to yes when using the interfaces parameter in order to limit access to machines that you can reach on those interfaces.

valid users Set this to allow the given users access. For example:

```
valid users = jruser, bill
```

guest ok Set this parameter to true to make a share available to anonymous users on the network.

guest only Set this parameter to true to allow anonymous access only.

browseable Set this to make shares viewable by network browsers. If you set this parameter to no for any shares, you'll still be able to access the shares on the Samba server, but you'll need to know their exact names in order to be able to access them.

12.4.3 Passwords

In general, you should only allow access to your Samba server with password authentication. Unfortunately, the basic password system on Unix is different than that on Windows, so unless you specify clear-text network passwords or authenticate passwords with a Windows server, you must set up an alternative password system. This section shows you how to set up an alternative password system using Samba's Trivial Database (TDB) backend, which is appropriate for small networks.

First, use these entries in your *smb.conf* [global] section to define the Samba password database characteristics:

```
# use the tdb  for Samba to enable encrypted passwords
security = user
passdb backend = tdbsam
obey pam restrictions = yes
smb passwd file = /etc/samba/passwd_smb
```

These lines allow you to manipulate the Samba password database with the smbpasswd command. The obey pam restrictions parameter ensures that any user changing their password with the smbpasswd command must obey any rules that PAM enforces for normal password changes. For the passdb backend parameter, you can add an optional pathname for the TDB file after a colon; for example, tdbsam:/etc/samba/private/passwd.tdb.

If you have access to a Windows domain, you can set security = domain *to make Samba use the domain's usernames and eliminate the need for a password database. However, in order for domain users to access the machine running Samba, each domain user must have a local account with the same username on the machine running Samba.*

Adding and Deleting Users

The first thing you need to do in order to give a Windows user access to your Samba server is to add the user to the password database with the smbpasswd -a command:

```
# smbpasswd -a username
```

The *username* parameter to the smbpasswd command must be a valid username on your Linux system.

Like the regular system's passwd program, smbpasswd asks you to enter the new user's password twice. If the password passes any necessary security checks, smbpasswd confirms that it has created the new user.

To remove a user, use the -x option to smbpasswd:

```
# smbpasswd -x username
```

To temporarily deactivate a user instead, use the -d option; the -e option will reenable the user:

```
# smbpasswd -d username
# smbpasswd -e username
```

Changing Passwords

You can change a Samba password as the superuser by using smbpasswd with no options or keywords other than the username:

```
# smbpasswd username
```

However, if the Samba server is running, any user can change their own Samba password by entering smbpasswd by itself on the command line.

Finally, here's one place in your configuration to beware of. If you see a line like this in your *smb.conf* file, be careful:

```
unix password sync = yes
```

This line causes smbpasswd to change a user's normal password *in addition* to the Samba password. The result can be very confusing, especially when a user changes their Samba password to something that's not their Linux password and discovers that they can no longer log in. Some distributions set this parameter by default in their Samba server packages!

12.4.4   Starting the Server

You may need to start your server if you didn't install Samba from a distribution package. To do so, run nmbd and smbd with the following arguments, where *smb_config_file* is the full path of your *smb.conf* file:

```
# nmbd -D -s smb_config_file
# smbd -D -s smb_config_file
```

The nmbd daemon is a NetBIOS name server, and smbd does the actual work of handling share requests. The -D option specifies daemon mode. If you alter the *smb.conf* file while smbd is running, you can notify the daemon of the changes with a HUP signal or use your distribution's service restart command (such as systemctl or initctl).

12.4.5   Diagnostics and Log Files

If something goes wrong when starting one of the Samba servers, an error message appears on the command line. However, runtime diagnostic messages go to the *log.nmbd* and *log.smbd* log files, which are usually in a */var/log* directory, such as */var/log/samba*. You'll also find other log files there, such as individual logs for each individual client.

12.4.6   Configuring a File Share

To export a directory to SMB clients (that is, to share a directory with a client), add a section like this to your *smb.conf* file, where *label* is what you would like to call the share and *path* is the full directory path:

```
[label]
path = path
comment = share description
guest ok = no
writable = yes
printable = no
```

These parameters are useful in directory shares:

guest ok   Allows guest access to the share. The public parameter is a synonym.

writable   A yes or true setting here marks the share as read-write. Do not allow guest access to a read-write share.

printable   Specifies a printing share. This parameter must be set to no or false for a directory share.

veto files   Prevents the export of any files that match the given patterns. You must enclose each pattern between forward slashes (so that it looks like */pattern/*). This example bars object files, as well as any file or directory named *bin*:

```
veto files = /*.o/bin/
```

12.4.7 Home Directories

You can add a section called [homes] to your *smb.conf* file if you want to export home directories to users. The section should look like this:

```
[homes]
comment = home directories
browseable = no
writable = yes
```

By default, Samba reads the logged-in user's */etc/passwd* entry to determine their home directory for [homes]. However, if you don't want Samba to follow this behavior (that is, you want to keep the Windows home directories in a different place than the regular Linux home directories), you can use the %S substitution in a path parameter. For example, here's how you would switch a user's [homes] directory to */u/user*:

```
path = /u/%S
```

Samba substitutes the current username for the %S .

12.4.8 Sharing Printers

You can export all of your printers to Windows clients by adding a [printers] section to your *smb.conf* file. Here's how the section looks when you're using CUPS, the standard Unix printing system:

```
[printers]
comment = Printers
browseable = yes
printing = CUPS
path = cups
printable = yes
writable = no
```

To use the printing = CUPS parameter, your Samba installation must be configured and linked against the CUPS library.

NOTE   *Depending on your configuration, you may also want to allow guest access to your printers with the* guest ok = yes *option rather than give a Samba password or account to everyone who needs to access the printers. For example, it's easy to limit printer access to a single subnet with firewall rules.*

12.4.9 Using the Samba Client

The Samba client program smbclient can print to and access remote Windows shares. This program comes in handy when you are in an environment where you must interact with Windows servers that don't offer a Unix-friendly means of communication.

To get started with smbclient use the -L option to get a list of shares from a remote server named *SERVER*:

```
$ smbclient -L -U username SERVER
```

You do not need -U *username* if your Linux username is the same as your username on *SERVER*.

After running this command, smbclient asks for a password. To try to access a share as a guest, press ENTER; otherwise, enter your password on *SERVER*. Upon success, you should get a share list like this:

```
Sharename    Type       Comment
---------    ----       -------
Software     Disk       Software distribution
Scratch      Disk       Scratch space
IPC$         IPC        IPC Service
ADMIN$       IPC        IPC Service
Printer1     Printer    Printer in room 231A
Printer2     Printer    Printer in basement
```

Use the Type field to help you make sense of each share and pay attention only to the Disk and Printer shares (the IPC shares are for remote management). This list has two disk shares and two printer shares. Use the name in the Sharename column to access each share.

12.4.10   *Accessing Files as a Client*

If you need only casual access to files in a disk share, use the following command. (Again, you can omit the -U *username* if your Linux username matches your username on the server.)

```
$ smbclient -U username '\\SERVER\sharename'
```

Upon success, you will get a prompt like this, indicating that you can now transfer files:

```
smb: \>
```

In this file transfer mode, smbclient is similar to the Unix ftp, and you can run these commands:

get *file*   Copies *file* from the remote server to the current local directory.

put *file*   Copies *file* from the local machine to the remote server.

cd *dir*   Changes the directory on the remote server to *dir*.

lcd *localdir*   Changes the current local directory to *localdir*.

pwd   Prints the current directory on the remote server, including the server and share names.

!*command*   Runs *command* on the local host. Two particularly handy commands are !pwd and !ls to determine directory and file status on the local side.

help   Shows a full list of commands.

Using the CIFS Filesystem

If you need frequent, regular access to files on a Windows server, you can attach a share directly to your system with mount. The command syntax is shown below. Notice the use of *SERVER:sharename* rather than the normal *\\SERVER\sharename* format.

```
# mount -t cifs SERVER:sharename mountpoint -o user=username,pass=password
```

In order to use mount like this, you must have the Common Internet File System (CIFS) utilities available for Samba. Most distributions offer these as a separate package.

12.5   NFS Clients

The standard system for file sharing among Unix systems is NFS; there are many different versions of NFS for different scenarios. You can serve NFS over TCP and UDP, with a large number of authentication and encryption techniques. Because there are so many options, NFS can be a big topic, so we'll just stick to the basics of NFS clients.

To mount a remote directory on a server with NFS, use the same basic syntax as for mounting a CIFS directory:

```
# mount -t nfs server:directory mountpoint
```

Technically, you don't need the -t nfs option because mount should figure this out for you, but you may want to investigate the options in the nfs(5) manual page. (You'll find several different options for security using the sec option. Many administrators on small, closed networks use host-based access control. However, more sophisticated methods, such as Kerberos-based authentication, require additional configuration on other parts of your system.)

When you find that you're making greater use of filesystems over a network, set up the automounter so that your system will mount the filesystems only when you actually try to use them in order to prevent problems with dependencies on boot. The traditional automounting tool is called automount, with a newer version called amd, but much of this is now being supplanted by the automount unit type in systemd.

12.6   Further Network File Service Options and Limitations

Setting up an NFS server to share files to other Linux machines is more complicated than using a simple NFS client. You need to run the server daemons (mountd and nfsd) and set up the */etc/exports* file to reflect the directories that you're sharing. However, we won't cover NFS servers primarily because shared storage over a network is often made much more convenient by simply purchasing an NAS device to handle it for you. Many of these devices are Linux based, so they'll naturally have NFS server support. Vendors add value to their NAS devices by offering their own administration tools to take the pain out of tedious tasks such as setting up RAID configurations and cloud backups.

Speaking of cloud backups, another network file service option is cloud storage. This can be handy when you need the extra storage that comes with automatic backups and you don't mind an extra hit on performance. It's especially useful when you don't need the service for a long time or don't need to access it very much. You can usually mount Internet storage much as you would NFS.

Although NFS and other file-sharing systems work well for casual use, don't expect great performance. Read-only access to larger files should work well, such as when you're streaming audio or video, because you're reading data in large, predictable chunks that don't require much back-and-forth communication between the file server and its client. As long as the network is fast enough and the client has enough memory, a server can supply data as needed.

Local storage is much faster for tasks involving many small files, such as compiling software packages and starting desktop environments. The picture becomes more complicated when you have a larger network with many users accessing many different machines, because there are tradeoffs between convenience, performance, and ease of administration.

13

USER ENVIRONMENTS

This book's primary focus is on the Linux system that normally lies underneath server processes and interactive user sessions. But eventually, the system and the user have to meet somewhere. Startup files play an important role at this point, because they set defaults for the shell and other interactive programs. They determine how the system behaves when a user logs in.

Most users don't pay close attention to their startup files, only touching them when they want to add something for convenience, such as an alias. Over time, the files become cluttered with unnecessary environment variables and tests that can lead to annoying (or quite serious) problems.

If you've had your Linux machine for a while, you may notice that your home directory accumulates a bafflingly large array of startup files over time. These are sometimes called *dot files* because they nearly always start with a dot (.). Many of these are automatically created when you first run a program, and you'll never need to change them. This chapter primarily covers shell startup files, which are the ones you're most likely to modify or rewrite from scratch. Let's first look at how much care you need to take when working on these files.

13.1   Guidelines for Creating Startup Files

When designing startup files, keep the user in mind. If you're the only user on a machine, you don't have much to worry about because errors only affect you and they're easy enough to fix. However, if you're creating startup files meant to be the defaults for all new users on a machine or network, or if you think that someone might copy your files for use on a different machine, your task becomes considerably more difficult. If you make an error in a startup file for 10 users, you might end up fixing this error 10 times.

Keep two essential goals in mind when creating startup files for other users:

Simplicity   Keep the number of startup files small, and keep the files as small and simple as possible so that they are easy to modify but hard to break. Each item in a startup file is just one more thing that can break.

Readability   Use extensive comments in files so that the users get a good picture of what each part of a file does.

13.2   When to Alter Startup Files

Before making a change to a startup file, ask yourself whether you really should be making that change. Here are some good reasons for changing startup files:

- You want to change the default prompt.
- You need to accommodate some critical locally installed software. (Consider using wrapper scripts first, though.)
- Your existing startup files are broken.

If everything in your Linux distribution works, be careful. Sometimes the default startup files interact with other files in */etc*.

That said, you probably wouldn't be reading this chapter if you weren't interested in changing the defaults, so let's examine what's important.

13.3   Shell Startup File Elements

What goes into a shell startup file? Some things might seem obvious, such as the path and a prompt setting. But what exactly *should* be in the path, and what does a reasonable prompt look like? And how much is too much to put in a startup file?

The next few sections discuss the essentials of a shell startup file—from the command path, prompt, and aliases through the permissions mask.

13.3.1   The Command Path

The most important part of any shell startup file is the command path. The path should cover the directories that contain every application of interest to a regular user. At the very least, the path should contain these components, in order:

```
/usr/local/bin
/usr/bin
/bin
```

This order ensures that you can override standard default programs with site-specific variants located in */usr/local*.

Most Linux distributions install executables for nearly all packaged software in */usr/bin*. There are occasional differences, such as putting games in */usr/games* and graphical applications in a separate location, so check your system's defaults first. And make sure that every general-use program on the system is available through one of the directories listed above. If not, your system is probably getting out of control. Don't change the default path in your user environment to accommodate a new software installation directory. A cheap way to accommodate separate installation directories is to use symbolic links in */usr/local/bin*.

Many users use a *bin* directory of their own to store shell scripts and programs, so you may want to add this to the front of the path:

```
$HOME/bin
```

NOTE   *A newer convention is to place binaries in $HOME/.local/bin.*

If you're interested in systems utilities (such as traceroute, ping, and lsmod), add the *sbin* directories to your path:

```
/usr/local/sbin
/usr/sbin
/sbin
```

Adding Dot (.) to the Path

There is one small but controversial command path component to discuss: the dot. Placing a dot (.) in your path allows you to run programs in the current directory without using ./ in front of the program name. This may seem convenient when writing scripts or compiling programs, but it's a bad idea for two reasons:

- It can be a security problem. You should *never* put a dot at the *front* of the path. Here's an example of what can happen: An attacker could put a Trojan horse named ls in an archive distributed on the Internet. Even if a dot were at the end of the path, you'd still be vulnerable to typos such as sl or ks.

- It is inconsistent and can be confusing. A dot in a path can mean that a command's behavior will change according to the current directory.

13.3.2   The Manual Page Path

The traditional manual page path was determined by the MANPATH environment variable, but you shouldn't set it because doing so overrides the system defaults in */etc/manpath.config.*

13.3.3   The Prompt

Experienced users tend to avoid long, complicated, useless prompts. In comparison, many administrators and distributions drag everything into a default prompt. Your choice should reflect your users' needs; place the current working directory, hostname, and username in the prompt if it really helps.

Above all, avoid characters that mean something significant to the shell, such as these:

```
{ } = & < >
```

NOTE   *Take extra care to avoid the > character, which can cause erratic, empty files to appear in your current directory if you accidentally copy and paste a section of your shell window (recall that > redirects output to a file).*

Even a shell's default prompt isn't ideal. For example, the default bash prompt contains the shell name and version number.

This simple prompt setting for bash ends with the customary $ (the traditional csh prompt ends with %):

```
PS1='\u\$ '
```

The \u is a substitution for the current username (see the PROMPTING section of the bash(1) manual page). Other popular substitutions include the following:

\h   The hostname (the short form, without domain names)

\!   The history number

\w   The current directory. Because this can become long, you can limit the display to just the final component with \W.

\$ $ if running as a user account, # if root

13.3.4   Aliases

Among the stickier points of modern user environments is the role of *aliases*, a shell feature that substitutes one string for another before executing a command. These can be efficient shortcuts that save some typing. However, aliases also have these drawbacks:

- It can be tricky to manipulate arguments.
- They are confusing; a shell's built-in which command can tell you if something is an alias, but it won't tell you where it was defined.
- They are frowned upon in subshells and noninteractive shells; they do not work in other shells.

Given these disadvantages, you should probably avoid aliases whenever possible because it's easier to write a shell function or an entirely new shell script. Modern computers can start and execute shells so quickly that the difference between an alias and an entirely new command should mean nothing to you.

That said, aliases do come in handy when you wish to alter a part of the shell's environment. You can't change an environment variable with a shell script, because scripts run as subshells. (You can also define shell functions to perform this task.)

13.3.5   The Permissions Mask

As described in Chapter 2, a shell's built-in umask (permissions mask) facility sets your default permissions. You should run umask in one of your startup files to make certain that any program you run creates files with your desired permissions. The two reasonable choices are these:

077   This mask is the most restrictive permissions mask because it doesn't give any other users access to new files and directories. This is often appropriate on a multi-user system where you don't want other users to look at any of your files. However, when set as the default, it can sometimes lead to problems when your users want to share files but don't understand how to set permissions correctly. (Inexperienced users have a tendency to set files to a world-writable mode.)

022   This mask gives other users read access to new files and directories. This can be important on a single-user system because many daemons that run as pseudo-users are not be able to see files and directories created with the more restrictive 077 umask.

NOTE   *Certain applications (especially mail programs) override the umask, changing it to 077 because they feel that their files are the business of no one but the file owner.*

13.4   Startup File Order and Examples

Now that you know what to put into shell startup files, it's time to see some specific examples. Surprisingly, one of the most difficult and confusing parts of creating startup files is determining which of several startup files to use. The next sections cover the two most popular Unix shells: bash and tcsh.

13.4.1   The bash Shell

In bash, you can choose from the startup filenames *.bash_profile*, *.profile*,
.bash_login, and *.bashrc*. Which one is appropriate for your command path,
manual page path, prompt, aliases, and permissions mask? The answer is
that you should have a *.bashrc* file accompanied by a *.bash_profile* symbolic
link pointing to *.bashrc* because there are a few different kinds of bash shell
instance types.

The two main shell instance types are interactive and noninteractive,
but of those, only interactive shells are of interest because noninteractive
shells (such as those that run shell scripts) usually don't read any startup
files. Interactive shells are the ones that you use to run commands from a
terminal, such as the ones you've seen in this book, and they can be classi-
fied as *login* or *non-login*.

Login Shells

Traditionally, a login shell is what you get when you first log in to a system with the terminal using a program such as */bin/login*. Logging in
remotely with SSH also gives you a login shell. The basic idea is that the
login shell is an initial shell. You can tell if a shell is a login shell by running echo $0; if the first character is a -, the shell's a login shell.

When bash runs as a login shell, it runs */etc/profile*. Then it looks for a
user's *.bash_profile*, *.bash_login*, and *.profile* files, running only the first one
that it sees.

As strange as it sounds, it's possible to run a noninteractive shell as a
login shell to force it to run startup files. To do so, start the shell with the
-l or --login option.

Non-Login Shells

A non-login shell is an additional shell that you run after you log in. It's
simply any interactive shell that's not a login shell. Windowing system terminal programs (xterm, GNOME Terminal, and so on) start non-login shells
unless you specifically ask for a login shell.

Upon starting up as a non-login shell, bash runs */etc/bash.bashrc* and
then runs the user's *.bashrc*.

The Consequences of Two Kinds of Shells

The reasoning behind the two different startup filesystems is that in the old
days, users logged in through a traditional terminal with a login shell, then
started non-login subshells with windowing systems or the screen program.
For the non-login subshells, it was deemed a waste to repeatedly set the
user environment and run a bunch of programs that had already been run.
With login shells, you could run fancy startup commands in a file such as
.bash_profile, leaving only aliases and other "lightweight" things to your *.bashrc*.

Nowadays, most desktop users log in through a graphical display manager (you'll learn more about these in the next chapter). Most of these start
with one noninteractive login shell in order to preserve the login versus

non-login model described above. When they do not, you need to set up your entire environment (path, manual path, and so on) in your *.bashrc*, or you'll never see any of your environment in your terminal window shells. However, you *also* need a *.bash_profile* if you ever want to log in on the console or remotely, because those login shells don't ever bother with *.bashrc*.

Example .bashrc

In order to satisfy both non-login and login shells, how would you create a *.bashrc* that can also be used as your *.bash_profile*? Here's one very elementary (yet perfectly sufficient) example:

```
# Command path.
PATH=/usr/local/bin:/usr/bin:/bin:/usr/games
PATH=$HOME/bin:$PATH

# PS1 is the regular prompt.
# Substitutions include:
# \u username \h hostname \w current directory
# \! history number \s shell name \$ $ if regular user
PS1='\u\$ '

# EDITOR and VISUAL determine the editor that programs such as less
# and mail clients invoke when asked to edit a file.
EDITOR=vi
VISUAL=vi

# PAGER is the default text file viewer for programs such as man.
PAGER=less

# These are some handy options for less.
# A different style is LESS=FRX
# (F=quit at end, R=show raw characters, X=don't use alt screen)
LESS=meiX

# You must export environment variables.
export PATH EDITOR VISUAL PAGER LESS

# By default, give other users read-only access to most new files.
umask 022
```

As described earlier, you can share this *.bashrc* file with *.bash_profile* via a symbolic link, or you can make the relationship even clearer by creating *.bash_profile* as this one-liner:

```
. $HOME/.bashrc
```

Checking for Login and Interactive Shells

With a *.bashrc* matching your *.bash_profile*, you don't normally run extra commands for login shells. However, if you want to define different actions for login and non-login shells, you can add the following test to your *.bashrc*, which checks the shell's $- variable for an i character:

```
case $- in
 *i*) # interactive commands go here
    command
    --snip--
    ;;
 *)   # non-interactive commands go here
    command
    --snip--
    ;;
esac
```

13.4.2   The tcsh Shell

The standard csh on virtually all Linux systems is tcsh, an enhanced C shell that popularized features such as command-line editing and multimode filename and command completion. Even if you don't use tcsh as the default new user shell (we suggest using bash), you should still provide tcsh startup files in case your users happen to come across tcsh.

You don't have to worry about the difference between login shells and non-login shells in tcsh. Upon startup, tcsh looks for a *.tcshrc* file. Failing this, it looks for the csh shell's *.cshrc* startup file. The reason for this order is that you can use the *.tcshrc* file for tcsh extensions that don't work in csh. You should probably stick to using the traditional *.cshrc* instead of *.tcshrc*; it's highly unlikely that anyone will ever use your startup files with csh. And if a user actually does come across csh on some other system, your *.cshrc* will work.

Example .cshrc

Here is sample *.cshrc* file:

```
# Command path.
setenv PATH /usr/local/bin:/usr/bin:/bin:$HOME/bin

# EDITOR and VISUAL determine the editor that programs such as less
# and mail clients invoke when asked to edit a file.
setenv EDITOR vi
setenv VISUAL vi

# PAGER is the default text file viewer for programs such as man.
setenv PAGER less

# These are some handy options for less.
setenv LESS meiX

# By default, give other users read-only access to most new files.
umask 022

# Customize the prompt.
```

```
# Substitutions include:
# %n username %m hostname %/ current directory
# %h history number %l current terminal %% %
set prompt="%m%% "
```

13.5   Default User Settings

The best way to write startup files and choose defaults for new users is to experiment with a new test user on the system. Create the test user with an empty home directory and refrain from copying your own startup files to the test user's directory. Write the new startup files from scratch.

When you think you have a working setup, log in as the new test user in all possible ways (on the console, remotely, and so on). Make sure that you test as many things as possible, including the windowing system operation and manual pages. When you're happy with the test user, create a second test user, copying the startup files from the first test user. If everything still works, you now have a new set of startup files that you can distribute to new users.

The following sections outline reasonable defaults for new users.

13.5.1   Shell Defaults

The default shell for any new user on a Linux system should be bash because:

- Users interact with the same shell that they use to write shell scripts (for example, csh is a notoriously bad scripting tool—don't even think about it).
- bash is standard on Linux systems.
- bash uses GNU readline, and therefore its interface is identical to that of many other tools.
- bash gives you fine, easy-to-understand control over I/O redirection and file handles.

However, many seasoned Unix wizards use shells such as csh and tcsh simply because they can't bear to switch. Of course, you can choose any shell you like, but choose bash if you don't have any preference, and use bash as the default shell for any new user on the system. (A user can change his or her shell with the chsh command to suit individual preferences.)

NOTE   *There are plenty of other shells out there (rc, ksh, zsh, es, and so on). Some are not appropriate as beginner shells, but zsh and fish are sometimes popular with new users looking for an alternative shell.*

13.5.2   Editor

On a traditional system, the default editor should be vi or emacs. These are the only editors virtually guaranteed to exist on nearly any Unix system, which means they'll cause the least trouble in the long run for a new user. However, Linux distributions often configure nano to be the default editor, because it's easier for beginners to use.

As with shell startup files, avoid large default editor startup files. A little set showmatch in the *.exrc* startup file never hurt anyone but steer clear of anything that significantly changes the editor's behavior or appearance, such as the showmode feature, auto-indentation, and wrap margins.

13.5.3   Pager

It's perfectly reasonable to set the default PAGER environment variable to less.

13.6   Startup File Pitfalls

Avoid these in startup files:

*   Don't put any kind of graphical command in a shell startup file.
*   Don't set the DISPLAY environment variable in a shell startup file.
*   Don't set the terminal type in a shell startup file.
*   Don't skimp on descriptive comments in default startup files.
*   Don't run commands in a startup file that print to the standard output.
*   Never set LD_LIBRARY_PATH in a shell startup file (see Section 15.1.4).

13.7   Further Startup Topics

Because this book deals only with the underlying Linux system, we won't cover windowing environment startup files. This is a large issue indeed, because the display manager that logs you in to a modern Linux system has its own set of startup files, such as *.xsession, .xinitrc*, and the endless combinations of GNOME- and KDE-related items.

The windowing choices may seem bewildering, and there is no one common way to start a windowing environment in Linux. The next chapter describes some of the many possibilities. However, when you determine what your system does, you may get a little carried away with the files that relate to your graphical environment. That's fine, but don't carry it over to new users. The same tenet of keeping things simple in shell startup files works wonders for GUI startup files, too. In fact, you probably don't need to change your GUI startup files at all.

14

A BRIEF SURVEY OF THE LINUX DESKTOP

This chapter is a quick introduction to the components found in a typical Linux desktop system. Of all of the different kinds of software that you can find on Linux systems, the desktop arena is one of the wildest and most colorful because there are so many environments and applications to choose from, and most distributions make it relatively easy for you to try them out.

Unlike other parts of a Linux system, such as storage and networking, there isn't much of a hierarchy of layers involved in creating a desktop structure. Instead, each component performs a specific task, communicating with other components as necessary. Some components do share common building blocks (in particular, libraries for graphical toolkits), and these can be thought of as simple abstraction layers, but that's about as deep as it goes.

This chapter offers a high-level discussion of desktop components in general, but we'll look at two pieces in a little more detail: the X Window System, which is the core infrastructure behind most desktops, and D-Bus, an interprocess communication service used in many parts of the system. We'll limit the hands-on discussion and examples to a few diagnostic utilities that, while not terribly useful day-to-day (most GUIs don't require you to enter shell commands in order to interact with them), will help you understand the underlying mechanics of the system and perhaps provide some entertainment along the way. We'll also take a quick look at printing.

14.1   Desktop Components

Linux desktop configurations offer a great deal of flexibility. Most of what the Linux user experiences (the "look and feel" of the desktop) comes from applications or building blocks of applications. If you don't like a particular application, you can usually find an alternative. And if what you're looking for doesn't exist, you can write it yourself. Linux developers tend to have a wide variety of preferences for how a desktop should act, which makes for a lot of choices.

In order to work together, all applications need to have something in common, and at the core of nearly everything on most Linux desktops is the X (X Window System) server. Think of X as sort of the "kernel" of the desktop that manages everything from rendering windows to configuring displays to handling input from devices such as keyboards and mice. The X server is also the one component that you won't easily find a replacement for (see Section 14.4).

The X server is just a server and does not dictate the way anything should act or appear. Instead, X *client* programs handle the user interface. Basic X client applications, such as terminal windows and web browsers, make connections to the X server and ask to draw windows. In response, the X server figures out where to place the windows and renders them. The X server also channels input back to the client when appropriate.

14.1.1   Window Managers

X clients don't have to act like windowed user applications; they can act as services for other clients or provide other interface functions. A *window manager* is perhaps the most important client service application because it figures out how to arrange windows on screen and provides interactive decorations like title bars that allow the user to move and minimize windows. These elements are central to the user experience.

There are many window manager implementations. Examples such as Mutter/GNOME Shell and Compiz are meant to be more or less stand-alone, while others are built into environments such as Xfce. Most window managers included in the standard Linux distributions strive for maximum user comfort, but others provide specific visual effects or take a minimalist approach. There's not likely to ever be a standard Linux window manager because user tastes and requirements are diverse and constantly changing; as a result, new window managers appear all the time.

14.1.2 Toolkits

Desktop applications include certain common elements, such as buttons and menus, called *widgets*. To speed up development and provide a common look, programmers use graphical *toolkits* to provide these elements. On operating systems such as Windows or Mac OS X, the vendor provides a common toolkit, and most programmers use that. On Linux, the GTK+ toolkit is one of the most common, but you'll also frequently see widgets built on the Qt framework and others.

Toolkits usually consist of shared libraries and support files such as images and theme information.

14.1.3 Desktop Environments

Although toolkits provide the user with a uniform outward appearance, some details of a desktop require a degree of cooperation between different applications. For example, one application may wish to share data with another or update a common notification bar on a desktop. To provide for these needs, toolkits and other libraries are bundled into larger packages called *desktop environments*. GNOME, KDE, Unity, and Xfce are some common Linux desktop environments.

Toolkits are at the core of most desktop environments, but to create a unified desktop, environments must also include numerous support files, such as icons and configurations, that make up themes. All of this is bound together with documents that describe design conventions, such as how application menus and titles should appear and how applications should react to certain system events.

14.1.4 Applications

At the top of the desktop are applications, such as web browsers and the terminal window. X applications can range from crude (such as the ancient xclock program) to complex (such as the Chrome web browser and LibreOffice suite). These applications normally stand alone, but they often use interprocess communication to become aware of pertinent events. For example, an application can express interest when you attach a new storage device or when you receive new email or an instant message. This communication usually occurs over D-Bus, described in Section 14.5.

14.2   A Closer Look at the X Window System

The X Window System (*http://www.x.org/*) has historically been very large, with the base distribution including the X server, client support libraries, and clients. Due to the emergence of desktop environments such as

GNOME and KDE, the role of the X distribution has changed over time, with the focus now more on the core server that manages rendering and input devices, as well as a simplified client library.

The X server is easy to identify on your system. It's called X. Check for it in a process listing; you'll usually see it running with a number of options like this:

```
/usr/bin/X :0 -auth /var/run/lightdm/root/:0 -nolisten tcp vt7 -novtswitch
```

The :0 shown here is called the *display*, an identifier representing one or more monitors that you access with a common keyboard and/or mouse. Usually, the display just corresponds to the single monitor you attach to your computer, but you can put multiple monitors under the same display. When using an X session, the DISPLAY environment variable is set to the display identifier.

NOTE *Displays can be further subdivided into screens, such as :0.0 and :0.1, but this has become increasingly rare because X extensions, such as RandR, can combine multiple monitors into one larger virtual screen.*

On Linux, an X server runs on a virtual terminal. In this example, the vt7 argument tells us that it's been told to run on */dev/tty7* (normally, the server starts on the first virtual terminal available). You can run more than one X server at a time on Linux by running them on separate virtual terminals, but if you do, each server needs a unique display identifier. You can switch between the servers with the CTRL-ALT-FN keys or the chvt command.

14.2.1   Display Managers

You normally don't start the X server with a command line because starting the server doesn't define any clients that are supposed to run on the server. If you start the server by itself, you'll just get a blank screen. Instead, the most common way to start an X server is with a *display manager*, a program that starts the server and puts a login box on the screen. When you log in, the display manager starts a set of clients, such as a window manager and file manager, so that you can start to use the machine.

There are many different display managers, such as gdm (for GNOME) and kdm (for KDE). The lightdm in the argument list for the X server invocation above is a cross-platform display manager meant to be able to start GNOME or KDE sessions.

To start an X session from a virtual console instead of using a display manager, you can run the startx or xinit command. However, the session you get will likely be a very simple one that looks completely unlike that of a display manager, because the mechanics and startup files are different.

14.2.2   Network Transparency

One feature of X is network transparency. Because clients talk to the server using a protocol, it's possible to run clients across a network to a server running on a different machine directly over the network, with the X server listening for TCP connections on port 6000. Clients connecting to that port could authenticate, then send windows to the server.

Unfortunately, this method does not normally offer any encryption and is insecure as a result. To close this hole, most distributions now disable the X server's network listener (with the -nolisten tcp option to the server, as seen on page 300). However, you can still run X clients from a remote machine with SSH tunneling, as described in Chapter 10, by connecting the X server's Unix domain socket to a socket on the remote machine.

14.3   Exploring X Clients

Although one doesn't normally think of working with a graphical user interface from the command line, there are several utilities that allow you to explore the parts of the X Window System. In particular, you can inspect clients as they run.

One of the simplest tools is xwininfo. When run without any arguments, it asks you to click on a window:

```
$ xwininfo
xwininfo: Please select the window about which you
          would like information by clicking the
          mouse in that window.
```

After you click, it prints a list of information about the window, such as its location and size:

```
xwininfo: Window id: 0x5400024 "xterm"

  Absolute upper-left X:  1075
  Absolute upper-left Y:  594
--snip--
```

Notice the window ID here—the X server and window managers use this identifier to keep track of windows. To get a list of all window IDs and clients, use the xlsclients -l command.

NOTE   *There is a special window called the root window; it's the background on the display. However, you may never see this window (see "Desktop Background" on page 304).*

14.3.1   X Events

X clients get their input and other information about the state of the server through a system of events. X events work like other asynchronous inter-process communication events such as udev events and D-Bus events: The X server receives information from a source such as an input device, then redistributes that input as an event to any interested X client.

You can experiment with events with the xev command. Running it opens a new window that you can mouse into, click, and type. As you do so, xev generates output describing the X events that it receives from the server. For example, here's sample output for mouse movement:

```
$ xev
--snip--
MotionNotify event, serial 36, synthetic NO, window 0x6800001,
    root 0xbb, subw 0x0, time 43937883, (47,174), root:(1692,486),
    state 0x0, is_hint 0, same_screen YES

MotionNotify event, serial 36, synthetic NO, window 0x6800001,
    root 0xbb, subw 0x0, time 43937891, (43,177), root:(1688,489),
    state 0x0, is_hint 0, same_screen YES
```

Notice the coordinates in parentheses. The first pair represents the x- and y-coordinates of the mouse pointer inside the window, and the second (root:) is the location of the pointer on the entire display.

Other low-level events include key presses and button clicks, but a few more advanced ones indicate whether the mouse has entered or exited the window, or if the window has gained or lost focus from the window manager. For example, here are corresponding exit and unfocus events:

```
LeaveNotify event, serial 36, synthetic NO, window 0x6800001,
    root 0xbb, subw 0x0, time 44348653, (55,185), root:(1679,420),
    mode NotifyNormal, detail NotifyNonlinear, same_screen YES,
    focus YES, state 0

FocusOut event, serial 36, synthetic NO, window 0x6800001,
    mode NotifyNormal, detail NotifyNonlinear
```

One common use of xev is to extract keycodes and key symbols for different keyboards when remapping the keyboard. Here's the output from pressing the L key; the keycode here is 46:

```
KeyPress event, serial 32, synthetic NO, window 0x4c00001,
    root 0xbb, subw 0x0, time 2084270084, (131,120), root:(197,172),
    state 0x0, keycode 46 (keysym 0x6c, l), same_screen YES,
    XLookupString gives 1 bytes: (6c) "l"
    XmbLookupString gives 1 bytes: (6c) "l"
    XFilterEvent returns: False
```

You can also attach xev to an existing window ID with the -id *id* option. (Use the ID that you get from xwininfo as *id*) or monitor the root window with -root.)

14.3.2   Understanding X Input and Preference Settings

One of the most potentially baffling characteristics of X is that there's often more than one way to set preferences, and some methods may not work. For example, one common keyboard preference on Linux systems is to remap the Caps Lock key to a Control key. There are a number of ways to do this, from making small adjustments with the old xmodmap command to providing an entirely new keyboard map with the setxkbmap utility. How do you know which ones (if any) to use? It's a matter of knowing which pieces of the system have responsibility, but determining this can be difficult. Keep in mind that a desktop environment may provide its own settings and overrides.

With this said, here are a few pointers on the underlying infrastructure.

Input Devices (General)

The X server uses the *X Input Extension* to manage input from many different devices. There are two basic types of input device—keyboard and pointer (mouse)—and you can attach as many devices as you like. In order to use more than one of the same type of device simultaneously, the X Input Extension creates a "virtual core" device that funnels device input to the X server. The core device is called the master; the physical devices that you plug in to the machine become slaves.

To see the device configuration on your machine, try running the xinput --list command:

```
$ xinput --list
  Virtual core pointer                        id=2    [master pointer  (3)]
      Virtual core XTEST pointer              id=4    [slave  pointer  (2)]
      Logitech Unifying Device                id=8    [slave  pointer  (2)]
  Virtual core keyboard                       id=3    [master keyboard (2)]
      Virtual core XTEST keyboard             id=5    [slave  keyboard (3)]
      Power Button                            id=6    [slave  keyboard (3)]
      Power Button                            id=7    [slave  keyboard (3)]
      Cypress USB Keyboard                    id=9    [slave  keyboard (3)]
```

Each device has an associated ID that you can use with xinput and other commands. In this output, IDs 2 and 3 are the core devices, and IDs 8 and 9 are the real devices. Notice that the power buttons on the machine are also treated as X input devices.

Most X clients listen for input from the core devices, because there is no reason for them to be concerned about which particular device originates an event. In fact, most clients know nothing about the X Input Extension. However, a client can use the extension to single out a particular device.

Each device has a set of associated *properties*. To view the properties, use xinput with the device number, as in this example:

```
$ xinput --list-props 8
Device 'Logitech Unifying Device. Wireless PID:4026':
        Device Enabled (126):   1
        Coordinate Transformation Matrix (128): 1.000000, 0.000000, 0.000000,
0.000000, 1.000000, 0.000000, 0.000000, 0.000000, 1.000000
        Device Accel Profile (256):     0
        Device Accel Constant Deceleration (257):       1.000000
        Device Accel Adaptive Deceleration (258):       1.000000
        Device Accel Velocity Scaling (259):    10.000000
--snip--
```

As you can see, there are a number of very interesting properties that you can change with the --set-prop option (See the xinput(1) manual page for more information.)

Mouse

You can manipulate device-related settings with the xinput command, and many of the most useful pertain to the mouse (pointer). You can change many settings directly as properties, but it's usually easier with the specialized --set-ptr-feedback and --set-button-map options to xinput. For example, if you have a three-button mouse at *dev* on which you'd like to reverse the order of buttons (this is handy for left-handed users), try this:

```
$ xinput --set-button-map dev 3 2 1
```

Keyboard

The many different keyboard layouts available internationally present particular difficulties for integration into any windowing system. X has always had an internal keyboard-mapping capability in its core protocol that you can manipulate with the xmodmap command, but any reasonably modern system uses the XKB (the X keyboard extension) to gain finer control.

XKB is complicated, so much so that many people still use xmodmap when they need to make quick changes. The basic idea behind XKB is that you can define a keyboard map and compile it with the xkbcomp command, then load and activate that map in the X server with the setxkbmap command. Two especially interesting features of the system are these:

- You can define partial maps to supplement existing maps. This is especially handy for tasks such as changing your Caps Lock key into a Control key, and it is used by many graphical keyboard preference utilities in desktop environments.
- You can define individual maps for each attached keyboard.

Desktop Background

The old X command xsetroot allows you to set the background color and other characteristics of the root window, but it produces no effect on most machines because the root window is never visible. Instead, most desktop environments place a big window in the back of all of your other windows in order to enable features such as "active wallpaper" and desktop file browsing. There are ways to change the background from the command line (for example, with the gsettings command in some GNOME installations), but if you actually *want* to do this, you probably have too much time on your hands.

xset

Probably the oldest preference command is xset. It's not used much anymore, but you can run a quick xset q to get the status of a few features. Perhaps the most useful are the screensaver and *Display Power Management Signaling (DPMS)* settings.

14.4 The Future of X

As you were reading the preceding discussion, you may have gotten the feeling that X is a really old system that's been poked at a lot in order to get it to do new tricks. You wouldn't be far off. The X Window System was first developed in the 1980s. Although its evolution over the years has been significant (flexibility was an important part of its original design), you can push the original architecture only so far.

One sign of the age of the X Window System is that the server itself supports an extremely large number of libraries, many for backward compatibility. But perhaps more significantly, the idea of having a server manage clients, their windows, and act as an intermediary for the window memory has become a burden on performance. It's much faster to allow applications to render the contents of their windows directly in the display memory, with a lighter-weight window manager, called a *compositing window manager*, to arrange the windows and do minimal management of the display memory.

A new standard based on this idea, Wayland, has started to gain traction. The most significant piece of Wayland is a protocol that defines how clients talk to the compositing window manager. Other pieces include input device management and an X-compatibility system. As a protocol, Wayland also maintains the idea of network transparency. Many pieces of the Linux desktop now support Wayland, such as GNOME and KDE.

But Wayland isn't the only alternative to X. As of this writing, another project, Mir, has similar goals, though its architecture takes a somewhat different approach. At some point, there will be widespread adoption of at least one system, which may or may not be one of these.

These new developments are significant because they won't be limited to the Linux desktop. Due to its poor performance and gigantic footprint, the X Window System is not suitable for environments such as tablets and smartphones, so manufacturers have so far used alternative systems to drive embedded Linux displays. However, standardized direct rendering can make for a more cost-effective way to support these displays.

14.5 D-Bus

One of the most important developments to come out of the Linux desktop is *the Desktop Bus (D-Bus)*, a message-passing system. D-Bus is important because it serves as an interprocess communication mechanism that allows desktop applications to talk to each other, and because most Linux systems use it to notify processes of system events, such as inserting a USB drive.

D-Bus itself consists of a library that standardizes interprocess communication with a protocol and supporting functions for any two processes to talk to each other. By itself, this library doesn't offer much more than a fancy version of normal IPC facilities such as Unix domain sockets. What makes D-Bus useful is a central "hub" called dbus-daemon. Processes that need to react to events can connect to dbus-daemon and register to receive certain kinds of events. Processes also create the events. For example, the process udisks-daemon listens to ubus for disk events and sends them to dbus-daemon, which then retransmits the events to applications interested in disk events.

14.5.1   System and Session Instances

D-Bus has become a more integral part of the Linux system, and it now goes beyond the desktop. For example, both systemd and Upstart have D-Bus channels of communication. However, adding dependencies to desktop tools inside the core system goes against a core design rule of Linux.

To address this problem, there are actually two kinds of dbus-daemon instances (processes) that can run. The first is the system instance, which is started by init at boot time with the --system option. The system instance usually runs as a D-Bus user, and its configuration file is */etc/dbus-1/system.conf* (though you probably shouldn't change the configuration). Processes can connect to the system instance through the */var/run/dbus/system_bus_socket* Unix domain socket.

Independent of the system D-Bus instance, there is an optional session instance that runs only when you start a desktop session. Desktop applications that you run connect to this instance.

14.5.2   Monitoring D-Bus Messages

One of the best ways to see the difference between the system and session dbus-daemon instances is to monitor the events that go over the bus. Try using the dbus-monitor utility in system mode like this:

```
$ dbus-monitor --system
signal sender=org.freedesktop.DBus -> dest=:1.952 serial=2 path=/org/
freedesktop/DBus; interface=org.freedesktop.DBus; member=NameAcquired
    string ":1.952"
```

The startup message here indicates that the monitor connected and acquired a name. You shouldn't see much activity when you run it like this, because the system instance usually isn't very busy. To see something happen, try plugging in a USB storage device.

By comparison, session instances have much more to do. Assuming you've logged in to a desktop session, try this:

```
$ dbus-monitor --session
```

Now move your mouse around to different windows; if your desktop is D-Bus aware, you should get a flurry of messages indicating activated windows.

14.6 Printing

Printing a document on Linux is a multistage process. It goes like this:

1. The program doing the printing usually converts the document into PostScript form. This step is optional.
2. The program sends the document to a print server.
3. The print server receives the document and places it on a print queue.
4. When the document's turn in the queue arrives, the print server sends the document to a print filter.
5. If the document is not in PostScript form, a print filter might perform a conversion.
6. If the destination printer does not understand PostScript, a printer driver converts the document to a printer-compatible format.
7. The printer driver adds optional instructions to the document, such as paper tray and duplexing options.
8. The print server uses a backend to send the document to the printer.

The most confusing part of this process is why so much revolves around PostScript. PostScript is actually a programming language, so when you print a file using it, you're sending a program to the printer. PostScript serves as a standard for printing in Unix-like systems, much as the *.tar* format serves as an archiving standard. (Some applications now use PDF output, but this is relatively easy to convert.)

We'll talk more about the print format later; first, let's look at the queuing system.

14.6.1 CUPS

The standard printing system in Linux is *CUPS* (*http://www.cups.org/*), which is the same system used on Mac OS X. The CUPS server daemon is called cupsd, and you can use the lpr command as a simple client to send files to the daemon.

One significant feature of CUPS is that it implements *Internet Print Protocol (IPP)*, a system that allows for HTTP-like transactions among clients and servers on TCP port 631. In fact, if you have CUPS running on your system, you can probably connect to *http://localhost:631/* to see your current configuration and check on any printer jobs. Most network printers and print servers support IPP, as does Windows, which can make setting up remote printers a relatively simple task.

You probably won't be able to administer the system from the web interface, because the default setup isn't very secure. Instead, your distribution likely has a graphical settings interface to add and modify printers. These tools manipulate the configuration files, normally found in */etc/cups*. It's usually best to let these tools do the work for you, because configuration can be complicated. And even if you do run into a problem and need to configure manually, it's usually best to create a printer using the graphical tools so that you have somewhere to start.

14.6.2   Format Conversion and Print Filters

Many printers, including nearly all low-end models, do not understand PostScript or PDF. In order for Linux to support one of these printers, it must convert documents to a format specific to the printer. CUPS sends the document to a Raster Image Processor (RIP) to produce a bitmap. The RIP almost always uses the Ghostscript (gs) program to do most of the real work, but it's somewhat complicated because the bitmap must fit the format of the printer. Therefore, the printer drivers that CUPS uses consult the PostScript Printer Definition (PPD) file for the specific printer to figure out settings such as resolution and paper sizes.

14.7   Other Desktop Topics

One interesting characteristic of the Linux desktop environment is that you can generally choose which pieces you want to use and stop using the ones that you dislike. For a survey of many of the desktop projects, have a look at the mailing lists and project links for the various projects at *http://www.freedesktop.org/*. Elsewhere, you'll find other desktop projects, such as Ayatana, Unity, and Mir.

Another major development in the Linux desktop is the Chromium OS open source project and its Google Chrome OS counterpart found on Chromebook PCs. This is a Linux system that uses much of the desktop technology described in this chapter but is centered around the Chromium/Chrome web browsers. Much of what's found on a traditional desktop has been stripped away in Chrome OS.

15

DEVELOPMENT TOOLS

Linux and Unix are very popular with programmers, not just due to the overwhelming array of tools and environments available but also because the system is exceptionally well documented and transparent. On a Linux machine, you don't have to be a programmer to take advantage of development tools, but when working with the system, you should know something about programming tools because they play a larger role in managing Unix systems than in other operating systems. At the very least, you should be able to identify development utilities and have some idea of how to run them.

This chapter packs a lot of information into a small space, but you don't need to master everything here. You can easily skim the material and come back later. The discussion of shared libraries is likely the most important thing that you need to know. But to understand where shared libraries come from, you first need some background on how to build programs.

15.1   The C Compiler

Knowing how to run the C programming language compiler can give you a great deal of insight into the origin of the programs that you see on your Linux system. The source code for most Linux utilities, and for many applications on Linux systems, is written in C or C++. We'll primarily use examples in C for this chapter, but you'll be able to carry the information over to C++.

C programs follow a traditional development process: You write programs, you compile them, and they run. That is, when you write a C program and want to run it, you must *compile* the source code that you wrote into a binary low-level form that the computer understands. You can compare this to the scripting languages that we'll discuss later, where you don't need to compile anything.

NOTE   *By default, most distributions do not include the tools necessary to compile C code because these tools occupy a fairly large amount of space. If you can't find some of the tools described here, you can install the build-essential package for Debian/Ubuntu or the "Development Tools" yum groupinstall for Fedora/CentOS. Failing that, try a package search for "C compiler."*

The C compiler executable on most Unix systems is the GNU C compiler, gcc, though the newer clang compiler from the LLVM project is gaining popularity. C source code files end with *.c*. Take a look at the single, self-contained C source code file called *hello.c*, which you can find in *The C Programming Language*, 2nd edition, by Brian W. Kernighan and Dennis M. Ritchie (Prentice Hall, 1988):

```
#include <stdio.h>

main() {
    printf("Hello, World.\n");
}
```

Put this source code in a file called *hello.c* and then run this command:

```
$ cc hello.c
```

The result is an executable named *a.out*, which you can run like any other executable on the system. However, you should probably give the executable another name (such as *hello*). To do this, use the compiler's -o option:

```
$ cc -o hello hello.c
```

For small programs, there isn't much more to compiling than that. You might need to add an extra include directory or library (see Sections 15.1.2 and 15.1.3), but let's look at slightly larger programs before getting into those topics.

15.1.1 Multiple Source Files

Most C programs are too large to reasonably fit inside a single source code file. Mammoth files become too disorganized for the programmer, and compilers sometimes even have trouble parsing large files. Therefore, developers group components of the source code together, giving each piece its own file.

When compiling most *.c* files, you don't create an executable right away. Instead, use the compiler's -c option on each file to create *object files*. To see how this works, let's say you have two files, *main.c* and *aux.c*. The following two compiler commands do most of the work of building the program:

```
$ cc -c main.c
$ cc -c aux.c
```

The preceding two commands compile the two source files into the two object files *main.o* and *aux.o*.

An object file is a binary file that a processor can almost understand, except that there are still a few loose ends. First, the operating system doesn't know how to run an object file, and second, you likely need to combine several object files and some system libraries to make a complete program.

To build a fully functioning executable from one or more object files, you must run the *linker*, the ld command in Unix. Programmers rarely use ld on the command line, because the C compiler knows how to run the linker program. So to create an executable called *myprog* from the two object files above, run this command to link them:

```
$ cc -o myprog main.o aux.o
```

Although you can compile multiple source files by hand, as the preceding example shows, it can be hard to keep track of them all during the compiling process when the number of source files multiplies. The make system described in Section 15.2 is the traditional Unix standard for managing compiles. This system is especially important in managing the files described in the next two sections.

15.1.2 Header (Include) Files and Directories

C *header files* are additional source code files that usually contain type and library function declarations. For example, *stdio.h* is a header file (see the simple program in Section 15.1).

Unfortunately, a great number of compiler problems crop up with header files. Most glitches occur when the compiler can't find header files and libraries. There are even some cases where a programmer forgets to include a required header file, causing some of the source code to not compile.

Fixing Include File Problems

Tracking down the correct include files isn't always easy. Sometimes there are several include files with the same names in different directories, and it's not clear which is the correct one. When the compiler can't find an include file, the error message looks like this:

```
badinclude.c:1:22: fatal error: notfound.h: No such file or directory
```

This message reports that the compiler can't find the *notfound.h* header file that the *badinclude.c* file references. This specific error is a direct result of this directive on line 1 of *badinclude.c*:

```
#include <notfound.h>
```

The default include directory in Unix is */usr/include*; the compiler always looks there unless you explicitly tell it not to. However, you can make the compiler look in other include directories (most paths that contain header files have *include* somewhere in the name).

NOTE *You'll learn more about how to find missing include files in Chapter 16.*

For example, let's say that you find *notfound.h* in */usr/junk/include*. You can make the compiler see this directory with the -I option:

```
$ cc -c -I/usr/junk/include badinclude.c
```

Now the compiler should no longer stumble on the line of code in *badinclude.c* that references the header file.

You should also beware of includes that use double quotes (" ") instead of angle brackets (< >), like this:

```
#include "myheader.h"
```

Double quotes mean that the header file is not in a system include directory but that the compiler should otherwise search its include path. It often means that the include file is in the same directory as the source file. If you encounter a problem with double quotes, you're probably trying to compile incomplete source code.

What Is the C Preprocessor (cpp)?

It turns out that the C compiler does not actually do the work of looking for all of these include files. That task falls to the *C preprocessor*, a program that the compiler runs on your source code before parsing the actual program. The preprocessor rewrites source code into a form that the compiler understands; it's a tool for making source code easier to read (and for providing shortcuts).

Preprocessor commands in the source code are called *directives*, and they start with the # character. There are three basic types of directives:

Include files An #include directive instructs the preprocessor to include an entire file. Note that the compiler's -I flag is actually an option that causes the preprocessor to search a specified directory for include files, as you saw in the previous section.

Macro definitions A line such as #define BLAH something tells the preprocessor to substitute something for all occurrences of BLAH in the source code. Convention dictates that macros appear in all uppercase, but it should come as no shock that programmers sometimes use macros whose names look like functions and variables. (Every now and then, this causes a world of headaches. Many programmers make a sport out of abusing the preprocessor.)

NOTE *Instead of defining macros within your source code, you can also define macros by passing parameters to the compiler: -DBLAH=something works like the directive above.*

Conditionals You can mark out certain pieces of code with #ifdef, #if, and #endif. The #ifdef *MACRO* directive checks to see whether the preprocessor macro *MACRO* is defined, and #if *condition* tests to see whether *condition* is nonzero. For both directives, if the condition following the "if statement" is false, the preprocessor does not pass any of the program text between the #if and the next #endif to the compiler. If you plan to look at any C code, you'd better get used to this.

An example of a conditional directive follows. When the preprocessor sees the following code, it checks to see whether the macro DEBUG is defined and, if so, passes the line containing fprintf() on to the compiler. Otherwise, the preprocessor skips this line and continues to process the file after the #endif:

```
#ifdef DEBUG
  fprintf(stderr, "This is a debugging message.\n");
#endif
```

NOTE *The C preprocessor doesn't know anything about C syntax, variables, functions, and other elements. It understands only its own macros and directives.*

On Unix, the C preprocessor's name is cpp, but you can also run it with gcc -E. However, you'll rarely need to run the preprocessor by itself.

15.1.3   Linking with Libraries

The C compiler doesn't know enough about your system to create a useful program all by itself. You need *libraries* to build complete programs. A C library is a collection of common precompiled functions that you can build into your program. For example, many executables use the math library because it provides trigonometric functions and the like.

Libraries come into play primarily at link time, when the linker program creates an executable from object files. For example, if you have a program that uses the gobject library but you forget to tell the compiler to link against that library, you'll see linker errors like this:

```
badobject.o(.text+0x28): undefined reference to 'g_object_new'
```

The most important parts of these error messages are in bold. When the linker program examined the *badobject.o* object file, it couldn't find the function that appears in bold, and as a consequence, it couldn't create the executable. In this particular case, you might suspect that you forgot the gobject library because the missing function is g_object_new().

NOTE   *Undefined references do not always mean that you're missing a library. One of the program's object files could be missing in the link command. It's usually easy to differentiate between library functions and functions in your object files, though.*

To fix this problem, you must first find the gobject library and then use the compiler's -l option to link against the library. As with include files, libraries are scattered throughout the system (*/usr/lib* is the system default location), though most libraries reside in a subdirectory named *lib*. For the preceding example, the basic gobject library file is *libgobject.a*, so the library name is gobject. Putting it all together, you would link the program like this:

```
$ cc -o badobject badobject.o -lgobject
```

You must tell the linker about nonstandard library locations; the parameter for this is -L. Let's say that the badobject program requires *libcrud.a* in */usr/junk/lib*. To compile and create the executable, use a command like this:

```
$ cc -o badobject badobject.o -lgobject -L/usr/junk/lib -lcrud
```

NOTE   *If you want to search a library for a particular function, use the nm command. Be prepared for a lot of output. For example, try this:* **nm libgobject.a**. *(You might need to use the* locate *command to find* libgobject.a; *many distributions now put libraries in architecture-specific subdirectories in* /usr/lib.)*

15.1.4   Shared Libraries

A library file ending with *.a* (such as *libgobject.a*) is called a *static library*. When you link a program against a static library, the linker copies machine code from the library file into your executable. Therefore, the final executable does not need the original library file to run, and furthermore, the executable's behavior never changes.

However, library sizes are always increasing, as is the number of libraries in use, and this makes static libraries wasteful in terms of disk space and memory. In addition, if a static library is later found to be inadequate or insecure, there's no way to change any executable linked against it, short of recompiling the executable.

Shared libraries counter these problems. When you run a program linked against one, the system loads the library's code into the process memory space only when necessary. Many processes can share the same shared library code in memory. And if you need to slightly modify the library code, you can generally do so without recompiling any programs.

Shared libraries have their own costs: difficult management and a somewhat complicated linking procedure. However, you can bring shared libraries under control if you know four things:

- How to list the shared libraries that an executable needs
- How an executable looks for shared libraries
- How to link a program against a shared library
- The common shared library pitfalls

The following sections tell you how to use and maintain your system's shared libraries. If you're interested in how shared libraries work or if you want to know about linkers in general, you can check out *Linkers and Loaders* by John R. Levine (Morgan Kaufmann, 1999), "The Inside Story on Shared Libraries and Dynamic Loading" by David M. Beazley, Brian D. Ward, and Ian R. Cooke (*Computing in Science & Engineering*, September/October 2001), or online resources such as the Program Library HOWTO (*http://dwheeler .com/program-library/*). The ld.so(8) manual page is also worth a read.

Listing Shared Library Dependencies

Shared library files usually reside in the same places as static libraries. The two standard library directories on a Linux system are */lib* and */usr/lib*. The */lib* directory should not contain static libraries.

A shared library has a suffix that contains *.so* (shared object), as in *libc-2.15.so* and *libc.so.6*. To see what shared libraries a program uses, run ldd *prog*, where *prog* is the executable name. Here's an example for the shell:

```
$ ldd /bin/bash
    linux-gate.so.1 =>  (0xb7799000)
    libtinfo.so.5 => /lib/i386-linux-gnu/libtinfo.so.5 (0xb7765000)
    libdl.so.2 => /lib/i386-linux-gnu/libdl.so.2 (0xb7760000)
    libc.so.6 => /lib/i386-linux-gnu/libc.so.6 (0xb75b5000)
    /lib/ld-linux.so.2 (0xb779a000)
```

In the interest of optimal performance and flexibility, executables alone don't usually know the locations of their shared libraries; they know only the names of the libraries, and perhaps a little hint about where to find them. A small program named ld.so (the *runtime dynamic linker/loader*) finds and loads shared libraries for a program at runtime. The preceding ldd output shows the library names on the left—that's what the executable knows. The right side shows where ld.so finds the library.

The final line of output here shows the actual location of ld.so:
ld-linux.so.2.

How ld.so Finds Shared Libraries

One of the common trouble points for shared libraries is that the dynamic linker cannot find a library. The first place the dynamic linker *should* normally look for shared libraries is an executable's preconfigured *runtime library search path (rpath)*, if it exists. You'll see how to create this path shortly.

Next, the dynamic linker looks in a system cache, */etc/ld.so.cache*, to see if the library is in a standard location. This is a fast cache of the names of library files found in directories listed in the cache configuration file */etc/ld.so.conf*.

> **NOTE** *As is typical of many of the Linux configuration files that you've seen,* ld.so.conf *may include a number of files in a directory such as /etc/ld.so.conf.d.*

Each line in *ld.so.conf* is a directory that you want to include in the cache. The list of directories is usually short, containing something like this:

```
/lib/i686-linux-gnu
/usr/lib/i686-linux-gnu
```

The standard library directories */lib* and */usr/lib* are implicit, which means that you don't need to include them in */etc/ld.so.conf*.

If you alter *ld.so.conf* or make a change to one of the shared library directories, you must rebuild the */etc/ld.so.cache* file by hand with the following command:

```
# ldconfig -v
```

The -v option provides detailed information on libraries that ldconfig adds to the cache and any changes that it detects.

There is one more place that ld.so looks for shared libraries: the environment variable LD_LIBRARY_PATH. We'll talk about this soon.

Don't get into the habit of adding stuff to */etc/ld.so.conf*. You should know what shared libraries are in the system cache, and if you put every bizarre little shared library directory into the cache, you risk conflicts and an extremely disorganized system. When you compile software that needs an obscure library path, give your executable a built-in runtime library search path. Let's see how to do that.

Linking Programs Against Shared Libraries

Let's say you have a shared library named *libweird.so.1* in */opt/obscure/lib* that you need to link myprog against. Link the program as follows:

```
$ cc -o myprog myprog.o -Wl,-rpath=/opt/obscure/lib -L/opt/obscure/lib -lweird
```

The `-Wl,-rpath` option tells the linker to include a following directory into the executable's runtime library search path. However, even if you use `-Wl,-rpath`, you still need the `-L` flag.

If you have a pre-existing binary, you can also use the `patchelf` program to insert a different runtime library search path, but it's generally better to do this at compile time.

Problems with Shared Libraries

Shared libraries provide remarkable flexibility, not to mention some really incredible hacks, but it's also possible to abuse them to the point where your system becomes an utter and complete mess. Three particularly bad things can happen:

- Missing libraries
- Terrible performance
- Mismatched libraries

The number one cause of all shared library problems is the environment variable named `LD_LIBRARY_PATH`. Setting this variable to a colon-delimited set of directory names makes `ld.so` search the given directories *before* anything else when looking for a shared library. This is a cheap way to make programs work when you move a library around, if you don't have the program's source code and can't use `patchelf`, or if you're just too lazy to recompile the executables. Unfortunately, you get what you pay for.

Never set `LD_LIBRARY_PATH` in shell startup files or when compiling software. When the dynamic runtime linker encounters this variable, it must often search through the entire contents of each specified directory more times than you'd care to know. This causes a big performance hit, but more importantly, you can get conflicts and mismatched libraries because the runtime linker looks in these directories for *every* program.

If you *must* use `LD_LIBRARY_PATH` to run some crummy program for which you don't have the source (or an application that you'd rather not compile, like Mozilla or some other beast), use a wrapper script. Let's say your executable is */opt/crummy/bin/crummy.bin* and needs some shared libraries in */opt/crummy/lib*. Write a wrapper script called `crummy` that looks like this:

```
#!/bin/sh
LD_LIBRARY_PATH=/opt/crummy/lib
export LD_LIBRARY_PATH
exec /opt/crummy/bin/crummy.bin $@
```

Avoiding `LD_LIBRARY_PATH` prevents most shared library problems. But one other significant problem that occasionally comes up with developers is that a library's application programming interface (API) may change slightly from one minor version to another, breaking installed software. The best solutions here are preventive: Either use a consistent methodology to install shared libraries with `-Wl,-rpath` to create a runtime link path or simply use the static versions of obscure libraries.

15.2 make

A program with more than one source code file or that requires strange compiler options is too cumbersome to compile by hand. This problem has been around for years, and the traditional Unix compile management utility that eases these pains is called make. You should know a little about make if you're running a Unix system, because system utilities sometimes rely on make to operate. However, this chapter is only the tip of the iceberg. There are entire books on make, such as *Managing Projects with GNU Make* by Robert Mecklenburg (O'Reilly, 2004). In addition, most Linux packages are built using an additional layer around make or a similar tool. There are many build systems out there; we'll look at one named autotools in Chapter 16.

make is a big system, but it's not very difficult to get an idea of how it works. When you see a file named *Makefile* or *makefile*, you know that you're dealing with make. (Try running make to see if you can build anything.)

The basic idea behind make is the *target*, a goal that you want to achieve. A target can be a file (a *.o* file, an executable, and so on) or a label. In addition, some targets depend on other targets; for instance, you need a complete set of *.o* files before you can link your executable. These requirements are called *dependencies.*

To build a target, make follows a *rule*, such as a rule for how to go from a *.c* source file to a *.o* object file. make already knows several rules, but you can customize these existing rules and create your own.

15.2.1 A Sample Makefile

The following very simple Makefile builds a program called myprog from *aux.c* and *main.c*:

```
# object files
OBJS=aux.o main.o

all: myprog

myprog: $(OBJS)
        $(CC) -o myprog $(OBJS)
```

The # in the first line of this Makefile denotes a comment.

The next line is just a macro definition; it sets the OBJS variable to two object filenames. This will be important later. For now, take note of how you define the macro and also how you reference it later ($(OBJS)).

The next item in the Makefile contains its first target, all. The first target is always the default, the target that make wants to build when you run make by itself on the command line.

The rule for building a target comes after the colon. For all, this Makefile says that you need to satisfy something called myprog. This is the first dependency in the file; all depends on myprog. Note that myprog can be an actual file or the target of another rule. In this case, it's both (the rule for all and the target of OBJS).

To build myprog, this Makefile uses the macro $(OBJS) in the dependencies. The macro expands to *aux.o* and *main.o*, so myprog depends on these two files (they must be actual files, because there aren't any targets with those names anywhere in the Makefile).

This Makefile assumes that you have two C source files named *aux.c* and *main.c* in the same directory. Running make on the Makefile yields the following output, showing the commands that make is running:

```
$ make
cc    -c -o aux.o aux.c
cc    -c -o main.o main.c
cc -o myprog aux.o main.o
```

A diagram of the dependencies is shown in Figure 15-1.

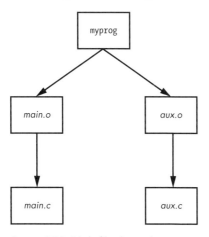

Figure 15-1: Makefile dependencies

15.2.2 Built-in Rules

So how does make know how to go from *aux.c* to *aux.o*? After all, *aux.c* is not in the Makefile. The answer is that make follows its built-in rules. It knows to look for a *.c* file when you want a *.o* file, and furthermore, it knows how to run cc -c on that *.c* file to get to its goal of creating a *.o* file.

15.2.3 Final Program Build

The final step in getting to myprog is a little tricky, but the idea is clear enough. After you have the two object files in $(OBJS), you can run the C compiler according to the following line (where $(CC) expands to the compiler name):

```
    $(CC) -o myprog $(OBJS)
```

The whitespace before $(CC) is a tab. You *must* insert a tab before any real command, on its own line.

Watch out for this:

```
Makefile:7: *** missing separator.  Stop.
```

An error like this means that the Makefile is broken. The tab is the separator, and if there is no separator or there's some other interference, you'll see this error.

15.2.4   Staying Up-to-Date

One last make fundamental is that targets should be up-to-date with their dependencies. If you type make twice in a row for the preceding example, the first command builds myprog, but the second yields this output:

```
make: Nothing to be done for 'all'.
```

This second time through, make looked at its rules and noticed that myprog already exists, so it didn't build myprog again because none of the dependencies had changed since it was last built. To experiment with this, do the following:

1. Run **touch aux.c**.
2. Run **make** again. This time, make determines that *aux.c* is newer than the *aux.o* already in the directory, so it compiles *aux.o* again.
3. myprog depends on *aux.o*, and now *aux.o* is newer than the preexisting myprog, so make must create myprog again.

This type of chain reaction is very typical.

15.2.5   Command-Line Arguments and Options

You can get a great deal of mileage out of make if you know how its command-line arguments and options work.

One of the most useful options is to specify a single target on the command line. For the preceding Makefile, you can run make aux.o if you want only the *aux.o* file.

You can also define a macro on the command line. For example, to use the clang compiler, try

```
$ make CC=clang
```

Here, make uses your definition of CC instead of its default compiler, cc. Command-line macros come in handy when testing preprocessor definitions and libraries, especially with the CFLAGS and LDFLAGS macros that we'll discuss shortly.

In fact, you don't even need a Makefile to run make. If built-in make rules match a target, you can just ask make to try to create the target. For example, if you have the source to a very simple program called *blah.c*, try `make blah`. The `make` run proceeds like this:

```
$ make blah
cc   blah.o   -o blah
```

This use of `make` works only for the most elementary C programs; if your program needs a library or special include directory, you should probably write a Makefile. Running `make` without a Makefile is actually most useful when you're dealing with something like Fortran, Lex, or Yacc and don't know how the compiler or utility works. Why not let `make` try to figure it out for you? Even if `make` fails to create the target, it will probably still give you a pretty good hint as to how to use the tool.

Two `make` options stand out from the rest:

-n   Prints the commands necessary for a build but prevents `make` from actually running any commands

-f *file*   Tells `make` to read from *file* instead of *Makefile* or *makefile*

15.2.6   Standard Macros and Variables

`make` has many special macros and variables. It's difficult to tell the difference between a macro and a variable, so we'll use the term *macro* to mean something that usually doesn't change after `make` starts building targets.

As you saw earlier, you can set macros at the start of your Makefile. These are the most common macros:

CFLAGS   C compiler options. When creating object code from a *.c* file, `make` passes this as an argument to the compiler.

LDFLAGS   Like `CFLAGS`, but they're for the linker when creating an executable from object code.

LDLIBS   If you use `LDFLAGS` but do not want to combine the library name options with the search path, put the library name options in this file.

CC   The C compiler. The default is `cc`.

CPPFLAGS   C *preprocessor* options. When `make` runs the C preprocessor in some way, it passes this macro's expansion on as an argument.

CXXFLAGS   GNU `make` uses this for C++ compiler flags.

A `make` *variable* changes as you build targets. Because you never set `make` variables by hand, the following list includes the $.

$@   When inside a rule, this expands to the current target.

$*   Expands to the *basename* of the current target. For example, if you're building *blah.o*, this expands to *blah*.

The most comprehensive list of `make` variables on Linux is the `make` info manual.

Keep in mind that GNU make has many extensions, built-in rules, and features that other variants do not have. This is fine as long as you're running Linux, but if you step off onto a Solaris or BSD machine and expect the same stuff to work, you might be in for a surprise. However, that's the problem that multi-platform build systems such as GNU autotools solve.

15.2.7   Conventional Targets

Most Makefiles contain several standard targets that perform auxiliary tasks related to compiles.

clean   The clean target is ubiquitous; a make clean usually instructs make to remove all of the object files and executables so that you can make a fresh start or pack up the software. Here's an example rule for the myprog Makefile:

```
clean:
        rm -f $(OBJS) myprog
```

distclean   A Makefile created by way of the GNU autotools system always has a distclean target to remove everything that wasn't part of the original distribution, including the Makefile. You'll see more of this in Chapter 16. On very rare occasions, you might find that a developer opts not to remove the executable with this target, preferring something like realclean instead.

install   Copies files and compiled programs to what the Makefile thinks is the proper place on the system. This can be dangerous, so always run a make -n install first to see what will happen without actually running any commands.

test or check   Some developers provide test or check targets to make sure that everything works after performing a build.

depend   Creates dependencies by calling the compiler with -M to examine the source code. This is an unusual-looking target because it often changes the Makefile itself. This is no longer common practice, but if you come across some instructions telling you to use this rule, make sure to do so.

all   Often the first target in the Makefile. You'll often see references to this target instead of an actual executable.

15.2.8   Organizing a Makefile

Even though there are many different Makefile styles, most programmers adhere to some general rules of thumb. For one, in the first part of the Makefile (inside the macro definitions), you should see libraries and includes grouped according to package:

```
MYPACKAGE_INCLUDES=-I/usr/local/include/mypackage
MYPACKAGE_LIB=-L/usr/local/lib/mypackage -lmypackage
```

```
PNG_INCLUDES=-I/usr/local/include
PNG_LIB=-L/usr/local/lib -lpng
```

Each type of compiler and linker flag often gets a macro like this:

```
CFLAGS=$(CFLAGS) $(MYPACKAGE_INCLUDES) $(PNG_INCLUDES)
LDFLAGS=$(LDFLAGS) $(MYPACKAGE_LIB) $(PNG_LIB)
```

Object files are usually grouped according to executables. For example, say you have a package that creates executables called boring and trite. Each has its own *.c* source file and requires the code in *util.c.* You might see something like this:

```
UTIL_OBJS=util.o

BORING_OBJS=$(UTIL_OBJS) boring.o
TRITE_OBJS=$(UTIL_OBJS) trite.o

PROGS=boring trite
```

The rest of the Makefile might look like this:

```
all: $(PROGS)

boring: $(BORING_OBJS)
        $(CC) -o $@ $(BORING_OBJS) $(LDFLAGS)

trite: $(TRITE_OBJS)
        $(CC) -o $@ $(TRITE_OBJS) $(LDFLAGS)
```

You could combine the two executable targets into one rule, but it's usually not a good idea to do so because you would not easily be able to move a rule to another Makefile, delete an executable, or group executables differently. Furthermore, the dependencies would be incorrect: If you had just one rule for boring and trite, trite would depend on *boring.c*, boring would depend on *trite.c*, and make would always try to rebuild both programs whenever you changed one of the two source files.

NOTE   *If you need to define a special rule for an object file, put the rule for the object file just above the rule that builds the executable. If several executables use the same object file, put the object rule above all of the executable rules.*

15.3   Debuggers

The standard debugger on Linux systems is gdb; user-friendly frontends such as the Eclipse IDE and Emacs systems are also available. To enable full debugging in your programs, run the compiler with -g to write a symbol table and other debugging information into the executable. To start gdb on an executable named *program*, run

```
$ gdb program
```

You should get a (gdb) prompt. To run *program* with the command-line argument *options*, enter this at the (gdb) prompt:

```
(gdb) run options
```

If the program works, it should start, run, and exit as normal. However, if there's a problem, gdb stops, prints the failed source code, and throws you back to the (gdb) prompt. Because the source code fragment often hints at the problem, you'll probably want to print the value of a particular variable that the trouble may be related to. (The print command also works for arrays and C structures.)

```
(gdb) print variable
```

To make gdb stop the program at any point in the original source code, use the breakpoint feature. In the following command, *file* is a source code file, and *line_num* is the line number in that file where gdb should stop:

```
(gdb) break file:line_num
```

To tell gdb to continue executing the program, use

```
(gdb) continue
```

To clear a breakpoint, enter

```
(gdb) clear file:line_num
```

This section has provided only the briefest introduction to gdb, which includes an extensive manual that you can read online, in print, or buy as *Debugging with GDB*, 10th edition, by Richard M. Stallman et al. (GNU Press, 2011). *The Art of Debugging* by Norman Matloff and Peter Jay Salzman (No Starch Press, 2008) is another guide to debugging.

NOTE *If you're interested in rooting out memory problems and running profiling tests, try Valgrind (*http://valgrind.org/*).*

15.4 Lex and Yacc

You might encounter Lex and Yacc when compiling programs that read configuration files or commands. These tools are building blocks for programming languages.

- Lex is a *tokenizer* that transforms text into numbered tags with labels. The GNU/Linux version is named flex. You may need a -ll or -lfl linker flag in conjunction with Lex.

- Yacc is a *parser* that attempts to read tokens according to a *grammar*. The GNU parser is bison; to get Yacc compatibility, run bison -y. You may need the -ly linker flag.

15.5 Scripting Languages

A long time ago, the average Unix systems manager didn't have to worry much about scripting languages other than the Bourne shell and awk. Shell scripts (discussed in Chapter 11) continue to be an important part of Unix, but awk has faded somewhat from the scripting arena. However, many powerful successors have arrived, and many systems programs have actually switched from C to scripting languages (such as the sensible version of the whois program). Let's look at some scripting basics.

The first thing you need to know about any scripting language is that the first line of a script looks like the shebang of a Bourne shell script. For example, a Python script starts out like this:

```
#!/usr/bin/python
```

Or this:

```
#!/usr/bin/env python
```

In Unix, *any* executable text file that starts with #! is a script. The pathname following this prefix is the scripting language interpreter executable. When Unix tries to run an executable file that starts with a #! shebang, it runs the program following the #! with the rest of the file as the standard input. Therefore, even this is a script:

```
#!/usr/bin/tail -2
This program won't print this line,
but it will print this line...
and this line, too.
```

The first line of a shell script often contains one of the most common basic script problems: an invalid path to the scripting language interpreter. For example, say you named the previous script myscript. What if tail were actually in */bin* instead of */usr/bin* on your system? In that case, running myscript would produce this error:

```
bash: ./myscript: /usr/bin/tail: bad interpreter: No such file or directory
```

Don't expect more than one argument in the script's first line to work. That is, the -2 in the preceding example might work, but if you add another argument, the system could decide to treat the -2 *and* the new argument as one big argument, spaces and all. This can vary from system to system; don't test your patience on something as insignificant as this.

Now, let's look at a few of the languages out there.

15.5.1   Python

Python is a scripting language with a strong following and an array of powerful features, such as text processing, database access, networking, and multithreading. It has a powerful interactive mode and a very organized object model.

Python's executable is python, and it's usually in */usr/bin*. However, Python isn't used just from the command line for scripts. One place you'll find it is as a tool to build websites. *Python Essential Reference*, 4th edition, by David M. Beazley (Addison-Wesley, 2009) is a great reference with a small tutorial at the beginning to get you started.

15.5.2   Perl

One of the older third-party Unix scripting languages is Perl. It's the original "Swiss army chainsaw" of programming tools. Although Perl has lost a fair amount of ground to Python in recent years, it excels in particular at text processing, conversion, and file manipulation, and you may find many tools built with it. *Learning Perl*, 6th edition, by Randal L. Schwartz, brian d foy, and Tom Phoenix(O'Reilly, 2011) is a tutorial-style introduction; a larger reference is *Modern Perl* by Chromatic (Onyx Neon Press, 2014).

15.5.3   Other Scripting Languages

You might also encounter these scripting languages:

PHP   This is a hypertext-processing language often found in dynamic web scripts. Some people use PHP for standalone scripts. The PHP website is at *http://www.php.net/*.

Ruby   Object-oriented fanatics and many web developers enjoy programming in this language (*http://www.ruby-lang.org/*).

JavaScript   This language is used inside web browsers primarily to manipulate dynamic content. Most experienced programmers shun it as a standalone scripting language due to its many flaws, but it's nearly impossible to avoid when doing web programming. You might find an implementation called Node.js with an executable name of node on your system.

Emacs Lisp   A variety of the Lisp programming language used by the Emacs text editor.

Matlab, Octave   Matlab is a commercial matrix and mathematical programming language and library. There is a very similar free software project called Octave.

R A popular free statistical analysis language. See *http://www.r-project .org/* and *The Art of R Programming* by Norman Matloff (No Starch Press, 2011) for more information.

Mathematica Another commercial mathematical programming language with libraries.

m4 This is a macro-processing language, usually found only in the GNU autotools.

Tcl Tcl (tool command language) is a simple scripting language usually associated with the Tk graphical user interface toolkit and Expect, an automation utility. Although Tcl does not enjoy the widespread use that it once did, don't discount its power. Many vetcran developers prefer Tk, especially for its embedded capabilities. See *http://www.tcl.tk/* for more on Tk.

15.6 Java

Java is a compiled language like C, with a simpler syntax and powerful support for object-oriented programming. It has a few niches in Unix systems. For one, it's often used as a web application environment, and it's popular for specialized applications. For example, Android applications are usually written in Java. Even though it's not often seen on a typical Linux desktop, you should know how Java works, at least for standalone applications.

There are two kinds of Java compilers: native compilers for producing machine code for your system (like a C compiler) and bytecode compilers for use by a bytecode interpreter (sometimes called a *virtual machine*, which is different from the virtual machine offered by a hypervisor, as described in Chapter 17). You'll practically always encounter bytecode on Linux.

Java bytecode files end in *.class*. The Java runtime environment (JRE) contains all of the programs you need to run Java bytecode. To run a bytecode file, use

```
$ java file.class
```

You might also encounter bytecode files that end in *.jar*, which are collections of archived *.class* files. To run a *.jar* file, use this syntax:

```
$ java -jar file.jar
```

Sometimes you need to set the JAVA_HOME environment variable to your Java installation prefix. If you're really unlucky, you might need to use CLASSPATH to include any directories containing classes that your program expects. This is a colon-delimited set of directories like the regular PATH variable for executables.

If you need to compile a *.java* file into bytecode, you need the Java Development Kit (JDK). You can run the javac compiler from JDK to create some *.class* files:

```
$ javac file.java
```

JDK also comes with jar, a program that can create and pick apart *.jar* files. It works like tar.

15.7 Looking Forward: Compiling Packages

The world of compilers and scripting languages is vast and constantly expanding. As of this writing, new compiled languages such as Go (golang) and Swift are gaining popularity.

The LLVM compiler infrastructure set (*http://llvm.org/*) has significantly eased compiler development. If you're interested in how to design and implement a compiler, two good books are *Compilers: Principles, Techniques, and Tools*, 2nd edition, by Alfred V. Aho et al. (Addison-Wesley, 2006) and *Modern Compiler Design*, 2nd edition, by Dick Grune et al. (Springer, 2012). For scripting language development, it's usually best to look for online resources, as the implementations vary widely.

Now that you know the basics of the programming tools on the system, you're ready to see what they can do. The next chapter is all about how you can build packages on Linux from source code.

16

INTRODUCTION TO COMPILING SOFTWARE FROM C SOURCE CODE

Most nonproprietary third-party Unix software packages come as source code that you can build and install. One reason for this is that Unix (and Linux itself) has so many different flavors and architectures that it would be difficult to distribute binary packages for all possible platform combinations. The other reason, which is at least as important, is that widespread source code distribution throughout the Unix community encourages users to contribute bug fixes and new features to software, giving meaning to the term *open source*.

You can get nearly everything you see on a Linux system as source code—from the kernel and C library to the web browsers. It's even possible to update and augment your entire system by (re-)installing parts of your system from the source code. However, you probably *shouldn't* update your machine by installing *everything* from source code, unless you really enjoy the process or have some other reason.

Linux distributions typically provide easier ways to update core parts of the system, such as the programs in */bin*, and one particularly important property of distributions is that they usually fix security problems very quickly. But don't expect your distribution to provide everything for you. Here are some reasons why you may want to install certain packages yourself:

- To control configuration options.
- To install the software anywhere you like. You can even install several different versions of the same package.
- To control the version that you install. Distributions don't always stay up-to-date with the latest versions of all packages, particularly add-ons to software packages (such as Python libraries).
- To better understand how a package works.

16.1   Software Build Systems

There are many programming environments on Linux, from traditional C to interpreted scripting languages such as Python. Each typically has at least one distinct system for building and installing packages in addition to the tools that a Linux distribution provides.

We're going to look at compiling and installing C source code in this chapter with only one of these build systems—the configuration scripts generated from the GNU autotools suite. This system is generally considered stable, and many of the basic Linux utilities use it. Because it's based on existing tools such as make, after you see it in action, you'll be able to transfer your knowledge to other build systems.

Installing a package from C source code usually involves the following steps:

1. Unpack the source code archive.
2. Configure the package.
3. Run make to build the programs.
4. Run make install or a distribution-specific install command to install the package.

NOTE   *You should understand the basics in Chapter 15 before proceeding with this chapter.*

16.2   Unpacking C Source Packages

A package's source code distribution usually comes as a *.tar.gz*, *.tar.bz2*, or *.tar.xz* file, and you should unpack the file as described in Section 2.18. Before you unpack, though, verify the contents of the archive with tar tvf or tar ztvf, because some packages don't create their own subdirectories in the directory where you extract the archive.

Output like this means that the package is probably okay to unpack:

```
package-1.23/Makefile.in
package-1.23/README
package-1.23/main.c
package-1.23/bar.c
--snip--
```

However, you may find that not all files are in a common directory (like *package-1.23* in the preceding example):

```
Makefile
README
main.c
--snip--
```

Extracting an archive like this one can leave a big mess in your current directory. To avoid that, create a new directory and cd there before extracting the contents of the archive.

Finally, beware of packages that contain files with absolute pathnames like this:

```
/etc/passwd
/etc/inetd.conf
```

You likely won't come across anything like this, but if you do, remove the archive from your system. It probably contains a Trojan horse or some other malicious code.

16.2.1   Where to Start

Once you've extracted the contents of a source archive and have a bunch of files in front of you, try to get a feel for the package. In particular, look for the files *README* and *INSTALL*. Always look at any *README* files first because they often contain a description of the package, a small manual, installation hints, and other useful information. Many packages also come with *INSTALL* files with instructions on how to compile and install the package. Pay particular attention to special compiler options and definitions.

In addition to *README* and *INSTALL* files, you will find other package files that roughly fall into three categories:

- Files relating to the make system, such as *Makefile*, *Makefile.in*, *configure*, and *CMakeLists.txt*. Some very old packages come with a Makefile that you may need to modify, but most use a configuration utility such as GNU autoconf or CMake. They come with a script or configuration file (such as *configure* or *CMakeLists.txt*) to help generate a Makefile from *Makefile.in* based on your system settings and configuration options.

- Source code files ending in *.c, .h,* or *.cc.* C source code files may appear just about anywhere in a package directory. C++ source code files usually have *.cc, .C,* or *.cxx* suffixes.

- Object files ending in *.o* or binaries. Normally, there aren't any object files in source code distributions, but you might find some in rare cases when the package maintainer is not permitted to release certain source code and you need to do something special in order to use the object files. In most cases, object (or binary executable) files in a source distribution mean that the package wasn't put together well, and you should run make clean to make sure that you get a fresh compile.

16.3   GNU Autoconf

Even though C source code is usually fairly portable, differences on each platform make it impossible to compile most packages with a single Makefile. Early solutions to this problem were to provide individual Makefiles for every operating system or to provide a Makefile that was easy to modify. This approach evolved into scripts that generate Makefiles based on an analysis of the system used to build the package.

GNU autoconf is a popular system for automatic Makefile generation. Packages using this system come with files named *configure, Makefile.in,* and *config.h.in.* The *.in* files are templates; the idea is to run the configure script in order to discover the characteristics of your system, then make substitutions in the *.in* files to create the real build files. For the end user, it's easy; to generate a Makefile from *Makefile.in,* run configure:

```
$ ./configure
```

You should get a lot of diagnostic output as the script checks your system for prerequisites. If all goes well, configure creates one or more Makefiles and a *config.h* file, as well as a cache file (*config.cache*), so that it doesn't need to run certain tests again.

Now you can run make to compile the package. A successful configure step doesn't necessarily mean that the make step will work, but the chances are pretty good. (See Section 16.6 for troubleshooting failed configures and compiles.)

Let's get some firsthand experience with the process.

NOTE   *At this point, you must have all of the required build tools available on your system. For Debian and Ubuntu, the easiest way is to install the build-essential package; in Fedora-like systems, use the "Development Tools" groupinstall.*

16.3.1   An Autoconf Example

Before discussing how you can change the behavior of autoconf, let's look at a simple example so that you know what to expect. You'll install the GNU coreutils package in your own home directory (to make sure that you don't mess up your system). Get the package from *http://ftp.gnu.org/gnu/coreutils/* (the latest version is usually the best), unpack it, change to its directory, and configure it like this:

```
$ ./configure --prefix=$HOME/mycoreutils
checking for a BSD-compatible install... /usr/bin/install -c
checking whether build environment is sane... yes
--snip--
config.status: executing po-directories commands
config.status: creating po/POTFILES
config.status: creating po/Makefile
```

Now run make:

```
$ make
  GEN      lib/alloca.h
  GEN      lib/c++defs.h
--snip--
make[2]: Leaving directory '/home/juser/coreutils-8.22/gnulib-tests'
make[1]: Leaving directory '/home/juser/coreutils-8.22'
```

Next, try to run one of the executables that you just created, such as *./src/ls*, and try running make check to run a series of tests on the package. (This might take a while, but it's interesting to see.)

Finally, you're ready to install the package. Do a dry run with make -n first to see what make install does without actually doing the install:

```
$ make -n install
```

Browse through the output, and if nothing seems strange (such as installing anywhere other than your *mycoreutils* directory), do the install for real:

```
$ make install
```

You should now have a subdirectory named *mycoreutils* in your home directory that contains *bin*, *share*, and other subdirectories. Check out some of the programs in *bin* (you just built many of the basic tools that you learned in Chapter 2). Finally, because you configured the *mycoreutils* directory to be independent of the rest of your system, you can remove it completely without worrying about causing damage.

16.3.2 Installing Using a Packaging Tool

On most distributions, it's possible to install new software as a package that you can maintain later with your distribution's packaging tools. Debian-based distributions such as Ubuntu are perhaps the easiest; rather than running a plain make install, you can do it with the checkinstall utility, as follows:

```
# checkinstall make install
```

Use the `--pkgname=`*name* option to give your new package a specific name.

Creating an RPM package is a little more involved, because you must first create a directory tree for your package(s). You can do this with the `rpmdev-setuptree` command; when complete, you can use the `rpmbuild` utility to work through the rest of the steps. It's best to follow an online tutorial for this process.

16.3.3   configure Script Options

You've just seen one of the most useful options for the `configure` script: using `--prefix` to specify the installation directory. By default, the `install` target from an autoconf-generated Makefile uses a *prefix* of */usr/local*—that is, binary programs go in */usr/local/bin*, libraries go in */usr/local/lib*, and so on. You will often want to change that prefix like this:

```
$ ./configure --prefix=new_prefix
```

Most versions of `configure` have a `--help` option that lists other configuration options. Unfortunately, the list is usually so long that it's sometimes hard to figure out what might be important, so here are some essential options:

`--bindir=`*directory* Installs executables in *directory*.

`--sbindir=`*directory* Installs system executables in *directory*.

`--libdir=`*directory* Installs libraries in *directory*.

`--disable-shared` Prevents the package from building shared libraries. Depending on the library, this can save hassles later on (see Section 15.1.4).

`--with-`*package*`=`*directory* Tells `configure` that *package* is in *directory*. This is handy when a necessary library is in a nonstandard location. Unfortunately, not all `configure` scripts recognize this type of option, and it can be difficult to determine the exact syntax.

Using Separate Build Directories

You can create separate build directories if you want to experiment with some of these options. To do so, create a new directory anywhere on the system and, from that directory, run the `configure` script in the original package source code directory. You'll find that `configure` then makes a symbolic link farm in your new build directory, where all of the links point back to the source tree in the original package directory. (Some developers prefer that you build packages this way, because the original source tree is never modified. This is also useful if you want to build for more than one platform or configuration option set using the same source package.)

16.3.4   Environment Variables

You can influence `configure` with environment variables that the `configure` script puts into make variables. The most important ones are `CPPFLAGS`, `CFLAGS`, and `LDFLAGS`. But be aware that `configure` can be very picky about environment variables. For example, you should normally use CPPFLAGS instead of CFLAGS for header file directories, because configure often runs the preprocessor independently of the compiler.

In bash, the easiest way to send an environment variable to configure is by placing the variable assignment in front of ./configure on the command line. For example, to define a DEBUG macro for the preprocessor, use this command:

```
$ CPPFLAGS=-DDEBUG ./configure
```

NOTE *You can also pass a variable as an option to configure; for example:*

```
$ ./configure CPPFLAGS=-DDEBUG
```

Environment variables are especially handy when configure doesn't know where to look for third-party include files and libraries. For example, to make the preprocessor search in *include_dir*, run this command:

```
$ CPPFLAGS=-Iinclude_dir ./configure
```

As shown in Section 15.2.6, to make the linker look in **lib_dir**, use this command:

```
$ LDFLAGS=-Llib_dir ./configure
```

If **lib_dir** has shared libraries (see Section 15.1.4), the previous command probably won't set the runtime dynamic linker path. In that case, use the -rpath linker option in addition to -L:

```
$ LDFLAGS="-Llib_dir -Wl,-rpath=lib_dir" ./configure
```

Be careful when setting variables. A small slip can trip up the compiler and cause configure to fail. For example, say you forget the - in -I, as shown here:

```
$ CPPFLAGS=Iinclude_dir ./configure
```

This yields an error like this:

```
configure: error: C compiler cannot create executables
See 'config.log' for more details
```

Digging through the *config.log* generated from this failed attempt yields this:

```
configure:5037: checking whether the C compiler works
configure:5059: gcc  Iinclude_dir conftest.c  >&5
gcc: error: Iinclude_dir: No such file or directory
configure:5063: $? = 1
configure:5101: result: no
```

16.3.5   Autoconf Targets

Once you get `configure` working, you'll find that the Makefile that it generates has a number of other useful targets in addition to the standard `all` and `install`:

make clean   As described in Chapter 15, this removes all object files, executables, and libraries.

make distclean   This is similar to `make clean` except that it removes all automatically generated files, including Makefiles, *config.h*, *config.log*, and so on. The idea is that the source tree should look like a newly unpacked distribution after running `make distclean`.

make check   Some packages come with a battery of tests to verify that the compiled programs work properly; the command `make check` runs the tests.

make install-strip   This is like `make install` except that it strips the symbol table and other debugging information from executables and libraries when installing. Stripped binaries require much less space.

16.3.6   Autoconf Log Files

If something goes wrong during the configure process and the cause isn't obvious, you can examine *config.log* to find the problem. Unfortunately, *config.log* is often a gigantic file, which can make it difficult to locate the exact source of the problem.

The general approach to finding the problem is to go to the very end of *config.log* (for example, by pressing G in `less`) and then page back up until you see the problem. However, there is still a lot of stuff at the end because `configure` dumps its entire environment there, including output variables, cache variables, and other definitions. So rather than going to the end and paging up, go to the end and search backward for a string such as `for more details` or some other part near the end of the failed `configure` output. (Remember that you can initiate a reverse search in `less` with the ? command.) There's a good chance that the error will be just above what your search finds.

16.3.7   pkg-config

There are so many third-party libraries that keeping all of them in a common location can be messy. However, installing each with a separate prefix can lead to problems when building packages that require these third-party libraries. For example, if you want to compile OpenSSH, you need the OpenSSL library. How do you tell the OpenSSH configuration process the location of the OpenSSL libraries and which libraries are required?

Many libraries now use the `pkg-config` program not only to advertise the locations of their include files and libraries but also to specify the exact flags that you need to compile and link a program. The syntax is as follows:

```
$ pkg-config options package1 package2 ...
```

For example, to find the libraries required for OpenSSL, you can run this command:

```
$ pkg-config --libs openssl
```

The output should be something like this:

```
-lssl -lcrypto
```

To see all libraries that `pkg-config` knows about, run this command:

```
$ pkg-config --list-all
```

How pkg-config Works

If you look behind the scenes, you will find that `pkg-config` finds package information by reading configuration files that end with *.pc*. For example, here is *openssl.pc* for the OpenSSL socket library, as seen on an Ubuntu system (located in */usr/lib/i386-linux-gnu/pkgconfig*):

```
prefix=/usr
exec_prefix=${prefix}
libdir=${exec_prefix}/lib/i386-linux-gnu
includedir=${prefix}/include

Name: OpenSSL
Description: Secure Sockets Layer and cryptography libraries and tools
Version: 1.0.1
Requires:
Libs: -L${libdir} -lssl -lcrypto
Libs.private: -ldl -lz
Cflags: -I${includedir} exec_prefix=${prefix}
```

You can change this file, for example, by adding `-Wl,-rpath=${libdir}` to the library flags to set a runtime dynamic linker path. However, the bigger question is how `pkg-config` finds the *.pc* files in the first place. By default, `pkg-config` looks in the *lib/pkgconfig* directory of its installation prefix. For example, a `pkg-config` installed with a */usr/local* prefix looks in */usr/local/lib/pkgconfig*.

Installing pkg-config Files in Nonstandard Locations

Unfortunately, by default, `pkg-config` does not read any *.pc* files outside its installation prefix. So a *.pc* file that's in a nonstandard location, such as */opt/openssl/lib/pkgconfig/openssl.pc*, will be out of the reach of any stock `pkg-config` installation. There are two basic ways to make *.pc* files available outside of the `pkg-config` installation prefix:

- Make symbolic links (or copies) from the actual *.pc* files to the central *pkgconfig* directory.

- Set your `PKG_CONFIG_PATH` environment variable to include any extra *pkgconfig* directories. This strategy does not work well on a system-wide basis.

16.4 Installation Practice

Knowing *how* to build and install software is good, but knowing *when* and *where* to install your own packages is even more useful. Linux distributions try to cram in as much software as possible at installation, and you should always check whether it would be best to install a package yourself instead. Here are the advantages of doing installs on your own:

- You can customize package defaults.
- When installing a package, you often get a clearer picture of how to use the package.
- You control the release that you run.
- It's easier to back up a custom package.
- It's easier to distribute self-installed packages across a network (as long as the architecture is consistent and the installation location is relatively isolated).

Here are the disadvantages:

- It takes time.
- Custom packages do not automatically upgrade themselves. Distributions keep most packages up-to-date without requiring much work. This is a particular concern for packages that interact with the network, because you want to ensure that you always have the latest security updates.
- If you don't actually use the package, you're wasting your time.
- There is a potential for misconfiguring packages.

There's not much point in installing packages such as the ones in the coreutils package that you built earlier in the chapter (`ls`, `cat`, and so on) unless you're building a very custom system. On the other hand, if you have a vital interest in network servers such as Apache, the best way to get complete control is to install the servers yourself.

16.4.1 Where to Install

The default prefix in GNU autoconf and many other packages is */usr/local*, the traditional directory for locally installed software. Operating system upgrades ignore */usr/local*, so you won't lose anything installed there during an operating system upgrade and for small local software installations, */usr/local* is fine. The only problem is that if you have a lot of custom software installed, this can turn into a terrible mess. Thousands of odd little files can make their way into the */usr/local* hierarchy, and you may have no idea where the files came from.

If things really start to get unruly, you should create your own packages as described in Section 16.3.2.

16.5 Applying a Patch

Most changes to software source code are available as branches of the developer's online version of the source code (such as a git repository). However, every now and then, you might get a *patch* that you need to apply against source code to fix bugs or add features. You may also see the term *diff* used as a synonym for patch, because the diff program produces the patch.

The beginning of a patch looks something like this:

```
--- src/file.c.orig     2015-07-17 14:29:12.000000000 +0100
+++ src/file.c   2015-09-18 10:22:17.000000000 +0100
@@ -2,16 +2,12 @@
```

Patches usually contain alterations to more than one file. Search the patch for three dashes in a row (---) to see the files that have alterations and always look at the beginning of a patch to determine the required working directory. Notice that the preceding example refers to *src/file.c*. Therefore, you should change to the directory that contains *src* before applying the patch, *not* to the *src* directory itself.

To apply the patch, run the patch command:

```
$ patch -p0 < patch_file
```

If everything goes well, patch exits without a fuss, leaving you with an updated set of files. However, patch may ask you this question:

```
File to patch:
```

This usually means that you are not in the correct directory, but it could also indicate that your source code does not match the source code in the patch. In this case, you're probably out of luck: Even if you could identify some of the files to patch, others would not be properly updated, leaving you with source code that you could not compile.

In some cases, you might come across a patch that refers to a package version like this:

```
--- package-3.42/src/file.c.orig     2015-07-17 14:29:12.000000000 +0100
+++ package-3.42/src/file.c   2015-09-18 10:22:17.000000000 +0100
```

If you have a slightly different version number (or you just renamed the directory), you can tell patch to strip leading path components. For example, say you were in the directory that contains *src* (as before). To tell patch to ignore the *package-3.42/* part of the path (that is, strip one leading path component), use -p1:

```
$ patch -p1 < patch_file
```

16.6 Troubleshooting Compiles and Installations

If you understand the difference between compiler errors, compiler warnings, linker errors, and shared library problems as described in Chapter 15, you shouldn't have too much trouble fixing many of the glitches that arise when building software. This section covers some common problems. Although you're unlikely to run into any of these when building using autoconf, it never hurts to know what these kinds of problems look like.

Before covering specifics, make sure that you can read certain kinds of make output. It's important to know the difference between an error and an ignored error. The following is a real error that you need to investigate:

```
make: *** [target] Error 1
```

However, some Makefiles suspect that an error condition might occur but know that these errors are harmless. You can usually disregard any messages like this:

```
make: *** [target] Error 1 (ignored)
```

Furthermore, GNU make often calls itself many times in large packages, with each instance of make in the error message marked with [*N*], where *N* is a number. You can often quickly find the error by looking at the make error that comes *directly* after the compiler error message. For example:

```
[compiler error message involving file.c]
make[3]: *** [file.o] Error 1
make[3]: Leaving directory '/home/src/package-5.0/src'
make[2]: *** [all] Error 2
make[2]: Leaving directory '/home/src/package-5.0/src'
make[1]: *** [all-recursive] Error 1
make[1]: Leaving directory '/home/src/package-5.0/'
make: *** [all] Error 2
```

The first three lines practically give it away: The trouble centers around *file.c* located in */home/src/package-5.0/src*. Unfortunately, there is so much extra output that it can be difficult to spot the important details. Learning how to filter out the subsequent make errors goes a long way toward digging out the real cause.

16.6.1 Specific Errors

Here are some common build errors that you might encounter.

Problem

Compiler error message:

```
src.c:22: conflicting types for 'item'
/usr/include/file.h:47: previous declaration of 'item'
```

Explanation and Fix

The programmer made an erroneous redeclaration of `item` on line 22 of *src.c*. You can usually fix this by removing the offending line (with a comment, an #ifdef, or whatever works).

Problem

Compiler error message:

```
src.c:37: 'time_t' undeclared (first use this function)
--snip--
src.c:37: parse error before '...'
```

Explanation and Fix

The programmer forgot a critical header file. The manual pages are the best way to find the missing header file. First, look at the offending line (in this case, line 37 in *src.c*). It's probably a variable declaration like the following:

```
time_t v1;
```

Search forward for `v1` in the program for its use around a function call. For example:

```
v1 = time(NULL);
```

Now run `man 2 time` or `man 3 time` to look for system and library calls named `time()`. In this case, the section 2 manual page has what you need:

```
SYNOPSIS
    #include <time.h>

    time_t time(time_t *t);
```

This means that `time()` requires *time.h*. Place #include <time.h> at the beginning of *src.c* and try again.

Problem

Compiler (preprocessor) error message:

```
src.c:4: pkg.h: No such file or directory
(long list of errors follows)
```

Explanation and Fix

The compiler ran the C preprocessor on *src.c* but could not find the *pkg.h* include file. The source code likely depends on a library that you need to install, or you may just need to provide the compiler with the nonstandard include path. Usually, you will just need to add a

-I include path option to the C preprocessor flags (CPPFLAGS). (Keep in mind that you might also need a -L linker flag to go along with the include files.)

If it doesn't look as though you're missing a library, there's an outside chance that you're attempting a compile for an operating system that this source code does not support. Check the Makefile and *README* files for details about platforms.

If you're running a Debian-based distribution, try the apt-file command on the header filename:

```
$ apt-file search pkg.h
```

This might find the development package that you need. For distributions that provide yum, you can try this instead:

```
$ yum provides */pkg.h
```

Problem

make error message:

```
make: prog: Command not found
```

Explanation and Fix

To build the package, you need *prog* on your system. If *prog* is something like cc, gcc, or ld, you don't have the development utilities installed on your system. On the other hand, if you think *prog* is already installed on your system, try altering the Makefile to specify the full pathname of *prog*.

In rare cases, make builds *prog* and then uses *prog* immediately, assuming that the current directory (.) is in your command path. If your $PATH does not include the current directory, you can edit the Makefile and change *prog* to *./prog*. Alternatively, you could append . to your path temporarily.

16.7   Looking Forward

We've only touched on the basics of building software. Here are some more topics that you can explore after you get the hang of your own builds:

- **Understanding how to use build systems other than autoconf, such as CMake and SCons.**

- **Setting up builds for your own software.** If you're writing your own software, you want to choose a build system and learn to use it. For GNU autoconf packaging, *Autotools* by John Calcote (No Starch Press, 2010) can help you out.

- **Compiling the Linux kernel.** The kernel's build system is completely different from that of other tools. It has its own configuration system tailored to customizing your own kernel and modules. The procedure is straightforward, though, and if you understand how the boot loader works, you won't have any trouble with it. However, you should be careful when doing so; make sure that you always keep your old kernel handy in case you can't boot with a new one.

- **Distribution-specific source packages.** Linux distributions maintain their own versions of software source code as special source packages. Sometimes you can find useful patches that expand functionality or fix problems in otherwise unmaintained packages. The source package management systems include tools for automatic builds, such as Debian's `debuild` and the RPM-based `mock`.

Building software is often a stepping-stone to learning about programming and software development. The tools you've seen in the past two chapters take the mystery out of where your system software came from. It's not difficult to take the next steps of looking inside the source code, making changes, and creating your own software.

17

BUILDING ON THE BASICS

The chapters in this book have covered the fundamental components of a Linux system, from low-level kernel and process organization, to networking, to some of the tools used to build software. With all of that behind you, what can you do now? Quite a lot, as it turns out! Because Linux supports nearly every kind of non-proprietary programming environment, it's only natural that a plethora of applications is available. Let's look at a few application areas where Linux excels and see how what you've learned in this book relates.

17.1 Web Servers and Applications

Linux is a popular operating system for web servers, and the reigning monarch of Linux application servers is the Apache HTTP Server (usually referred to as just "Apache"). Another web server that you'll often hear about is Tomcat (also an Apache project), which provides support for Java-based applications.

By themselves, web servers don't do much—they can serve files, but that's about it. The end goal of most web servers such as Apache is to provide an underlying platform to serve web applications. For example, Wikipedia is built on the MediaWiki package, which you can use to set up your own wiki. Content management systems like Wordpress and Drupal let you build your own blogs and media sites. All of these applications are built on programming languages that run especially well on Linux. For example, MediaWiki, Wordpress, and Drupal are all written in PHP.

The building blocks that make up web applications are highly modular, so it's easy to add your own extensions and create applications with frameworks such as Django, Flask, and Rails, which offer facilities for common web infrastructure and features, such as templates, multiple users, and database support.

A well-functioning web server depends on a solid operating system foundation. In particular, the material in Chapters 8 through 10 is particularly important. Your network configuration must be flawless, but perhaps more importantly, you must understand resource management. Adequately-sized, efficient memory and disk are critical, especially if you plan to use a database in your application.

17.2 Databases

Databases are specialized services for storing and retrieving data, and many different database servers and systems run on Linux. Two primary features of databases make them attractive: They offer easy, uniform ways to manage individual pieces and groups of data, and superior access performance.

Databases make it easier for applications to examine and alter data, especially when compared with parsing and changing text files. For example, the */etc/passwd* and */etc/shadow* files on a Linux system can become difficult to maintain over a network of machines. Instead, you can set up a database that offers user information LDAP (Lightweight Directory Access Protocol) to feed this information into the Linux authentication system. The configuration on the Linux client side is easy; all you need to do is edit the */etc/nsswitch.conf* file and add a little extra configuration.

The primary reason that databases generally offer superior performance when retrieving data is that they use indexing to keep track of data locations. For example, say you have a set of data representing a directory containing first and last names and telephone numbers. You can use a database to place an index on any of these attributes, like the last name. Then, when looking up a person by last name, the database simply consults the index for the last name rather than searching the entire directory.

17.2.1 Types of Databases

Databases come in two basic forms: relational and non-relational. *Relational databases* (also called *Relational Database Management Systems*, or *RDBMS*), such as MySQL, PostgreSQL, Oracle, and MariaDB, are general-purpose databases that excel in tying different sets of data together. For example, say you have two sets of data, one with postal (ZIP) codes and names, and another with the postal codes and their corresponding states. A relational database would allow you to very quickly retrieve all of the names located in a particular state. You normally talk to relational databases using a programming language called SQL (Structured Query Language).

Non-relational databases, sometimes known as *NoSQL* databases, tend to solve particular problems that relational databases don't easily handle. For example, document-store databases, such as MongoDB, attempt to make storing and indexing entire documents easier. Key-value databases, such as redis, tend to focus on performance. NoSQL databases don't have a common query language like SQL for access. Instead, you'll talk to them using a variety of interfaces and commands.

The disk and memory performance issues discussed in Chapter 8 are extremely important in most database implementations because there's a trade-off between how much you can store in RAM (which is fast) versus on disk. Most larger database systems also involve significant networking because they're distributed over many servers. The most common such network setup is called *replication*, where one database is basically copied to a number of database servers to increase the number of clients that connect to the servers.

17.3   Virtualization

In most large organizations, it's inefficient to dedicate hardware to specific server tasks because installing an operating system tailored to one task on one server means that you're limited to that task until you reinstall it. Virtual machine technology makes it possible to simultaneously install one or more operating systems (often called *guests*) on a single piece of hardware, and then activate and deactivate the systems at will. You can even move and copy the virtual machines to other machines.

There are many virtualization systems for Linux, such as the kernel's KVM (kernel virtual machine) and Xen. Virtual machines are especially handy for web servers and database servers. Although it's possible to set up a single Apache server to serve several websites, this comes at a cost of flexibility and maintainability. If those sites are all run by different users, you have to manage the servers and the users together. Instead, it's usually preferable to set up virtual machines on one physical server with their own supporting users, so that they don't interfere with each other and you can alter and move them at will.

The software that operates virtual machines is called a *hypervisor*. The hypervisor manipulates many pieces of the lower levels of a Linux system that you've seen in this book with the result that, if you install a Linux guest on a virtual machine, it should behave just like any other installed Linux system.

17.4   Distributed and On-Demand Computing

To ease local resource management, you can build sophisticated tools on top of virtual machine technology. The term *cloud computing* is a catch-all term that's often used as label for this area. More specifically, *infrastructure as a service (IaaS)* refers to systems that allow you to provision and control basic computing resources such as CPU, memory, storage, and networking on a remote server. The OpenStack project is one such API and platform that includes IaaS.

Moving up past the raw infrastructure, you can also provision platform resources such as the operating system, database servers, and web servers. Systems that offer resources on this level are said to be *platform as a service (PaaS)*.

Linux is central to many of these computing services, as it's often the underlying operating system behind all of it. Nearly all of the elements that you've seen in this book, starting with the kernel, are reflected throughout these systems.

17.5   Embedded Systems

An *embedded system* is anything designed to serve a specific purpose, such as a music player, video streamer, or thermostat. Compare this to a desktop or server system that can handle many different kinds of tasks (but may not do one specific thing very well).

You can think of embedded systems as almost the opposite of distributed computing; rather than expanding the scale of the operating system, an embedded system usually (but not always) shrinks it, often into a small device. Android is perhaps the most widespread embedded version of Linux in use today.

Embedded systems often combine specialized hardware with software. For example, you can set up a PC to do anything a wireless router can by adding enough network hardware and correctly configuring a Linux installation. But it's usually preferable to buy a smaller, dedicated device consisting of the necessary hardware and eliminate any hardware that isn't necessary. For example, a router needs more network ports than most desktops but doesn't need video or sound hardware. And once you have custom hardware, you must tailor the system's software, such as the operating system internals and user interface. OpenWRT, mentioned in Chapter 9, is one such customized Linux distribution.

Interest in embedded systems is increasing as more capable small hardware is introduced, particularly system-on-a-chip (SoC) designs that can cram a processor, memory, and peripheral interfaces into a small space. For example, the Raspberry Pi and BeagleBone single-board computers are based around such a design, with several Linux variants to choose from as an operating system. These devices have easily accessible output and sensor input that connects to language interfaces such as Python, making them popular for prototyping and small gadgets.

Embedded versions of Linux vary in how many features from the server/desktop version can be carried over. Small, very limited devices must strip out everything except the bare minimum because of lack of space, which often means that even the shell and core utilities come in the form of a single BusyBox executable. These systems tend to exhibit the most differences between a full-featured Linux installation, and you'll often see older software on them, such as System V init.

You'll normally develop software for embedded devices using a regular desktop machine. More powerful devices, such as the Raspberry Pi, have the luxury of more storage and the power to run newer and more complete software, so you can even natively run many development tools on them.

Regardless of the differences, though, embedded devices still share the Linux genes described in this book: You'll see a kernel, a bunch of devices, network interfaces, and an init alongside a bunch of user processes. Embedded kernels tend to be close (or identical) to regular kernel releases, simply with many features disabled. As you work your way up through user space, though, the differences become more pronounced.

17.6 Final Remarks

Whatever your goals for gaining a better understanding of Linux systems, I hope that you've found this book to be helpful. My goal has been to instill you with confidence when you need to get inside your system to make changes or do something new. At this point, you should feel like you're really in control of your system. Now go and push it around a little and have some fun.

BIBLIOGRAPHY

Abrahams, Paul W., and Bruce Larson, *UNIX for the Impatient*, 2nd ed. Boston: Addison-Wesley Professional, 1995.

Aho, Alfred V., Brian W. Kernighan, and Peter J. Weinberger, *The AWK Programming Language*. Boston: Addison-Wesley, 1988.

Aho, Alfred V., Monica S. Lam, Ravi Sethi, and Jeffrey D. Ullman, *Compilers: Principles, Techniques, and Tools*, 2nd ed. Boston: Addison-Wesley, 2006.

Barrett, Daniel J., Richard E. Silverman, and Robert G. Byrnes, *SSH, The Secure Shell: The Definitive Guide*, 2nd ed. Sebastopol: O'Reilly, 2005.

Beazley, David M., *Python Essential Reference*, 4th ed. Boston: Addison-Wesley, 2009.

Beazley, David M., Brian D. Ward, and Ian R. Cooke, "The Inside Story on Shared Libraries and Dynamic Loading." *Computing in Science & Engineering* 3, no. 5 (September/October 2001): 90-97.

Calcote, John, *Autotools: A Practitioner's Guide to GNU Autoconf, Automake, and Libtool*. San Francisco: No Starch Press, 2010.

Carter, Gerald, Jay Ts, and Robert Eckstein, *Using Samba: A File and Print Server for Linux, Unix & Mac OS X*, 3rd ed. Sebastopol: O'Reilly, 2007.

Christiansen, Tom, brian d foy, Larry Wall, and Jon Orwant, *Programming Perl: Unmatched Power for Processing and Scripting*, 4th ed. Sebastopol: O'Reilly, 2012.

Chromatic, *Modern Perl*, rev. ed. Hillsboro: Onyx Neon Press, 2014.

Davies, Joshua, *Implementing SSL/TLS Using Cryptography and PKI*. Hoboken: Wiley, 2011.

Filesystem Hierarchy Standard Group, "Filesystem Hierarchy Standard, Version 2.3," edited by Rusty Russell, Daniel Quinlan, and Christopher Yeoh, 2004, *http://www.pathname.com/fhs/*.

Friedl, Jeffrey E. F., *Mastering Regular Expressions: Understand Your Data and Be More Productive*, 3rd ed. Sebastopol: O'Reilly, 2006.

Gregg, Brendan, *Systems Performance: Enterprise and the Cloud*. Upper Saddle River: Prentice Hall, 2013.

Grune, Dick, Kees van Reeuwijk, Henri E. Bal, Ceriel J.H. Jacobs, and Koen Langendoen, *Modern Compiler Design*, 2nd ed. New York: Springer, 2012.

Hopcroft, John E., Rajeev Motwani, and Jeffrey D. Ullman, *Introduction to Automata Theory, Languages and Computation*, 3rd ed. Upper Saddle River: Prentice Hall, 2006.

Kernighan, Brian W., and Rob Pike, *The UNIX Programming Environment*. Upper Saddle River: Prentice Hall, 1983.

Kernighan, Brian W., and Dennis M. Ritchie, *The C Programming Language*, 2nd ed. Upper Saddle River: Prentice Hall, 1988.

Kochan, Stephen G., and Patrick Wood, *Unix Shell Programming*, 3rd ed. Indianapolis: SAMS Publishing, 2003.

Levine, John R., *Linkers and Loaders*. San Francisco: Morgan Kaufmann, 1999.

Liu, Cricket, and Paul Albitz, *DNS and BIND*, 5th ed. Sebastopol: O'Reilly, 2006.

Lucas, Michael W., *SSH Mastery: OpenSSH, PuTTY, Tunnels and Keys*. Tilted Windmill Press, 2012.

Matloff, Norman, *The Art of R Programming: A Tour of Statistical Software Design*. San Francisco: No Starch Press, 2011.

Matloff, Norman, and Peter Jay Salzman, *The Art of Debugging with GDB, DDD, and Eclipse*. San Francisco: No Starch Press, 2008.

Mecklenburg, Robert, *Managing Projects with GNU Make: The Power of GNU Make for Building Anything*, 3rd ed. Sebastopol: O'Reilly, 2004.

The New Hacker's Dictionary, 3rd ed. Edited by Eric S. Raymond. Cambridge: MIT Press, 1996.

Peek, Jerry, Grace Todino Gonguct, and John Strang, *Learning The UNIX Operating System: A Concise Guide for the New User*, 5th ed. Sebastopol: O'Reilly, 2001.

Pike, Rob, Dave Presotto, Sean Dorward, Bob Flandrena, Ken Thompson, Howard Trickey, and Phil Winterbottom, "Plan 9 from Bell Labs." *Bell Labs*. Accessed July 10, 2014, *http://plan9.bell-labs.com/sys/doc/9.html*.

Robbins, Arnold, *sed & awk Pocket Reference: Text Processing with Regular Expressions*, 2nd ed. Sebastopol: O'Reilly, 2002.

Robbins, Arnold, Elbert Hannah, and Linda Lamb, *Learning the vi and Vim Editors: Unix Text Processing*, 7th ed. Sebastopol: O'Reilly, 2008.

Salus, Peter H., *The Daemon, the Gnu, and the Penguin*. Reed Media Services, 2008.

Samar, V., and R. Schemers, "Unified Login with Pluggable Authentication Modules (PAM)," October 1995, Open Software Foundation (RFC 86.0), *http://www.opengroup.org/rfc/mirror-rfc/rfc86.0.txt*.

Schneier, Bruce, *Applied Cryptography: Protocols, Algorithms, and Source Code in C*, 2nd ed. Hoboken: Wiley, 1996.

Shotts, William E. Jr., *The Linux Command Line: A Complete Introduction*. San Francisco: No Starch Press, 2012

Schwartz, Randal L., brian d foy, and Tom Phoenix, *Learning Perl: Making Easy Things Easy and Hard Things Possible*, 6th ed. Sebastopol: O'Reilly, 2011.

Silberschatz, Abraham, Peter B. Galvin, and Greg Gagne, *Operating System Concepts*, 9th ed. Hoboken: Wiley, 2012.

Stallman, Richard M., *GNU Emacs Manual*, 17th ed. Boston: Free Software Foundation, 2012. *http://www.gnu.org/software/emacs/manual/*.

Stallman, Richard M., Roland Pesch, Stan Shebs, Etienne Suvasa, and Matt Lee, *Debugging with GDB: The GNU Source-Level Debugger*, 10th ed. Boston: GNU Press, 2011. *http://sourceware.org/gdb/current/onlinedocs/gdb/*.

Stevens, W. Richard, *UNIX Network Programming, Volume 2: Interprocess Communications*, 2nd ed. Upper Saddle River: Prentice Hall, 1998.

Stevens, W. Richard, Bill Fenner, and Andrew M. Rudoff, *Unix Network Programming, Volume 1: The Sockets Networking API*, 3rd ed. Boston: Addison-Wesley Professional, 2003.

Tanenbaum, Andrew S., and Herbert Bos, *Modern Operating Systems*, 4th ed. Upper Saddle River: Prentice Hall, 2014.

Tanenbaum, Andrew S., and David J. Wetherall, *Computer Networks*, 5th ed. Upper Saddle River: Prentice Hall, 2010.

INDEX

V

/var, 41
/var/log, 151–153
VFS, 73, 90
vi, 24–25
vipw, 155–156
virtual console, 51–52, 113,
        135–136, 300
virtual machine, 327, 347–348
virtual memory, 6, 85. *See also*
        memory: management
vmstat, 183–185

W

wallpaper. *See* desktop background
warning messages, 29
Wayland, 305
web application, 346
web server, 271, 346
WEP, 228
while, 262–263
who -r, 113
widget, 299
wildcard. *See* glob
window manager, 298–299
Windows
    boot, 106–107
    file sharing, 278–285
    partition, 73
    password, 280–281
    printer sharing, 283
wireless network, 202–204. *See also*
        Ethernet: wireless
worker process, 232–233
WPA, 228

X

xargs, 267–268
xev, 302
X event, 301–302
xinetd, 237
xinput, 303–304
XKB, 304
xlsclients, 301
xmodmap, 302, 304
xset, 305
X Window System
    application, 299
    client, 298, 301
    diagnostics, 301–305
    display (*see* display)
    event, 301–302
    future, 305
    input, 302–304
    network transparency, 300–301
    preferences, 302–305
    server, 51, 298–300
    tunneling, 233–234, 301
    window manager, 298–299
xwininfo, 301
xz, 39

Y

Yacc, 324–325

Z

zcat, 39
zip, 39

How Linux Works, 2nd Edition is set in New Baskerville, TheSansMono Condensed, Futura, and Dogma. The book was printed and bound by Edwards Brothers Malloy in Ann Arbor, Michigan. The paper is 60# Husky Opaque, which is certified by the Sustainable Forestry Initiative (SFI).

The book uses a RepKover binding, in which the pages are bound together with a cold-set, flexible glue and the first and last pages of the resulting book block are attached to the cover with tape. The cover is not actually glued to the book's spine, and when open, the book lies flat and the spine doesn't crack.

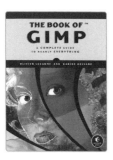